Ken Akamatsu

TRANSLATED AND ADAPTED BY

Alethea Nibley and Athena Nibley

LETTERED BY

Joe Caramagna

Negima! Omnibus volume 3 is a work of fiction. Names, characters, places, and incidents are the products of the author's imagination or are used fictitiously. Any resemblance to actual events, locales, or persons, living or dead, is entirely coincidental.

A Kodansha Comics Trade Paperback Original.

Published in the United States by Kodansha Comics, an imprint of Kodansha USA Publishing, LLC, New York.

Publication rights for this English edition arranged through Kodansha Ltd., Tokyo.

First published in Japan in 2004-2005 by Kodansha Ltd., Tokyo as *Maho sensei Negima!* volumes 7, 8 and 9.

ISBN 978-1-935429-64-7

Printed in the United States of America.

www.kodansha.us

3 4 5 6 7 8 9

Translator: Alethea Nibley and Athena Nibley
Lettering: Joe Caramagna

CONTENTS

Honorifics Explained

Throughout the Kodansha Comics books, you will find Japanese honorifics left intact in the translations. For those not familiar with how the Japanese use honorifics and, more important, how they differ from American honorifics, we present this brief overview.

Politeness has always been a critical facet of Japanese culture. Ever since the feudal era, when Japan was a highly stratified society, use of honorifics—which can be defined as polite speech that indicates relationship or status—has played an essential role in the Japanese language. When addressing someone in Japanese, an honorific usually takes the form of a suffix attached to one's name (example: "Asuna-san"), is used as a title at the end of one's name, or appears in place of the name itself (example: "Negi-sensei," or simply "Sensei!").

Honorifics can be expressions of respect or endearment. In the context of manga and anime, honorifics give insight into the nature of the relationship between characters. Many English translations leave out these important honorifics and therefore distort the feel of the original Japanese. Because Japanese honorifics contain nuances that English honorifics lack, it is our policy at Kodansha Comics not to translate them. Here, instead, is a guide to some of the honorifics you may encounter in Kodansha Comics books.

-san: This is the most common honorific and is equivalent to Mr., Miss, Ms., or Mrs. It is the all-purpose honorific and can be used in any situation where politeness is required.

-sama: This is one level higher than "-san" and is used to confer great respect.

-dono: This comes from the word "tono," which means "lord." It is an even higher level than "-sama" and confers utmost respect.

-kun: This suffix is used at the end of boys' names to express familiarity or endearment. It is also sometimes used by men among friends, or when addressing someone younger or of a lower station.

-chan: This is used to express endearment, mostly toward girls. It is also used for little boys, pets, and even among lovers. It gives a sense of childish cuteness.

Bozu: This is an informal way to refer to a boy, similar to the English terms "kid" and "squirt."

Sempai/
Senpai: This title suggests that the addressee is one's senior in a group or organization. It is most often used in a school setting, where underclassmen refer to their upperclassmen as "sempai." It can also be used in the workplace, such as when a newer employee addresses an employee who has seniority in the company.

Kohai: This is the opposite of "sempai" and is used toward underclassmen in school or newcomers in the workplace. It connotes that the addressee is of a lower station.

Sensei: Literally meaning "one who has come before," this title is used for teachers, doctors, or masters of any profession or art.

-[blank]: This is usually forgotten in these lists, but it is perhaps the most significant difference between Japanese and English. The lack of honorific means that the speaker has permission to address the person in a very intimate way. Usually, only family, spouses, or very close friends have this kind of permission. Known as yobisute, it can be gratifying when someone who has earned the intimacy starts to call one by one's name without an honorific. But when that intimacy hasn't been earned, it can be very insulting.

魔法先生
ネギま!
MAGISTER NEGI MAGI
7
Ken
Akamatsu
赤松 健

ASUNA: !?

N-NOT A PART OF--!? HOW DARE YOU TALK LIKE THAT AFTER EVERYTHING WE'VE BEEN THROUGH!? NEGI-BOZU!

NEGI: WA-WA-WAH! ASUNA-SAN? I CAN'T BREATHE!

NO, IT'S JUST THAT YOU'RE A NORMAL PERSON! YOU'RE NOT PART OF IT! I DIDN'T WANT YOU GETTING INTO ANY DANGER!

CONTENTS

MN...
...HUH? WHERE... AM I?
CRACKLE
パチ
CRACKLE
パチ..
もぞ...
SQUIRM
A DESERT?
HEY THERE.
I SEE YOU'RE AWAKE.
OOH! WHO'S THE RUGGED OLD GUY!?

YOU CAN WASH YOUR FACE OVER THERE.
'KAY...
HEY, WHERE ARE YOU GOING? LET ME SEE HIM SOME MORE!
I WANNA SEE THE OLD GUY!

...NN?
パシャ...
SPLASH

IS THIS... ME...?
ME... WHEN I WAS LITTLE?

THE STARS ARE SO PRETTY...
WHAT AM I *DOING* HERE?!
I'M BACK!
WHOA. THAT WAS FAST.
ZSH ZSH
I CAUGHT US THREE RAT-LOOKING THINGS!
RAT-"LOOKING"? AND WE'RE SUPPOSED TO EAT THEM?
OH! *YOU'RE* UP EARLY.
DANGLE
HUH? I... KNOW THIS MAN.
ZSH
BUT HOLD ON. HOW DO I KNOW HIM?
I MEAN, HE'S SUPPOSED TO BE THE BRAT'S--
GOOD MORN-ING, NAGI...

CHECK OUT THE SKY OVER THERE, ASUNA.
THE DAWN IS GOR-GEOUS.

MINISTRA MAGI ASUNA
NEGIMA!
MAGISTER NEGI MAGI
54TH PERIOD:
A MAP, A FEVER, AND CHOCOLATE ♡

...
CHIRP チュン CHIRP チュン...
WHAT A WEIRD DREAM ...
TWEET TWEET TWEET チ...
HUH ?
NOON, ALREADY ...?
...RIGHT, WE'RE BACK FROM THE SCHOOL TRIP.
TWEET TWEET TWEET チチチ
AND IT'S SUNDAY...
I CAME BACK FROM MY PAPER ROUTE AND WENT BACK TO SLEEP.
NN?
SKRITCH SKRITCH SKRITCH カリ カリ
SKRIT SKRIT SKRIT カリ カリ カリ
SKRITCH SKRITCH SKRITCH SKRITCH カリ カリ カリ

YOU'RE SCRITCHING AWAY ALREADY? WE ONLY JUST GOT BACK, NEGI.
OH, GOOD MORNING, ASUNA-SAN!
YO!
SKRITCH
SKRITCH
ALLEY-OOP!
I'M COMING IN!
SCRITCH SCRITCH
BOFF
TEP
WHEN DID THIS LOFT TURN INTO YOUR AND CHAMO'S PERMANENT RESIDENCE?
NOT THAT I MIND, BUT...
TMP

NN?
CHOCOLATE?
LOOKS YUMMY! DON'T MIND IF I DO!
YOINK
SMACK
...I'VE BEEN INVESTIGATING THE CLUE CHIEF-SAN GAVE ME.
OH YEAH! SO WHAT KIND OF A CLUE IS IT?
YOU'LL NEVER GUESS! IT'S A BUNDLE OF MAPS OF THE ACADEMY!
FWOOSH
MAHORA
THEY'RE WHAT MY FATHER WAS RESEARCHING THE LAST TIME HE WAS AT THAT HOUSE.

WHAT!? MAPS OF MAHORA ACADEMY!? WH-WH-WHY?
I DON'T KNOW. IT'S WRITTEN IN CODE. I WAS TRYING TO DECIPHER IT, BUT... WELL...
HMMM? YOU SEEM UNUSUALLY CHIPPER.
ER... EH HEH HEH.
WE DID RUN INTO SOME BAD PEOPLE AND STRONG ENEMIES, BUT...
...I GOT TO SEE MY FATHER'S HOUSE, AND I EVEN GOT A CLUE TO FINDING HIM.
SO I'M REALLY EAGER TO GET BACK TO SEARCHING AGAIN.

AFTER EVERY-THING THAT HAP-PENED ON THE TRIP, THERE ARE LOTS OF THINGS I NEED TO DO.
IT WON'T BE EASY. I STILL HAVE MY TEACH-ING DUTIES, AFTER ALL...
BUT JUST YOU WATCH, ASUNA-SAN.
I CAN DO THIS!

CHECK OUT THE SKY OVER THERE, ASUNA.
...
SWOO... よろっ..
?
GASP
IS SOME-THING WRONG, ASUNA-SAN?
PEER ひょいっ
EH!?
B-DMP ドキ..
I-IT'S NOTHING!
MRPHLE!?
FSHH

DING-DONG DING-DONG ♪
FORGIVE OUR INTRUSION, NEGI-SENSEI ♡
HO HO HO
BAM
BUT WOULD YOU JOIN ME FOR TEA ON THIS FINE SUNDAY AFTER-NOON?

PLEASE, HELP YOURSELF TO THESE NAMA YATSUHASHI I BROUGHT BACK FROM KYOTO. ♡
CHIPPER CHIPPER
AS FOR TEA, I HAVE A NEW BLEND FROM MOUNT ALI IN TAIWAN.
O-OH. THANK YOU.
ALTHOUGH I DID GO TO KYOTO, TOO...
HEY, CLASS REP! WHAT ARE YOU DOING, BARGING INTO OUR ROOM LIKE THIS!?
ASUNA, IT'S THE MIDDLE OF THE DAY, AND YOU'RE STILL IN YOUR PJS?
I CAN WEAR WHAT I WANT!

NEGI-KUUUN! WANNA HANG OUT WITH US?
B-BAM
WE DON'T HAVE ANY CLUB-STUFF TODAY!
NEGI-SENSEI!
ZBAM
WE CAN PLAY NINJAS!
LET'S HAVE FUN! ♡

NEGI-KUN, LET'S GO SING KARAOKE ♪
D-DUN

KACHAK
I'M HOME!
EEP!? WHERE'D ALL THESE PEOPLE COME FROM?
CO-OP

CLAMOR
OOOH, SO THIS IS NEGI-KUN'S ROOM! IT'S SO CUTE! ♡
WOW
HO HO...
SO ABOUT THOSE CARDS OF YOURS, NEGI-KUN! CAN I STILL GET ONE IF I KISS YOU? I WANT ONE! ♪
CLAMOR
CHUCKLE CHUCKLE
EXCUSE ME! YUNA-SAN, KAKIZAKI-SAN! THAT TEA IS FOR NEGI-SENSEI.
CLAMOR
OH NO, OH NO! I NEED TO GET OUT SOME TEA, AND SNACKS!
OOH, LET ME SEE...!
UM, WELL...
GLINT
YOU MUST BE TIRED, NEGI-KUN. LET ME GIVE YOU A BACK RUB!
YOU GUYS... THIS IS NOT YOUR ROOM...
TWITCH TWITCH
あたふた
PANIC PANIC
LET'S SEE, ONE, TWO, THREE...
YAY!
KYA HA HA HA!
IT'S A PARTY IN HERE ♪
ドタドタ
STOMP STOMP
GET OUT ———!!!
AH HA HA
WAAAH! KYAAA ♡
UGH! IT'S SUNDAY RIGHT AFTER OUR CLASS TRIP. YOU'D THINK THEY COULD WIND DOWN A LITTLE
YOU'RE SO POPULAR, NEGI-KUN.

...WELL?
WHAT ARE ALL THESE "THINGS YOU NEED TO DO"?
...WELL, AFTER THE TRIP, I REALIZED JUST HOW WEAK I AM.
SO FIRST...
...I WANT TO ASK HER TO TRAIN ME.
HUH?
TRAIN YOU?

NEGI-SENSEI...
WELCOME TO OUR HUMBLE HOME.
BOW...
CHA-CHA-MARU-SAN?!
THEN THIS HOUSE BELONGS TO...
BOW
AND THAT MEANS WHEN YOU SAID YOU WANT "HER" TO TRAIN YOU, YOU MEANT...
E-E-EVA-CHAN?!
ARE YOU INSANE!? SHE'S STILL AFTER YOUR BLOOD, YOU KNOW!
OH, ASUNA-SAN. YOU KNOW THAT EVANGELINE-SAN ISN'T A BAD PERSON.
BUT--
IT'S ALL RIGHT, ASUNA-SAN
DON'T WORRY SO MUCH.
BESIDES, RIGHT NOW I WANT TO GET STRONGER.
I WANT THE STRENGTH TO PROTECT WHAT'S IMPOR-TANT.

THE NEXT TIME SOMETHING HAPPENS...I WANT TO BE ABLE TO PROTECT KONOKA-SAN
AND I WANT TO PROTECT YOU, ASUNA-SAN.
GH
....
B-DMP
GASP!
WH-WHAT? WHY DID MY HEART SKIP A BEAT AGAIN?
AND HEY, WE DON'T WANT ANYTHING TO HAPPEN!

WHAT?
TRAIN YOU?
ARE YOU STUPID?
SNIFFLE
SNIFFLE
ぐすぐす
HAY FEVER
WE'RE TECHNICALLY STILL ENEMIES! AND I HAVEN'T LET GO OF MY GRUDGE AGAINST THAT THOUSAND MASTER FATHER OF YOURS!
BESIDES, I DON'T TAKES DISCIPLES!
IF YOU WANT TO LEARN TO FIGHT, GO ASK TAKAMICHI!

I KNEW ALL OF THOSE THINGS WHEN I CAME HERE!
AND TAKAMICHI'S NOT AT THE ACADEMY! HE KEEPS GOING OVERSEAS...
BUT MORE THAN ANY OF THAT, AFTER SEEING YOU IN KYOTO, I REALIZED THAT IF I WANT TO LEARN HOW TO FIGHT A WIZARD'S BATTLE, YOU'RE THE ONLY ONE WHO CAN TEACH ME!
TWITCH
...SO IN OTHER WORDS, YOU WERE IMPRESSED WITH MY POWER.
SNIFF
YES!
...REALLY?
SMIRK
YES!!
HMPH!
FINE. IF YOU INSIST.
HOWEVER! LET ME REMIND YOU, SINCE YOU SEEM TO HAVE FORGOTTEN, THAT I'M AN EVIL WIZARD.
EH...?
WHEN YOU ASK AN EVIL WIZARD FOR A FAVOR, THEN YOU'D BETTER BE PREPARED TO PAY THE PRICE.
HEH HEH HEH.
NN?

ZWIP
YOU CAN START BY LICKING MY FEET.
OH! SHE'S SHOWING HER EVIL SIDE!
ZOOM
AND SWEAR ETERNAL FEALTY TO ME AS MY SLAVE. THEN WE'LL TALK.
DUN
DUN
DUN
DUN
DUN
DUN
ARE YOU STUPID!?
THWACK!
SHE IS FAST.
HBLEHH!!?
WHAT ARE YOU DOING, GOING ALL ADULT ON A KID LIKE THAT!?
WOW, ANE-SAN
ARGH, CURSE YOU, ASUNA KAGURAZAKA!! I MAY BE IN A WEAKENED STATE, BUT I'M STILL A PUREBLOOD! YOU CAN'T GO IGNORING MY MAGIC BARRIER!!
TREMBLE
TREMBLE
STING
STING
BESIDES, EVA-CHAN! NEGI'S PUTTING HIS HEART AND SOUL INTO THIS REQUEST! DON'T YOU THINK YOU'RE BEING A LITTLE MEAN?
AND WOULDN'T THE WORLD BE A WONDERFUL PLACE IF WE COULD ALL GET EVERYTHING WE WANTED JUST BY BOWING OUR HEADS AND BEING A LITTLE HUMBLE!!
STING
STING
Ha.
BUT ANY-WAY.
SMIRK

WHY ARE YOU SO DETERMINED TO HELP THE KID?
IT'S NOT LIKE YOU'RE RELATED.
HEH HEH HEH.
WHAT ARE YOU, IN LOVE? WITH A TEN-YEAR-OLD BRAT?
B-DMP!
WHA--!?
BLUSH
I A-A-A-AM NOT!
NEGI'S JUST A KID!
RAR
HA HA HA! WHAT'S WRONG? YOU'RE BLUSHING UP TO YOUR EARS! YOU'RE SO ADORABLE, ASUNA KAGURAZAKA!
I-I'M NOT! I'M JUST-
RAR
METHINKS SHE DOTH PROTEST TOO MUCH! HA HA HA! THAT MEANS I'M RIGHT!
I AM NOT!!
KER-THWACK!
WH-WH-WHY YOU! YOU HIT ME TWICE!
SH-SHUT UP! TAKE THAT BACK, YOU FAKE-Y VAMPIRE!
WHAT'D YOU CALL ME!?
BONK
KONK
UHHHH?
CHATTER
CHATTER
ASUNA-SAN IS THE ONLY ONE WHO CAN ENGAGE IN PHYSICAL SLAPSTICK WITH THE MISTRESS.
ER, UM...
WHEEZE WHEEZE
GASP
HFF HFF
ALL RIGHT. ALL RIGHT ALREADY.
COME HERE AGAIN NEXT SATURDAY. I'LL GIVE YOU A TEST TO SEE IF YOU'RE WORTHY OF BECOMING MY DISCIPLE. IS THAT GOOD ENOUGH FOR YOU?
EH...?
TH...
THANK YOU SO MUCH!

THAT'S GREAT, ANIKI!
IT IS! AND IT'S ALL THANKS TO ASUNA-SAN'S PERSISTENCE.
I-IT WAS NOTHING. I WAS JUST MAD AT EVA-CHAN FOR SAYING ALL THAT STUFF.
AAAAAUGHH. THIS IS SO NOT GOOD. I THINK MY FACE IS STILL RED. WH-WHAT IS WRONG WITH ME?
D-DON'T TELL ME SHE'S RIGHT!? DID I...AT SOME POINT DURING THE SCHOOL TRIP...WITHOUT REALIZING IT...?
NO WAY! NEGI'S JUST A KID, AND MY FEELINGS WOULDN'T CHANGE THIS SUDDENLY, RIGHT...?
B-DMP B-DMP
B-DMP B-DMP
B-BUT WHY IS MY HEART STILL POUNDING?
B-DMP

THANK YOU FOR ALL YOUR HELP.
STARBOOKS COFFEE
MURMUR MURMUR
'TWAS NOTHING.
ARE YOU ALL RIGHT, HEADMASTER?
AND, UM...IF MY SECRET GETS OUT, I'LL BE TURNED INTO AN ERMINE... SO PLEASE...
WE UNDERSTAND, NEGI-SENSEI.
AYE-AYE!
OUR LIPS VERY TIGHT ♡
OH, PLEASE. THIS IS NOTHING. I'M JUST GLAD KONOKA IS SAFE.
YOU DID VERY WELL, NEGI-KUN.
NO, NO!
OWWW

YOOHOO, NEGI-SENSEI! ♪
WHAT DID YOU WANT TO SHOW US?
陰陽道と西洋魔術
ONMYŌDŌ AND WESTERN MAGIC
THIS.
RUSTLE!
...I SEE. THIS IS FASCINATING.
HE SAID NEGI'S DAD WAS RESEARCHING IT.
YES. IF THIS IS ACCURATE, THEN THERE ARE SECRETS AT THIS SCHOOL EVEN BIGGER THAN LIBRARY ISLAND.
WOOOW, NEGI-KUN! NOT EVEN THE COL-LEGE CLUB MEMBERS HAVE MAPS LIKE THIS!
ALL RIGHT. WE MEMBERS OF THE LIBRARY EXPLORATION CLUB WILL DO EVERYTHING IN OUR POWER TO HELP YOU.
THANK YOU VERY MUCH!
TROT
TROT
TROT
YUE-YUE!
TEP
...ER.
THEY DIDN'T HAVE ANY TOMATO MILK... OH!
N-NEGI-SENSEI...
BLUSH

UM...
N-NODOKA-SAN! UM...
PFFT HEH.
KONK
H... HELLO!
ABUH-BUH!
I'M SORRY!
OWWW.
OWW, I-I-I-I'M SO SORRY!
LOOKS LIKE THEY'RE NERVOUS SEEING EACH OTHER AFTER THE CLASS TRIP. THEY'RE SO CUTE AND INNOCENT ♡
SMIRK
SMIRK
...
BUT LOOK HOW FLUSTERED NEGI-KUN IS ♡
CHUCKLE CHUCKLE
MAYBE NODOKA HAS A CHANCE AFTER ALL ♪
TWINGE
ERK...? SEEING THEM TOGETHER IS MAKING MY CHEST HURT?
N-NO! DOES THAT MEAN I REALLY AM...
GLINT!
OHO!?
HEH HEH HEH HEH! I SMELL IT. I SMELL IT! OVER THERE--THE A FAINT, BITTERSWEET FRAGRANCE...OF THE LOVE STENCH!!
FWIP!
LOVE STENCH !?
WHAT IS THIS TERRIBLY-NAMED THING OF WHICH YOU SPEAK!?
I AM NOT "STENCHING" !!

BACAW! BACAW! アホー アホー
GOOD WORK, ANIKI!
I GUESS THAT'S ENOUGH FOR TODAY.
THIS IS BAD. THIS IS REALLY BAD...
SWEAT SWEAT
JUST LOOKING AT HIM GETS MY HEART GOING NOW.
NO! NO, IT CAN'T BE TRUE!
B-DMP ドキ ドキ ドキ B-DMP B-DMP

FOR ONE THING, I REALLY DO HATE KIDS!!
THEY CAN'T DO ANYTHING FOR THEMSELVES, BUT THEY STILL TALK LIKE THEY'RE SO IMPORTANT, AND THEY COMPLAIN ABOUT EVERYTHING WITHOUT TRYING TO DO ANYTHING ABOUT IT...!
GH-GH
O-OKAY, SO MAYBE NEGI IS DIFFERENT, BUT...
AND HE WAS KINDA COOL ON THE CLASS TRIP SOMETIMES, AND WHAT HE SAID BACK THERE WASN'T ANYTHING YOU'D REALLY HEAR A KID SAY... BUT, BUT...
THE NEXT TIME SOMETHING HAPPENS, I WANT TO BE ABLE TO PROTECT KONOKA-SAN.
ドキ B-DMP ドキ B-DMP ドキ B-DMP ドキ B-DMP

?
キラリン♡ SPARKLE
ドッキーン B-DMP
WAAAAHHH! NOOOO! I'M JUST AS BAD AS CLASS REP!
I'M A F-F-FREAK!!
EEEK!? WHAT'S THE MATTER, ASUNA-SAN?
THRASH わたたっ
FLAIL FLAIL じたばた
WINCE びくっ

ARE YOU ALL RIGHT, ASUNA-SAN? ACK! YOUR FACE IS ALL RED!
HUH? OH, NO, IT'S NOTHING. REALLY...
よろろっ WOBBLE
IT IS NOT. COME ON, SIT DOWN.
LET ME SEE YOUR FOREHEAD.
HUH? MY FOREHEAD?
PLOP

YES, I'M CHECKING YOUR TEMPERATURE.
!!
BLUSH
STICK
WAIT A--
NEGI...
EH... ?
S-STOOOOOP!!
WAAAH !?
GULP...
NGH...

NO! I'M NOT LIKE THAT! I'M NOT!!
WHAM WHAM WHAM
KRACK
WAAAH!
RUMBLE
GYRAAA! ASUNA-SAN, NO!
CRUMBLE
PATTER PATTER
DASH
I'M NOT LIKE THAT!
GONG
HEY... YOU OKAY ?
NNNGH.

WHAT'S YOUR PROBLEM, ANE-SAN? YOU'RE ACTING WEIRD TODAY.
UM... WELL...
HFF
はぁ…
WH-WHAT AM I GONNA DO? AM I REALLY... WITH NEGI...!?
HE'S FIVE YEARS YOUNGER THAN ME.
Graceful Angel
OH...I JUST REMEMBERED. I KNOW YOU'D KNOW BETTER, BUT...YOU DIDN'T EAT ANY OF THE CHOCOLATE ON MY DESK, DID YOU?
OH YEAH! WE FORGOT TO TELL YOU ABOUT THAT.
EH?
GULP!
YOU REMEMBER. WHEN I FIRST CAME HERE, I TRIED TO MAKE A LOVE POTION, AND IT DIDN'T WORK?
IT'S BEEN BOTHERING ME ALL THIS TIME, SO I ASKED CHAMO-KUN TO ORDER SOME FOR ME.
OVER MagiNet.
......
HUH?
LOVE ...?
JUST GIVE SOMEONE THAT CHOCOLATE, AND THEY INSTANTLY FALL IN LOVE WITH THE NEXT PERSON THEY SEE.
HEH HEH HEH. IT'S POWERFUL BLACK MARKET STUFF. USE THEM WISELY, ANE-SAN.
BUT THE EFFECTS ONLY LAST FOR ABOUT HALF A DAY.
L...LOVE... POTION?
YES. I'M SORRY YOU HAD TO WAIT SO LONG.
O...O...OH... IN THAT CASE...
?
TREMBLE TREMBLE
ふるふる

THWACK!
YOU SHOULD HAVE SAID SO!!
WA HYAAAAA!?
?
WH...WHAT A RELIEF!
IT WAS ALL BECAUSE OF THE LOVE POTION...
おほおおお〜っ
WHEEEEW.
...DON'T TELL ME YOU DID EAT SOME, ASUNA-SAN?
O-OF COURSE I DIDN'T! AH HA HA HA!
SHE TOTALLY DID.

AH
AAHH! NEGI-SENSEI, ASUNA-SAN! HELP!
WH-WH-WHAT'S GOING ON!?
TWITCH, TWITCH
ぴくぴく
I LOVE YOU! ~♡
OOOOHHH! I LOVE YOU, SET-CHAN!
NUZZLE
NUZZLE
I'LL JUST GET RID OF THESE.
HEY! I PAID A LOT FOR THOSE!
CLANG
DON'T WASTE FOOD!
PLOP
PLOP

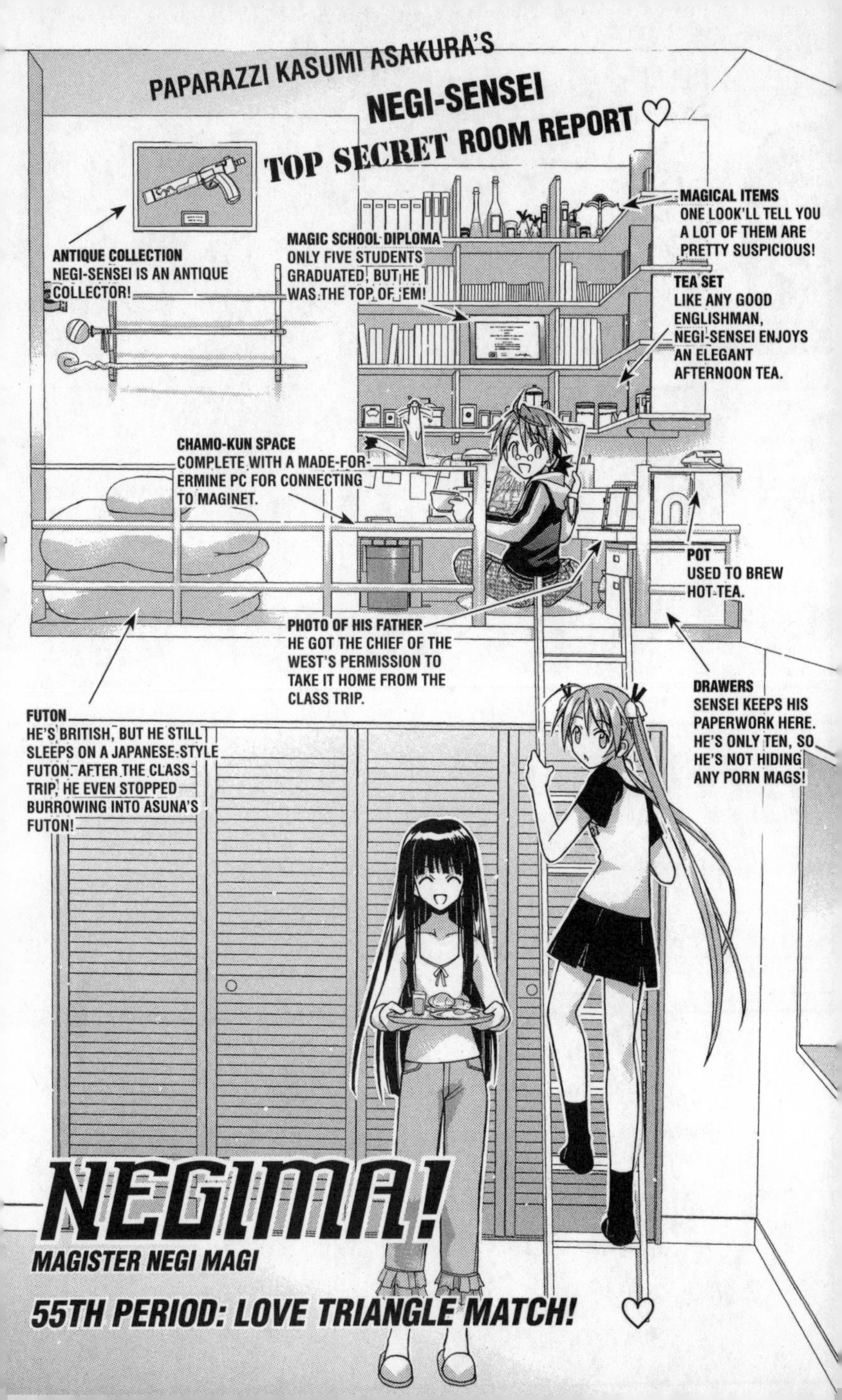
PAPARAZZI KASUMI ASAKURA'S
NEGI-SENSEI
TOP SECRET ROOM REPORT
MAGICAL ITEMS
ONE LOOK'LL TELL YOU A LOT OF THEM ARE PRETTY SUSPICIOUS!
ANTIQUE COLLECTION
NEGI-SENSEI IS AN ANTIQUE COLLECTOR!
MAGIC SCHOOL DIPLOMA
ONLY FIVE STUDENTS GRADUATED, BUT HE WAS THE TOP OF 'EM!
TEA SET
LIKE ANY GOOD ENGLISHMAN, NEGI-SENSEI ENJOYS AN ELEGANT AFTERNOON TEA.
CHAMO-KUN SPACE
COMPLETE WITH A MADE-FOR-ERMINE PC FOR CONNECTING TO MAGINET.
POT
USED TO BREW HOT TEA.
PHOTO OF HIS FATHER
HE GOT THE CHIEF OF THE WEST'S PERMISSION TO TAKE IT HOME FROM THE CLASS TRIP.
DRAWERS
SENSEI KEEPS HIS PAPERWORK HERE. HE'S ONLY TEN, SO HE'S NOT HIDING ANY PORN MAGS!
FUTON
HE'S BRITISH, BUT HE STILL SLEEPS ON A JAPANESE-STYLE FUTON. AFTER THE CLASS TRIP, HE EVEN STOPPED BURROWING INTO ASUNA'S FUTON!
NEGIMA!
MAGISTER NEGI MAGI
55TH PERIOD: LOVE TRIANGLE MATCH!

ALLLL-RIGHT! I'M GETTING BACK TO WORK TODAY!
MIDTERMS ARE COMING UP, SO STUDY HARD, ASUNA-SAN!
ERK... SH-SHUT UP!
AH HA HA! YOU'RE IN A GOOD MOOD, NEGI-KUN!
STOMP STOMP STOMP STO
ANYWAY...I'M GOING TO HAVE MY TEACHING DUTIES AND MY TRAINING TO GET STRONGER. ...IT'S GOING TO BE HARD, BUT I HAVE TO DO MY BEST!
TO BE A MAGISTER MAGI... TO CATCH UP TO MY FATHER...!
GH
THAT REMINDS ME. EVANGELINE-SAN SAID SHE WAS GOING TO TEST ME.
ON SATURDAY...
A DISCIPLE-SHIP TEST... I WONDER WHAT SHE'LL MAKE ME DO...
FIGHT! FIGHT!
50 TICKETS ON THE CAP-TAIN!!
HUH...? IS THAT...

KŪ FEI -SAN?!
DUN!
O-O-OH NO! KŪ FEI-SAN IS SURROUNDED BY BAD GUYS!!
HOP
'TIS NOTHING OUT OF THE ORDINARY.
TODAY WILL BE THE DAY WE FINALLY BEAT YOU, C-MAC CAPTAIN KŪ FEI!!
WHOOOOOAAA!
WHOOSH
C-MAC = CHINESE MARTIAL ARTS CLUB
WHAM
WHAP
KŪ'S IS THE CHAMPION OF THE SCHOOL'S MARTIAL ARTS TOURNAMENT.
THUS, SHE FACES NO END OF CHALLENGERS.
BANG
KONK
CRACK
WHACK
POW
POW
GAWK
ZSH!
YOU ALL SO WEAK!
THERE NO ONE STRONGER?
DU-DUN
TH-THAT'S OUR CAPTAIN... SHE'S STRONG...

NEGI-BŌZU, NIHAO!
CLAP CLAP
OHH
IT AIN'T OVER YET, CAPTAIN FEI!!
ROAR!
MAHORA HIGH "KARATE LOVERS KLUB"
NEGI-KUN, WATCH OUT!
AIEEEE!?
CLAMOR CLAMOR
GOOD MORNING, KŪ FEI-SAN!
IT...
GH-GH-GH
MURMUR
GWEEEHH!?
MAHORA HIGH
PAO QUAN!!!
WHAM!
Y-YOU OKAY, NEGI-BŌZU?
SORRY.
I-I'M FINE.
THANK YOU.
HA HA HA!
SHE'S GOOD!
OOOH
Z-ZNN
WHY-Y-Y?
CLAMOR CLAMOR

YOU'RE SO STRONG, KŪ FEI-SAN.
NYAH HA HAH! BUT I NO MATCH FOR KAEDE AND MANA.
MY SPECIALTY XING YIQUAN AND BAGUAZ HANG.
ALSO DABBLE IN BAJIQUAN AND XINYI LIUHEBA-FAQUAN, BECAUSE IS FAD.
WOW, THERE ARE SO MANY DIFFERENT KINDS OF CHINESE MARTIAL ARTS!
HMMM...
KŪ FEI-SANH...
GOOD MORNING, NEGI-SENSEI! ♡
HO HO HO
OH, GOOD MORNING, LADIES.
DANG DONG
I THINK THIS WILL BE ON THE TEST, SO MAKE SURE TO REVIEW IT.
AND THAT'S ALL FOR TODAY.
ALL STAND!
ALL BOW!
UMMM...ER, KŪ FEI-SAN, MAY I HAVE A WORD WITH YOU?
HUH?
W-WORD WITH ME?
MURMUR...

OH... BUT MAYBE NOT IN FRONT OF EVERYONE...
HMMM
OKAY!
WILL YOU COME SEE ME AFTER SCHOOL AT THE GIANT STEPS IN FRONT OF THE WORLD TREE, PLEASE?
I NO MIND ...
ガラッ
CLATTER
THANK YOU! I'LL SEE YOU LATER, THEN.
SHUT
しーん
HUSH
STOMP STOMP STOMP
WH-WH-WHAT IS THE MEANING OF THIS!? WHY WOULD KŪ FEI-SAN GET A PERSONAL INVITATION TO TALK TO NEGI-SENSEI!?
THE WORLD TREE PLAZA IS A POPULAR SPOT FOR LOVE CONFESSIONS!
WHAT!? SO NEGI-KUN'S GONNA TELL HER HE LOVES HER!?
ひそ
WHISPER
WELL, YOU KNOW, I HEAR HE WAS ATTACKED BY THUG THIS MORNING, AND KŪ-CHAN RESCUED HIM!
S-SO IT WAS LOVE AT FIRST SIGHT WITH KŪ-CHAN!?
NO WAY!
ARE YOU SERIOUS!? KŪ-CHAN WASN'T EVEN IN THE RUNNING UNTIL NOW!
WHISPER
ひそひそ
WHISPER
WHISPER
ひそ
THERE THEY GO AGAIN ...

じぃ...
STARE...
?

BUT KŪ-CHAN'S, LIKE, YOU KNOW. **REALLY STUPID.**
HE'D NEVER GO FOR HER.
WHISPER
ひそひそ
WHISPER
WHISPER
ひそ
うんうん
MM-HM.
YEAH, SHE IS.
THE FIGHTING FREAK, BAKA YELLOW.
AND SHE HAS NO SEX APPEAL.
GUESS IT CAN'T BE A CONFESSION.
YOU'RE STUPID, TOO, MAKIE.
THEY'RE ALL DONE. IT'S A NEW RECIPE TODAY... ♡
TRY IT.
キャッ
SQUEE
OOH, I WAIT FOR THIS!
YOU GIRLS EAT, TOO!
キャッ
SQUEE
YAY! THANK YOU!

AFTER ALL THAT TALK, HERE WE ARE SPYING.
IN A GROUP, NO LESS.
WE JUST CAN'T HELP BUT WONDER.
I REALLY DOUBT IT, THOUGH.
WONDER WHAT NEGI-BŌZU WANT TALK ABOUT.
KŪ FEI-SAN...!
SORRY I'M LATE!
OH! THERE'S NEGI-KUN!
HE'S SO CUTE IN HIS STREET CLOTHES! ♡
LICK
TROT TROT
WELL? WHAT YOU WANTING?
UMM, WELL...
GH

HYAAHH!!
GAP
OH!
YOINK
WHRR
WHOOM
SHPAH
CATCH
GRAB
ERK!
AAHH!
THEY'RE HUG-GING !?
BUZZ
BUZZ
S-S-SO HE REALLY IS CONFESSING HIS LOVE TO HER!!?
COME TO THINK OF IT, I DID HEAR THAT SOME-ONE SAW KU-CHAN SNEAK OUT OF HER ROOM ON THE THIRD DAY OF THE CLASS TRIP...
IS THAT WHEN...
DOES THAT MEAN THEY LOVE EACH OTHER!? ALREADY!?
WAAAAAH!
I COULDN'T TELL!
WHAT!? WHO INITIATED IT!?
HEH HEH...
YOU NO THINK IT WRONG, THROW SUCKER PUNCH AT STUDENT?
IF REAL FIGHT, I NOW KNOCK YOU OUT WITH PUNCH TO BACK OF HEAD.
KNOCK KNOCK
I-I'M IMPRESSED, KŪ FEI-SAN. E-ER...UM.
OOOH!
THE TRUTH IS, KŪ FEI-SAN...
I...
AAAAAHHH! HE REALLY IS GOING TO CONFESS!?

HEEEY! NEGI!
I KNEW WE'D FIND YOU HERE!
STAMP STAMP

OH! ASUNA-SAN!
OH!

SETSUNA-SAN SAYS SHE'S NEVER BEEN BOWLING OR TO KARAOKE BEFORE, SO WE'RE GONNA TAKE HER. WANNA COME?
YOU CAN COME, TOO, KŪ-CHAN!

OH, YES! I GO! I GO! ♡
I LOV BOWLING!
TAKING SETSUNA-SAN BOWLING... SOUNDS FUN. LET'S GO!
I GUESS I CAN ASK HER LATER...

BARGING IN RIGHT AT THE MOST IMPORTANT PART!
ARGH! I WON'T BE SATISFIED UNTIL I SEE THIS WHOLE THING THROUGH TO THE END!!
RUSTLE
RUSTLE
RUSTLE
AH! CLASS REP!?

OH, WHAT A COINCIDENCE, NEGI-SENSEI ♡ WHY, I'D LOVE TO GO BOWLING WITH YOU!
OH HO HO HO
THAT'S OUR CLASS REP
OOOH! WE'RE GOING BOWLING! ♡ I'LL LET EVERYONE KNOW!

TORI BOWL
24hours!
BOWLING FEST
WEEKDAY DISCOUNT

KRASH KER-CLUNK
CLAMOR
CLAMOR
WHOA, AWESOME! SEVEN STRIKES IN A ROW!!
AND WITH SUCH TERRIBLE FORM, TOO!
SET-CHAN'S TERRIBLE, JUST LIKE ME!
HEH HEH HEH. I HAVE 21 POINTS.
HA HA HA. IT'S HARD TO CONTROL MY STRENGTH PROPERLY.
55 POINTS.
WOW, THAT'S AMAZING, KŪ FEI-SAN!
I'M IMPRESSED!
CLAP CLAP CLAP
NYO HO HO HO! ♡
YOU JUST LEAVE TO ME. ♪
BURRN...
STEE-RIKE!

SORRY. I DON'T KNOW WHY WE HAVE MORE THAN HALF THE CLASS HERE.
IT'S ALL RIGHT...
ALLEY-OOP!
AH HA HA.
キャッ
HERE I GO!
キャッ
CHUCKLE CHUCKLE
HEE HEE
NN?
ズゴゴゴ...
RUMBLE RUMBLE RUMBLE
HRMM!
MAYBE I IMAGINE. I FEELING TERRIBLE CHI ENERGY.
HMPH!
MAYBE IS CHI MASTER NEARBY?
SIGH...BUT DOES NEGI-SENSEI REALLY LOVE KŪ FEI...?
WHAT WILL I DO IF HE DOES...?

HMMM... I DON'T MEAN TO BRAG, BUT I LIKE NEGI-KUN A LOT.
...CUZ HE'S SO CUTE!
HRRM.
BUT NEGI-KUN'S TEN, SO IT'S NOT LIKE A "I WANT HIM TO BE MY BOYFRIEND" KIND OF LIKE. ...BUT, BUT I'D HATE TO HAVE KŪ FEI TAKE HIM AWAY FROM ME...
TREMBLE TREMBLE
ぷるぷる
I...
I...
I CANNOT APPROVE OF THIS!
EVEN IF NEGI-SENSEI HAS MADE UP HIS MIND!!
I REFUSE TO SIT BACK AND LET DESTINY PLAY OUT LIKE THIS! EVEN IF THE GODS ALLOW IT, I, AYAKA YUKIHIRO, WILL NOT!
CLASS REP!?
AN EXPLOSION OF STUPID !?
THEREFORE, KŪ FEI-SAN, I CHALLENGE YOU TO A DUEL!!!
FWIP!
CATCH
HUH !?
DUEL? I ALWAYS ACCEPT CHALLENGE!
ARE YOU TWO READY!!? WHOEVER LOSES GIVES UP ON HIM!! NO HARD FEELINGS!
WHAAAT !?
HOLD ON, CLASS REP!
RAR
I NOT KNOW WHAT GOING ON, BUT YOU SURE, CLASS REP?
I GOOD AT EVERYTHING BUT STUDY.
SMIRK
GLINT!
HEH HEH HEH HEH HEH. I'LL MAKE YOU CRY.

WHAT IS CHAL-LENGE!?
CLAMOR ワイ。
CLAMOR ワイ
ONE GAME OF BOWLING!!
HEY, GIRLS! THEY'RE STARTING A DUEL!
OOH! SOME-THING'S HAPPEN-ING OVER THERE!
GOOD LUCK, GIRLS!
TEN TICK-ETS ON KŪ FEI!!
FIVE ON CLASS REP!!
WOW.
CLAP パチ パチ CLAP
?
HO HO HO!
パカァ
HA!
バッキャァーン
KER-SMASH
KER-CRASH
NNNN...
TAKE THAT!
WAAH
WAAH
ゴト
CLUNK
!?
ゴトッ CLUNK
ゴロゴロゴロ ROLL ROLL ROLL
OOO HHH !?
EEP!
!?
ドヨドヨドヨ BUZZ BUZZ BUZZ

KER-SMASH!
WHOA! EIGHT STRIKES IN A ROW!!
WHO *IS* THAT GIRL?

HEY, DID SOMETHING HAPPEN WITH THEM?
CLASS REP IS SCARY...
UM, WELL... YOU SEE...

WHAAAAT!? ~?! NEGI LIKES KŪ FEI?!
←TOILET

KER-CRASH
AH HA HA HA. NO, NO. NO WAY. BOOKSTORE-CHAN IS ONE THING, BUT KŪ FEI AND NEGI? NOT A CHANCE.
CRASH
BUT HARUNA SAID IT WAS PRACTICALLY SET IN STONE.
IT'S TRUE, ASUNA! WE SAW THEM HUGGING, AND HE WAS RIGHT ABOUT TO CONFESS HIS LOVE!

AND HEY, WHY ARE YOU ASKING *ME* ABOUT THIS?
WELL, YOU'RE BAKA RED, AND YOU'RE NEGI-KUN'S GUARDIAN...
ERK...
SO, ASUNA. WHAT DO YOU THINK WE SHOULD DO?
SHOULD WE TELL KŪ-CHAN?
KŪ-SAN'S NOT VERY BRIGHT ABOUT LOVE.
HMMM, BUT I CAN'T REALLY TRUST PARU'S INFO...
WELL *EXCUSE* ME!

ANYWAY, LET'S JUST KEEP AN EYE ON THEM. I THINK IT'S BETTER NOT TO TELL KŪ FEI.
Y-YEAH. YOU'RE RIGHT.
KER-CRASH

269
229
17
AYAKA YUKIHIRO 269
MAKIE SASAKI 229
NODOKA MIYAZAKI 17
DRR

KŪ FEI 300
300
DU-DUN!

I WIN~~~~♪
WHOOOOOAA!
I'VE NEVER SEEN A PERFECT GAME BEFORE!
PSHH
AAAUGH, THERE'S NO WAY WE COULD BEAT THAT!
WHIMPER.
BUT A LOSS IS A LOSS. AND THAT WAS A BIG ONE.
SIGH...

GOOD WORK MAKIE-SAN! YOU WERE REALLY GOOD OUT THERE, TOO!
...EH?
CLASP
NEGI-KUN...
I'LL SUPPORT YOU IN ANY LOVE YOU MAY PURSUE, NEGI-KUN... GOOD LUCK!
HUH?
OH NO, I LOST. WH-WH-WHAT DO I DO?
OH, STOP IT, NODOKA! HOW COULD YOU PARTICIPATE IN SOMETHING SO IDIOTIC?
B-B-BUT NEGI-SENSEI...
THAT'S NO REASON TO PLAY ALONG WITH THEIR LITTLE BOWLING CHALLENGE! UGH, YOU'RE SO DUMB.

NODOKA! ARE YOU REALLY GOING TO LET KŪ FEI TAKE NEGI-KUN AWAY FROM YOU!?
I THINK THAT'S JUST A STUPID RUMOR.
SHAKE
SHAKE
SHAKE
BUT NEGI-SENSEI HAS MADE UP HIS MIND. THERE'S NOTHING I CAN DO ABOUT IT.
HOW CAN YOU SAY THAT!? LOVE IS WAR!! YOU'VE ALREADY TOLD HIM YOU LOVE HIM! YOU'RE LIKE TWO STEPS AHEAD OF HER!
YOU JUST NEED TO FIND A WAY TO GET HIM ALONE, PUSH HIM DOWN, AND KISS HIM OR SOMETHING! GET YOUR LEAD BACK! TAKE HIS LOVE BY FORCE!!
P... PUSH...
F... FORCE ...?
I CAN'T DO THAT!
YES YOU CAN!!
RAR
EEEEK!
LOOK! HE'S GOING TO THE BATH-ROOM!
NOW'S YOUR CHANCE !!
R... RIGHT.
OKAY...
SHE'S RIGHT... I HAVE TO WORK AT THIS... FIGHT, NODOKA!
GH
H...HERE GOES!
IS SHE GOING TO BE OKAY?
SO SHE'S GOING TO PUSH DOWN A TEN-YEAR-OLD, HUH?
HMM-MM.
SO I GOT A LITTLE CAR-RIED AWAY.
OH...
WH... WHAT'S THE MATTER, NODOKA-SAN?
B-DMP
B-DMP
B-DMP
B-DMP
B-DMP
B-DMP
B-DMP
UH, UM...
CRASH
KA-CRASH
CRASH
KA-CRASH
SHE SURE IS TAKING HER TIME.
KA-CRASH
OH!

THEY'RE BACK!
AH HA HA
HEE HEE HEE!

HUH? WHAT? WHAT HAPPENED!? THEY'RE REALLY HITTING IT OFF!
CAN IT BE? CAN IT BE?
...
NODOKA!! HOW DID IT GO?

IT WAS A B-B-BIG SUCCESS!
SQUEEE!
SERIOUSLY!? SO, WHAT DID YOU DO!? DID YOU PUSH HIM DOWN!? DID YOU KISS HIM!?

I MADE A LOT OF SMALL TALK WITH HIM
I'M IN HEAVEN!
IF I DIED THIS YEAR, I'D BE HAPPY!
SEVEN MINUTES OF SMALL TALK... THAT'S A NEW RECORD.
BEEP

THAT WASN'T THE PLAN!
MORON!
SMACK!
I'M SORRY!!

THIS IS NO TIME FOR SLAPSTICK COMEDY, YOU TWO.

NEGI-SENSEI'S GONE TO TALK TO KŪ FEI-SAN.
WHAT!?

STOMP STOMP STOMP
AH!
ZSH!
UMM, WE GOT INTER-RUPTED EARLIER.
SO I'D LIKE TO START OVER. THERE'S SOME-THING I'D LIKE TO ASK YOU, KŪ FEI-SAN.
O-OH NO! IT'S LOVE CONFES-SION TIME FOR REAL NOW!
UM... THAT IS...
KŪ FEI-SAN?
I...
LUNGE
NEGI-SEN--
NO, CLASS REP! YOU CAN'T STOP HIM! THAT'D BE UNFAIR!
I...
DUN!
I WANT YOU TO TEACH ME CHINESE MARTIAL ARTS!
......
...I KNEW IT.
HUH?

OHO!
CHINESE MARTIAL-ART?
YES. I FOUGHT A VERY STRONG BOY ONCE, AND HE USED THE SAME TECHNIQUE YOU USED THIS MORNING.
AND THERE'S THIS OTHER BOY NAMED KOTARO. HE'S REALLY STRONG, TOO.
WHAM!
MRPLE!?
WHAM!
SO I WAS HOPING YOU WOULD TEACH ME, KŪ FEI-SAN.

SO...
...YOU WANT TO GET STRONGER.
YES.
HA HA HA! OKAY, I DO IT ♡
I LOVE STRONG BOYS!
YOU GETTING STRONG ENOUGH, YOU BE MY HUSBAND!
BAM
BAM
BAM
EH!? H-HUS-BAND!?
HA HA HA HA! JOKE, JOKE!
FOR NOW.
HA HA HA HA!
RUMBLE RUMBLE RUMBLE
NN?
DID YOU HAVE TO PUT US THROUGH THAT?
AIEEEEEE! WHAT I DO!?
LADIES, PLEASE!
OOO-HHH.
I FIGURED THAT'S WHAT WAS GOING ON.
B-DUMP CHING

超包子

ポ
BOUND
チャレッ♪
TRALA
ワ
WAAH
ッ
SHE'S DONE IT! MAKIE SASAKI, THE PINK ALBATROSS OF MAHORA ACADEMY, HAS DONE IT!
EH...?
UH...
SHE'S WON THE NATIONAL CHAMPION-SHIP!!
NIKH

NEGIMA!
MAGISTER NEGI MAGI
56TH PERIOD:
NEGI, MAKIE, AND THE DISCIPLESHIP TEST

CON-GRATU-LATIONS, MAKIE-SAN!!
YOU DID IT, MAKIE!
THANK YOU, NEGI-KUN! THANK YOU, EVERY-ONE! I DID IT ♡
WAAH
WAAH
...E-SAN.
MAKIE-SAN!
I WON ...
...MNYAH.
...FNYAH !?
WHAT?!
HUH? NEGI-KUN!!
BOLT
DUN
I'M GLAD YOU WANT TO WIN THE GYMNASTICS CHAMPIONSHIPS, BUT I HOPE YOU'LL WORK HARD AT ENGLISH, TOO.
AH HA HA!

S-SORRY, NEGI-KUN. I WOKE UP EARLY FOR PRACTICE, SO I DIDN'T GET ENOUGH SLEEP.
I SEE.

YOU MUST REALLY LOVE GYMNASTICS, MAKIE-SAN.
OH, WELL, I...
BLUSH

TROT TROT

I'M MAKIE SASAKI, AGE 14! I'M IN MY THIRD YEAR AT MAHORA ACADEMY JUNIOR HIGH!!
MY GRADES AREN'T REALLY THE BEST, BUT I'VE GOT AWESOME REFLEXES. I'M A BRIGHT AND CHEERFUL, SPORTY GIRL. ♡
MY LIKES INCLUDE NEGI-KUN ♡
MAKIE!
BUT WHAT I LIKE EVEN MORE IS RHYTHMIC GYMNASTICS!!
I WAS JUST ABOUT TO GO SEE COACH NINOMIYA.
I'LL GO WITH YOU PART-WAY.
I'VE BEEN DOING GYMNASTICS SINCE I WAS FIVE, SO I THINK I'M PRETTY GOOD!
THEN LET'S RACE ♡
HEY, NO FAIR!
WHEN IT COMES TO RHYTHMIC GYMNASTICS, I WON'T LET ANYONE BEAT ME ♪
IT'S NOT EVERY DAY WE SEE YOU IN THE GYM'S FACULTY ROOM, SHIZUNA.
HOW ARE THINGS GOING WITH THE LITTLE BOY TEACHER?
NEGI-KUN'S A GOOD BOY. HE'S DOING WELL. ...WHAT ARE YOU WATCHING?
OH, THAT'S MAKIE-CHAN.
IS THIS THE VIDEO OF LAST YEAR'S TOURNAMENT?
OUR TEAM IS HAVING PRELIMINARIES FOR THE SUMMER TOURNAMENT ON SUNDAY.
I'M STUDYING UP.

MAKIE-CHAN DOES WORK HARD AT HER CLUB ACTIVITIES. HOW IS SHE DOING?
TRC TROT TROT
NINO-MIYA-SENS...
MAKIE?
TO BE HONEST, I DON'T THINK SHE'LL MAKE THE TOURNAMENT.
SWOOP

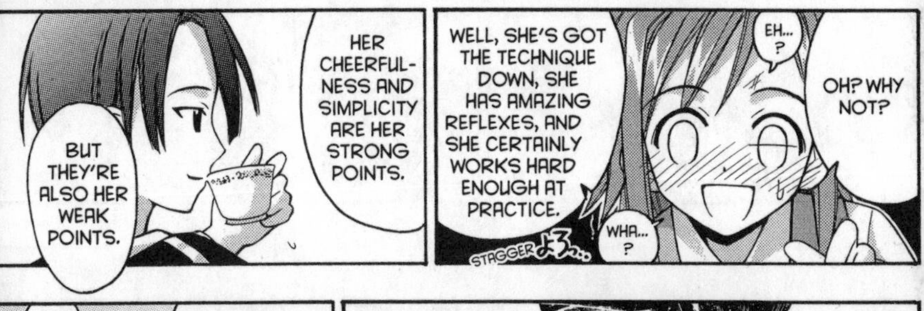
OH? WHY NOT?
EH...?
WELL, SHE'S GOT THE TECHNIQUE DOWN, SHE HAS AMAZING REFLEXES, AND SHE CERTAINLY WORKS HARD ENOUGH AT PRACTICE.
WHA...?
STAGGER
HER CHEERFUL-NESS AND SIMPLICITY ARE HER STRONG POINTS.
BUT THEY'RE ALSO HER WEAK POINTS.

TO PUT IT CHARITABLY, SHE'S SIMPLE AND INNOCENT.
NOT SO CHARITABLY, HER PERFORMANCES CHILDISH. LIKE SOMETHING YOU OUT OF A GRADE SCHOOL.
CLANG
SHE'S HAVING A HARD TIME OVERCOMING THAT; SHE CAN'T GET PAST THAT PLATEAU.
HOW UN-SPARING OF YOU.
UM... MAKIE...
GRADE SCHOOL
CHILDISH
SIMPLE
STAGGER...
ERK...

WHAM!
AH!
OH! NEGI-KUN!!
MAKIE-SAN!?
WAAH!
CRY
CRY
WH-WHAT'S THE MATTER?
DASH!
WAAAA-AHHH!
MAKIE !?

AH!
D-DASH!
IT'S NOTHING!

I-I WONDER WHAT HAPPENED.
I... HAVE NO IDEA.

TWEET TWEET
THE NEXT MORNING...

662 IZUMI, AKO
SASAKI, MAKI
JR. HIGH GIRLS' DORM

WAKE...

SIT
SIGH...

COME ON, EVA-CHAN! WHY ARE YOU BEING SO MEAN TO NEGI-KUN? WHAT'S WRONG WITH MAKING HIM YOUR DISCIPLE?
I DON'T KNOW WHAT KIND OF DISCIPLE, BUT STILL.
IT WOULD APPEAR THAT SHE IS JEALOUS.
YOU LIKE THE BRAT THAT MUCH, HUH?
SHAKE
SHAKE
I SAID! I'M NOT JEALOUS!
HMPH! PLAYING GAMES WITH LITTLE KIDS ISN'T MY THING.
AND NEITHER IS TALKING TO CHILDISH BRATS LIKE YOU, MAKIE SASAKI.
WHA--!?
BRAT
SNAP
LOOK WHO'S TALKING, EVA-CHAN! YOU'VE GOT THE BODY OF A LITTLE KID!
UGH!
WELL NYAH-NYAH! I DON'T CARE! I SAW IT! NEGI-KUN WAS SUUUUUPER STRONG!
HE DOESN'T NEED YOUR HELP! HE'LL BE A MASTER IN NO TIME WITHOUT YOU! SO THERE!
EH? JUST A-- MAKIE-SAN...
MAHORA
POP
GRR...
SO SHE REMEMBERS THAT, HUH?
SHE WAS MY SLAVE, DARNIT...
MAKIE-SAN, YOU REMEMBER?
HUH? REMEMBER WHAT?
FINE. I JUST DECIDED HOW I'M GOING TO TEST YOU.
USE YOUR LITTLE WANNABE KUNG-FU TO LAND A PUNCH ON CHACHAMARU.
IF YOU CAN DO IT, YOU PASS.
...BUT REMEMBER, IT'S ONE-ON-ONE.

GREAT ♪ WE ACCEPT !!
DUN
THAT'LL BE A PIECE OF CAKE FOR NEGI-KUN!
M-M-MAKIE-SAN...!
TEACH HIM A LESSON, CHACHAMARU.
YES, MISTRESS. BUT...
NO BUTS. JUST DO IT.
YOU DON'T HAVE TO HURT HIM.
YES, MISTRESS.
I BEG YOUR PARDON, NEGI-SENSEI.
ZSH!
HUH?
!
DUN!
CHACHAMARU
!?
DSH
WHAM!
KAPOW
GYA!
UNGH!
AH!
NEGI-KUN!
NNNNGH...
FSHH...

MAKIE... YOU OFF TO MORNING PRACTICE?
NOPE. SELF-TRAINING.
...HAVE YOU BEEN CRY-ING?
ARE YOU OKAY?
I WASN'T CRY-ING!
MM!
FLOP
べたー
NNN!
HUFF!
HUFF!
MAYBE I'LL HEAD TOWARD WORLD TREE HILL.
MAHO
STEP STEP
チチチチ...
CHIRP
チュン
CHIRP
チュン
CHIRP
チュチュン...
HUFF
HUFF
WHEW.
CHILDISH, HUH? ..WHAT AM I MISSING?
SMACK
パ
WHAP
SMACK
パ
WHAP
パ
HM...?
WHAT'S THAT SOUND...?

HUH...? NEGI-KUN ?
SMACK
WHACK
ZSH!
HFF
は
HFF
は
WHAT'S HE DOING HERE SO EARLY IN THE MORNING?
SS
HA!
SMACK
WHAP
HA!
ZSH
OH...
HA!

OKAY! NEXT.
ZSH
NEEEGI-KUN!♡
ばーん!
WHAM!
わたたたっ
WA-WA-WAH!
H-HUH? MAKIE-SAN? OUT FOR A MORNING JOG?
WHACHA DOIN', NEGI-KUN?
IS THAT THE CHINESE MARTIAL ARTS YOU WERE TALKING ABOUT THE OTHER DAY?

Y-YES. KU FEI-SAN HAS BEEN TEACHING ME FOR TWO DAYS NOW.
RUFFLE RUFFLE
くしゃくしゃ
WOW. YOU'RE LOOKING GOOD FOR JUST TWO DAYS OF TRAINING.
I'M IMPRESSED!

HEY, HEY, NEGI-KUN. ARE YOU GONNA BE IN THE SCHOOL'S MARTIAL ARTS TOURNAMENT?
N-NO, THAT'S NOT WHY I...
HMMMM?
YOU'RE ALL SWEATY AND STINKY, NEGI-KUN ♡
ふにふに
SQUISH SQUISH

NEGI-KUN...
IS IT JUST ME, OR HAVE YOU GOTTEN A LITTLE MORE GROWN-UP SINCE THE CLASS TRIP?
EHEH HEH HEH ♡

EH...?
Y-YOU THINK SO?
びくっ
WINCE

HEY, HEY! DO THAT ONE AGAIN ♡
YEAH ♡
OH. ALL RIGHT.
HMPH. ...KUNG FU, HUH?
ZSH

BOW
ペコリ…
WELL AREN'T WE JUST FULL OF ENTHUSIASM.
HUH? EVA-SAMA, CHACHAMARU-SAN? GOOD MORNING ♡
OH, GOOD MORNING!
ARE YOU HERE ON A JOB?
SO YOU DECIDED TO TRAIN IN KUNG-FU, HUH?
THEN I GUESS YOU WON'T MIND IF WE FORGET ABOUT THIS WHOLE DISCIPLE THING.
むすっ…
SULK
URP !?
SHOCK
HUH...? WHY'D I CALL HER "SAMA"?
OH, NO, THIS IS JUST... I'M RESEARCHING THAT BOY'S FIGHTING STYLE...!
FLAIL FLAIL
I DON'T CARE. I NEVER HAD ANY INTENTION OF TAKING YOU ON AS A DISCIPLE ANYWAY.
BUT-NO! IT'S NOT WHAT YOU THINK!
WHAT ARE YOU TALKING ABOUT, NEGI-KUN?
UM, WELL! I WANTED EVANGELINE-SAN TO LET ME BE HER DISCIPLE!
HRM
LATER.
IT'S APPROPRIATE, REALLY. A LITTLE KID PLAYING "KUNG-FU FIGHTER."
AH...! WAIT, PLEASE!
GOOD GRIEF.
KID...
ARE YOU JEALOUS, MISTRESS?
HEH HEH HEH
WHA...?
N-NO!

BOW
IF YOU CAN'T EVEN LAND ONE HIT ON CHACHAMARU, YOU'VE GOT NO POTENTIAL ANYWAY.
HA HA HA HA HA.
WE'LL MEET HERE. I'LL GIVE YOU UNTIL MIDNIGHT SUNDAY MORNING.
DO WHAT YOU CAN.

NEGI !?
NEGI-BŌZU!
NEGI-SENSEI !!
HEY! ARE YOU OKAY? WHAT HAP-PENED?
YOU HANG-ING IN THERE!
DID...DID I DO SOME-THING...
REALLY BAD?
DUN

DING
DONG
DANG
DONG
AFTER SCHOOL...

YOU'RE DEFI-NITELY NOT HAPPY, MAKIE. ARE YOU OKAY?
...YEAH.
FIDGET FIDGET
WHAT DO I DO? NEGI-KUN'S IN A BIG MESS, AND ALL BECAUSE OF ME.
I HAVE TO DO SOME-THING... BUT WHAT?
YEAH... OKAY!
GH
RAAAAHH!!
DASH
AH! MAKIE!

YOU FIGURE OUT SO QUICK, NEGI-BŌZU...
I THINK YOU HAVE TALENT, TOO, BUT...
HARD TO LEARN MUCH IN TWO DAYS.
WHAP
WHAP
GOOD LUCK!
WH-WHAP
CLOP
WAH!
YOU LOSE!
EEEEP!
SWOOP
DOES THAT MEAN HE WON'T GET TO BE EVA-CHAN'S DISCIPLE?
HMMM.
NEGI-SENSEI IS ONLY AN AMATEUR WHEN IT COMES TO PHYSICAL COMBAT.
STOMP STOMP STOMP STOMP STOMP
NEGI-KUUUN!
I MADE LOOOOTS OF LUNCH FOR YOU
STAC
DU-DUN!
EH!? ER...
THANK YOU VERY MUCH!?
IF YOU'RE GOING TO WIN A FIGHT, THE FIRST THING YOU NEED IS STAMINA.
OOH! LOOKS YUMMY!
DOESN'T IT? I'M A GOOD COOK! EAT LOTS
YOU MAKE AWFUL LOT.
OOH!
OSECHI!
COME, EAT UP! THE YAKINIKU'S REALLY GOOD!
CLAMOR
CLAMOR
THIS TOO, THIS TOO!
I BROUGHT STEAK, TOO
OH, RIGHT. THANKS.
MUNCH MUNCH
MRPHLE!
MWRM!

ぽっちゃり～～ん
BLOAT
HE...HE EVEN WEAKER NOW!
HE FAT-FU FIGHTER!
WOH-PAH!
NEGI-KUN!?
EH!?

I-I-I'M SORRY, NEGI-KUN!
I'M HOKAY..
B-B-BUT THAT'S OKAY! MY TEAM HAS PASSED DOWN A SECRET DIETING TECHNIQUE FOR GENERATIONS!
FIRST, WRAP YOUR WHOLE BODY IN PLASTIC WRAP.
THEN YOU PUT ON THREE BLANKETS.
ワイワイ
CLAMOR CLAMOR
キャー
KYAA
AND THEN YOU SPEND THREE HOURS IN THE SCHOOL SAUNA.
THAT WOULD KILL HIM?!
AAAH! HE EVEN MORE WEAKER...
げそ～～ん
EMACIATE
ピクピク
TWITCH TWITCH
よろよろ
WOBBLE WOBBLE
ガクガクガク
SHAKE SHAKE
WOOOH-PAAAH...
NEGI-KUN-N-N-N!!
NOOOOOOO~~!?

HA HA HA.
フラフラ
SWAY SWAY
IT'S ALL RIGHT.
I'M SOOOOO SORRY, NEGI-KUN! THIS IS ALL MY FAULT!
I JUST WANTED TO HELP, BUT I ONLY MADE IT WORSE...
NO, REALLY, MAKIE-SAN. IT'S OKAY.
B-BUT IT'S ONLY TWO DAYS UNTIL SUNDAY.
...WAIT. SUNDAY?
アホーアホー
BACAW BACAW

AAAAHHH!
I FORGOT!!
I'VE GOT PRELIMINARIES FOR THE TOURNAMENT ON SUNDAY!
WHAT!? REALLY!? ARE YOU GONNA BE OKAY!?
SO SHE HAD FORGOTTEN...
WELL, UM...
I'M NOT FEELING GOOD ABOUT IT AT ALL.
WAAAH!
WHAT? WHY NOT?
SENSEI SAID MY PERFORMANCE IS CHILDISH...
SNIFFLE
ぐす
AND ALL I EVER DO IS MAKE THINGS WORSE FOR NEGI-KUN, TOO. I'M HOPELESS...
WH-WH--
WHAT YOU SAYING?
BAKA-PINK.
THIS ISN'T LIKE YOU!
CHEER UP.
YEAH.
I KNOW! WHY DON'T YOU LET US SEE SOME GYMNASTICS, MAKI-CHAN?
I LIKE THE RIBBON! ♡
WHAAAT? I CAN'T!
SURE YOU CAN! SHOW US, SHOW US!
BUT --
OH...I WOULD LIKE TO SEE IT, TOO. I'VE NEVER SEEN YOU PERFORM, MAKIE-SAN.
NGH...
NEGI-KUN...
...O-OKAY, JUST A LITTLE...
もじ FIDGET

AHEM...
コホン...
トソッ
TMP

TRA-LA
...
UM...
TWIST TWIST
IT... I-IT--
IT'S KINDA...LIKE THAT...
W--
WOO-OOW!
WE COULD TOTALLY SEE YOUR PANTIES.
CLAP CLAP CLAP
OOOH!
THAT WAS SO GOOD! I DON'T SEE ANY REASON TO WORRY!
BUT SENSEI, SHE SAYS I LOOK LIKE A GRADE SCHOOLER...
YOU DO NOT!!
I DON'T KNOW ANYTHING ABOUT GYMNAS-TICS, BUT THAT WAS WONDERFUL!
BEAUTIFUL, HONEST, AND STRAIGHT-FORWARD--JUST LIKE YOU, MAKIE-SAN!
HE'S DEFI-NITELY NOT JAPANESE. LAYING ON THE PRAISE WITHOUT A HINT OF BASHFUL-NESS.
AND HOW!
REALLY ?
REALLY! I WAS AMAZED!
TH...
THANK YOU, GI-KUN.
GLOOOM
BUT THE TEST IS IN THREE DAYS...
THAT'S TRUE, BUT...
YOU'VE ALREADY COME THIS FAR. IT WOULD BE A SHAME TO TURN BACK NOW.
SIGH

WE HAVE TWO DAYS.
LET'S PRACTICE TO-GETHER!
OKAY, MAKIE-SAN?
OH... OKAY...
..NEGI-KUN.
COME, NEGI-BŌZU. WE KEEP TRAIN-ING.
RIGHT!
WHAP WHAP
RIGHT HAND TOO SLOW!
R-RIGHT!
MAKE FIRST MOVE OR GET BEAT UP
WHAP WHAP WHAP
ASUNA ...
NN ?
NEGI-KUN ISN'T JUST CUTE.
HE'S KINDA COOL, TOO.
EH ?

TWEET
TWEET
チュンチュン
CHIRP
CHIRP
チチチ…
FRIDAY
4:00 A.M.
PUFF
PUFF
パフパフ
ANYWAY
HM HMMM
~ん♪
PUFF
PUFF
PUFF...
パフパフパフ..
MAKIE... MORNING PRACTICE AGAIN?
SCRIT
SCRIT
カキカキ
MMMM.
Y... YOU'RE GOING TO PRAC-TICE. RIGHT?
YUP ♪
YUP ♡ WITH NEGI-KUN!
PFFFT!
WHO ARE YOU!?
SPIN
くるっ
CUPIE
ぎゅぴーーん
DRIP
タラー
WELL, I'M OFF!
WHA !?
WAIT, WAIT! YOU'RE NOT GOING OUT LIKE THAT, ARE YOU?
YOUR LIP GLOSS IS DRIPPING! HERE, LET ME SEE YOUR FACE!

NEGIMA!

MAGISTER NEGI MAGI

57TH - 58TH PERIOD: LAND THAT PUNCH!

I'M MAKIE SASAKI, AGE 14. I'M IN MY THIRD YEAR AT MAHORA ACADEMY'S JUNIOR HIGH!
I'M A LITTLE DUMB, BUT I HAVE GREAT REFLEXES AND I'M A CHIPPER, SPORTY GIRL ♡
MY LIKES INCLUDE RHYTHMIC GYMNASTICS!
HFF! HFF!
OH!
GOOD MORNING, MAKIE-SAN!
NEGI-KUU-UN...!
OH!
GOOD MORNING, MAKIE-SAN!

MORNING, NEGI-KUN!!
WOW, WHAT HAPPENED?
YOU'RE LOOKING ESPECIALLY CUTE TODAY!
EH?
REALLY?
YAY!
SQUEE
HEE HEE! I'M GLAD YOU NOTICED ♡ I DECIDED TO DRESS UP A LITTLE TODAY!
SPIN
UM, BUT... WE'RE PRACTICING, RIGHT?
YUP ♪ IT'S EASY TO MOVE IN.
ANYWAY, NEGI-KUN...
YES! MAKIE-SAN.
YOU HAVE PRELIMINARIES THE DAY AFTER TOMORROW!
AND YOU HAVE A DISCIPLESHIP TEST TOMORROW NIGHT AT MIDNIGHT!
GH!
GH!
CLASP
HEH HEH.
LET'S GO FOR IT!
FUH-FUH...

SINCE WE DO ONLY HAVE TWO DAYS, WE HAVE A SPECIAL COACH COMING TO GIVE US A CRASH COURSE.
OOOOH! WHO IS IT?
HO HO HO!
IT IS I.
WHOOSH
YOU... YOU'RE ...!
!?
NEGI-BŌZU. FROM TODAY, YOU CALL ME KŪ-RŌSHI, YES.
HO
HO
HO
DUN
AN IDIOT!?
I MEAN, KŪ FEI!?
NEGI-BŌZU. IT DIFFICULT LANDING HIT ON MASTER FIGHTER WITH ONLY TWO DAYS TRAINING.
TMP
THNK
SO TRAIN-ING LITTLE SEVERE. YOU READY?
WHY THE BEARD?
YES!!!

OOH! THAT SOUNDS KINDA FUN! I'LL DO IT, TOO!
MM. VERY WELL.
IT MIGHT HELP ME!

FIRST IS TRAINING TO IMPROVE BALANCE!
IF CAN DODGE ALL PIECE OF WOOD, YOU PASS TEST!!

ZSH
ZSH
ZSH
KYAAAH—!!
HO!
PWAH
ZSHH
WAH!
WHAT THE HECK—!?
DANGLE
KH!
WHAP
WHAP
WHAP
WHAP
BONK
BONK
BONK
TWANG
EEEEEK! WAIT! WAIT, KŪ FEI!
I'M ALL TANGLED UP! AND MY PANTIES--
EEEEEP!!!
MM.
SAW THAT COMING, MAKIE.

IS TOO SOON FOR GIVING UP, YES.
NEXT!!
WH-WHAT ARE THOSE!?
MNN
AAH
DU-DU-DUN
NOW IS TIME FOR CHINESE MARTIAL ARTS CLUB SPECIALTY: "TRUE WOODEN MEN FIST."
THESE AUTOMATIC WOODEN MAN MADE BY ROBOTICS CLUB. VERY ACCURATE ATTACK.
DODGE THEIR ATTACKS AND GO TO BASE OF HILL.
KIDS THESE DAYS WON'T GET THAT REFERENCE...
Y-YES, ROSHI!
DASH
WHOOM
WH-WHOOM
BWAP
WA-WA-WAH!
TH-TH-THIS IS REALLY HARD!
I CAN'T GET ANYWHERE!
BWAP
BASH
HEY.
YOU GO, TOO, MAKIE.
YEEK !?
YANK!
AGAIN —!?
NOOOOOOO!
WHOOSH
MAKIE-SAN !?
KAPOW!
EEEEEP!

WHAT! YOU TIRED ALREADY!? PATHETIC!!
YOU STILL HAVING IRON GETA SHOES 10K MARATHON, ONE INCH PUNCH, PLUS MANY MORE TRAINING...
HEAVY
I...I'M SORRY.
MNN
AAH
HFF
HFF
AND YOU STRETCHED OUT MY PANTIES!
MORNING TRAINING ISN'T SUPPOSED TO BE LIKE THIS!
CHIRP CHIRP
TWEET TWEET
WHAT ARE YOU DOING? THAT'S SO STUPID.
OH! SETSUNA AND ASUNA ♡
YOU FINISH DELIVERY?
BESIDES, THAT'S THE KIND OF THING YOU NEED TO TRAIN EVERY DAY FOR.
HM! YOU THINKING SO?
MAYBE IS MISTAKE USING OLD MANGA AND MOVIES FOR NIGHTMAR TRAINING IDEAS.
KŪRŌSHI!?
KŪ FEI, YOU DUMMY!!
YOU'RE HOPELESS!

DING
DONG
SO IN THIS CASE, YOU'D WANT A PREPOSITION AND...
NEO HORIZON
SIGH...NEGI-KUN SURE IS TOUGH... EVEN AFTER THAT TRAINING, HE'S STILL UP THERE...
BUT I CAN HARDLY KEEP MY EYES OPEN...
DAZE

NYAH HA HA! SORRY ABOUT THIS MOR-NING.
NOW WE BE SERIOUS.
UGH, KEEP IT TOGETHER, KŪ FEI.
OKAY, NEGI-BŌZU. WE THINK OF WAY TO BEAT CHACHAMARU. COME THIS WAY.
YES, RŌSHI.
OKAY, SETSUNA-SAN, LET'S START WHERE WE LEFT OFF THIS MORNING.
ALL RIGHT.
WHAP
OOF!
WAH!
WHAM
WHAP
WHAP WHAP
YOU'RE HAVING SETSUNA-SAN TEACH YOU KENDO, ASUNA?
USING A FOLDING FAN...
HUH? YEAH.
I PRACTICE A LITTLE AFTER MY PAPER ROUTE, TOO.
AND NEGI-KUN'S IN TRAINING, TOO... WHY, ALL OF A SUDDEN?
UM, WELL, A LOT HAP-PENED ON THE CLASS TRIP...

IN MY CASE, IT JUST KIND OF ENDED UP THIS WAY.
IT'S NOT LIKE I NEED TO DO IT...
BUT IT'S FUN PRACTICING WITH SETSUNA-SAN LIKE THIS.
ON THE OTHER HAND, I THINK NEGI'S GOT A REASON...
GLINT!
キラーン
EH? WHAT, WHAT? SO NEGI-KUN DOES HAVE A REASON?
YEAH. HE... HUH? I DON'T KNOW IF IT'S OKAY FOR ME TO TELL YOU.
IT'S NOT LIKE I KNOW ALL THE DETAILS.
EEEHH!? COME ON, DON'T BE MEAN! TELL ME!
WHY DON'T YOU TRY ASKING HIM?
THWACK
POW POW POW
EVEN IF ONLY NEEDING HIT ONCE, IF GO TOO LONG AGAINST MASTER, DIS-ADVANTAGE
YOU HAVE TWO CHOICE: TRICK HER INTO RELAX AND SURPRISE ATTACK...OR MAKE HER STRIKE FIRST THEN COUNTER-ATTACK.
EITHER WAY, IF FIRST PUNCH MISS, NO SECOND CHANCE. UNDERSTAND?
BASH
Y-YES, RŌSHI!
SURPRISE ATTACK HARD IN FAIR FIGHT.
SO I TEACH YOU MANY DIFFERENT COUNTER ATTACK. IS MOST SPECIAL OF CHINESE MARTIAL ART SPECIALTY.
NEGI-KUUU...
WHAP
WHAP
YES, KŪ-RŌSHI!
. . . . .

OH, MAKIE-SAN! CAN I HELP YOU?
HFF HFF
EH? OH, NO. IT'S NOTHING.
HMMM.
I HAVE TO WORK HARD, TOO!
GH...
LET'S GO FOR IT, NEGI-KUN?!
OOHH !?
EH? ER, YES!!
ALLLRIGHT! TOMORROW'S SATURDAY, AND WE DON'T HAVE SCHOOL! SO LET'S PRACTICE ALL THE WAY UNTIL GO-TIME!
YEAH
YEAH-H-H!!
COME ON, GUYS. MAKE SURE YOU GET SOME SLEEP.
THE NEXT DAY, SATURDAY, 4 PM.
EIGHT HOURS UNTIL NEGI'S DISCIPLESHIP TEST.
OKAY, NEGI-BŌZU! IS ENOUGH.
THIS EVERYTHING I CAN TEACH
IN TIME I HAVING!

ANYTHING ELSE IN HANDS OF FATE! USE NEXT EIGHT HOURS FOR REST AND REVIEW! UNDERSTAND?
ZSH!
YES! KŪ-RŌSHI!
HEY-Y-Y~~~~!
NEGI-KUN! I HEARD YOU'VE GOT SOME KIND OF A MATCH TONIGHT?
WE MADE YOU A DELUXE SPECIAL DINNER BENTŌ TO PERK YOU UP!
CLAMOR
ワイ
CLAMOR
ワイ
SQUEE
キャッ
SQUEE
キャ♡
SO, YOU THINK YOU CAN WIN?
SNAP
パ
キャッ
NEGI-BŌZU SO GOOD AT LEARNING, IT SHOULD BE AGAINST RULES.
MOVE THAT TAKE ONE MONTH TO GET GOOD AT, HE LEARN IN THREE HOURS.
WHAT UP WITH THIS KID?
WORLD NOT FAIR.
WOW!
...BUT IF HE WASN'T AT LEAST THAT GOOD A LEARNER, HE COULDN'T BE TEACHING AT TEN YEARS OLD...

OH YEAH! WELL, THAT'S OUR GENIUS BOY, THEN!! IT'LL BE A CINCH!!
おおーーっ!!
YEAH!!
A TOTAL PIECE OF CAKE ♪
YEAH
NYOH-HO-HO.
NO, UM, I DON'T KNOW...
NN...?
SNIFF
HEY, NEGI. YOU'RE KINDA SMELLY.
SNIFF SNIFF SNIFF
EH?
GULP
DON'T TELL ME YOU HAVEN'T BEEN BATHING AGAIN.
WHEN WAS YOUR LAST BATH?
NO, UM...!
EEEEHHH!?
SKID
YOU...
MURMUR MURMUR BUZZ BUZZ
YOU WORKED UP ALL THAT SWEAT AND YOU DIDN'T--?
N-NO WAY...
UNBE-LIEV-ABLE!
BUT I HEAR THERE ARE A LOT OF BRITISH PEOPLE WHO DON'T TAKE BATHS.
NO, UM! IT'S JUST, I KIND OF... FORGOT...
WHISPER WHISPER WHISPER WHISPER
ABUH-ABUH!
RUMBLE
NO EXCUSES! YOU'RE COMING WITH ME!! I'LL WASH YOU UP!
UGH, YOU'RE STUPID
DRAG DRAG DRAG
EEEEP!
BUT ASUNA, WHERE?
GYM NO.2'S SHOWER ROOM IS CLOSE TO HERE.
BUT I THOUGHT BOYS WEREN'T ALLOWED IN THERE.

OH ♡ WE'RE OKAY.
THERE'S NO ONE HERE RIGHT NOW.
SHOWER ROOM NO. 8

ABUH-BUH--! ASUNA-SAN, I CAN DO IT MYSELF!
SCRUB
SCRUB
SCRUB
DON'T LIE TO ME!! IF I LET YOU DO IT YOURSELF, YOU'LL JUST GET YOUR HAIR WET AND TELL ME YOU'RE DONE!
SCRUB
SCRUB
WAAAAH
RAR
RAR
HA HA HA! THEY'RE LIKE BROTHER AND SISTER.
ARE THEY ALWAYS LIKE THAT?
HMMM. YEAH, PRETTY MUCH.
SQUEEZE
SO HEY, WHY IS NEGI-KUN STAYING IN YOUR ROOM?
BECAUSE MY GRAND-PA'S THE HEAD-MASTER.
OHHH, SO IT WAS THE HEAD-MASTER'S IDEA.
...
HEY, ASUNA.
NN?
RAR
RAR
ASUNA, ARE YOU GOING OUT WITH NEGI-KUN?
KERSMASH

WHY DOES EVERY-BODY KEEP ASKING ME THAT?!
BLUS-S-SH
I'VE SAID IT A MILLION TIMES--HE'S A LITTLE KID! TEN YEARS OLD!!
AAH!
AH HA HA. OH YEAH.
HE'S JUST SUCH A LITTLE BRAT SOMETIMES, *SOMEBODY* HAS TO LOOK AFTER HIM!
THERE, ALL CLEAN!!
SQUEAKY
NOW WE HAVE TO SNEAK OUT OF HERE.
SNEAK
こそ
こそ
SNEAK
LEAV-ING AL-READY?
OOOOH! THIS IS SO THRILLING! WHAT IF A TEACHER OR CLASS REP FINDS US HERE?
ZSH
ZSH
ZSH
HO HO HO.
ホホホ
WHEW. I WORKED UP QUITE A SWEAT TODAY.
SPIN
くるっ
SPIN
くるっ
OH, ASUNA-SAN, MAKIE-SAN. ALL OF YOU.
AH HA HA!! CLASS REP! BACK FROM EQUES-TRIAN CLUB ALREADY?
WHY ARE YOU IN THE SHOWER TOGETHER?
OH, UM, WE'RE WASHING EACH OTHER'S BACKS!!
REEEALLY. I DIDN'T REALIZE YOU TWO WERE THAT CLOSE.
WELL, YOU ARE BOTH BAKA RANGERS
SQUEEZE
ABUH-BUH!!
I CAN'T BREATHE!
STOMP
STOMP
STOMP
STOMP
STOMP

THIS IS R-R-R-REALLY BAD, ASUNA!
TWITCH
ぴくぴく
TWITCH
MMPH!
ぎゅうぎゅう
SQUISH
SQUISH
THERE'S NOTHING WE CAN DO! WE JUST HAVE TO WAIT UNTIL CLASS REP LEAVES!
EEEP!
OH NO, ASUNA!
EH!?
WHAT?
NEGI-KUN'S YOU-KNOW-WHAT IS TOUCHING MY BUTT!!
I DON'T NEED TO KNOW THAT!!
DUN!
UWAHHH?!
WHAT!?
FLASH
I THINK IT'S STARTING TO GET BIGGER!!
どぎゃん
SHOCK!
HEY! STOP MAKING STUFF UP!!
AND YOU BE CAREFUL, TOO!
B...BUT I DIDN'T DO ANYTHING!!
?
UH-OH! CLASS REP'S LOOKING AT US FUNNY!
PRETEND YOU'RE WASHING!
HURRY!

キャッ SQUEE
キャッ SQUEE
WHEW...
IT'S SAFE NOW.
シャア... FSHH
BY THE WAY, NEGI...
HOW DO YOU FEEL ABOUT YOUR MATCH TONIGHT?
THINK YOU CAN BEAT CHA-CHAMARU-SAN?
WELL...I DON'T KNOW...
BUT I'VE DONE EVERY-THING I CAN.
ALL THAT'S LEFT IS TO DO MY BEST.
OH.
...
ZSHH
HEY, NEGI-KUN.
WHY DO YOU...
TRY SO HARD AT EVERY-THING?
EH?
ER...
WELL, UM...
THERE'S SOME-ONE... I LOOK UP TO...
I WANT TO CATCH UP TO THAT PERSON.
AND TO DO THAT, I'VE DECIDED I'LL DO... WHATEVER I HAVE TO.

HMM... OKAY...
NEGI-KUN... YOU'RE SO GROWN-UP.

EH...?

WELL, IF YOU'LL EXCUSE ME.
YOU TWO ARE TAKING AN AWFULLY LONG SHOWER.
WELL, WE'RE JUST, YOU KNOW. AH HA HA.
SKID
WHEW
THAT WAS CLOSE

NOW, MAKI-CHAN. DO YOU MEAN THAT? LOOK AT THIS KID! HE'S JUST A LITTLE BRAT!
PINCH
WHAT? NO, HE'S NOT!
YOU'RE VERY MATURE. RIGHT, NEGI-KUN?
EH? ...I--

YOU'RE STILL JUST A KID DOWN HERE, THOUGH ♡
FLIP
GYAAAAAH
?!!
PFFT!
WHAT ARE YOU DOING!?
GYAA
KYAA
I WAS JUST CHECKING.
MORON!!
CHECKING WHAT!?
OH, YES. I ALMOST FORGOT.
RATTLE
THERE'S SOMETHING I'D LIKE TO ASK YOU, ASUNA-SAN...
HO HO HO
DO YOU KNOW NEGI-SENSEI'S PLANS FOR GOLDEN WEEK?
......
SHAKE SHAKE
UH.
...
WH-WH-WH-WHAT DO YOU THINK YOU THREE ARE DOING!?
WAAH
KYAA
IT'S NOT WHAT YOU THINK, CLASS REP!
OOPS, SHE CAUGHT 'EM.
FIVE HOURS UNTIL NEGI'S DISCIPLESHIP TEST.

HEY, MISTRESS. I CAN'T SEE THE MATCH FROM HERE.
SET ME DOWN SOME-WHERE WITH A BETTER VIEW, WOULD YOU!?
UGH. YOU'RE AWFULLY WHINY FOR SOMEBODY SO USE-LESS.
I CAN'T HELP IT. I CAN'T MOVE.
IT'S YOUR FAULT, MIS-TRESS.
ARE YOU CERTAIN ABOUT THIS, MISTRESS?
THE PROB-ABILITY OF NEGI-SENSEI LANDING A BLOW ON ME IS LESS THAN THREE PERCENT.
AND WOULD NEGI-SENSEI'S FAILURE TO PASS THE TEST NOT BE AGAINST YOUR TRUE WISHES?
...HEY. DON'T GET ANY FUNNY IDEAS, CHA-CHAMARU.
HEH. HEH HEH.
I REALLY DON'T WANT A DISCIPLE.
THEY'RE TOO MUCH WORK.
BESIDES, I'M ONLY MAKING HIM HIT YOU ONCE. I'M BEING EXTREMELY GENEROUS HERE.
IF HE STILL CAN'T HACK IT, IT'S HIS OWN FAULT.
UNDER-STAND, CHA-CHAMARU? DON'T EVEN THINK ABOUT GOING EASY ON HIM.
YES, MIS-TRESS.
I UNDER-STAND.
IT'S ALMOST TIME...
EVANGELINE -SAAAAN!

NEGI SPRINGFIELD, REPORTING FOR HIS DISCIPLESHIP TEST!
ZSH!
Dash CheeSe
BOW.
ペコ…
I'M SURPRISED TO SEE YOU HERE, BŌYA
WELL, LET'S GET THIS STARTED.
TICK.
K-CHAK
HEH HEH...

IF YOU CAN LAND A SINGLE PUNCH ON CHACHAMARU WITH YOUR LITTLE "KUNG-FU," YOU PASS.
IF SHE KNOCKS YOU OUT BEFORE YOU TOUCH HER, YOU'RE OUT.
UNDER-STAND?
......
SMIRK
AND THAT'S THE ONLY CONDI-TION?
NN? YEAH, THAT'S ALL.
...BUT FIRST,
WHAT'S WITH THE PEANUT GALLERY?
FWIP!
THEY'RE EVERY-WHERE!
CLAMOR
CLAMOR
GO FOR IT!
YEAH!
CLAMOR
UM... THEY JUST FOLLOWED ME...

NEGI-SENSEI... !
GET HER, NEGI-KUN!
GOOD LUCK, NEGI-SENSEI!
NEGI-KUN!
ARE YOU GOING TO BE OKAY, NEGI-KUN?
YOU CAN COUNT ON ME, MAKIE-SAN.
THIS IS WHAT I'VE BEEN TRAINING FOR!!
NEGI ...
ANIKI !
IT'S ALL RIGHT, CHAMO-KUN. ASUNA-SAN.
WAAH
WAAH
KEEP FOCUS, OKAY ?
I WILL, KŪ-RŌSHI!
... HMPH

CHA-CHA-MARU-SAN.
IF YOU PLEASE!
THEN LET US BEGIN.
H-HE WILL BE OKAY, RIGHT, KŪ FEI?!
DON'T KNOW... I HEARING CHACHAMARU VERY STRONG.
IF GO ON TOO LONG, MIGHT LOSE!!
IF NO CAN COUNTER IN FIRST MINUTE, NEGI-BŌZU NO WIN.
N-NO...
NEGI.
ANIKI.
NEGI-KUN...
GOOD LUCK...!
BAM
LET IT BEGIN!!

I BEG YOUR PAR- DON.
SIM IPSE PARS PER NON- AGINTA SECUN- DAS!
FWOOM
NEGIUS SPRING- FIELDES!
WHOOM
WHACK
SHWOONG
WHAM
WHAP
WHOOSH
OH!
OOHH!?
HWHIRL
GSHH
BAJIQUAN!
GSHH
ZHUAN JUAN KUA DA!!
NGH!
SO CLOSE!

WH-WH-WH-WHAT'S GOING ON!?
WHACK WHACK
WHACK
WHOA.
WHAM
I THOUGHT THEY WERE JUST GONNA HIT EACH OTHER! WHAT ARE THEY!?
SO FAST! YOU GOOD, NEGI-BŌZU!!
CHACHAMARU INCREDIBLE, TOO.
B-BUT HE...
YEAH.
HMPH. AN ORIGINAL SPELL TO MAGICALLY ENHANCE HIS ABILITIES, HUH?
HOW PUSHY CAN A SPELL GET?
ANYWAY, WITH ONLY TWO DAYS OF TRAIN-ING,
WHACK!
NGH!
YOU MAY BE ABLE TO MATCH HER SPEED AND POWER, BUT YOU WON'T BE ABLE TO BEAT HER.
SHNK!
ERGH...
ZSH
NEGI-KUN!!
NO, IS ALL PART OF PLAN!! HE LURE HER IN!!

LURE ?!
!
YES!
NGH!!
BOOF
GOOD !!
FWOOM
NOW HE COUNTER !
GWIP
BAJI-QUAN LIU DA KAI: DING
HUO DA DING ZHOU !!!
FWOOM
LIGHTNING ELBOW-STRIKE!!
TAP
DSH!
!?
WHA --?!
Z-POW

B-BAM BAM!
ZSH!
SKIID
ROLL
ROLL ROLL
SHH
AH...
KH...
...TO
!
IS THAT IT?
GRIT
HMPH. THAT'S ABOUT WHAT I EXPECTED.
SOME-ONE'S IN A BAD MOOD.
HEH HEH HEH.
TOO BAD, BŌYA. BUT THAT'S ALL YOU'VE GOT.
WASH UP AND TRY AGAIN LATER.
NEG!!
NEGI-KUN!
AH?
HEH... HEH HEH.
GH...

GH...
NOT YET... I'M NOT DOWN FOR THE COUNT YET.
EVANGE-LINE-SAN.
HFF HFF
NEGI-KUN!
GH-GH-GH...
SHAKE
NN...? WHAT ARE YOU BLATH-ERING ABOUT?
SHOO, SHOO
THIS FIGHT IS OVER. BE A GOOD BOY AND GO HOME TO BED.
GO ON!
THE BRAT CONCENTRATED HIS MAGIC INTO A BARRIER RIGHT BEFORE SHE HIT.
HFF HFF...
...BUT YOU SAID I HAVE UNTIL SHE KNOCKS ME OUT.
I DON'T REMEMBER ANYTHING ABOUT A TIME LIMIT.
SMIRK
WH... WHAT!?
DON'T TELL ME YOU --
HEH HEH... THAT'S RIGHT. YOU WON'T GET RID OF ME UNTIL I LAND A HIT, EVEN IF IT TAKES HOURS.
GH
SKUFF
...CHA-CHAMARU-SAN, PLEASE CON-TINUE!!
B-BUT, SENSEI ...
!?

WHACK!
DUN
BAM!
KAPOW
EEK, OW!
ERK! LONG TIME BATTLE NO GOOD! AND SUDDENLY SPEED MUCH LESS! WHAT WRONG?
H-HIS CONTRACT EXECUTION TIMED OUT...
ANIKI!...
NEGI...!
BUT HE CAN STILL MOVE BETTER THAN THE AVERAGE ADULT.
CHACHAMARU-SAN... P-PLEASE DON'T HOLD BACK. PASSING THIS TEST WON'T MEAN ANYTHING IF YOU WERE GOING EASY ON ME.
HFF... HFF
B... BUT --
BASH
WHOOM
...VERY WELL.
THWACK!
NGAH
N-N-N-NEGI-KUN!
NGH!
WHACK
NEGI-SENSEI! HE'S NOT GOING TO STOP?
CRACK
KONK
AWAH
BUT THE WAY THINGS ARE GOING...
Y-YEAH. HE DOESN'T STAND A CHANCE...
BRAKK
WHACK
NEGI-KUN...
CRACK!
NGH...

CRACK!
WHACK!
POW!
CRACK!
WHAM!
BONK!
CRUNCH!
SCRUNCH!
BAFF!
HFF
HFF
HFF
CRUNCH
HFF
THRASHED
NEGI-SENSEI ...
HFF
DU-DUN!
HFF
HFF
C-COME ON, BŌYA. THAT'S ENOUGH.
I DON'T CARE HOW MUCH MAGIC YOU HAVE TO DEFEND YOURSELF; EVENTUALLY, YOU'RE GOING RUN OUT.
ARGH...
HE'S SURE GOT GUTS.
YOU'RE DETERMINED. I GET IT.
N-NO. NOT YET...
I HA'N'T GI'EN UP YET.
SMIRK
GASH!
DMP!
HYOOP
KAPOW!
HYAH-H-H!
SENSEI, STOP —!
HE'S BEEN AT IT FOR MORE THAN AN HOUR.
N-NEGI-KUN, WHY DO YOU KEEP PUSHING YOUR-SELF!?

WHACK
CRACK
NGH!
I-I CAN'T WATCH THIS ANYMORE! I HAVE TO STOP THIS!!
ZSH!
G-GO, ASUNA!
N--

NO, ASUNA, YOU CAN'T!!
DON'T STOP HIM !!
BAM!

...
B-BUT --

LOOK AT HIM! HE'S FALL-ING APART!
HE SHOULDN'T HAVE TO PUSH HIMSELF THROUGH ALL THIS!

I KNOW! I KNOW, BUT...

IT WOULD BE MORE CRUEL TO NEGI-KUN IF YOU STOPPED HIM NOW.
...I THINK.
I MEAN, NEGI-KUN SAID HE WAS GOING TO DO HIS BEST AT EVERYTHING HE COULD!

MAKI-CHA...

BUT...! HE'S JUST BEING A STUBBORN KID RIGHT NOW! I HAVE TO STOP HIM, OR...
NO! NEGI-KUN'S NOT A KID!
M-MAKI-CHAN, YOU SAID THE SAME THING IN THE SHOWER,
BUT THERE'S NO WAY YOU CAN POS-SIBLY THINK THAT--!
NOBODY COULD GO THAT FAR IF THEY WERE JUST BEING A STUB-BORN KID.
I-I CAN'T REALLY EXPLAIN IT.
BUT I THINK N... N... NEGI-KUN KNOWS WHAT HE'S GOTTEN HIMSELF INTO.
H-HE KNOWS?
YEAH. NEGI-KUN HAS A GOAL... AND HE DECIDED THAT HE'LL GIVE HIS ALL TO ACHIEVE IT.
ASUNA, THINK ABOUT YOURSELF, YOUR FRIENDS--EVEN YOUR UPPERCLASSMEN, OR JUST SOME BOYS YOU KNOW. DO YOU KNOW ANYONE WHO HAS A GOAL, LIKE NEGI-KUN?
NOT JUST A VAGUE DREAM, BUT A REAL GOAL, THAT HE'S DECIDED TO LIVE TO PURSUE?
W-WELL...
WHAT THE...
S...SO NAIVE...
GUESS THAT'S YOUTH FOR YA.

NEGI-KUN'S GROWN UP.
HE'S WORKING HARD FOR A GOAL.
THAT'S WHY... THAT'S WHY YOU SHOULDN'T STOP HIM NOW.
......
MAKI-CHAN...
HMM. NOT BAD FOR A THIRD-YEAR JUNIOR HIGH BRAT...
STOP BLUSHING, MISTRESS.
MAKIE-SAN...
STAGGER
よろ
AH...!
HEY. CHACHA-MARU!
EH?

STUMBLE
ひょろっ…
...SBAP
...AH!
WHA?!A
OH!
...!
THUD
I...I HI' YOU...
AH... !

HE DID IT—!
NEGI-KUUUN! ♡
DAM-MIT, CHA-CHA-MARU!
I-I-I I AM TERRIBLY SORRY, MIS-TRESS!
チュン
CHIRP
チュン
CHIRP
チチチ...
TWEET TWEET

ERK...
H... HUH?
WH...WHAT HAP-PENED? HOW DID THE TEST GO...?
IT'S OKAY, NEGI.
YOU PASSED, NEGI-KUN ♡

...FINE. I LOST, BŌYA.
AS PROM-ISED, I'LL TRAIN YOU. COME TO MY CABIN WHENEVER YOU'RE READY.
...OH, AND ONE MORE THING.
GO AHEAD AND KEEP DOING YOUR LITTLE "KUNG-FU" TRAINING.
EITHER WAY, YOU'RE GOING TO NEED PHYSICAL FIGHTING SKILLS.
AND CHINESE MARTIAL ARTS ARE A GOOD MATCH FOR A THINKER LIKE YOU.
ペコ...
BOW
LATER.

TH-THANK YOU.
EVA'GELINE-SAN.
CLAMOR
YOU DO SO GOOD, NEGI-BŌZU!!
GOOD! GOOD!
CLAMOR
THAT WAS AWE-SOME, NEGI-KUN!
I SEE YOU IN A NEW LIGHT!
I'LL MAKE YOU A YUMMY BREAK-FAST AS A REWARD, NEGI-KUN!

GOOD WORK... NEGI-KUN.
IT'S NUFF-ING...
YOU DO YOUR BEST, TOO, MAKIE-PHAN...

I WILL!
YOU CAN COUNT ON ME, NEGI-KUN!

NEXT IS NUMBER 5, MAKIE SASAKI.
HERE!

YOU'RE USING THE RIBBON, RIGHT?
YES.
NN ?
MAKIE, DID SOMETHING HAPPEN? I DIDN'T RECOG-NIZE YOU FOR A SECOND.
CLAMOR CLAMOR
EH...? NOTHING HAP-PENED.
OH, REEEALLY. ARE YOU SURE YOU DIDN'T FALL IN *LOVE* WITH SOMEONE?
なに
STOP TALKING LIKE AN OLD MAN, NINOMIYA-SENSEI!
HA HA HA. I'M KID-DING.
UGH ~~~!
NOW, NUMBER FIVE, MAKIE SASAKI! BEGIN YOUR ROUTINE!
YES, MA'AM !!

59TH PERIOD: A CLUE FOR YOU...
OKAY, NEGI-KUN, HOLD STILL.
PAT
ポン
PAT
ポン
OWWW.
NNNGH...
WOW, NEGI-KUN, I DIDN'T REALIZE YOU WERE SUCH A HOT HEAD. FIGHTING UNTIL YOU'RE BLACK AND BLUE.
I-I-I-I'M SORRY!
BUT HEY, KONOKA.
CAN'T YOU JUST FIX HIM UP WITH YOUR MAGIC, LIKE YOU DID DURING THE CLASS TRIP?
HMMM, BACK THEN, I JUST DID WHAT EVA-CHAN TOLD ME.
NEGIMA!
MAGISTER NEGI MAGI
AND BESIDES, I DON'T KNOW HOW TO USE MAGIC.
I DON'T KNOW MUCH HEALING MAGIC, EITHER...
I GUESS THAT'S TRUE.
IT MIGHT BE A GOOD IDEA TO GO ASK HER TO TEACH YOU SOME TIME.
EVANGELINE-SAN, I MEAN.
BUT MAN, YOU DID GOOD, ANIKI!

YEAH! NOW I CAN GET EVANGELINE-SAN TO TEACH ME ALL KINDS OF THINGS, AND KŪ FEI-SAN SAID SHE'D KEEP TRAINING ME, TOO.
NOW I JUST HAVE TO WORK AT IT!
BUT IT'LL ONLY GET HARDER FROM HERE, ANIKI.
YOU GONNA BE OKAY?
...INDEED. ESPECIALLY THE MARTIAL ARTS. YOU CAN'T JUST LEARN THEM WITH YOUR HEAD.
YOU NEED LONG HOURS OF PRACTICE TO GET YOUR BODY TO REMEMBER THE PROPER FORMS AND HOW TO USE THEM, OR YOU'LL NEVER BE ABLE TO WIN A FIGHT LIKE YESTERDAY'S WITH CHACHAMARU-SAN.
BUT YOU WERE STILL AMAZING.
GOOD LUCK WITH YOUR TRAINING, SENSEI.
THANK YOU, SETSUNA-SAN.
ALLLRIGHT... I'M GONNA DO THIS!
WHAT I'M CONCERNED ABOUT NOW IS--
OH YEAH, NEGI. WHAT HAPPENED TO THAT MAP CLUE?
OH, ABOUT THAT.
DING-DONG
COMING!
OH? CHA-CHAMARU-SAN.
WHAT BRINGS YOU HERE?
NEGI-KUN? YES, HE'S HERE.
EH?
OH! H-H-H-HELLO, CHACHAMARU-SAN!

...OH. N-NEGI-SENSEI...
HOW ARE YOU FEELING?
I'M FINE. I'M NOT IN NEARLY AS BAD SHAPE AS I LOOK.
I THINK I HAVE YOU TO THANK, FOR GOING EASY ON ME.
THAT IS GOOD.
UM...THIS IS FROM THE MISTRESS. ...I UNDERSTAND IT IS A RATHER EFFECTIVE SALVE.
SS...
EH...? OH, TH-THANK YOU.
AND...THIS IS FROM ME. ...IT IS A DELICIOUS TEA.
RUSTLE
OH... THAT'S SO KIND OF YOU. THANK YOU.
...UM...I REALIZE THAT IT WAS A SPARRING MATCH, BUT... NEGI-SENSEI... I...
THAT IS...?
WHISPER WHISPER
FIDGET FIDGET
...HUH?
...W-WELL, IF YOU WILL EXCUSE ME.
TEK TEK
AAAHH! CHACHAMARU-SAN! WAIT, WAIT!
?
YOU COULD STAY AND VISIT FOR A WHILE!
UGH
...MAY I? THEN I WILL PUT ON SOME TEA.
STOMP
STOMP
STOMP
NEGI-KUN, NEGI-KUUUN!!
I PASSED! I PASSED THE PRE-LIMINAR-IES!!
BAM!
ANY WAY

EEHH!? REALLY, MAKIE-SAN!?
I DID, NEGI-KUN! I REALLY DID!!
CLAMOR
CON-GRATULA-TIONS!
CLAMOR
WOW, THAT'S PERFECT! WE'LL HAVE A TEA PARTY TO CELEBRATE!
OH! I LIKE THAT IDEA ♡
AAAAHH!? IT'S CH-CHA-CHACHA-MARU-SAN?!
SKID
OH, COME ON. DON'T BE SCARED OF HER. CHA-CHAMARU-SAN IS ACTUALLY A VERY NICE PERSON.
CLAMOR CLAMOR
SQUEE
SQUEE
THIS ROOM IS NEVER QUIET, IS IT?
SQUEE SQUEE
DING DONG
COMING!
KACHAK
SQUEE SQUEE
AH HA HA
HUH? YUE-CHAN, BOOK-STORE-CHAN!
ASUNA-SAN. ...ACTUALLY, WE HAVE SOMETHING TO TALK TO NEGI-SENSEI ABOUT. PRIVATELY...
HUH?
CLAMOR
CLAMOR

EEEEHHHH!?
YOU FOUND A CLUE IN THE MAP!?

B-BUT THAT CODE WAS ALMOST IMPOSSIBLE TO BREAK... YOU REALLY *ARE* VERY SMART, YUE-SAN...
RUSTLE
IT WAS NOTHING. ...LET'S SEE, ON THE EIGHTH PAGE OF THE COPY YOU GAVE US, THERE'S A PART WITH AN ENLARGED MAP OF THE ILLUSORY UNDER-GROUND READING ROOM.

LET ME MAKE SURE I UNDER-STAND THIS PROP-ERLY.
YOU'RE LOOKING FOR YOUR LONG-LOST FATHER, RIGHT, NEGI-SENSEI?

YES.
AND THESE MAPS HOLD A CLUE TO FINDING HIM?
YES!

PLEASE TAKE A GOOD LOOK AT THIS PART HERE.
RUSTLE
WH-WHERE? WHERE'S THE CLUE TO FINDING MY FATHER?
THOSE BRUISES LOOK PAIN-FUL...
RIGHT HERE. THIS IS YOUR CLUE...

LET'S SEE, WHERE IS IT?
GAAAA
DANGER
THIS WAY
CLUE TO FINDING ME
CLUE...
...TO FINDING ME?
IT'S A CLUE!?
IT'S NOT EVEN IN CODE!
SHOCK!
H-HUH? THAT'S WEIRD. MAYBE I MISSED IT BECAUSE IT'S IN JAPANESE.
AWA-WAH!
UM, HE DREW HIS FACE, TOO...
NEGI... YOU'RE REALLY STUPID SOMETIMES, YOU KNOW THAT?
BUT THIS IS GREAT, NEGI!
YES! WE'LL HAVE TO INVESTIGATE!
...ABOUT THAT, NEGI-SENSEI.
THERE'S ONE THING I WANT TO MAKE VERY CLEAR.
EH?
IT PAINS ME TO USE SUCH FANTASTICAL VOCABULARY SO SERIOUSLY...
BUT AFTER WHAT I SAW ON THE CLASS TRIP, I HAVE NO CHOICE BUT TO ACCEPT IT.
NEGI-SENSEI...
WHIP
ZNN
YOU'RE A WIZARD, AREN'T YOU?

EEP!
I, WELL--
DU-DUN!
ズドギャーン!
DON'T WORRY. I'VE ONLY TALKED ABOUT THIS WITH NODOKA. WE'RE KEEPING IT FROM HARUNA.
I DO WONDER WHY YOU NEED TO KEEP THAT FACT A SECRET...
BUT RIGHT NOW, I HAVE A PLETHORA OF QUESTIONS I'M MORE INTERESTED IN ANSWERING.
FIRST OF ALL, FROM CERTAIN CONVERSATIONS, I HAVE DEDUCED THAT EVANGELINE-SAN IS A VERY POWERFUL WIZARD.
ERK!
FURTHERMORE, KONOKA-SAN IS ALSO A WIZARD! AS IS THE HEADMASTER.
EEP!
THESE THINGS ALONE ARE ENOUGH TO DEFY COMMON SENSE...I MEAN, ENOUGH TO SURPRISE ANYONE.
BUT IF I WERE TO DRAW ANY CONCLUSIONS FROM WHAT KONOKA'S FATHER WAS SAYING, IT WOULD BE THAT THERE IS AN ENTIRE COMMUNITY OF WIZARDS, ALL OVER THE WORLD.
EEEEEP!
WELL, SENSEI?
N-NO, UM... I CAN'T ANSWER THAT...
言い訳不可能!!
I HAVE NO EXCUSES!!
あわわわ
AWAWAWAH!
IN ADDITION, I BELIEVE...
...THAT THE MYSTERIES OF THIS SCHOOL--THE LARGE UNDERGROUND READING ROOM, THE MOVING STONE STATUE...
AND EVEN THE ENORMOUS WORLD TREE.

I BELIEVE THAT ALL THESE MYSTERIES...
RAR!
わっ
...MAKE SO MUCH MORE SENSE, WHEN YOU ASSUME THAT THIS ACADEMY...
...WAS BUILT BY YOU WIZARDS!

EEEEP!
SHE'S A SHARP ONE.
I-IS THAT TRUE, NEGI?
Y-YOU'RE PROBABLY RIGHT!
HA-WA-WAH!
HUH.
THEN, TO THE POINT, NEGI-SENSEI.
IF YOU'RE GOING TO INVESTIGATE THAT CLUE, WE WANT YOU TO TAKE US WITH YOU.
WE WANT TO KNOW MORE ABOUT LIBRARY ISLAND AND THE SECRETS OF THIS SCHOOL... AND ABOUT YOU WIZARDS.

B-B-B-BUT YUE-SAN. UM, I MEAN--
AS I'M SURE YOU LEARNED ON THE CLASS TRIP,
THERE'S NO TELLING WHAT DANGER MIGHT BE WAITING IN OUR WORLD.
RUMBLE RUMBLE

I DON'T CARE, SENSEI!
CLAMP!
ACK!

UM. THAT IS.
AWAH
AWA-WA-WAH

I-I-I-I'M SORRY! I CAN'T!
D-DASH!
AH! NEGI!?
HE RAN AWAY!

NEGI! DON'T YOU THINK THAT WAS A LITTLE MEAN? THEY *DID* FIND YOUR CLUE FOR YOU AND ALL.
B-BUT...
I CAN'T LET DELICATE GIRLS LIKE NODOKA-SAN AND YUE-SAN GET WRAPPED UP IN MY WORLD.
OOHH, SO YOU'RE SAYING I'M NOT DELICATE?
N-NO, I DIDN'T MEAN--
DID SOMETHING HAPPEN?
WELL, SHE'S *NOT* DELICATE.
NOPE.
LISTEN, KONOKA! YUE-CHAN...
OOOHH?
YUP
...OKAY.
TWEET TWEET
CHIRP CHIRP
ASUNA-SAN IS ON HER PAPER ROUTE...
SO NOW'S MY CHANCE.
SNEAK
SNEAK
MMM~? NEGI-KUN?
SHIFT
WINCE!
MORE MORNING TRAINING? BUT YOU SHOULD REST UNTIL YOU'RE ALL HEALED UP.
N-NO.
I HAVE TO TRAIN EVERY DAY TO STAY IN GOOD FORM.
B-DMP
B-DMP
B-DMP
HMM...
DAZE
WELL DON'T PUSH YOURSELF.
THAT WAS CLOSE!
SNEAK
SNEAK
...
MYAH...
BEEP

ANIKI, YOU OKAY?
I CAN'T ALWAYS BE BOTHERING ASUNA-SAN, CAN I?
TUG
TUG
HEH HEH HEH! SHE IS A DELICATE GIRL, AFTER ALL.
HOO HEH HEH HEH.
BESIDES, I HAVE A CLUE TO MY FATHER RIGHT IN FRONT OF ME.
HOW CAN I SIT STILL? I HAVE TO GO CHECK IT OUT!
YEAH!
ZSH!
OKAY!
GOOD MORNING, NEGI-SENSEI!
!?
WINCE!
W-WAH! YUE-SAN, NODOKA-SAN!?
GOOD MORNING!
SWAY SWAY
HEH HEH HEH. WE THOUGHT THIS MIGHT HAPPEN. SO WE ASKED KONOKA-SAN TO LET US KNOW IF YOU TRIED ANYTHING.
JUST GOT OUT OF BED.
DUN!
YOU'RE GOING TO THE LIBRARY, AND WE'RE IN THE LIBRARY EXPLORATION CLUB. YOU CAN TRY TO LOSE US, BUT WE'LL FIND YOU.
HEH HEH HEH HEH
SLEEPY
SWAY SWAY

YOU OWE
US FOR
FINDING
THAT CLUE
FOR YOU.
NNNGH.
I DON'T
THINK WE'RE
BEING
UNREASONABLE.

B-
BUT-
...
あせあせ
SWEAT
SWEAT
ず〜ん
STARE
IT'S NO
USE, ANIKI.
THEY WANT
IT TOO
BAD.
ど〜ん
GLOOM
NNNGH...
THEN I
HAVE NO
CHOICE.

ALL
RIGHT.
GET
ON.
EH...
?
♡
GET
ON?

ふわっ...
FWAH
EEP!
ERK
...
BUT IF I'M
LETTING YOU
COME, THEN
WE'RE TURN-
ING BACK AT
THE SLIGHT-
EST SIGN OF
DANGER.

YOU'VE
RIDDEN
MY WAND
BEFORE,
RIGHT,
NODOKA-
SAN?
UM...
YES!

EEEEEEK!?
ヒュウウウ..
WHOOSH
...AH.

WOW ...

AS YOU CAN SEE,
I'M A REAL WIZARD.

THERE'S A FIELD AROUND THE WAND THAT KEEPS US FROM FALLING OFF.
BUT IF YOU GET SCARED, THEN HOLD ON TIGHT, OKAY?
A-ALL RIGHT.
SQUEEZE
YOU DON'T HAVE TO HOLD ON *THAT* TIGHT.

WON'T ANY-ONE...
SEE US FROM BELOW?
THERE'S A LITTLE ANTI-RECOGNITION SPELL ON US, SO NORMAL PEOPLE WON'T.
DOES THAT MAKE SENSE?
...I SEE.

B-DMP B-DMP
.....

...IT'S JUST LIKE IN A PICTURE BOOK.

SQUEEZE
ギュッ…

WE CAN FLY THIS TIME, SO THIS SHOULD BE MUCH EASIER THAN THE LAST TIME WE WERE HERE.
Y... YES... RIGHT ...
WHOOSH
ビュオオオ…

TH-TH-THIS WIND IS SO STRONG!
KYAAAAA! KYAAAAA!
WE'RE FALLING!
IT'S OKAY, DON'T WORRY.
YOU'RE NOT GOING TO FALL.
WHOOSH
BLECH!! WHAT IS A SPIDER'S WEB IN MID-AIR!?
TWANG
EEE-YEHKK!
IT'S STICKING ALL OVER ME!
WAAAH! PLEASE DON'T COVER MY EYES!
IT'S ALL RIGHT. CALM DOWN.
AREN'T YOU TWO SUPPOSED TO BE IN THE EXPLORATION CLUB?
M-MY APOLOGIES.
I LOST MY WITS.
I-I-I'M SORRY!
WE'LL WALK FROM HERE. THERE MIGHT BE SOME MAGICAL TRAPS.
PLEASE DON'T LET GO OF MY HAND.
COME ON, YUE-SAN. YOU, TOO
OH... RIGHT.
CLICK
RUMBLE RUMBLE RUMBLE
NN?

WAAH!
ROLL
ROLL
ROLL
I SHOULD HAVE SEEN THIS COMING!
H-HOW COULD I HAVE BEEN SO CARE-LESS?
RUMBLE RUMBLE RUMBLE
RUMBLE RUMBLE
OOHH
KYAA!
EEK!
......

ZSH
HUFF, HUFF... WE'RE HERE.
WE...WE ALWAYS KNEW YOU HAVE TO EXPECT THE UNEX-PECTED AT LIBRARY ISLAND...
STAGGER
STAGGER
ZSH

BEHIND THIS DOOR...
HFF HFF
TATTERED
...LIES THE CLUE?
HFF HFF
SO THIS IS THE ILLUSORY...
HFF HFF
THIS IS EVEN DEEPER THAN WHERE WE FELL LAST TIME.
YES. THERE'S A FORCE FIELD AROUND IT, SO I DON'T THINK ANY NORMAL PEOPLE COULD MAKE IT THIS FAR.
A... FORCE FIELD?
YUE-YUE! THE MAP HERE...
WHAT IS IT?
WHAT DO YOU THINK THIS IS?
DANGER
IT SAYS "DANGER"...
IS THAT A CAT...? OR MAYBE A DOG?
CAN YOU OPEN IT?
I'LL TRY. YOU TWO GET SOME REST.
SPLAT
SPLORP
WAH! WE'RE ALL STICKY?
WHAT IS THIS STUFF ...?

HUH ...?
SPLAT
GLARE
HUH ?
HAA...
CRASH!
YEEK
D-D-D-

GRRR
ROOARR
ゴアアアア!!!
DRAGON!!?
R-RUN...! YUE-SAN, NODOKA-SAN, RUN!

YUE-SAN, NODOKA-SAN—!?
SNAP OUT OF IT!
RARRR!
THIS DOESN'T USUALLY HAPPEN IN THE PICTURE BOOKS...
EHEH HEH HEH HEH
NO, NO. THIS IS NOT HAPPENING. THERE WOULD NEVER BE SUCH A FANTASY-TYPE SITUATION A MERE FEW HUNDRED METERS UNDER A PLACE WHERE PEOPLE NORMALLY GO TO SCHOOL. HA HA
HEH HEH HEH HEH HEH HEH.
FIRST OF ALL, EVEN IF SUCH A CREATURE WERE TO EXIST, IT WOULD REQUIRE VAST AMOUNTS OF FOOD TO MAINTAIN ITS ENORMOUS SIZE. IT DOESN'T HAVE ARMS; DOES THAT MEAN IT'S A WYVERN TYPE DRAGON? IN THAT CASE, IT MIGHT NOT BE VERY STRONG.
GZHN!
NGH!
!?
DASH!
Z-ZNN
SWIPE
CHA... CH-CHA-CHAMARU-SAN!?
EH...?
R-RIGHT!
ZSH!
WE MUST ESCAPE, NEGI-SENSEI!
GRRARR
KYAA KYAA
FWOOSH
B-BOM
WHOOSH
KYAAA! EEEEK!
NOOOO!
GYAAA! IT BREATHED SOMETHING AT US!

TWEET
TWEET
チュンチュン
チチチ…
CHIRP
CHIRP
CHIRP
WHEEZE WHEEZE
ゼェゼェ…
HFF HFF
ハァハァ…
THANK YOU SO MUCH, CHA-CHAMARU-SAN.
...WHY DID YOU COME TO HELP US?
HFF HFF
ハァ
I... I AM NOT SURE, MYSELF...

EITHER WAY, I DON'T THINK WE'LL BE ABLE TO GO ANY FURTHER UNTIL WE'VE DEALT WITH THAT THING.
YOU DON'T STAND A CHANCE AT YOUR LEVEL, ANIKI. IT IS A DRAGON.
I GUESS THAT MEANS IT'S TIME TO TRAIN.
GOOD GRIEF.

HEH...HEH HEH HEH. HOW DARE THAT OVER-GROWN LIZARD DROOL ALL OVER ME...
GLINT
ギュピー
YUE-SAN?
NEGI-SENSEI!! WE NEED TO GO BACK!! WE HAVE TO TEACH THAT LIZARD A LESSON!!
EH...?
W-WE WILL!!

SOMEDAY, WE WILL BE BACK FOR REVENGE!
LIZARD!
YEAH—!!
Y-YEAH...
THAT DRAGON IS A MAGICAL CREATURE. I DO NOT BELIEVE LOW LEVEL MAGIC WILL HAVE ANY EFFECT AGAINST IT.
IT'LL BE YEARS BEFORE YOU CAN BEAT THAT THING...

OKAY. NOW GET STARTED.
SETSUNA, SUPPRESS YOUR CHI ENERGY.
WITHOUT ENOUGH PRACTICE, THE MAGIC POWER AND CHI ENERGY WILL ONLY CONFLICT WITH EACH OTHER.

YES, EVAN-GELINE-SAN.
HERE I GO.
I THOUGH AS MUCH.

SISTIS MEAE PARTES PER CENTUM OCTOGINTA SECUNDAS!
FLASH

60TH PERIOD: THE RIGHT WAY TO USE A CARD?

NEGIMA!

MAGISTER NEGI MAGI

MINISTR NEGII, CONO CONOC
BWOH
EEP!
MIJAZACI NODOCA
BWOH
AH!
CAGU-RAZACA ASUNA
MM
SACURA-ZACI SETUNA.
BWOFF
B-BWOH
NGH...
EE HEE HE IT TIC LES.
EEP ...
IT'S HARD TO GET USED TO THIS.
IS IT? I DON'T THINK SO...
NKH!
HROAR

OKAY, NEXT. CREATE AN OMNIDI-RECTIONAL ANTI-MATERIAL SHIELD, FULL POWER!
RIGHT!

NEXT! FULL POWER ANTI-MAGIC SHIELD!!
TOMATO JUICE
VNN!
RIGHT!
....
AFTER YOU'VE HELD THAT FOR THREE MINUTES, SHOOT 199 MAGIC ARROWS INTO THE NORTHERN SKY!!
I'VE SET UP A FORCE FIELD, SO DON'T HOLD BACK!
NGH...!
R-RIGHT!!

UNDE-
DUCENTI
SPIRITUS
LUCIS!
COEUNTES
INIMICUM
SAGITENT!
HFF
HFF
WHEEZE
WHEEZE
BAM!
BOOM
KA-SHOOM!
KER-RACK!
OOHH!
SO
THIS...IS
MAGIC.
YEAH,
WELL.
KNG KNG
KNNG
IT'S
BEAUTI-
FUL...
WHOA
LIKE
FIRE-
WORKS
♡
SWAY
EEEEP?
HMPH.
YOU
FAINTED
AFTER
THAT? I
CAN'T EVEN
TALK TO
YOU.
I DON'T
CARE IF YOU
DID INHERIT
VAST
AMOUNTS
OF MAGICAL
POWER
FROM *HIM*.
IF YOU CAN'T
USE IT, IT'S
WASTED ON
YOU.
SMACKITY
SEN-
SEI
?
NEGI-
KUN!
TOMATO
JUICE

YO, YO, EVANGELINE-SAN. GIVE HIM A BREAK. ANIKI'S ONLY TEN.
EXECUTING FOUR SEPARATE CONTRACTS FOR THREE MINUTES, PLUS 199 MAGIC ARROWS--HE DIDN'T EVEN USE THAT MUCH MAGIC ON THE CLASS TRIP.
'COURSE HE FAINTED. ANY AVERAGE SPELL-CASTER, AND THAT'D BE ENOUGH TO--
NNGH.
SILENCE. SO AN "AVERAGE SPELLCASTER" IS ENOUGH FOR YOU, SUB-CREATURE?
ZNN
...I'LL BOIL YOU INTO A STEW.
YOU ARE AN ILLEGAL IMMIGRANT, AFTER ALL.
THERE, THERE. I KNOW SHE'S SCARY.
YOU'RE THE ONE WHO BEGGED ME TO BE YOUR MASTER. DON'T THINK YOU'RE GOING TO GET OFF WITH SOME HALF-BAKED TRAINING.
SHAKE SHAKE
TREMBLE TREMBLE
BAM

LISTEN UP, BŌYA. I HEREBY FORBID YOU FROM ANY BACKTALK OR WHINING.
HEH HEH HEH HEH.
RUMBLE RUMBLE
IF I HEAR THE TINIEST COMPLAINT, I'LL DRAIN YOUR LIFE'S BLOOD...

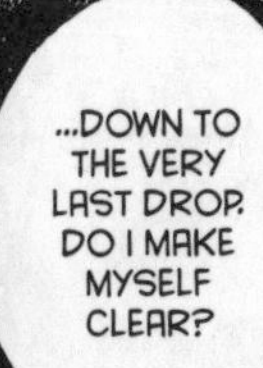
...DOWN TO THE VERY LAST DROP. DO I MAKE MYSELF CLEAR?

L-LIFE'S BLOOD !?
AWA-WAH!
GH...!
YES!
CRYSTAL CLEAR, EVANGELINE-SAN!
HRM ...?
CRINGE
C-CALL ME MASTER.
IT WON'T BE EASY WITH THIS KID.
Y-YES, MASTER! UM, BY THE WAY...

HOW LONG DO I HAVE TO TRAIN BEFORE I CAN BEAT A DRAGON?
WHAT? ?
...SAY THAT AGAIN.
I WANT TO BEAT A DRAGON ...
OH, I SEE. A DRAGON ...
YES!
ARE YOU STUPID !?
KAPOW!
PF-PF-FAH !?

WHO'S GONNA FIGHT A DRAGON IN 21ST CENTURY JAPAN!?
IF YOU HAVE TIME TO SPOUT THAT GARBAGE, USE THAT TIME TO LEARN A SPELL OR SOMETHING!
EEEP ~?
AH ...
...?
HEY, WHAT'S THIS ABOUT A DRAGON ?
LIKE, IN A VIDEO GAME ?
UM, WELL... THAT IS...I DON'T KNOW IF YOU'LL BELIEVE THIS, BUT YESTER-DAY...
?

NEVER MIND. THAT'S ENOUGH FOR TODAY.
DISMISSED !
I'M TIRED OF THIS.
Y-YES, MASTER!
I'D LIKE TO THANK ALL OF YOU FOR COMING TO HELP.
BOW
W-WE DON'T MIND. ...W-WELL, WE'LL BE GOING NOW...
IS NOTHING!
HUH? ASUNA-SAN?
......

IS SOMETHING THE MATTER, ASUNA-SAN?
... NO.
...I HEARD.
YOU WENT TO LIBRARY ISLAND YESTERDAY WITHOUT TELLING ME.
EH!? ER, UM, THAT WAS...
...WHY DIDN'T YOU TAKE ME WITH YOU?
GLARE
UM, WELL, I DIDN'T KNOW WHAT KIND OF DANGER MIGHT BE WAITING THERE...
I HEARD ABOUT THAT, TOO! I DON'T ABOUT DRAGONS, BUT THERE WAS SOMETHING BIG!
THAT'S DANGEROUS! WHY DIDN'T YOU TELL ME, YOU STUPID BRAT!?
B-BRAT!? ASUNA-SAN!
MRK!
peaceful

YOU WERE NEVER A PART OF OUR WORLD, ASUNA-SAN.
I WAS THINKING OF YOU. I CAN'T BOTHER YOU WITH MY PROBLEMS FOREVER...
!?
HEH HEH HEH. YOU'RE SUCH A DELICATE WOMAN, ANE-SAN.
SNAP

YANK
N-NOT A PART OF--!? HOW DARE YOU TALK LIKE THAT AFTER EVERYTHING WE'VE BEEN THROUGH!? NEGI-BŌZU!
WA-WA-WAH! ASUNA-SAN?
I CAN'T BREATHE!
AWA-WAH!
NO, IT'S JUST THAT YOU'RE A NORMAL PERSON! YOU'RE NOT PART OF IT! I DIDN'T WANT YOU GETTING INTO ANY DANGER!
NOT PART OF IT... YOU LITTLE... WHY DO YOU THINK I'M HAVING SETSUNA-SAN TEACH ME KENDŌ, WHEN I BARELY HAVE ANY TIME FOR MYSELF!?
EEEHH!? I NEVER ASKED YOU TO DO ANYTHING LIKE THAT!
WHY ARE YOU SO MAD, ASUNA-SAN?
"WHY AM I"...!? THIS IS WHY I HATE KIDS...
NOW I KNOW WHAT YOU REALLY THINK OF ME! BRAT!! PIP-SQUEAK!!
RAR
BONK
WH-WH-WH-WHAT DID YOU SAY? THAT'S BIG TALK COMING FROM A KID WITH NO FACIAL HAIR!!
WELL YOU'RE THE PAIPAN WITH BEAR PANTIES!!
RAR
U-HHH...
THEY HAVEN'T FOUGHT LIKE THIS IN A WHILE.
I ASKED ABOUT THAT WORD! IT MEANS SOMEONE WITH NO HAIR DOWN THERE!
Y-YOU'RE THE IMMATURE ONE, ASUNA-SAN! AND YOU'RE SUPPOSED TO BE OLDER! GROUCH! MONKEY!!
WHAT ARE THEY DOING?
THEY APPEAR TO BE FIGHTING.
WHA--
BLUSH

YOU LITTLE...
ADEAT...
EEP
!
DE-
FLEXIO
...
MORON!
パキャアァアン
SHATTER
EEEEEP!
スパ
THWACK!
AH...
!
SORRY!
NGH
...
JUST...
LEAVE
ME
ALONE!
DASH!
ダッ
STUPID
!
SWAY
SWAY
フラフラ
AH!
ASUNA
!
A...
ASUNA-
SAN...
STAGGER
よろ...
...UGH.
WHAT ARE
YOU STUPID
BRATS
DOING?
THAT FAN
SHOULD BE
AGAINST
THE RULES.
BŌYA.
KONOKA
KONOE. WE
NEED TO
TALK.
STOP BY
MY PLACE
ON THE
WAY HOME.
EH...
?

YOU TWO HAVE ENORMOUS MAGICAL CAPACITY.
THAT'S SOMETHING THAT'S DIFFICULT TO IMPROVE THROUGH TRAINING. IN OTHER WORDS, YOU HAVE TO BE BORN WITH IT. CONSIDER YOURSELVES LUCKY.
BUT CAPACITY ALONE JUST MAKES YOU GIANT MAGIC FUEL TANKS.
SPLISH たぽたぽ
MAGIC ENERGY
SPLISH SPLISH たっぽん
MAGIC ENERGY
IN ORDER TO MASTER THAT POWER, YOU NEED TO RAISE YOUR SPELL EFFICIENCY.
OR TO STRENGTHEN YOUR MENTAL CAPACITY SO YOU CAN HANDLE IT. BOTH REQUIRE TRAINING.
1. To stre
power of mi
2. To highten
of witchcraft
CLACK
INCIDENTALLY, IN ORDER TO HANDLE "MAGIC ENERGY," YOU NEED TO BE STRONG MENTALLY,
WHILE USING CHI ENERGY CAN BE LIKE AN INNER BATTLE OF PHYSICAL STRENGTH.

HEY, I'M TALKING HERE!
NNNNGH, I HAD A FIGHT WITH ASUNA... WHAT DO I DO?
NOW, NOW, NEGI-KUN.

KEEP SNIVEL-LING, AND I'LL THROTTLE YOU, KID!
NNNGH, BUT ASUNA-SAN'S...
HMPH. I LIKE SEEING YOU TWO AT ODDS WITH EACH OTHER.
HEH HEH HEH.
WHEN YOU'RE TOGETHER, YOU GIVE ME NOTH-ING BUT TROUBLE.
KEEP IT UP!
KONOKA. I HAVE A MESSAGE FROM EISHUN FOR YOU.
FROM DADDY?
NOW THAT YOU KNOW THE TRUTH, IF YOU WANT,
HE WANTS ME TO TEACH YOU ALL ABOUT MAGIC.
MUTTER MUTTER
MAN, WHAT A PAIN.

WITH YOUR POWER,
YOU COULD BECOME A MAGISTER MAGI.

MAGI... IS THAT WHAT NEGI-KUN WANTS TO BE?
KONOKA-SAN...

YES. THAT POWER OF YOURS MIGHT HELP THE WORLD SOMEDAY. THINK IT OVER.

HMMM-M-M...
HM. HM. HM.
OJŌ-SAMA...

NOW FOR YOU, BŌYA.

I WANT YOU TO CHOOSE YOUR FIGHTING STYLE
SO I KNOW WHICH WAY TO GO WITH YOUR TRAINING.
MY FIGHTING STYLE?

YES. AFTER WATCHING YOU FIGHT ON THE CLASS TRIP, I CAN SEE TWO OPTIONS FOR YOU.
LET ME LAY 'EM OUT FOR YOU.

YOU CAN BE A TRADITIONAL MAGE.
LEAVE FRONTAL DEFENSE ALMOST ENTIRELY TO YOUR MINISTER,
AND RELEASE POWERFUL SPELLS FROM THE REAR.
IT'S A WELL-BALANCED STYLE.

OR YOU CAN BE A MAGIC SWORDSMAN.
ENHANCE YOUR PHYSICAL ABILITIES WITH MAGIC AND FIGHT ALONGSIDE YOUR MINISTER ON THE FRONT LINES.
YOU CAN ALSO USE SPELLS, BUT SPEED IS KEY.
IT'S A VERY VERSATILE STYLE.

A *MAGE* OR A *MAGIC SWORDSMAN*...
IT'S LIKE A VIDEO GAME!
THEY'RE JUST ROUGH CATEGORIZATIONS TO DEFINE YOUR TRAINING.
BOTH HAVE PROS AND CONS.
I THINK A CLEVER LITTLE BOY LIKE YOU WOULD MAKE A GOOD *MAGE*, PERSONALLY.
HEH HEH HEH..
...
MAY I ASK A QUESTION?
WHAT?
WHAT STYLE DID THE THOUSAND MASTER USE?
HEH...
I FIGURED YOU'D ASK THAT.
...AS YOU CAN TELL FROM WATCHING ME AND THE WHITE-HAIRED KID FIGHT,
WHEN YOU GET STRONG ENOUGH, THESE CATEGORIES DON'T MEAN MUCH.
WHAM
WHAM
WHAM
BUT IF I HAD TO SAY,

HE WAS A MAGIC SWORDSMAN.
AND ONE SO POWERFUL THAT HE DIDN'T NEED A PARTNER.

I SEE YOU'RE NOT SURPRISED.
HUH? NO, I...
WELL, TAKE YOUR TIME, AND THINK IT OVER.
...
HM...
KONOKA. I HAVE MORE TO SAY TO YOU. COME DOWNSTAIRS.
UM, OKAY. COMING, EVA-CHAN.
WHAP!
MABU D'ING ZHOU
KAI-GONG SHI
FWIP
MUTTER MUTTER
UMM, ZUOYOU FEN ZHANG
ZHAO DU SHUANG ZHUANG
THMP
BAM
HE'S CERTAINLY ENTHUSI-ASTIC.
INTEREST-ING MOVES.
HFF HFF
WHEW... BUT I DOUBT I CAN BEAT A DRAGON WITH KUNG-FU.
HMMM
MAGE OR MAGIC SWORDS-MAN...?
SPIN
ASUNA-SAN, WHAT DO YOU THINK I SHOULD CHOOSE?
...OH.

OH YEAH! I MADE ASUNA-SAN MAD!
HERE I THOUGHT HE'D GOTTEN OVER IT.
BUT APPARENTLY HE'D ONLY FORGOTTEN.
ARE YOU ALL RIGHT, NEGI-SENSEI?
OH. THANK YOU.
HERE IS SOME TEA.
HEL-LO!
AAAAHHH! WHAT DO I DO, WHAT DO I DO?
WHAT'S WRONG WITH HIM?
NEGI-SENSEI AND ASUNA-SAN HAD A FIGHT.
WHAT WAS ASUNA-SAN ANGRY ABOUT?
WAAAH, I DON'T KNOW!
YOU'RE SUCH A STUPID BRAT. JUST APOLOGIZE, DUH.
OR JUST KILL HER.
CHACHAZERO-SAN...
B-BUT I DON'T REMEMBER DOING ANYTHING WRONG...
IN THAT CASE, IT'S BEST TO ANALYZE THE SITUATION, SENSEI.
CHACHAMARU, DO YOU STILL HAVE THE VOICE DATA FROM WHEN IT HAPPENED?
EH? UH...
YES.
ER, UM, WHY ARE YOU HERE, HAKASE-SAN?
HAKASE IS ON OUR SIDE. DO NOT WORRY.
CHA CHA CHA CHA CHA CHA

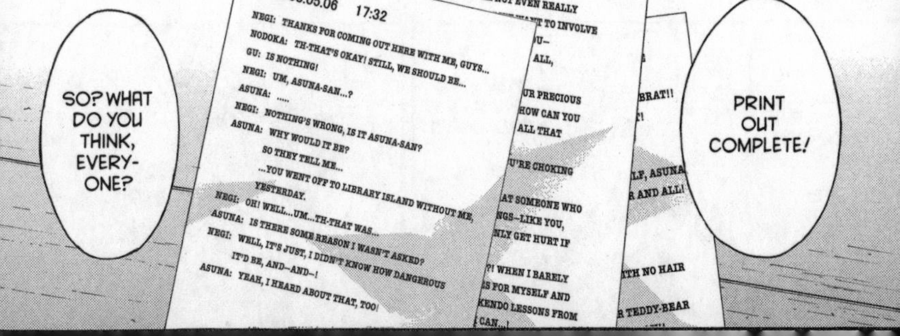
PRINT OUT COMPLETE!
NEGI: IT'S JUST...YOU'RE NOT EVEN REALLY
2003.05.06 17:32
NEGI: THANKS FOR COMING OUT HERE WITH ME, GUYS...
NODOKA: TH-THAT'S OKAY! STILL, WE SHOULD BE...
GU: IS NOTHING!
NEGI: UM, ASUNA-SAN...?
ASUNA: .....
NEGI: NOTHING'S WRONG, IS IT ASUNA-SAN?
ASUNA: WHY WOULD IT BE?
SO THEY TELL ME...
...YOU WENT OFF TO LIBRARY ISLAND WITHOUT ME, YESTERDAY.
NEGI: OH! WELL...UM...TH-THAT WAS...
ASUNA: IS THERE SOME REASON I WASN'T ASKED?
NEGI: WELL, IT'S JUST, I DIDN'T KNOW HOW DANGEROUS IT'D BE, AND--AND--!
ASUNA: YEAH, I HEARD ABOUT THAT, TOO!
SO? WHAT DO YOU THINK, EVERYONE?

HMMMM.
WELCOME TO THE "LEAST LIKELY TO KNOW HOW GIRLS THINK" CLUB.
IT SEEMS TO ME THAT SHE IS ANGRY ABOUT BEING LEFT OUT...
ERK!
BUT YOU CAN TELL THAT HE REALLY JUST DIDN'T WANT TO PUT HER IN DANGER!
NGH...
MAYBE HE HURT HER FEELINGS WHEN HE CALLED HER A MON-KEY...?
HMM, BUT THAT'S NOTHING TO GET WORKED UP ABOUT.
YOU THINK IT WAS MAYBE THIS WORD THAT'S THE PROBLEM?
...YEAH, WELL. IT'S NEVER A GOOD IDEA TO THROW SOMEONE'S PHYSICAL SHORTCOM-INGS IN THEIR FACE.
ERK! BUT THAT WASN'T WHY SHE WAS MAD TO BEGIN WITH...
WHAT DOES THAT WORD MEAN?
IT'S RIGHT THERE IN THE NEXT LINE.
Y'KNOW, I THINK I'D BE DEPRESSED IF SOMEONE CALLED ME THAT, TOO...
EH!?
YOU REALLY THINK SO...?
I'M TELL-ING YOU THAT'S THE PROB-LEM.
HMMM, I GUESS WE'VE FOUND OUR ANSWER THEN.
HEY! COME ON!

YUP. UH-HUH. I THINK. I BELIEVE.
SHE'S MAD THAT YOU CALLED HER PAIPAN
WILL YOU PLEASE DROP IT!!
STAGGER STAGGER
MMMM, WHAT DO I DO?
I STILL HAVE NO IDEA.

DO YOU THINK ASUNA-SAN HATES ME NOW?
OF COURSE NOT.
WELL, YOU KNOW. JUST APOLOGIZE.
THIS STUFF IS SUCH A PAIN. WHOEVER APOLOGIZES FIRST, WINS.
OR JUST KILL HER.

I DO THINK THE BEST THING WOULD BE TO GO APOLOGIZE TO HER IN PERSON.
IF I KNOW ASUNA-SAN, SHE'LL LISTEN.
IF YOU DO NOT KNOW WHY SHE IS ANGRY, THE BEST SOLUTION WOULD BE TO ASK HER.

NGH ...
Dash Cheese
Y... YOU'RE RIGHT.
FIRST, I HAVE TO APOLOGIZE.
FOR INSULTING HER, TOO.
O-OKAY, NOW THAT IT'S SETTLED ...
I'M GOING TO APOLOGIZE!
HUH? SHE'S NOT ANSWERING HER PHONE.
ANIKI, USE THE CARD!
OH YEAH! LET'S SEE...
RUMMAGE RUMMAGE
...AH.
I-I'LL JUST STEP OUTSIDE.
CHUCKLE
くす...

643 KAGURAZAKA, ASUNA
KONOE, KONOKA
NEGI
FSHH
ASUNA-SAN! ASUNA-SAN!
NN?

ASUNA-SAN! ASUNA-SAN! I WANT TO TALK TO YOU...
UGH, HE'S SO ANNOY-ING!
WHAT DO YOU WANT!?
OH...! THANK GOOD-NESS, ASUNA-SAN.
SORRY TO BOTHER YOU, ASUNA-SAN. I WANT TO APOLOGIZE ABOUT EARLIER...
EH...?
WH-WHY?
ER... UM...
I DO THINK THE BEST THING WOULD BE TO GO APOLOGIZE TO HER IN PERSON.
IF I KNOW ASUNA-SAN SHE'LL LISTEN.
I-I KNOW! I WANT TO TALK TO YOU IN PERSON, SO I'M GOING TO SUMMON YOU, OKAY?
EH!?
OKAY, HERE GOES!
EH!? JUST A--
EVOCEM TE!!
GYAAAAA!! WAIT, WAIT, WAIT!
VNN
OH? WELL IF IT ISN'T NEGI-KUN.
I HEARD YOU HAD A HECK OF A TIME ON THE CLASS TRIP.
OH, TAKA-MICHI. WHAT BRINGS YOU HERE?
OH, I JUST HAVE A THANK YOU GIFT FOR EVA FROM THE WESTERN CHIEF.
WHAT'S THIS YOU'RE DOING HERE?

SHWAH-
BOOM

N--
N...
TREMBLE
TREMBLE
ふる
ふる...
TA...
KA..
SHOCK
UH...
I-I'M
SORRY
!!
AAAHH,
I MADE
HER EVEN
MORE
MAD!
FSHH
WELL,
THAT
WAS
A BIG
FLOP.
MAYBE I
DIDN'T
HAVE THE
BEST
TIMING.
WHAT
DO I DO?
I'M
SORRY,
NEGI-
KUN.

HM.
...

SI-I-IGH
ASUNA-SAN HASN'T SPOKEN TO ME IN THREE WHOLE DAYS...
NEGIMA!
MAGISTER NEGI MAGI
61ST PERIOD:
TROPICAL MARSHMALLOW EMPIRE
YOU'VE GOT THE PROBLEMS PILING UP AGAIN, ANIKI.
NNNGH...
HERE WE FINALLY FOUND A CLUE,
BUT THERE'S A GINORMOUS GUARDIAN BLOCKING THE WAY.
BUT WORST OF ALL THERE'S ASUNA-SAN!
WHY IS SHE MAD AT ME!? I DIDN'T MEAN TO GET IN A FIGHT WITH HER!
I DON'T UNDER-STAND WOMEN AT ALL!
DON'T WORRY; YOU'RE ONLY TEN. NO ONE EXPECTS YOU TO.
GUH HEH HEH HEH. NOT EASY BEING A LADIES' MAN, IS IT, ANIKI?
AND YOU'VE GOT THIS BIG DECISION IN FRONT OF YOU.
MAGE OR MAGIC SWORDS-MAN. THAT COULD CHANGE YOUR LIFE.
STUN
WHOAH!
VROOM
KONK
PRFF!
KREE

HO HO HO HO
ホホホホ
GOOD MORNING, NEGI-SENSEI!
GRRR!
GRRR!
CLASS REP-SAN!
I'VE HEARD THAT YOU'VE BEEN UNHAPPY THESE PAST FEW DAYS.
OH, NO, I--
DID YOU GO SOMEWHERE DURING GOLDEN WEEK?
NO, NO-WHERE...
OH, MY! WE CAN'T HAVE THAT!
IT IS THE WEEKEND, AFTER ALL. WHAT WOULD YOU SAY TO A GLORIOUS TROPICAL PARADISE? ♡
EH...? TROPICAL PARA-DISE...?
YUP! ♡ A SOUTHERN ISLAND...
THE BEACH.
EH...? THE B...
BEACH ...?
?

VRRON
OOOH~~!
IT'S REALLY A TROPICAL ISLAND!

THIS IS ONE OF THE YUKIHIRO GROUP'S RESORT ISLANDS. I'VE RESERVED IT FOR OUR OWN PRIVATE USE FOR THE ENTIRE DAY.
SPLISH SPLISH
WOW. I'M IMPRESSED, CLASS REP-SAN!
THE BEACH IS RIGHT OVER THERE--
ALLLL RIGHT!

LOVE
SQUEE
キャッ
SQUEE
キャッ
AH HA HA!
アハハ
GLOOM
どーん
WOW
HRNGRRRRR. WHAT ON EARTH--!? MY PLAN WAS TO SPEND TIME IN PARADISE ALL ALONE WITH NEGI-SENSEI.
H-H-HOW DID IT TURN INTO *THIS?* AND WITH MORE THAN HALF OF THE CLASS!
GRRR
ぐぎぎぎ
THIS IS WHAT HAPPENS WHEN YOU LET KAZUMI AND HARUNA-SAN IN ON YOUR PLANS, AYAKA.
WHAT ABOUT YOU TWO!?
YOU DIDN'T HAVE TO COME, EITHER!

OCEAN, HERE WE COME!!
MAN, THANKS FOR OFFERING THIS GREAT VACATION TO US POOR, PEN-NILESS JUNIOR HIGH GIRLS, CLASS REP ♡
RRRGH!!
NOW, NOW.
WE'VE GOT THE WHOLE ISLAND. WHO CARES HOW MANY OF US THERE ARE? ♡
WHY DID I HAVE TO COME?
WHAT AM I DOING AT CLASS REP'S FAMILY HOTEL?
NOW, NOW. YOU HAP-PENED TO HAVE TIME OFF FROM YOUR PAPER ROUTE, SO WHY NOT?

IF SHE HAS ENOUGH FUN PLAYING ON THE BEACH, MAYBE SHE'LL FORGET ABOUT HER FIGHT WITH NEGI-KUN ♡
...I HOPE SO.
OH... ASUNA-SAN.
HMPH!
HUFF!
ぷいっ
CLANG!
WHIMPER...
SHE'S STILL TOTALLY MAD AT ME.
WHAT, YOU EXPECTED MIRACLES?
WOW, A VACAY IN THE TROPICS.
IT'S LIKE HEAVEN ♡
SQUEE
キャッ
SQUEE
キャッ
WOW, CHIZURU REALLY DOES...
HAVE GIGANTIC BOOBS...
WELL, SHE IS NUMBER ONE IN THE CLASS.
HEH HEH HEH
フフフ
HMMM, BUT WITHOUT ANY GUYS HERE, THE TROPICS JUST AREN'T WHAT THEY SHOULD BE.
GUESS THAT'S WHAT NEGI-KUN'S FOR ♡

SIIIIGH...
ASUNA-SAN WON'T TALK TO ME. WHAT DO I DO?
SIGH...

SIIIGH...
I KNEW IT... THERE IS SOME-THING BOTHER-ING NEGI-SENSEI...

IN THAT CASE, I SHALL HAVE TO CHEER HIM UP!
AND WHEN I'VE SUCCEEDED, WE'LL HAVE A SWEET AVENTURE D'AMOUR...
HO HO HO
HA HA HA
SWIM
?
NEGI SEN --
HM ?
NEGI-SENSEI-- !!
SPLASH
LET'S PLAY ♡
WAAAH!?

HRM ?
EXCUSE ME, LADIES! I WAS GOING TO INVITE NEGI-SENSEI TO--
BOING!
NEGI-KUN, LET'S GO OVER THERE AND DO SOMETHING FUN!
UM, I...
SQUEE
SQUEE

OOH, ANOTHER BATTLE OVER NEGI-KUN!
EH?
LET'S GO!!
DON'T LET 'EM BEAT YOU!

PLAY WITH US, NEGI-KUN ♪
NO, HARUNA-SAN! I WAS HERE FIRST!
SQUEE
EEP! EEP!
SQUEE
YOU WERE NOT, CLASS REP!
NEGI-KUN'S GOING TO PLAY WITH US!
EEP!
UM...
ZER-PLASH!
I'M SORRY! I WANT TO BE ALONE TODAY!
AH! NEGI-KUN!
MRPHLE!?
FWUMP
MPHRPHLE!? WHAT ARE THESE SOFT, MARSHMALLOWY...
OH MY, MY?
BOING
MMPH! MMPH!!
FLAIL FLAIL
じたばた
OH, COME ON!
KER-SHOCK
CHIZURU-SAN—?

CH-CH-CHIZURU-SAN, WOULD YOU MIND EXPLAINING TO ME WHY YOU'VE INSERTED NEGI-SENSEI'S FACE INTO YOUR CLEAVAGE!?
OH, HE DID THIS ON HIS OWN.
OH, DEAR. HE CAN'T GET OUT.
MMPH MMPH
もがが
GASP! CAN IT BE ALL THIS TIME CHIZURU-SAN HAS ONLY **PRETENDED** TO HAVE NO INTEREST IN HIM?
AND NOW SHE'S POISED TO CHARM NEGI-SENSEI AWAY WITH HER WELL-ENDOWED, MOTHERLY PHYSIQUE!?
I REFUSE TO ALLOW IT, CHIZURU-SAN! RETURN NEGI-SENSEI AT ONCE!
BUT HE'S STUCK, AYAKA.
HEY, YOU! WHAT'S GOING ON OVER THERE!?
AWA-WAH!
OOOH! ARE WE HAVING ANOTHER BUST BATTLE?

NO ONE WILL BEAT ME IN SIZE ♪
TAKE THAT!
APSARAS
もぎゅ
SQUISH
ぷるるるんっ
JIGGLE JIGGLE
LADIES! WHAT IS THE MEANING OF THIS!?
もぎゅ
SQUISH
ARGHL-MRPHLE!
JIGGLE
ぷるんっ

WHAT'S HAPPENING?
IT'S A MARSHMALLOW NIGHTMARE!
BLUB BLUB
ブクブク
NEGI-SEN--
HUH?
ぷか BWOOP
...
OH NO! SENSEI'S DROWNING!
NOOOOOOOOO!!

SOMEBODY GIVE HIM MOUTH-TO-MOUTH!
ALLOW ME!
NO, ME!
WHAT ARE THEY DOING...? IDIOTS...
HA HA HA
POOR NEGI-KUN!

SQUEE
キャッ
SQUEE
キャッ
AH HA HA HA

VAIO

いひひ
EE HEE HEE!
くすくす
KYA HA HA HA!
GIGGLE GIGGLE

SORRY ABOUT EAR-LIER!
WOULD YOU LIKE A DRINK?
CLINK
カラン…

WHEW ...
Z-ZSHH
CRUNCH
CRUNCH
CRUNCH
I'M TERRIBLY SORRY ABOUT WHAT HAPPENED.
NEGI-SENSEI.
NEGI-SENSEI. ARE YOU STILL DEPRESSED? WHATEVER IS THE MATTER?
OH, NO... IT'S ALL RIGHT ...
WELL, UM, I...
WHAT !?
A BIG FIGHT WITH ASUNA-SAN?
Z-ZSH
YES...

I DON'T KNOW WHY SHE'S MAD, AND I JUST KEPT MAKING IT WORSE...
OH, MY...
OHO ...?
WHAT'S THIS...?
THIS COULD BE SOME PRICELESS TOP-SECRET INFORMATION. IT COULD GIVE CLASS REP HER BIG CHANCE.
INDEED. ALL SHE HAS TO DO IS GIVE HIM SOME KIND WORDS WHILE HE'S FEELING DOWN, AND HE'LL BE ALL HERS.
EEEP! WHAT WILL SHE DO?
ぎゅっ…
CLASP
I UNDERSTAND, NEGI-SENSEI.
OH!
ALLOW ME TO HELP YOU
PATCH THINGS UP WITH ASUNA-SAN.
EH...?
OH?
JUST LEAVE EVERYTHING TO ME ♡
HO HO HO HO HO
TH-THANK YOU SO MUCH, CLASS REP-SAN!
HUH...?
BESIDES, NEGI-SENSEI AND ASUNA-SAN WERE ALWAYS SO CLOSE. I FEEL SORRY FOR HIM, SEEING HIM LIKE THIS.
CLASS REP... YOU'RE ACTUALLY A NICE PERSON.
SHE'S GOING TO FAIL AT ROMANCE IN THE FUTURE. I JUST KNOW IT.
WAIT UP, CLASS REP! ARE YOU SURE ABOUT THIS?
THIS WAS YOUR BIG CHANCE TO PULL OUT AHEAD AND MAKE THE HEARTBROKEN NEGI-SENSEI YOURS!
WHAT!? I WOULD NEVER!!
LIKE TAKING IN A STRAY PUPPY! ♡
OOOHHH...!

THAT'S THE AYAKA I KNOW AND LOVE.
TOUCHED
TEARS
ホロリ…
ALL RIGHT. I'LL HELP, TOO.
OH, YOU, TOO, CHIZURU-SAN?
TH-THANK YOU!!
NOW THEN! LET US BEGIN OPERATION: GET NEGI-SENSEI AND ASUNA-SAN BACK TOGETHER!
YEAH !!
IT MIGHT BE A LITTLE DANGEROUS, BUT DON'T YOU WORRY, NEGI-SENSEI. YOU'LL BE OKAY ♡
?

WOW, THEY'RE ALL SUCH GOOD PEOPLE, AREN'T THEY, CHAMO-KUN?
BUT HEY, ANIKI.
WHY D'YOU THINK THE ANEGO WITH THE JUGS TOLD YOU TO WAIT HERE?

SS... す…
I'M JUST GONNA STARTLE YOU A LITTLE...
I'M SORRY, SENSEI!
!?
ずぼっ
PLUNGE!
SPLASH
SPLASH
バシャ バシャ
ABWUH! MRPHGLE!
WHAT'S WRONG, ANIKI!?
ASUNA, WHY DON'T YOU JUST FORGIVE NEGI-KUN?
I DON'T HAVE TO IF I DON'T WANT TO!
ASUNA-SAN! ASUNA-SAN!

HUFF
HUFF
IT'S T-T-TERRIBLE! NEGI-SENSEI GOT HIS FOOT CAUGHT! HE'S IN DEEP WATER!
ACT WORRIED, ACT WORRIED.
HE MIGHT REALLY DROWN THIS TIME!
WHAT!?
NEGI'S ...!?
SHUDDER
WHERE IS HE!!?
DASH!
SHE'S FAST!
ASUNA-SAN...
ASUNA!
ZSH!
THIS WAY!!
NEGI!!
DAAAH-NUH DAAAH-NUH
HUH?
YEEEK~!!
DA-NUH DA-NUH DA-NUH DA-NUH DAAAH-NUH!
HEEELP~!
UWAH-H-H!

SOME-BODY HELP ME!
SH-SH-SH-SH-SHARKS!?
NEGI!
URGH!
ASUNA-SAN!
BAM!
DA-DASH!
NEGI-SENS... MMPH!
CLAMP
CLAMP
NE-MRPHLE!?!
CALM DOWN, YOU TWO. THIS IS ALL PART OF THE PLAN. ASUNA'S STRONG SENSE OF JUSTICE WOULD NEVER LET HER ABANDON NEGI-KUN ♡
WE DIDN'T TELL NEGI-KUN, THOUGH.
B-B-BUT THE SHARKS!!
P... PLAN?
THAT'S TOO MUCH!
OH, YOU KNOW. THERE WASN'T ENOUGH SUSPENSE IF HE JUST DROWNING, SO WE SPICED IT UP ♡
NN HN HN ♡
INSIDE THE SHARKS
STUFFED SHARK FROM THE HOTEL LOBBY?
SHARK 1: KU-FEI
IS EASY JOB FOR 50 MEAL TICKET
SHARK 2: NATSUMI MURAKAMI
COSTUME
BUT WE NEVER GUESSED SHE'D JUMP RIGHT INTO THE WATER ♪

コポッ
BURBLE
ABLUB BLUB
あばばっ
YOU HAVE TO FIGHT BACK! IT'S THE ONLY WAY!!
BUT MY WAND --OH! I KNOW!
EEK!
NNNGH... I'M SCARED...
BUT ...
WHOOSH
BASH

THIS IS THE PERFECT TIME TO USE THE KUNG-FU I'M LEARNING FROM KŪ FEI,
BLUB BLUB BLUB
AND THE SIMPLIFIED MAGICAL ENHANCEMENT EVANGELINE-SAN TAUGHT ME...
ZSH!

DRAH!!
BLUB BLUB
GOOD JOB! A SHARK'S WEAKNESS IS ITS GILLS OR ITS NOSE, ANIKI!!

OOH! HE GOOD, MOVING LIKE THAT UNDERWATER.
FWAP WHAP WHAP WHAP
べしっ パンパンパン
GSH!
WHA--!?
BLUUUUB!
WARGHLE !?
BOING
YU CHI DA ZHANG!
EEK?!
NEGI-SENSEI -!

A SHARK'S USING KUNG-FU !?
HEELP! HEEELP!!
DA-NUH DA-NUH DA-NUH!
DA-NUH DA-NUH DA-NUH!
NYOH-HO-HOH! ♪
NEGI!!
ADEAT!!
MURMUR
FLASH
ZSHAM
BWOH
WHY, YOU--

WHAAA?!
KYAAH!!
KER-SPLASH!
STUPID SHARK !!
ZWAH-ZOOM
A—
ZOOOOO—
SH-SHE PARTED THE SEA!?
RIDICULOUS!
NEGI! NEGI!
ARE YOU OKAY?!
A... ASUNA-SAN.
THANK YOU!
NEGI...
Z-ZSHH...
SPLAT
...NN?
...HUH?
KSHH
WOW.

WHAT...IS GOING ON HERE?
RUMBLE RUMBLE
NO, THIS IS-- UM!
IT'S NOT WHAT YOU THINK, ASUNA-SAN! WE DID IT TO HELP YOU MAKE UP--
GH
YOU SNOT-NOSED LITTLE-- !!
SWOOSH
EEP!
......
BAP
?
PULLING... A PRANK LIKE THAT...
I WAS... REALLY WORRIED...
STUPID ...
EH...?
STUPID!
DASH!
FSHH...
W-WAS ASUNA-SAN CRY-ING?
ASUNA... !
AH-H-H-H?
MAYBE WE REALLY DID OVERDO IT A LITTLE.
I'M S-S-S-S-SO SORRY, NEGI-SENSEI.
TREMBLE
TREMBLE
OH, WHAT SHOULD I DO?
DOES ANE-SAN HAVE A THING FOR...?

NEGIMA!

MAGISTER NEGI MAGI

62ND PERIOD: SKIP A BEAT! DON'T OPEN UP IN THE TROPICS...

WAIT, ASUNA-SAN! PLEASE, LISTEN TO ME!
LEAVE ME ALONE!
AND STOP FOLLOW-ING ME!
WAA-AAH! WAIT!
STOMP
STOMP
STAMP
STOMP
W-WELL, HE IS ONLY TEN...
HE HAS HIS PATHETIC MOMENTS, TOO.
BUT IT'S CUTE.
...STILL, IF HE DOESN'T HAVE TO FIGHT, I THINK THAT'S GOOD, TOO.
PEACE IS THE BEST THING...
NN?
WHAT ARE YOU TALK-ING ABOUT, BOOKSTORE? IT'S NOT LIKE WE'RE TALKING ABOUT BEAT-ING UP BAD GUYS!
AH HA HA!
WE'RE TALK-ING ABOUT WORKING FOR YOUR DREAM--THAT KIND OF THING!
EEP.
SQUEE
SQUEE
....

SI-I-IGH
TRUDGE TRUDGE
NOW IS NOT THE TIME, CHAMO-KUN!
POUT
POUT
OH, RIGHT, RIGHT. ASUNA-ANESAN.
WHOA, LOOK, ANIKI! WHAT A SUNSET!
TALK ABOUT A PERFECT TROPICAL VACATION.
ZSHH...
DON'T WORRY ABOUT HER. SHE'LL CHEER UP SOONER OR LATER.
PFFT HEH HEH.
HRNGH, THAT'S NO WAY TO TAKE RESPONSI-BILITY...

ARE YOU ALL RIGHT, NEGI-SENSEI?
HAVE YOU FIXED THINGS WITH ASUNA-SAN YET?
OH.
HEL-LO.
Celtic Moon
Celtic Moon
BY THE WAY, HOW DID THIS ALL START?
WELL, ER...
WHAT? IT'S PARTLY BECAUSE YOU WENT TO LIBRARY ISLAND WITH US?
Z-ZSHH
HERE'S A TRAN-SCRIPT OF THE FIGHT.

I THINK THIS PART MAY BE THE PROBLEM.
EH !?
YOU'VE ALREADY FIGURED IT OUT?

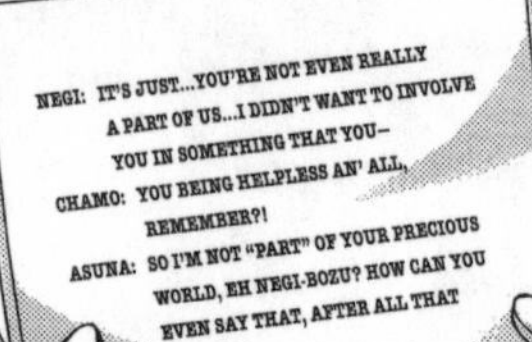

NEGI: IT'S JUST...YOU'RE NOT EVEN REALLY A PART OF US...I DIDN'T WANT TO INVOLVE YOU IN SOMETHING THAT YOU—

CHAMO: YOU BEING HELPLESS AN' ALL, REMEMBER?!

ASUNA: SO I'M NOT "PART" OF YOUR PRECIOUS WORLD, EH NEGI-BOZU? HOW CAN YOU EVEN SAY THAT, AFTER ALL THAT WE'VE—!!

THINK WHAT YOU WANTED TO SAY, NEGI-SENSEI, WAS, *"YOU WEREN'T PART OF THE FANTASY WORLD TO BEGIN WITH, SO I DON'T WANT TO CAUSE TROUBLE FOR YOU AND PUT YOU IN DANGER,"* BUT...

THE WAY YOU SAID IT, IT SOUNDS LIKE YOU'RE SAYING, *"YOU'RE NOT PART OF THIS, AND YOU'RE JUST A NORMAL JUNIOR HIGH GIRL, SO MIND YOUR OWN BUSINESS."*

STUN
EEHH!? I DIDN'T MEAN *THAT* AT ALL!

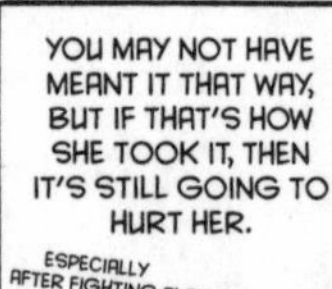

YOU MAY NOT HAVE MEANT IT THAT WAY, BUT IF THAT'S HOW SHE TOOK IT, THEN IT'S STILL GOING TO HURT HER.
ESPECIALLY AFTER FIGHTING ALONG-SIDE YOU.

N-NO ...
CLANG
CLANG
CLANG
SO THAT'S WHY...

TH-THANK YOU SO MUCH, YUE-SAN!!
I HAD NO IDEA!
YOU REALLY KNOW HOW GIRLS THINK!!
YUE-ANEKI!
I THINK IT'S ONLY COMMON SENSE...
IT'S NOT ABOUT HOW GIRLS THINK...

...NOW I'M SORRY TO CHANGE THE SUBJECT.
BUT THERE'S SOME-THING WE WOULD VERY MUCH LIKE TO ASK YOU.
EH ?

YOU'RE SURE, NODOKA ?
YES.

UM.
THAT IS...

NEGI-SENSEI...
WOULD IT BE POS-SIBLE... FOR US TO BECOME WIZARDS?
DUN!
THIS IS CONCEPT ART
... HUH ?
EEEHH!? YOU WANT TO BE WIZARDS!?
AND WHAT IS THAT CONCEPT ART?
W-WE'LL STUDY REALLY HARD...
STUN
IS IT IMPOS-SIBLE? SINCE WE'RE... NORMAL?
NO...! IT'S NOT NEC-ESSARILY IMPOS-SIBLE...
GH!
THEN, PLEASE!
YES, WELL ...
I MEAN, NO !
IT'S JUST LIKE WITH ASUNA-SAN; YOU STUDENTS AREN'T A PART OF MY WORLD. I CAN'T PUT YOU IN DANGER!
YES...THAT'S WHY WE MADE UP OUR MINDS, OF OUR OWN FREE WILL, TO SET FOOT INTO YOUR FANTASY WORLD--A WORLD FILLED WITH DANGER AND ADVENTURE.
WE'D LIKE TO TELL HARUNA ABOUT IT, TOO...
TO BE HONEST...
IT'S NOT FAIR OF US TO LEAVE YOU TO FIGHT THAT LIZARD ALL BY YOUR-SELVES...
WE WANT TO HELP IN SOME WAY...
YUE-SAN, NODOKA-SAN...

IF OUR FIRST CONCEPT PHOTO FAILED TO MEET WITH YOUR SATISFACTION, WE ARE PREPARED TO TAKE IT IN THIS DIRECTION...
AWA-WA-WA-WAH
MAGICAL GIRLS BIBLION ILLUSTRATION BY: PARU
HEY, HEY!
THERE AREN'T ANY WIZARDS LIKE THAT!
B-BUT I ONLY JUST GRADU-ATED MAGIC SCHOOL MYSELF...
AND ONE MORE THING! IF IT'S ALL RIGHT WITH YOU, NEGI-SENSEI...
I WOULD LIKE
ONE OF THOSE PROBA-TIONARY CONTRACTS, TOO!
GH...
EH...!?
!?
GLINT
EEEHH!?
A PACTIO!?
YES. I BELIEVE IT WOULD BE BEST TO HAVE AS MUCH FIREPOWER AS... HM? WHAT'S WRONG? WHY IS YOUR FACE SO RED?
OH! UM...
SPLASH
YOO-HOO!
WHACHA TALKIN' ABOUT?
OH! ASAKURA-NŌSAN!

ACTUALLY! YUE-ANEKI SAYS SHE WANTS TO MAKE A PACTIO WITH ANIKI.
HEY! CHAMO-KUN!
OOOHH. WHY NOT? I SAY GO FOR IT.
THAT'S RIGHT. EVERYONE WHO MAKES A PACTIO GETS A SPECIAL ITEM, RIGHT?
I KINDA WANT ONE MYSELF.
WILL YOU MAKE A PROBATIONARY CONTRACT WITH ME, NEGI-KUN?
NN HN HN
W-W-WAIT A SECOND!
OHO!
NN ?
? ? ?
...HUH ?
AHA. SO THEY DON'T KNOW HOW TO MAKE A PACTIO?
ARE YOU SURE ABOUT THIS, YUECCHI? THE RITUAL TO MAKE A PACTIO INVOLVES KISSING NEGI-SENSEI, YOU KNOW.
WHISPER WHISPER
ぼそぼそ
PSST PSST
ひそひそ
TUG
...EH !?
K-KISS!?
?

GASP! NOW THAT SHE MENTIONS IT...
THAT KISS WAS THE PACTIO...!?
I DIDN'T REALLY KNOW WHAT WAS GOING ON THEN.
WELL, YUECCHI? D'YOU WANNA MAKE A PACTIO, I MEAN KISS NEGI-KUN?
KYAAAAA!
KYAAAAA!
FLAIL
ぱた
FLAIL
ぱた
FLAIL
ぱた
YUE ...?
WHAT'S WRONG, YUE?
GULP!
ギックゥッ
O-OH, IT'S NOTHING, I SAY.

NEGI-KUUUUN! WE HAVE A QUESTION!
IS THERE A WAY TO MAKE A PACTIO THAT DOESN'T INVOLVE KISSING?
ZUH-PLAT!
ステーン
EH...? KISS-ING?
KISS-ING...?
YOU KISSED HIM ON THE CLASS TRIP, MIYAZAKI, REMEMBER? THAT'S WHY YOU...
KYAAAA!?
I-I-I-IT'S NOT WHAT YOU THINK, NODOKA!
WHAT BRINGS THIS UP ALL OF A SUDDEN, KONOKA-SAN?
OH, WELL, I'VE BEEN THINKING ABOUT IT, AND I DECIDED THAT I DO WANT TO STUDY TO BE A WIZARD.
WOW, REALLY!?
WOW
ほぉぉ～っ
CLAMOR CLAMOR
ワイワイ
YUP ♡
AND I WANT SET-CHAN TO BE MY PARTNER.
BUT SET-CHAN SAYS THAT GIRLS SHOULDN'T KISS EACH OTHER.
NO, I MEANT...
I WOULDN'T MIND, BUT...

KISS... EEP ?
がくがく
SHAKE SHAKE
NODOKA, IT'S NOT WHAT YOU THINK! I HAD ABSOLUTELY NO INTENTION OF--
OH, COME ON. IT'S JUST A LITTLE KISS.
WE'VE ALL GOOFED AROUND WITH KISSES BEFORE, HAVEN'T WE?
ワイ CLAMOR
N-NO, I BELIEVE WE SHOULD MAINTAIN SOME STANDARD OF...
ワイ CLAMOR
HM-MMM
BUT MAN, SUDDENLY WE'VE GOT A WHOLE TEAM.
THIS WILL MAKE STRATEGIZING MORE INTERESTING.
HEH HEH HEH. YOU'RE QUITE THE LADIES' MAN, ANIKI.
HEH, HEH, HEH
IF THOSE TWO BOTH LEARN MAGIC, THEN WE CAN USE THEM LATER. THEN WE'LL HAVE ATTACK, HEALING, AND SUPPORT MAGIC. OUR REAR GUARD WILL BE PERFECT.
WE'LL SAY ASAKURA-NŌSAN CAN FIND INFO AND BE A DYNAMIC FIGHTER... HMM, WE DON'T HAVE ENOUGH FOR OUR VANGUARD. EVEN IF WE ASK KŪ-RŌSHI TO HELP, THERE'S STILL...
ASA INTEL ATTACK
KO HEALING
YU ATTACK MAGICS?
NO EMPATHY, SUPPORT
NE MAGIC-USER?
COMBAT-MAGE?
SET SWORDSMAN
KU MARTIAL ARTS
STOP, CHAMO-KUN! YOU CAN'T JUST...
ぶつぶつ MUTTER MUTTER MUTTER
カリカリカリ SKRITCH SKRITCH SKRITCH

MEMBERS ASSEMBLED!? READY!!
"NEGI AND HIS MERRY MAIDENS"
カシャアッ KA-CRASH

. . .
HMMM, ANIKI. IT JUST DOESN'T LOOK RIGHT WITHOUT ASUNA-ANE-SAN.
VISUALLY OR STRATEGICALLY.
GASP!
OH YEAH! ASUNA-SAN!
I HAVE TO GO APOLOGIZE TO ASUNA-SAN!
EEEHH ?
YOU TWO HAVEN'T MADE UP YET?
ワイワイ CLAMOR CLAMOR

LET'S SEE... ASUNA-SAN IS IN ROOM 304...
OHO. CABINS ON THE WATER. NIIIICE ♪
OH? NEGI-SENSEI.
KACHAK
HUH? CLASS REP-SAN?
I-I'M SORRY... ASUNA-SAN SAYS SHE DOESN'T WANT TO SEE ANYONE...
EH...?
CLANG
I-I SEE...
GLOOM...
OH, B-BUT NEGI-SENSEI.
I'LL TALK TO HER AND TAKE RESPONSIBILITY FOR EVERYTHING THAT HAPPENED. IT WILL BE ALL RIGHT ♡
IT WAS MY MISTAKE THIS AFTERNOON.
DON'T WORRY. GO BACK TO YOUR ROOM AND GET SOME REST ♡

EH?
OH, TH-THANK YOU...
I'M SORRY TO PUT YOU THROUGH ALL OF THIS, CLASS REP-SAN...
TOUCHED
EH...? M-MY...
TWANG
OH, NEGI-SENSEI.
PLEASE DON'T CRY.
WIPE WIPE

HON-ESTLY!
HOW CAN YOU BE SO MEAN TO SUCH A SWEET LITTLE BOY! I DON'T BELIEVE YOU!
SHUT
I'M NOT BEING MEAN! WE'RE FIGHTING!
WHAT ARE YOU DOING IN MY ROOM, ANYWAY!?
I'M GETTING DRESSED, HERE!
I BOOKED THIS HOTEL. ALL ROOMS ARE MY ROOMS.
HO HO HO
YOU TRULY ARE A MONKEY!
INDRA
APSARAS
WHAT WAS THAT
!?
I CALLED YOU A MONKEY, YOU SIMPLETON! NOW WHY DON'T YOU STOP BEING SO STUB-BORN AND MAKE UP WITH HIM!?
SHUT UP, CLASS REP! YOU DON'T EVEN HAVE ANY IDEA WHAT'S GOING ON!!
SO WHAT IF I DON'T? YOU ARE SO IMMA-TURE! OHHH, THAT'S RIGHT, I REMEMBER. YOU'RE NOT MATURE PHYSI-CALLY EITHER, I HEAR! OH HO HO HO.
WH-WH-WHA!? I-I-I'LL KILL YOU FOR THAT!
BAM
BAM
BAM
BAM
BY ALL MEANS, TRY!! MORE IMPORTANTLY, HOW COULD YOU GET INTO A FIGHT WITH A LITTLE KID IN THE FIRST PLACE!?
BOFF
BOFF
BOFF
WELL, HE--!
NGH!
I...I CAN'T TELL YOU...
BUT HE SAID SOMETHING HOR-RIBLE TO ME, OKAY? REALLY, REALLY HORRIBLE.
WILL YOU LISTEN TO YOURSELF? HE'S TEN.
HONESTLY

YOU'VE CHANGED A LOT SINCE I FIRST MET YOU.
BUT YOU'RE STILL JUST AS STUBBORN AS YOU WERE THEN.
INDRA APSARAS
...YOU FOR-GAVE HIM LONG AGO, AND YOU KNOW IT.
ERK ...
HO HO HO HO
REALLY. HOW DID A QUIET, UNSOCIABLE BRAT WITH EYES LIKE *THIS*.
GROW UP TO BE SUCH A VIOLENT MONKEY?
IRK
....
BY ARGUING WITH YOU EVERY-DAY!
BATH ROOM
SLAM!
ERG-GH!?
ARE YOU RUN-NING AWAY FROM ME?
NEGI-SENSEI WAS *CRYING!* DON'T YOU FEEL SORRY FOR HIM?
ASUNA-SAAAN, OPEN THIS DOOR!
FSHH
POUND
POUND
POUND
......
I KNOW, I KNOW...
STUPID CLASS REP.
FSHH...

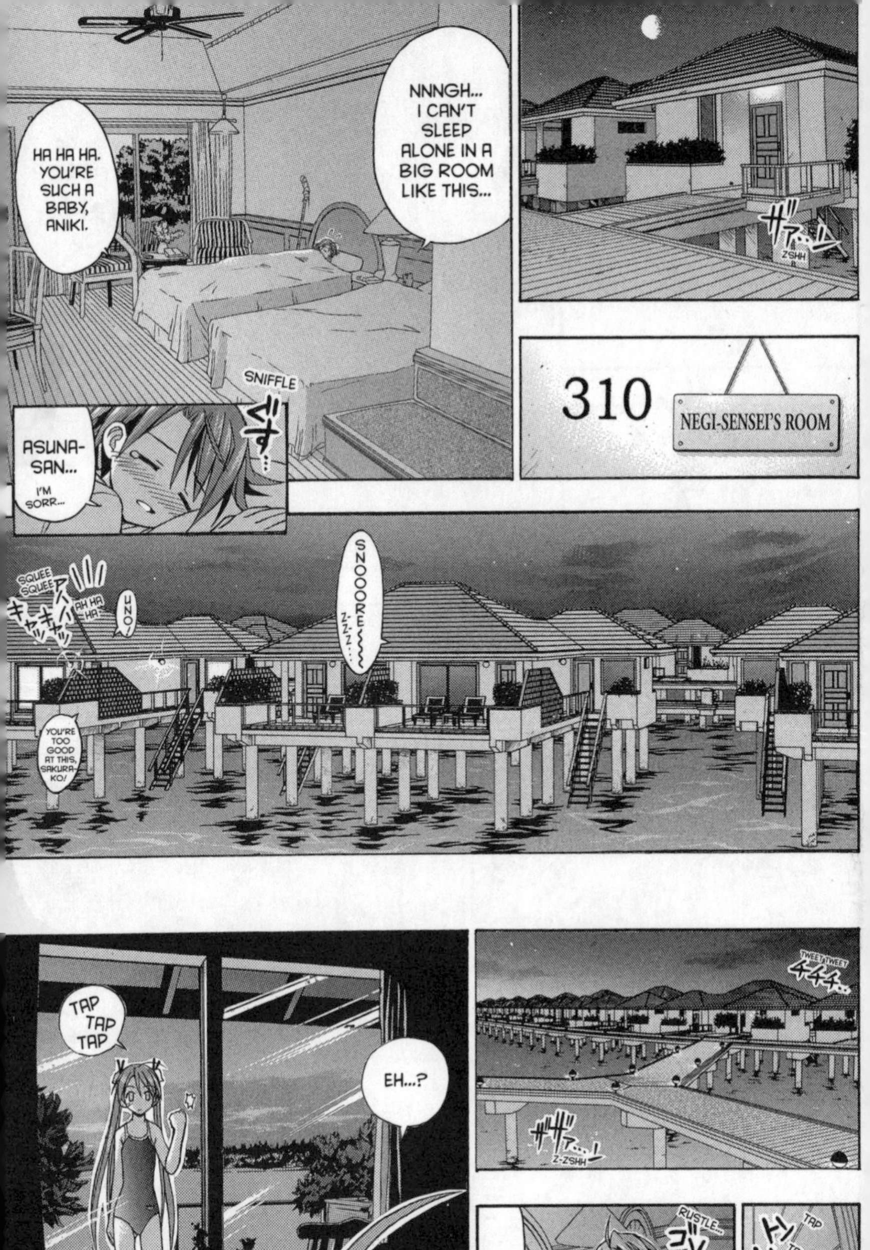

Z'SHH
310
NEGI-SENSEI'S ROOM
NNNGH... I CAN'T SLEEP ALONE IN A BIG ROOM LIKE THIS...
HA HA HA. YOU'RE SUCH A BABY, ANIKI.
SNIFFLE
ASUNA-SAN...
I'M SORR...
SNOOORE
Z-Z-Z...
UNO!
AH HA HA
SQUEE SQUEE
YOU'RE TOO GOOD AT THIS, SAKURAKO!
TWEET TWEET
Z-ZSHH
TAP TAP TAP
EH...?

TAP TAP
RUSTLE...
...NN ?

ASUNA-SAN?!
BECKON
ER, UM... ASUNA-SAN.
SS...
HUH? MY SWIM-SUIT?
...
TUG
EH...? JUST A-- ASUNA-SAN?
UM...
TMP
TMP
TMP
ASUNA-SAN?

OH, WOW ♡ I DIDN'T REALIZE.
THE VERANDA LEADS RIGHT DOWN INTO THE WATER!
IS THIS WHERE YOU CAME UP FROM?
SPLISH
SPLISH

YANK!
EEP?

WAAH--?!
KERSPLASH

SPLASH
PWHA ...?!
WH-WHA-BLUH! ASUNA-SA--
SPLASH
PFFT...
AH HA HA HA
YOU SHOULD SEE THE LOOK ON YOUR FACE! STUPID KID!
EH ...?
HIYA !
BAM
KYAAH — !?
KERSPLASH-ITY
FGY-AAAA-AHH —
WHAT ARE YOU DO-ING?
AHA-HA-HAH!
PAY BACK FOR THE OTHER DAY.
BLUH-BLUH! ASUNA-SAN!
SPLASH
SPLASH
SPLASH

TWEET TWEET
AH-HA-HA-HAH...
THAT WAS MEAN. SCARING ME LIKE THAT.
WHY WOULD YOU DO THAT?
STAGGER
STAGGER
SPLASH

...IT'S NO-THING.
I WAS JUST THINKING, HERE WE ARE ON THIS TROP-ICAL ISLAND, AND I HAVEN'T PLAYED WITH YOU AT ALL.

EH... ?
GLANCE
. . .
SPLASH
SPLASH
EEK ?
WHAT!?
WINCE
SPLASH
SHE-SHE'S GOING TO HIT ME!

SPLASH
EH...?
ASUNA-SAN...?
KOFF, KOFF...
I WAS WRONG TO IGNORE YOU ALL THIS TIME.
I APOLOGIZE...
I'M SORRY.
I'M SORRY, OKAY?
HUH?

ぎゅううう
SQUEEEEZE
TAKE THAT!
SABAORI!
ARGHLBEBWUHHH!?
UNCLE! UNCLE!
EH...?
EH...?
AH.....!
ER, UM --
UHH...

ME, TOO. I SHOULDN'T HAVE SAID YOU'RE NOT A PART OF MY WORLD.
I'M SORRY.
I DON'T CARE ABOUT THAT ANYMORE...
BESIDES...
?
THAT WASN'T THE ONLY THING!
SQUEEZE
きゅっ
GWEH?
...
...I'M JUST...
...WORRIED ABOUT YOU.

I DON'T KNOW WHY... BUT IT STARTED A LITTLE WHILE AGO.
DRIP
ポタ
I'M WORRIED YOU'LL GO OFF AND GET HURT WHEN I'M NOT LOOKING.
OR THAT YOU'LL GET KILLED.
YOU'RE TOO RECKLESS.
ASUNA-SAN...?
GH
BUT YOU'RE NOT GOING TO STOP LOOKING FOR YOUR DAD, NO MATTER WHAT I SAY, ARE YOU?
LET ME PROTECT YOU.
I WANT YOU TO SEE ME...
AS A REAL PARTNER.
NEGI.

A...
ASUNA...
SAN...
OKAY?
BLUSH
...
NO, UM, IT-IT'S NOT THAT I DON'T APPRECIATE YOUR FEELINGS-- I REALLY DO!
A REAL PARTNER?
BUT IT'S JUST SO SUDDEN.
I-I-I'M ONLY TEN, AND THERE ARE SO MANY PROBLEMS THAT COULD ARISE--
NN?
HUH...?
AH...!
BLUSH
YOU STUPID--! I DON'T MEAN IT LIKE THAT!
I JUST MEANT THAT YOU'RE SUCH A STUPID, CHILDISH, RECK-LESS BRAT, AND I'M SO WORRIED I CAN HARDLY LOOK AT YOU...
IF ONE-CHAN KNEW ABOUT THIS... WHAT WOULD SHE SAY!?
SHE MIGHT FAINT!
AWAWA-WAH! I-I-I-I COULDN'T!
I SAID IT'S NOT LIKE THAT! MORON!
BRAT! IDIOT! SIMPLETON!!
RAR
RAR
HMMM—?
WHAT'S GOING ON? IT'S TOO EARLY FOR THIS.
THEY'RE STILL FIGHTING.
DON'T THEY EVER GET TIRED?
MMNYA MMNYA
HEH HEH. I KNEW THERE WAS NOTHING TO WORRY ABOUT.
I GUESS ANE-SAN REALLY DOES HAVE A THING FOR ANIKI.
BUT IF I SAID IT OUT LOUD, SHE'D SQUEEZE ME INTO PASTE.

魔法先生
ネギま!
MAGISTER NEGI MAGI
8
Ken Akamatsu
赤松 健

CONTENTS

NKA!!
ZSH
ZSH
ZSH
ZSH
DUN!
KAPOW
GYAH!
BA-BAM

63RD PERIOD: SECRET TOWER FOR TWO ♡

NEGIMA!
MAGISTER NEGI MAGI
Z-SHAM
TMP
TMP
THMP
TMP
SHING
KA-SHING
FLANS
SCRUNCH
URGHMPH!
PARIES AERIALIS !!!
BWAH

SQUISH-
KYA-HA!
EEEEK!?
SHOONK!
FWMPH!
DUN
PUNT
EEEEK!?
LET'S KEEP GOING.
WHAT'S WRONG? IT'S ONLY BEEN TWELVE SECONDS.
I KNOW IT'S THREE ON ONE, BUT YOU COULD AT LEAST LAST A WHOLE MINUTE.
SQUISH SQUISH
むにむに♡
ANIKI!
CATCH
SWOOSH
SWOOSH
HEH-HEH!
IF THIS IS THE BEST YOU GOT, YOU'LL NEVER BEAT THAT WHITE-HAIRED KID.
WHACK
EEP!
DSH!
PWOH
PWOH
I'LL GO EASY ON YOU.
CRACKLE
DON'T LET THIS KILL YOU.
AWOO!!
LIC LAC LA LAC LILAC!
Κενοτητος ἀστράπσατω... δὲ τεμέω ...
SPARK

ΔΙΟΣ ΤΥΚΟΣ!
DUN!
...THAT WAS A HIGH ANCIENT LIGHTNING SPELL. IT'S PRETTY EFFECTIVE AS A FINISHING MOVE.
STEP
NNNGH... I-I'M NUMB ALL OVER ...
TWITCH TWITCH
ZAP ZAP
WHOOSH
...INCIDENTALLY, THAT WAS ONE OF THE THOUSAND MASTER'S FAVORITE COMBOS.
EH...?

IT WOULDN'T HURT YOU TO LEARN IT.
NOT THAT YOU COULD, AT YOUR LEVEL.
MY FATHER ...

I SEE... AN UNINCANTED CLOSE-RANGE SAGITTA MAGICA FOLLOWED BY AN UPPER MID-LEVEL HIGH ANCIENT SPELL WITH A FAST INCANTATION... A SIMPLE BUT USEFUL TACTIC.
STILL, I'M IMPRESSED. LIGHTNING'S FAR FROM HER SPECIALTY, BUT SHE JUST KEEPS SHOOTING 'EM OFF LIKE FIREWORKS.
ONCE YOU'VE RECOVERED, YOU HAVE TWO MORE HOURS OF COMBAT TRAINING.
Y-YES, MASTER !
EEEHHH? MORE!? YOU'VE ALREADY BEEN AT IT FOR FOUR HOURS!

MAN! THE TIME THEY SPEND TRAINING IS GETTING LONGER BY THE DAY!
I MEAN, I KNEW IT'D BE TOUGH, BUT I DIDN'T THINK EVANGELINE'S TRAINING WOULD BE *THIS* INTENSE.
IS ANIKI GONNA BE OKAY?
ALTHOUGH.
THIS RESORT OF HERS IS ANOTHER SURPRISE.
WHOOSH...
ERK...
TMP
MISTRESS—
TCH. ...I MUST HAVE GOTTEN A LITTLE CARRIED AWAY. YOU PROMISED, BŌYA. TIME TO PAY TODAY'S TRAINING FEE.
STAGGER
EH...? B-BUT YOU TOOK SO MUCH YESTERDAY...

THAT PIDDLY AMOUNT...?
HEH HEH HEH...
SS...
IT WAN'T *NEARLY* ENOUGH ♡

AH...
GH-GH...
E-EVANGELINE-SAN...

R-R-RIIING!

YES, HELLO?
OH, EISHUN!
WE SEEM TO HAVE A PROBLEM ...
I DON'T THINK IT'S MUCH TO WORRY ABOUT, BUT...
MM-HM... MM-HM...
WHAT? ESCAPED!?
STAGGER
ふらふら
I'M HOME!

WELCOME BACK, NEGI-KUN ♡
WEHHUM HOM!
OH, WOW! ARE YOU STUDYING, ASUNA-SAN?
SWAY SWAY
よろよろ
IT'S ALMOST TIME FOR MIDTERMS, AND I'VE BEEN SLACKING A LITTLE TOO MUCH.
WHAT WITH THE TROPICAL VACATION, PRACTICING WITH SETSUNA...
W-WELL, GOOD LUCK.
よろろろっ..
SWAAAY

HEY, NEGI! ARE YOU OKAY? YOU'RE NOT WALKING STRAIGHT.
STAGGER STAGGER
I-I'M ALL RIGHT. I HAVE TO PREPARE FOR TOMORROW'S CLASSES.
POOR NEGI-KUN SEEMS AWFULLY TIRED WHEN HE COMES BACK FROM PRACTICING WITH EVA-CHAN.
W-WELL, Y'KNOW. SHE'S A TOUGH TEACHER.
NNNGH MMNYA, MMNYA.
OH, NEGI-KUN...
YOU HAVE TO SLEEP IN YOUR BED.
UH, RIGHT...
BUT HEY. HE ONLY SPENDS TWO OR THREE HOURS AFTER SCHOOL AT EVA-CHAN'S. SHOULD HE REALLY BE THAT WOBBLY?
WELL, Y'KNOW, SHE... YOU KNOW. SHE'S A TOUGH TEACHER.
I DON'T CARE HOW TOUGH SHE IS.
I SMELL A RAT. YOU'RE NOT HIDING SOMETHING, ARE YOU?
SQUEEZE
I AIN'T HIDIN' NOTHIN'!
GOOD NIGHT, NEGI-KUN ♡
THANKS, KONOKA-SAN
PAT PAT
MMNYA
......

HA HA HA.
STAGGER
フラ
NEO HORIZON
O-OKAY, WHO WILL READ THE NEXT SECTION...? YOTSUBA-SAN?
NEGI-KUN LOOKS TIRED. OR MORE LIKE EX-HUASTED.
WHISPER WHISPER
SPRING FEVER?
OR AN IM-PATIENT SUMMER FEVER?
NEGI-SENSEI...
MURMUR MURMUR
ざわ ざわ
WILL HE BE OKAY?
DID SOME-THING HAP-PEN?
NO, HE...
DING DONG DANG
W-WELL, THAT WILL BE ALL FOR TODAY...
FUMP
パタン
SHUT
MRPH.
KONK
SWAY
よろっ
EEP!
STAGGER STAGGER
フラ フラ
BOW
ペコ
GOOD DAY...
STAGGER STAGGER
SNEAK
SOMETHING ISN'T RIGHT. HE SHOULD *NOT* BE THAT WASTED AFTER JUST TWO OR THREE HOURS OF TRAINING.
I'M GONNA FIND OUT WHAT'S GOING ON.

I SEE. SO IT'S BECAUSE OF HIS TRAINING WITH EVANGE-LINE-SAN.
HOP
ひょこっ
WAH?
POP
ひょい
THAT'S WHY HE'S SO BURNED OUT.
HE TIRED IN MY MORNING TRAINING, TOO. I WORRY-ING.
WH-WHAT?
YOU GUYS!
OH! HE MEET WITH EVA!
HRRRM...

BUT HE'S COMING HOME EXHAUSTED EVERY DAY, AFTER ONLY TWO OR THREE HOURS. THAT CAN ONLY MEAN ONE THING.
WHAT'S THAT?
OH, YOU KNOW. THAT TOP SECRET THING THAT YOU DON'T WANNA SAY TOO LOUD.
TOP SECRET
秘
HEY, HEY! HOW CAN YOU THINK THAT!?
?

ASUNA! WE'RE COMING-TOO!
ERK.
THEY'RE COMING OUT OF THE WOODWORK!
HEY, COME ON. WE CAN'T TAIL THEM LIKE THIS.
MOMMY, WHAT ARE THEY DOING?
LOOK AWAY!
CLAMOR
ワイ
CLAMOR
ノイ
SQUEEZE SQUEEZE
ぎゅうぎゅう
OH, IT'S RAIN-ING.
DRIP DROP
ポツポツ
OH...!
SHH
ザァァ
THEY'RE GOING INTO EVA-CHAN'S HOUSE! JUST THE TWO OF THEM!
ARE THEY TRAINING INSIDE BECAUSE OF THE RAIN?
NO WAY. NOT IN THAT TINY SPACE.

SO IT IS THE TOP SECRET...
HE'S TEN!!
UGH, WOULD YOU QUIT IT WITH THAT?
I DIDN'T EXPECT YOU TO BE SO SQUEAMISH ABOUT THAT KINDA THING.
SHH
WE DON'T HAVE THE WHOLE CLASS FOLLOWING US, DO WE?
HEY. DON'T UNDERESTIMATE MY ABILITY TO CONTROL INFORMATION.
SPLASH
SPLASH
SPLASH
SHH
...HUH.
NO ONE'S HERE?

THAT'S WEIRD. I KNOW THEY BOTH CAME IN HERE.
HMMM...
NO ONE IN TOILET OR BATH, EITHER.

H-HEY, GIRLS! OVER HERE!
DID YOU FIND SOMETHING?
UM...! IN THE BASEMENT...
A LOG CABIN WITH A BASEMENT. WHO KNEW?
WOW, THERE'S A LOT OF DOLLS.
CREAK...
...OH?

WHAT IS IT?
WHAT DO YOU THINK IT IS?
EVANGELINE'S RESORT

SOME KIND OF BUILDING... A MINIATURE TOWER?
IT'S LIKE A SHIP IN A BOTTLE.
IT'S A LITTLE TOO DETAILED FOR A MODEL. MAYBE IT'S A HOLOGRAM?
NODOKA SAYS SHE SAW NEGI-SENSEI INSIDE.

EH!? BUT HOW COULD--?
A REALLY SMALL NEGI-SENSEI WAS...
NN?
CLICK
...HWA?
HYOOP
CLICK
AH...
SS
CLICK
HMMM.
...HM?

FLICKA
OH?

HUH...? HEY, GUYS?
JUST A--WHERE DID YOU GO!?

SHH...
ザァァ...
SHH...
ザァァ...
I HOPE NEGI-SENSEI IS OKAY.
MAYBE HE'S CAUGHT A COLD...
OH?
HE'S DYING ON THE SIDE OF THE ROAD, NATSUMI.
DYING ON THE SIDE OF THE ROAD!?
OH, YOU... MEAN THAT DOG...
HFF HFF
POOR THING..

SHH...
サァァ..
AND HE'S HURT.
ACK! HE'S ALL DIRTY, CHIZU-NE.
SQUEEZE
ぎゅう..

GUYS ...!?
TMP
HYOOP
ひゅっ..
OH! YUE-CHAN, I'M GLAD I FOUND YOU.
YOU FINALLY MADE IT, ASUNA-SAN
WHERE DID YOU GO? I WAS LOOKING FOR YOU.
WHERE'S EVERYONE ELSE?
TAKE A LOOK AROUND.
AROUND?
EH... ?
WHOOSH
ゴォォォ..

WHA...
WH-WH-WH-WHERE ARE WE!!?
WHOOSH

WE WOULD APPEAR TO BE IN THE PLACE WE SAW IN THAT MINIATURE.
NNGH... I DIDN'T THINK ANYTHING COULD SURPRISE ME ANYMORE, BUT...
WHOOSH...
YEEK!
WHOOSH
ER, WAIT A SECOND! THIS BRIDGE IS WAY HIGH UP! WHY AREN'T THERE ANY GUARD RAILS!?
I KNOW IT'S FANTASY, BUT ENOUGH IS ENOUGH!

THIS WAY, ASUNA-SAN.
CAW
CAW
IT'S HOT HERE...
WE JUST CAME BACK FROM THE TROPICS...

YOU THINK SO? PERSON-ALLY, I FIND ALL THESE FANTASTICAL HAPPENINGS EXHILARATING.
THEY'RE SO MUCH MORE FULFILLING THAN OUR BORING CLASSES AT SCHOOL.
UM, BUT YUE-CHAN, YOUR KNEES ARE KNOCKING.
LET'S SAY I'M SHAKING WITH EXCITE-MENT...
KNOCK KNOCK

WE ALL TOOK A LOOK AROUND IN THE 30 MINUTES BEFORE YOU GOT HERE, ASUNA-SAN.
EH...? 30 MINUTES? BUT I WAS ONLY LOOKING FOR YOU FOR A MINUTE OR TWO.
HEEEEY! OVER HERE!
WE HEARD VOICES UNDER HERE!
AT THE BOTTOM OF THIS STAIR-WAY?
SO SHE SAYS
AWAWAH.
WHOSE VOICES?
UM, THEY WERE, WELL . . .
AWAH.
AWAH.
?
...HEH HEH HEH. YOU DON'T MIND, DO YOU? JUST A LITTLE MORE.
NN?
I-I CAN'T TAKE ANY MORE.
JUST TAKE A LITTLE BREAK AND YOU'LL BE FINE. YOU'RE YOUNG.
AH! NO!
JUST WHIP IT OUT ALREADY.
AWAWAWAWAWAH
SHAKE SHAKE
N-NO, EVANGELINE-SAN, I...
HEH HEH... CALL ME MASTER.
D-DON'T TELL ME THEY'RE REALLY...?
SNAP
HE-H-H-H-HEY!
WHAT DO YOU THINK YOU'RE DOING TO HIM!? HE'S JUST A KID!
BAM!!

NN?
SLURP
ちゅう
E-EVANGE-LINE-SAN, N-N-N-NO MORE!
SPLAT
ステーン
...WHAT ARE YOU DOING HERE?
WHAT ARE WE DOING HERE!? WHAT ARE YOU DOING!?
I'M JUST SUCKING HIS BLOOD AS PAY-MENT FOR TRAINING HIM.
I CAN'T KEEP UP WITH IT MYSELF IF I DON'T RECHARGE MY MAGIC SUPPLY.
IT'S NO WORSE THAN A BLOOD DONATION.
HA HA HA. I KNEW IT WAS SOME-THING LIKE THAT!!!
...WHAT DID YOU THINK WE WERE DOING?
SHUT UP!
I MADE THIS RESORT BACK IN THE DAY. I STOPPED USING IT A WHILE AGO,
BUT I DUG IT OUT OF STORAGE FOR THE BOY'S TRAINING.

WOW, YOU MAKE THIS? WIZARDS SURE AMAZ-ING!
UGH... NOW THAT YOU'VE GONE AHEAD AND LET YOUR-SELVES IN, I GUESS I SHOULD WARN YOU.
THIS RESORT WAS DESIGNED TO BE USED IN 24-HOUR INCREMENTS. YOU WON'T BE ABLE TO LEAVE FOR A WHOLE DAY.
WHAT—?!

SO WE NO LEAVING UNTIL TOMOR-ROW!?
NO ONE TOLD US THIS!
WHAT ABOUT CLASS TOMORROW?
CLAMOR
CLAMOR
OH, WOULD YOU JUST SHUT UP? RELAX.
ISN'T THERE SOME JAPA-NESE FOLK TALE ABOUT URASHIMA TARŌ AND RYŪGŪ PALACE?
THIS PLACE WORKS IN REVERSE OF THAT.
YOU CAN SPEND A DAY IN HERE, AND ONLY AN HOUR WILL PASS OUTSIDE.
WE USE THIS TO GIVE THE BOY A FULL DAY OF TRAINING EVERY DAY.
<NEGI'S CURRENT SCHEDULE>
A DAY INSIDE THE RESORT
0
SLEEP
INDEPENDENT MARTIAL ARTS TRAINING
6
BREAKFAST
BASIC TRAINING
LUNCH AND REST
12
COMBAT TRAINING
18
IN
OUT
DINNER
COMBAT TRAINING, MISC.
5-15 MINUTES AT THE END OF EACH DAY RESERVED FOR TRAINING AGAINST EVA. (CAN'T HANDLE MORE THAN THAT.)
A NORMAL DAY
SLEEP
MORNING TRAINING (KŪ)
6
BREAKFAST
SCHOOL
LUNCH
12
SCHOOL
AFTER-SCHOOL
18
EVA'S TRAINING
PREPARING FOR NEXT DAY, ETC.

EEEHH!? WHAT THE HECK!?
RAR
RAR
WHOA!
...SO YOU'RE SAYING THAT AFTER A DAY OF BEING A TEACHER,
NEGI-KUN SPENDS ANOTHER DAY HERE TRAINING?
WE WOULDN'T GET ANYWHERE IF HE ONLY TRAINED FOR A FEW MINUTES HERE AND THERE IN HIS SPARE TIME.

SO NEGI-BŌZU DOES TWO DAY IN ONE!?
WHAAAAA!?
THAT'S TOO MUCH!
CLAMOR
CLAMOR
NO WONDER HE'S SO WASTED! A WHOLE STRAIGHT DAY OF TRAINING FOLLOWED BY A BLOOD-SUCKING SESSION.
NEGI... DON'T YOU THINK YOU'RE OVERDOING IT AGAIN?
T'S ALL RIGHT, ASUNA-SAN.

I WOULDN'T WANT A REPEAT OF WHAT HAPPENED ON THE CLASS TRIP.
IF I WANT TO GET STRONGER, I CAN'T LET A LITTLE THING LIKE THIS GET ME DOWN!
......

SHH...
UGH, CHIZU-NĒ. ARE YOU SURE IT'S OKAY TO TAKE HIM IN LIKE THIS?
HE'S A STRAY!
NOW THAT WE'VE FOUND HIM, WHAT CHOICE DO WE HAVE?
WE OULDN'T JUST LEAVE HIM THERE, DYING.

I'M GOING TO BAN-DAGE HIM UP. WOULD YOU DRY HIM OFF A LITTLE FIRST?
YES, MA'AM!
LET ME FIND A TOWEL.
KYAAAAA!?
WHAT'S WRONG, NATSUMI?
I-I-I ONLY LOOKED AWAY FOR A SECOND!
THE DOG-- HE DISAP-PEARED...
FSHH
しゅううぅ…
AND THERE'S A NAKED BOY INSTEAD...?
......
OH, MY.

■「来たれ、虚空の雷、薙ぎ払え。『雷の斧』」

(κενότητος ἀστράπσατω δὲ τεμέτω. ΔΙΟΣ ΤΥΚΟΣ)

COME FORTH, LIGHTNING FROM THE VOID, MOW DOWN MY ENEMIES. LIGHTNING AXE."

As Hesiod says, "and again, [the Earth] bare the Cyclopes, overbearing in spirit, brontes, and steropes and stubborn-hearted arges, who gave Zeus the thunder and made the thunderbolt," (Theogony, 139-141, cf.501-505), Zeus, chief god of Ancient Greece, used the lightning bolt as his weapon. **ΙΟΣ** (dios) is the genitive case of **ΔΙΣ** (dis), which is an old name for **ΖΕΥΣ** (zeus). Therefore, **ΔΙΟΣ ΤΥΚΟΣ** (dios tykos) means Zeus's Axe.

Although the range of this spell is not very wide, the incantation is so short, and the lightning strike so quick, that it is extremely effective in eliminating targets in close to mid range.

NEGIMA!

MAGISTER NEGI MAGI

64TH PERIOD: AFTER THAT MAGIC TEACHER!!!

OM 665
NABA, CHIZURU
MURAKAMI, NATSUMI
YUKIHIRO, AYAKA
JR. HIGH GIRLS'
SHH
H-HELLO THERE...
I'M NATSUMI MURAKAMI, NUMBER 28 IN CLASS 3-A AT MAHORA ACADEMY.
Mardock Scramble 09
I'M AN AVERAGE, ORDINARY JUNIOR HIGH SCHOOL GIRL.
I FADE INTO THE BACKGROUND OF MY CLASS FULL OF CUTE GIRLS, AND I'M A BIT INSECURE ABOUT MY FRECKLES.
.....
SO IF YOU'RE WONDERING HOW A GIRL LIKE ME GOT INTO THIS DANGEROUS SITUATION...
EEP.
PRICK

しゅうう…
FSHH...
MY, MY...
WH-WHY IS THERE A BOY IN OUR ROOM...?
I WONDER IF THAT LITTLE PUPPY TURNED INTO THIS BOY.
BE SERI-OUS. BUT WHAT DO WE DO, CHIZU-NE?
OH, DEAR.
HE'S BURNING UP.
ハァ ハァ
HFF HFF...
HOLD ON.
WE'D BETTER CALL A DOCTOR. NAT-SUMI, CARRY HIM TO BED.
WHAT...? BUT HE'S A NAKED BOY...
WHAT ARE YOU SO EMBAR-RASSED ABOUT? HE'S JUST A CHILD. YOU'LL BE FINE. HE SHOULDN'T WEIGH ALL THAT MUCH.
NO, BUT-- HE LOOKS LIKE HE COULD BE THIRTEEN...

HE'S ACTUALLY KIND OF ATTRACTIVE, NOW THAT I LOOK AT HIM.
Mardock Scramble 09
...I WONDER WHAT THESE EAR THINGIES ARE?
HELLO? IS THIS THE DOCTOR'S OFFICE?
YES, UM...
BOP
UPSY-DAISY...
EH?
A TAIL ...?
TWITCH
EEK!?
LUNGE
WHOOSH
!?
SMASH
...DON'T.
YOU CAN'T TELL ANYONE I'M HERE.

...AND THAT BRINGS US TO NOW.
UH...
UM...
UM! WHO ARE YOU?
AND WHAT ARE YOU DOING?
QUIET!
HFF HFF
YESSIR!
Y...YOU THERE.
GET ME... SOME-THING TO WEAR.
AND SOME-THING TO EAT.
HFF HFF
.....

WHAT'S YOUR NAME?
WHERE DID YOU COME FROM?
WOULD YOU PLEASE TELL US?
WE MIGHT BE ABLE TO HELP YOU.

WH-WHAT...? NAME...? MY NAME? ...HUH?
?
STAGGER
WHO AM I ...?
NO.
THROB...
I HAVE TO FIND HIM...
HFF HFF

AND WHO MIGHT "HE" BE?
ZOOM
!?
ST-STAY BACK!
SWIPE!
!
SPURT
CHI...
CHIZU-NĒ!!
AH... !
...STOP.
DON'T MOVE AROUND SO MUCH. YOU'LL FAINT AGAIN.
SQUISH
YOUR FEVER IS NEARLY UP TO 40 DEGREES*.
*104 DEGREES FAHRENHEIT
EH...? WHA...?

OKAY?
SQUEEZE
AND I NEED TO TAKE CARE OF YOUR ARM.
FLOP
SLUMP
ERK...
DIZZY
WHA-WH-WH-WHAT HAPPENED?
IT'S ALL RIGHT. HE JUST FAINTED AGAIN.
WOW, CHIZU-NĒ, YOU'RE AMAZING! JUST WHAT I'D EXPECT FROM A FUTURE DAY-CARE TEACHER!
HO HO HO
I DO DEAL WITH THE SCHOOL'S PROBLEM CHILDREN EVERY DAY, WHILE I'M VOLUNTEERING.
BUT, SERIOUSLY. WHAT IS GOING ON WITH THIS BOY...?
WE KNOW ONE THING. HE'S NO ORDINARY RUNAWAY.
ER, KYAAAA!?
CHIZU-NĒ, BLOOD!! YOU'RE BLEEDING!!!
EEEEK!
POUR
OH, DEAR.

MEANWHILE...
EVANGELINE'S RESORT
MMM ♪ YUMMY!
HEY! STAY OUT OF THAT! THAT'S MY SECRET STASH!
あははは
AH HA HA HA
SUCH A PRETTY SUNSET ♡
YES.
CLAMOR
CLAMOR
HEY, STUPID! YOU'RE A MINOR! DON'T DRINK THAT!
SQUEE
SQUEE
WHAT? BUT IT SAYS "JUICE."
IT'S NOT JUST JUICE!
NOW, NOW, DON'T BE SUCH A BUZZ-KILL, EVA-CHAN ♡

...AND THERE YOU HAVE IT.
AH HA HA
SQUEE
SQUEE
...WHAT? MAGIC?
AND YOU WANT ME TO TEACH YOU?
WHY WOULD I GO OUT OF MY WAY TO TEACH YOU?
YOU HAVE A TEACHER RIGHT OVER THERE. GO ASK HIM. THE MAGIC TEACHER.
...

EEHH !?
TEACH YOU MAGIC? HERE? NOW?
UM, IS THAT ALL RIGHT, MASTER?
DO WHAT YOU WANT. JUST DON'T BLAME ME IF ANYTHING GOES WRONG.
YOU CAN TELL THE WHOLE CLASS FOR ALL I CARE.
A DAY A DOG
WELL, THERE'S MORE MAGIC IN HERE THAN THERE IS OUTSIDE, SO MAYBE EVEN AN AMATEUR COULD FIRE OFF A SPELL OR TWO.
THAT'S HOW I CAN MOVE, Y'KNOW.
HMMM.
A-ALL RIGHT, WE'LL START WITH THE SIMPLEST SPELLS.
YOU CAN EACH HAVE A BEGINNER'S WAND.
CHOOSE WHICHEVER YOU LIKE.
WAVE YOU WAND AND SAY, "PRACTE BIGI NAR, ARDESCAT."
AR YO WATC ING LIK THIS
PRACTE BIGI NAR. ARDESCAT.
WHOOSH
PWOH
CLAP CLAP CLAP
O-O-OH!
WELL, IT MIGHT BE FASTER TO JUST USE A LIGHTER, BUT IT'S A SPELL FOR BEGINNERS.
OH! WHAT HAVE WE HERE?
THAT LOOKS LIKE FUN.
I JOIN, TOO!
ME TOO! ME TOO!
EEEHH!? DO I HAVE ENOUGH WANDS?

P-PRACTE BIGI NAR!
BAM
ARDESCAT—!
OHHH. NOTHING HAPPENED.
DON'T WORRY. THERE'S NO RUSH.
SO IN OTHER WORDS, MAGICAL POWER IS THE ENERGY RESIDING IN ALL THINGS: AIR, WATER, ETC. CORRECT?
MM-HM.
YUE'S NOTES
BASICALLY, YES. AND YOU TAKE IN THAT ENERGY, JUST LIKE BREATHING THE AIR.
THEN IMAGINE FOCUSING IT AT THE TIP OF YOUR WAND.
BREATHE IN.
BREATHE OUT.
BREATHE IN.
BREATHE OUT.
...HERE I GO.
PRACTE BIGI NAR!
FLASH
B-BAM
ARDESCAT!
SILENCE
CHUCKLE CHUCKLE
すくす
しーーーん
...
AH HAHA!
THAT'S ALL RIGHT. IT USUALLY TAKES MONTHS OF PRACTICE.

PRACTE BIGI NAAAR! ...THIS IS KIND OF EMBARRASS-ING.
Y'KNOW?
HIYA! RAAH! AAAAAH! IT'S NOT DOING ANYTHING
IT'S NOT GOING TO WORK ON YOUR FIRST TRY
WAVE WAVE
YOU'RE NOT GOING TO TRY, SET-CHAN?
I CAN ALREADY DO IT.
ラン RAM
BWOH
EEEE! THAT'S AMAZING, SET-CHAN ♡
CLAP CLAP CLAP
CLAMOR
CLAMOR
PR-PR-PRA-PRACTE
TRY DROPPING YOUR SHOULDER A BIT...
PRACTE
HIYA!
RAAAR!
UGH... HOW CAN THEY ALL BE SO INTO IT...?
NN?
....

...PRACTE BIGI NAR. ARDESCAT.
WHISPER
しーーん
SILENCE
....
WHAT ARE YOU BLUSHING ABOUT, ASUNAC-CHI?
DUN
SHUT UP!!

OOH!? I DOING IT!!
WHAT!?
ARE YOU SERI-OUS!?
B-B-BWOH
DUN
OOOHHH!?

THAT'S A 100 YEN* LIGHTER!
YOU TRICKED US!
WAAAAH! IT JUST LITTLE GAG!
BONK
KONK
BASH
*ABOUT A DOLLAR
PRACTE!
AH, I SAW IT! NODOKA, I SAW IT! JUST FOR A SECOND!
CLAMOR CLAMOR
THAT WAS ONLY THE SUN REFLECTING OFF THE WAND.
SQUEE SQUEE
FIRE, COME!
COME FORTH!
ZSHH...

WHAP WHAP
BASH
THMP
WHAP
MMMM, PRACTE...
MMNYA MMNYA
SQUIRM...
...BATH-ROOM.
...UGH.
AGAIN ...?

CRACKLE
DSH!
RAS TEL MA SCIR MAGISTER. . . .
Κενότητος ἀστράπσατω... δὲ τεμέω...
B-BAM
ΔΙΟΣ ΤΎΚΘΣ!!!
DUN!
CLANK
OOOHH!?
WHOA! THAT'S MY ANIKI!! SHE SAID IT'D TAKE TWO OR THREE MONTHS, BUT AT THIS RATE, YOU'LL HAVE IT IN NO TIME!
YAHOO!
CLAP CLAP CLAP CLAP
NO, I WON'T. IT'S TOO WEAK, AND I HAVEN'T GOTTEN THE UNINCANTED SAGITTA MAGICA TO WORK AT ALL.
BESIDES, YOU KNOW IT'S EASIER TO DO MAGIC IN HERE THAN OUTSIDE, SO...
THAT'S OUR MAGIC TEACHER.
BOY GENIUSES REALLY ARE ON A WHOLE OTHER LEVEL.
ASUNA-SAN!
BUT...IF YOU JUST LET ME SAY ONE THING. NO GOOD'LL COME OF YOU GETTING YOURSELF SICK FROM PUSHING YOURSELF TOO HARD.
STRANGLE STRANGLE
NGGH! I-I'M SORRY! BUT I SPENT SO MUCH TIME PLAYING AROUND WITH EVERYONE TODAY...
I WANT TO MAKE UP FOR IT.
I'M TELLING YOU, TAKING TIME OFF TO PLAY IS PART OF TRAINING! YOU'RE WORKING TOO HARD!
UNCLE! I GIVE UP, ASUNA-SAN!
YOU LITTLE...
STILL, IT IS STRANGE.
Z-ZSHH

WE DID ALL THAT GOOFING OFF, EATING, AND SLEEPING, AND IT'S ONLY BEEN 20 MINUTES OUTSIDE.
ZSHH
HA HA HA. YEAH.
THAT'S THE POWER OF MAGIC FOR YA.
......
UM, ASUNA-SAN.
WINCE
EH? WHAT?
MAY I TELL YOU SOME-THING?
EH? WH-WHERE DID THIS COME FROM?
I THINK IT WOULD BE BEST IF YOU KNEW.
AS MY PARTNER.
EH... ?
B-DMP
W-WELL, OKAY... WHAT IS IT?
IT'S THE REASON I WORK SO HARD.

IT'S WHAT HAPPENED SIX YEARS AGO, WHEN I MET MY FATHER--
--THE THOUSAND MASTER.
MEANWHILE...
SHH...
WHAT SHOULD WE DO WITH HIM?
I WONDER WHAT AYAKA WILL SAY WHEN SHE GETS BACK.

...NN?
NNG --N-NEGI-...
NEGI...
HE'S TALK-ING IN HIS SLEEP. SOME-THING ABOUT NEGI...? LEEKS?
OH! ♡ NOW THAT YOU MENTION, I HAVE HEARD THAT POKING LEEKS UP YOUR BOTTOM IS GOOD FOR COLDS.
IT RAISES THE BODY TEMPERA-TURE...
AND HAPPEN TO HAVE SOME ♡ LET'S TRY IT!
SHOVE 'EM RIGHT UP
WAAAH! YOU CAN'T, CHIZU-NĒ! YOU'VE ONLY JUST MET HIM!
NNG...

I HAVE TO...
TELL HIM...
HFF...
HFF...
ハァ…ハァ…
DANGER... COMING CLOSER...

SHH
ザァァァ…

ZZ...
ズ…

...

NEGI SPRING-FIELD ....
ASUNA KAGU-RAZAKA ....
PLORP

...HMM, YOUR FATHER. HE WAS A VERY FAMOUS HERO... HE WAS LIKE SUPERMAN.
SUPERMAN?

YES ♡ WHENEVER ANYONE WAS IN TROUBLE, HE WOULD COME OUT OF NOWHERE AND SAVE THE DAY!
WOW, SUPERMAN. COOL...

DID HE EVER HELP YOU, NEKANE-ONĒCHAN?
HEH HEH HEH. THAT'S MY LITTLE SECRET ♡
BUT HE'S DEAD. THE RECKLESS IDIOT. AND HE ENDED UP LEAVING YOU ALL ALONE. ...HE WAS A FOOL.
OHH! STAN-SAN! DON'T TALK THAT WAY IN FRONT OF THE CHILD.
...HE'S "DEAD"?

THAT MEANS... YOU CAN'T EVER SEE HIM AGAIN.
NEGIMA!
MAGISTER NEGI MAGI
65TH PERIOD:
MY VERY OWN SUPERMAN!

Z-ZSHH
YOU'RE GOING TO TELL ME WHAT HAPPENED SIX YEARS AGO,
WHEN YOU MET YOUR FATHER?
WHY NOW, ALL OF A SUD-DEN?
OH, WELL, I WAS THINKING IT WOULD BE GOOD FOR EVERYONE TO KNOW...
BUT IF YOU DON'T WANT TO, THAT'S OKAY! I'M SORRY FOR SPRINGING IT ON YOU!
YANK
むんずっ
NO ONE'S SAYING THEY DON'T WANT TO HEAR IT, STUPID.

BUT, UM, YOU SAID YOU WANTED ME TO SEE YOU AS A PARTNER... SO, UM... I THOUGHT I SHOULD TALK TO YOU...
....

I DON'T MIND. TELL ME.
...I'VE BEEN WONDERING WHAT MAKES YOU SO RECKLESS.

MMNYA...
ムニャ...
WHERE'S THE BATH-ROOM...?
FIDGET.
もじ...
!
ドッキューン
B-DMP
LIKE THIS?
Y-YES. SINCE YOU'RE SO MUCH TALLER THAN I AM.
CLA-CLACK
カカカッ
WHA-WHAT ARE THEY DOING...?
B-DMP B-DMP B-DMP
ドキドキドキ
HMMM. THAT'S MIND SYNCHRONIZATION MAGIC.
EEYAH!
E-EH-EH-EVANGELINE-SAN!!
ビックウ!
WINCE!
HEH, HEH!
YOU'VE GOT THAT THING, RIGHT? THE "ARTIFACT" THAT CAN READ THE TOP LAYER OF PEOPLE'S MINDS? LEMME SEE IT. WE'LL WATCH THE BOY'S THOUGHTS.
EEEHH !? I-I-I CAN'T DO THAT...
THEY'RE GOING TO GO INTO HIS PAST. AREN'T YOU CURI-OUS?

I THINK KNOWING YOUR BELOVED'S PAST WOULD GIVE YOU THE UPPER HAND, DON'T YOU?
SMIRK
EEP!?
HOW DID YOU KNOW I--?
HE SAID HE WAS GOING TO TELL EVERYONE. IT'LL BE FINE.
I'M HIS MASTER. I HAVE A RIGHT TO KNOW.
GLINT
THAT ASUNA KAGURAZAKA ACTS LIKE A SISTER TO HIM. IF SHE'S THE ONLY ONE TO HEAR IT,
SHE COULD GET AN EDGE OVER YOU IN SO MANY WAYS.
IS THAT WHAT YOU WANT?
WELL? WHAT ARE YOU GOING TO DO, NODOKA MIYAZAKI?
SPIN SPIN
SO MANY WAYS?
UM!
SPIN
WELL...
J-J-JUST FOR A LITTLE WHILE...
SWOON
SWOON
VERY GOOD.
GOOD GIRL.
HEH, HEH, HEH, HEH!
KIDS ARE SO EASY.
NOW WE'LL JOIN HANDS AND PUT OUR FOREHEADS TOGETHER.
H-HEY, IS THIS REALLY GOING TO LET ME EXPERIENCE YOUR MEMORIES?

YES. THIS WILL BE EASIER THAN TELLING YOU. ...IS SOMETHING WRONG?
N-NOTHING.
WHAT'S MY PROBLEM? IT'S JUST MY FOREHEAD.
SOMETHING IS WRONG WITH ME LATELY...

ARE YOU READY?
READY.
ALL RIGHT, THEN.
MATER MUSARUM, MNEMOSYNE.
FLASH
AD SE NOS ALLICIAT.

HUH?
ちょん
BIP

WHERE AM I...?
THE SMALL VILLAGE IN THE MOUNTAINS WHERE I LIVED SIX YEARS AGO.
OH... ACK! WHY AM I NAKED!?
OH. I-I'M SORRY. THAT'S JUST HOW THE MAGIC WORKS.
IT CAN'T BE HELPED.
YOU'VE GOT TO BE KIDDING ME! IT'S SNOWING HERE!
YOU SHOULDN'T FEEL THE COLD.
THAT'S NOT THE PROBLEM!
I CAN'T EVER SEE HIM AGAIN? WHAT DOES THAT MEAN?
DID FATHER MOVE SOME-WHERE FAR AWAY?
...YES. HE WENT TO A FAR, FARAWAY LAND.
THAT'S WHAT "DEAD" MEANS.
HUH...? IS THAT YOU WHEN YOU WERE LITTLE, NEGI?
AND NEXT TO YOU IS YOUR ONE-CHAN YOU TOLD ME ABOUT.
I GUESS SHE DOES KINDA LOOK LIKE ME.
SO...SO... IF I'M IN TROUBLE...
WILL FATHER COME SAVE ME?
H-HMMM, WELL...
U'RE SO MB!

WHEN SOME-ONE'S DEAD, YOU'LL NEVER SEE THEM AGAIN!
YOU'RE THE THOUSAND MASTER'S SON AND YOU DON'T EVEN KNOW THAT?
HELLO, ANYA-CHAN.
IRK
TH- THAT'S NOT TRUE!
MY FATHER WILL COME!
RAR
RAR
GRR
YOU'RE SO DUMB!
YOU DON'T KNOW WHAT IT MEANS TO DIE!
WHO'S THAT?
SHE'S SO CUTE...
SMART FOR HER AGE.
MY FRIEND GROWING UP, ANYA. SHE'S A YEAR OLDER THAN I AM.
HERE, YOU CAN HAVE THIS, NEGI.
WHAT IS IT?
A PRACTICE WAND FOR BEGINNERS. YOU'RE COMING TO SCHOOL NEXT YEAR, RIGHT?
HMPH!
TOSS
IF YOU WANT TO BE LIKE YOUR DAD WHEN HE WAS ALIVE,
YOU'D BETTER START PRACTIC-ING.
...
PUB
white hart

DAMN THAT NAGI! ALL HE EVER DID WAS GIVE ME TROUBLE!
IF NOT FOR HIM, ME AND THIS WHOLE VILLAGE WOULD GET A LITTLE MORE PEACE!
STAN-SAN, YOU'VE HAD TOO MUCH TO DRINK.
OH, STAN-SAN... THERE HE GOES AGAIN...
......
WAS FATHER A BAD MAN?
MILK
YES. HE WAS A REAL BAD EGG!
HOW MANY TIMES HAVE I HAD TO CLEAN UP AFTER THAT FOOL?
ONCE, HE EVEN DRAGGED THE WHOLE VILLAGE INTO IT.
WHEW
HIC
HE DID US ALL A FAVOR WHEN HE DIED!
......
JANGLE JANGLE
DASH
AH! NEGI!
YOU DIDN'T HAVE TO PUT IT LIKE THAT, SIR.
HMPH!
I'M JUST TELLIN' IT LIKE IT IS!
THE BASTARD.
...
I'LL SEE YOU IN A MONTH.
TAKE CARE OF YOURSELF, NEGI.
I WILL.
YOU'D BETTER PRACTICE!
HUH?
WHAT? SHE'S LEAVING?
YES. SHE WAS A STUDENT AT A SCHOOL IN WALES, SO I COULD ONLY SEE HER WHEN SHE HAD TIME OFF.

VROOM
PRACTE BIGI NAR!
WAVE
WAVE
ARDES-CAT!
JINGLE
HIYA!
I THINK I SAW A LITTLE FIRE!
SO HE LIVES IN HIS UNCLE'S GUEST HOUSE. HE'S PRACTICALLY LIVING BY HIMSELF.
LIVING ALONE IN SUCH A BIG ROOM...
HERE I THOUGHT HE WAS LIVING HAPPILY WITH HIS ONĒ-CHAN...
HE SHOWS UP WHEN THERE'S TROUBLE ♪
GROO GROO
...
HE APPEARS OUT OF NOWHERE ♪

VERMILION
YELLOW
プッ… HEH

...HE REALLY DOES LOVE HIS FATHER.

NEGI-SENSEI... I FEEL KIND OF SORRY FOR HIM...
BOUNCE BOUNCE
HMPH...
NOT THAT I CARE, BUT THE PICTURES IN YOUR DIARY SUCK.
I HOPE SOMEONE DIES SOON.

YUECCHI, YUECCHI!
SHAKE SHAKE
ユサユサ

THERE'S SOMETHING GOING ON OVER THERE!
?

BOW WOW
BOW WOW
BOW WOW
BOW WOW
CREEP
SPRK
SNAP

BARK BARK
BOW! WOW!
AIEEEEEE!
WHAT AN IDIOT...
WHEW ......
I GUESS THAT'S NOT ENOUGH TROUBLE.
!
.....
EH...? NOW JUST A--
WH-WHAT DO YOU THINK YOU'RE DOING?
SPLOOSH
SPLASH
SPLASH
FA...
BAM
FATHER! IS IT TRUE THAT NEGI ALMOST DROWNED!?
OH, NEKANE. HE'S ALL RIGHT. ALTHOUGH, HE IS PASSED OUT WITH A FEVER OF 40*.
*104 DEGREES FAHRENHEIT
SEE, WHAT'D I TELL YOU? LIKE FATHER, LIKE SON.
ANY NORMAL HUMAN BEING WOULD'VE DIED.
AND HE'S BEEN JUMPING OUT OF TREES, TEASING DOGS... UGH.
NO, NO. IT'S GOOD FOR A BOY TO BE SO ENERGETIC.
CLAMOR
CLAMOR
YOU JUMPED INTO A FROZEN LAKE...?
WHAT WERE YOU THINKING, YOU IDIOT?
CHIRP CHIRP
TWEET TWEET
OH... WHY WOULD YOU DO THAT?
...WELL.

WELL I THOUGHT, IF I WAS IN TROUBLE...
HFF HFF...
FATHER WOULD COME SAVE ME...
...!
OH, NEGI...
SQUEEZE
DON'T THINK THAT...
PLEASE DON'T DO THIS ANYMORE.
PLEASE...
....
SNIFFLE
HIC
I'M SORRY, ONÉ-CHAN...
SOB
HIC
I WON'T DO IT AGAIN.
DON'T CRY. I'M SORRY...
....
HUH? IT'S SNOW-ING...
IT SHOULD ALMOST BE SPRING BUT IT'S SNOW-ING?
I MUST HAVE BEEN WATCH-ING A LONG STRETCH OF MEMO-RIES.
OH, ONÉ-CHAN.
VRROOM
ONE WHOLE MONTH!
I HOPE NEGI IS ALL RIGHT.
OH?

I WONDER WHAT THAT IS...
SPLISH
HE SHOWS UP WHEN THERE'S TROUBLE ♪
HE APPEARS OUT OF NOWHERE ♪
OH! THAT'S RIGHT!
NEKANE-ONĒCHAN IS COMING HOME TODAY!
I HAVE TO GET BACK TO THE VIL-LAGE!
TMP
HFF HFF HFF
ZSHH
HEH HEH. HE'S SO CUTE.
I HATE KIDS, BUT WHEN THEY'RE THIS LITTLE...
HFF HFF
NEKANE-ONĒ-CHAN!
BWAH
!?
EH?

ゴオオオオオオオ…
FWOOSH...
EH... ?
F-FIRE!? WH-WHAT THE HECK IS GOING ON!?
WHY IS THE VILLAGE ON FIRE!?
NEKANE-ONĒ-CHAN...
UNCLE!!
ゴオオオオ
FWOOSH
AH! NEGI! NO, IT'S TOO DANGER-OUS!
オオオオ…
WHOOSH
UN...
ゴオオオ オ オ オ
FWOOSH
CLE...?

IT-IT'S JUST LIKE ON THE CLASS TRIP...
HNNH...
IS-IS THIS...
BECAUSE I WANTED TO BE IN TROUBLE...?
EH...?
BECAUSE I THOUGHT FATHER WOULD COME IF I WAS IN TROUBLE...?
BECAUSE I DID ALL THAT STUFF...!?
D-DON'T BE STUPID! HOW CAN YOU SAY THAT?
OF COURSE IT'S NOT YOUR FAULT, YOU STUPID NEGI!
SMASH
!?
ZZ...
ZH ZH ZH
H...
HEY...
ZH ZH
WH... WHAT THE HECK?
ZH ZH ZH ZH
ZH ZH
WHAT ARE THESE GUYS...?
THIS IS LIKE THE CLASS TRIP, TOO...

NEGI!! WH-WH-WHAT'S HAPPEN-ING!!?
L-L-L-LIT-TLE NEGI'S GONNA BE KILLED!
HEY !!
SHAKE
SHAKE
!?
ZLR
BWOH
LOOM
NEGI — !!
N-NEG
NEGI, RUN!
FATHER
FATHER
FATHER
IT'S ALL M FAUL

DUN!

IS...IS THAT...!?

NEGIMA!

MAGISTER NEGI MAGI

64TH-65TH PERIOD SPELL GLOSSARY

■「火よ、灯れ。」

LIGHT, FIRE. (ARDESCAT)

A spell that creates a flame at the tip of the caster's wand to light fires. It may appear plain at a glance, but it can create flame out of thin air. This is because, unlike a natural flame--that is to say, light and heat brought about from a chemical reaction (between oxygen and carbon, for example)--a magical flame is one of the types of matter known as the four elements, along with earth, water, and air. (Though of course, the premodern concepts of matter differ greatly from those of modern classical mechanics.)

Negi observed that using a lighter might be faster, but there is great significance in beginning wizards starting their training with a spell that produces fire. For example, Plato's *Protagoras* relates the following incident:

"Once upon a time there were gods only, and no mortal creatures. But when the time came that these also should be created, the gods fashioned them out of earth and fire and various mixtures of both elements in the interior of the earth; and when they were about to bring them into the light of day, they ordered Prometheus and Epimetheus to equip them, and to distribute to them severally their proper qualities. Epimetheus said to Prometheus: 'Let me distribute, and do you inspect'.... The appointed hour was approaching when man in his turn was to go forth into the light of day; and Prometheus, not knowing how he could devise his salvation, stole the mechanical arts of Hephaestus and Athene, and fire with them (they could neither have been acquired nor used without fire), and gave them to man. Thus man had the wisdom necessary to the support of life..." (320c–321d).

As can be seen from the tale of this mythological Greek hero, fire plays an important role, being intimately related to the learned arts. In other words, the mastery of fire symbolizes the beginning of a single art. Negi himself started practicing magic with a fire spell, because fire has such a mythological and symbolic background.

■

RAN

According to *Shugen Hashira Moto Shinpo*, (roughly "the universe according to shugen"), the five seed syllables making up the mahavairocana tathagata mantra in the mandala of the womb realm, (a vi ra hum kha)-- (a), (va), (ra), (ka), (kha)--each represent one the five elements: earth, water, fire, wind, and void, respectively. Of them, when the anusvara diacritical mark [dot] is added to the character that corresponds with fire, (ra), it becomes (ram), and "the character is the fire of knowledge, burning away the ignorance of beasts."

■「ムーサ達の母、ムネーモシュネーよ。おのがもとへと我らを誘え。」

(MATER MUSARUM, MNEMOSYNE. AD SE NOS ALLICIAT.)

A spell that allows its target to experience the memories of the caster. Mnemosyne is "memory" in ancient greek, and she is the mother of the goddesses of the arts, the muses (cf. *Theogony*, ll. 51-54, 914-917). Normally, it is impossible to perceive the past in the form of clear images and sounds. Images and sound are always phenomena experienced in the present (*praesentia*) and the past never appears within these phenomena. Ergo, it is essentially impossible to experience the past as it happened in the form of concrete images and sound. The past is unseeable and untouchable, and it is memories that give it being in one form or another--in other words, it would not exist if not for the human consciousness. For example, aristotle presents the following concept: "there would not be time unless there were soul, but only that of which time is an attribute." (Physics, 223a 26-27)

CREAK
CREAK
KRAK
KRA-KRAK
SMUS-S-SH
CREAK
IS... IS THAT...?
IT CAN'T BE...
CRACK
κενότητος ἀστραπαία
δέ τελείω

ΔΙΟΣ ΤΥΚΟΣ!
LIGHTNING-AXE!!!
P-POW
NEGIMA!
MAGISTER NEGI MAGI
66TH PERIOD:
THE TRUTH OF THAT SNOWY DAY
WHOA...
WH...
FWOOSH
BOMP
FWOOM
B-BAM
Z-ZAM
DUN DUN DUN
W-WATCH OUT!!

WHAM!
KA-FWAM
ZSH ZSH ZSH
ZSH ZSH ZSH
KERSMASH!
BAM
veniant spiritus aeriales fulgurientes
cum fulguratione flet tempestas austrina

JOVIS TEMPESTAS FULGURIENS !!!
ZPOW

WHAM!
WHOOSH
BOOM
GWAH!
KYAAA!!!
KER-SHOOM

FWOOM
FWOOM
OH... SO YOU'RE... THE ONE...
GH
GH
GH
HEH... THE DIFFERENCE IN OUR POWER...
IT'S HARD TO TELL WHICH OF US IS THE MONSTER...
SMIRK
CRUNCH
WINCE
S... SOMEHOW...
NEGI?
SHUDDER SHUDDER SHUDDER
AH! NEGI, WAIT!
TEP
WHOOSH
THUD

NEGI, DON'T!
THERE'S STILL LOTS OF MONSTERS AROUND...
HFF HFF
ZSH
!
GWOP
FLASH
NEGI!!
BA-SHING
WHOOSH
EH...?
GNNH...
KRAK
ZAM
NGH...
STAGGER
O... ONĒ-CHAN...
KRIK
KRAK
KRIK
KRAK
KRAK
KRIK
KRAK

KER-SNAP
ONĒ-CHAN!
ZSH ZSH ZSH ZSH
BAM
ZH ZH
HEXA-GRAMMA ET PENTA-GRAMMA
ZSH ZSH
MALOS SPIRITUS SIGILLENT!
LAGENA SIGNA-TORIA!!
GH-KZHNG
SNAP!
GH-KZHNG
WHOO
WHEW. YOU ALL RIGHT, BOY?
FWOOM
OJI...
OJI'I-CHAN...
KRIK KRAK
SBOP
HN... THIS MUST HAVE BEEN DONE BY SOMEONE WITH A GRUDGE AGAINST ONE OF OUR VIL-LAGERS.
THIS VILLAGE IS FULL OF ODD DUCKS WHO CAME HERE FOR LOVE OF NAGI, AFTER ALL.
KRIK KRAK
DUN
KRIK
HRNGH...
STAN-OJI'I-CHAN!
BUT THE SHEER NUMBER AND POWER OF LESSER DEMONS...
WHOEVER SUMMONED THEM IS NO ORDINARY SPELL-CASTER.
WHEN WE RALLY OUR FORCES... THIS VILLAGE IS STRONG ENOUGH... TO FACE A BATTALLION, BUT THIS... NGH!
OJI'I-CHAN...

RUN, BOY. TAKE NEKANE AND RUN.
THERE'S NO HOPE FOR ME. THIS IS A POWERFUL PETRIFICATION SPELL. THERE'S NO WAY...TO REVERSE IT.
ペキ.. KRIK...
PLEASE... SAVE YOURSELF...
NO MATTER WHAT HAPPENS, I MUST PROTECT YOU.
HEH
SMIRK
THAT'S THE PROMISE I MADE...TO THAT DEAD FOOL.
FIND ANY HEALER YOU CAN THAT'S STILL ALIVE... IF YOU DON'T STOP THE PETRIFICATION...NEKANE WON'T MAKE IT...
OJI...
ペキ ペキ KRIK KRAK
GO ON, BOY. I'M AN OLD MAN... LEAVE... ME...
CHAN...
パキ KRAK
CRACK
OJI'I-CHAN!
STAN-OJI'I-CHAN...
TUG
TUG
WHOOSH...
ONĒ-CHAN
GET UP, ONĒ-CHAN.
ONĒ-CHAN!
SHAKE SHAKE...
ZSH
WINCE
WHOOSH

WHOOSH
I'M SORRY...
I WAS TOO LATE...
ぐっ…
CLENCH
!!
ZSH
....
YOU'RE
...

...I SEE.
YOU'RE... NEGI...
...ARE YOU TRYING
TO PROTECT YOUR COUSIN?
ZSH
ZSH
ZSH
ZSH
ぎゅっ
SQUEEZE
くしゃ..
RUFFLE
YOU'RE SO BIG...
...OH, I KNOW.
HERE...
TAKE THIS WAND.
CALL IT A LEGACY.

...FA--
FATHER ...?
HA HA HA. TOO HEAVY FOR YOU, HUH?
STAGGER
EEP!
THUD
... THERE'S NO TIME.
EH?
NEKANE WILL BE FINE. I STOPPED THE PETRIFICATION.
YOU'LL EED TO GET HER HEALED COM-LETELY.
SORRY.
I WISH I COULD DO MORE.
...FATHER?
FATHER!
I DON'T HAVE ANY RIGHT TO SAY THIS, BUT...
GROW STRONG.
BE HAPPY!
FATH--

THUD
WHOOSH
FA... THER...
CLENCH
FATHEEER—!!!
WAAAAH!
WAAAH!
NEGI...
I-I'M SORRY YOU HAD TO SEE ME LIKE THAT.
WINCE!
OH! NO, THAT'S OKAY!
WHAT HAPPENED AFTER THIS?
WELL...
DON'T STARTLE ME LIKE THAT.
B-DMP
B-DMP

THREE DAYS LATER, ON-CHAN AND I WERE RESCUED, AND WE MOVED TO A TOWN OF WIZARDS DEEP IN THE MOUNTAINS OF WALES.
AFTER THAT, I STUDIED AT THE MAGIC SCHOOL EVERY DAY FOR FIVE YEARS.
WHAT HAPPENED TO THE REST OF THE VILLAGERS?
I DON'T KNOW. I WAS A CHILD, SO ALL THEY WOULD TELL ME IS THAT THEY WERE ALL OKAY, AND THERE WAS NOTHING TO WORRY ABOUT.
I WAS SO TERRIFIED OF THAT SNOWY NIGHT...
WHAT? STILL STUDYING?
FOR SOME REASON, I STARTED TO PUT EVERYTHING I HAD INTO MY STUDIES
ALL I WANTED WAS TO SEE MY FATHER AGAIN...
I WANTED TO MEET THE GREAT WIZARD...WHO SAVED ME...
BUT EVEN NOW, I STILL WONDER.
I WONDER IF WHAT HAPPENED THAT NIGHT
WAS MY PUNISHMENT
FOR THINKING THAT IF I WAS IN TROUBLE, MY FATHER WOULD COME SAVE ME.
EH...?
WHA--!?

HOW CAN YOU SAY THAT!? OF COURSE IT WASN'T!!
DON'T BE STUPID! IT WAS THOSE WEIRD MON-STERS!!
BAM

I DIDN'T SEE A SINGLE THING IN ALL OF THAT THAT MADE IT YOUR FAULT!!
IT'S OKAY!! YOU'LL SEE YOUR FATHER AGAIN!! HE'S ALIVE!!

A...
ASUNA-SAN...
MM-HM

LEAVE IT TO ME! I'LL MAKE SURE YOU GET TO SEE...
NN?

UWAH?!
SOB!
CRY CRY
...
EH...?
I LIKED WHEN HE SNAPPED THE GUY'S NECK.
THAT WAS FUN.

HNNM... WHO KNEW NEGI-KUN HAD SUCH A TRAGIC PAST...
TEARS
NEGI-SENSEI...
OJI-OJI-CHAN...

NEGI-KUUN!
NEGI-SENSEI!
STOMP STOMP
WAAAAAAH!
C-CARE-FUL!

キャ
SQUEE
キャ
SQUEE
Y-Y-YOU WERE ALL LISTENING!?
NEGI-KUN!! IT MAY NOT BE MUCH, BUT I'LL DO WHATEVER I CAN TO HELP YOU FIND YOUR FATHER!!
ME, TOO!
HELP ME...? NO, YOU CAN'T!
AWAWAH!
EVA-- MASTER, PLEASE! SAY SOMETHING!
I HELPING TOO!
NO, UM, WELL
M-M-ME, TOO...
UM...WELL, I SUPPOSE I COULD HELP, TOO...
SNIFFLE
YOU CRYING?
NO! THAT'S NOT WHAT I MEANT!
WHAT ARE YOU SNIFFLING FOR!?

ALL RIGHT, HERE'S TO FINDING NEGI-KUN'S FATHER!
CHEERS!♪
カンパーイ!
CHEERS!
AH HA HA HA HA
ワイワイ
CLAMOR
CLAMOR
YOU'RE PARTYING AGAIN!?
NNNGH, NNNNGH!
YOUR FATHER AMAZING!
WAS THAT ALL TRUE, NEGI-KUN?
キャッ
SQUEE
キャッ
SQUEE

ザァァ...
SHHH...
ROOM 665
NABA, CHIZURU
MURAKAMI, NATSUMI
YUKIHIRO, AYAKA
JR. HIGH GIRLS'

MUNCH
MUNCH
CHOMP
CHOMP
NOM NOM
WHOA...
MMM... YEAH, THIS IS GOOD!! REALLY GOOD!
YOU SURE EAT A LOT.
I'M GLAD YOU LIKE IT ♡ EAT AS MUCH AS YOU LIKE.
OKAY! SEC-ONDS, PLEASE!
THANKS FOR EVERY-THING. I MEAN IT.
YUM!
MUNCH
MUNCH
HE BOUNCES BACK FAST. HIS FEVER'S ALREADY GONE.
SO YOUR NAME IS KOTARŌ-KUN. DO YOU REMEMBER ANYTHING ELSE YET?
NO... I DON'T ...
IT'S LIKE THERE'S THIS FOG IN MY BRAIN...
OH... WELL, THERE'S NO HELPING THAT.
IN THAT CASE...
WE'VE ALL BEEN WAITING TO TRY SOME LEEKS UP YOUR REAR. LET'S SEE IF IT HELPS ♡
SHOVE
THE SHOCK MIGHT BRING BACK YOUR MEMORY.

LAST TIME, YOU WOKE UP RIGHT BEFORE I COULD TRY IT.
HOO HEH HEH HEH HEH HEH HEH.
ウフフフフ
CHIZŪ-NE... TOLD YOU. HIS FEVER IS GONE.
RUB
キュッ
RUB
キュッ
NOOOO! DON'T DO IT!
I'M JUST KIDDING ♡ NOW LET'S GET YOU WASHED UP.
FLAIL
じた
FLAIL
ばた
W-W-WAIT! I CAN WASH MYSELF!
NO ♡ YOU'RE JUST TOO FILTHY, YOU WIDDLE BOY
OH, THIS TAIL ACCESSORY IS STUCK RIGHT TO YOUR BODY. NATSUMI, COME TAKE A LOOK!
WAAAAH! DON'T TAKE OFF MY PANTS!
POOR KOTARŌ— HE'S ALREADY CHIZU-NĒ'S PLAYTHING... I PRAY FOR YOUR SOUL...
AH...
MM?
WHAT?
THAT SCRATCH ...
I-I'M SORRY... MY HEAD WAS SO CLOUDED UP, I...
OH, THAT'S ALL RIGHT. IT'S NOT VERY DEEP.
NO, BUT, I'M NOT SUPPOSED TO HURT GIRLS... WHAT IF IT LEAVES A SCAR...?
DON'T WORRY ABOUT IT.
MORE IMPORTANTLY ...

YOU'RE WELCOME TO STAY HERE AS LONG AS YOU NEED TO, UNTIL YOU CAN REMEMBER SOMETHING, KOTARŌ-KUN.
I WON'T TELL ANYONE, SINCE YOU OBVIOUSLY HAVE YOUR REASONS FOR NOT WANTING ME TO.
SMILE
EH... ?
YEAH... OKAY...
SORRY.
TH... THANK YOU...

...KOTARŌ-KUN. JUST LETTING YOU KNOW, YOU'D BETTER NOT FALL IN LOVE WITH CHIZU-NĒ.
WHISPER WHISPER
PSST PSST
...SHE'S SCARY.
HUH ?
N-NO ONE'S FALLING IN LOVE, OKAY!
HO HO HO
NATSUMI-SAN. DID YOU SAY SOME-THING?
NO! NOTH-ING!
SHH
RUMBLE RUMBLE

FLASH
CRASH
RUMBLE RUMBLE RUMBLE
HO HO HO. NATSUMI-SAAAN!
KYAAA! KYAAA!
HMMM... I FEEL LIKE I HAD SOMETHING IMPORTANT TO DO ...

66TH PERIOD SPELL GLOSSARY

■「六芒の星と五芒の星よ、悪しき霊に封印を。『封魔の瓶』」

(HEXAGRAMMA ET PENTAGRAMMA, MALOS SPIRITUS SIGILLENT. LAGENA SIGNATORIA) A spell that uses a powerful magical item to neutralize and confine beings with relatively high spiritual natures. Such beings continue to exist, even after their flesh (caro) is destroyed (for example, even after his body was frozen at an extremely low temperature and shattered, it was still necessary to seal ryomen sukuna no kami away again; see 53rd period). Ergo, at present, humans have no way to remove the threat they pose but to confine them within a seal and render them powerless.

In 66th period, Mr. Stan sealed away something called a devil (demon), but devil (or Akuma in the Japanese) is not the most appropriate translation of "demon." The english demon, as well as the german dämon, come from the latin "daemon, daemonium," which extends farther back to the ancient greek, δαίμων, δαιμόνιον In ancient greek, δαίμων, and δαιμόνιον are general terms referring to spiritual beings--from gods to other beings on the deity level. For example, The Apology Of Socrates records the following conversation:

> Socrates: 'do we not believe that the (demons) are either gods or children of gods? Yes or no?'
>
> Meletus: 'certainly yes.'" (27D-e)

As we can see from the above, a demon is a being on par with the gods, and possesses an extremely high spiritual nature. As such, the δαίμων, δαιμόνιον were assigned the role of devil, the only beings opposite the gods, because of unfortunate distortions brought about by the mixing of the polytheistic cultures that made the δαίμων, δαιμόνιον an object of their faith, and the monotheistic cultures of the semitic peoples. The "gospel of matthew" contains the following famous episode:

> "But when the Pharisees heard it, they said, 'This fellow doth cast out devils, but by Beelzebub the prince of the devils.'" (Matthew 12:24) also Mark 3:22, Luke 11:15-16)

In this passage, the words δαίμων, δαιμόνιον were permanently given the meaning of devil, the opposite of god. However, originally, δαίμων, δαιμόνιον meant nothing more than a being with a highly spiritual nature, whether it be good or evil, beneficial or malevolent, and the terms were only assigned the position of "devil" because of the narrow point of view of a demonology based on semitic monotheism.

67TH PERIOD: RUB-A-DUB-DUB THERE'S SLIME IN THE TUB

RUMBLE RUMBLE
THANKS FOR HAVING US!
SHH
WHOA, IT'S POURING OUT THERE!
I ONLY HAVE ONE UMBRELLA.
EVA-CHAN, LET ME USE YOUR RESORT AGAIN WHEN I NEED MORE TIME TO STUDY FOR TESTS.
♪
YOU CAN IF YOU WANT, BUT...I WOULDN'T RECOMMEND IT.
YOU'LL STILL AGE.
ERK!! I WILL?
NO WORRYING.
WHAT'S WRONG WITH AGING AN EXTRA TWO OR THREE DAYS?
YOU ONLY SAY THAT 'CAUSE YOU'RE YOUNG.
KYAAA
GOOD GRIEF. FINALLY SOME PEACE AND QUIET.
SPLASH SPLASH
I THOUGHT YOU WERE ENJOYING THEIR COMPANY, MISTRESS.
......
NN... ?
IS SOMETHING THE MATTER?
NO...
I MUST BE IMAGINING IT.

KYAAA
AH HA HA
SQUEE SQUEE

CALL US IF ANYTHING HAPPENS. WE'LL DO WHATEVER WE CAN, NEGI-KUN.
...
TH-THANK YOU.
OH, BOTHER.
WHAT ?

WHEN I TOLD YOU WHAT HAPPENED SIX YEARS AGO,
WHAT I MEANT TO SAY WAS I MIGHT RUN INTO MORE DANGER LIKE THAT, SO YOU SHOULD THINK HARD BEFORE GETTING INVOLVED WITH MY LIFE.
SO? THEY'RE SAYING THEY WANT TO HELP.
I MEANT IT FOR YOU, TOO, ASUNA-SAN.
NNGH.

BUT HMMM...
NO, I REALLY DO NEED TO GET STRONGER.
GH...
OKAY! I'LL WORK EVEN HARDER AT MY TRAIN-ING!
WAIT A SECOND! IF YOU WORK ANY HARDER, YOU'LL KNOCK YOURSELF OUT! LITER-ALLY!
I'LL BE ALL RIGHT, ASUNA-SAN!

UGH. THERE HE GOES, WORKING HIMSELF UP AGAIN.
OH, MAN. DO YOU THINK HE'LL GET ALL WOBBLY AGAIN?
NEGI-KUN *IS* THE TYPE TO PUSH HIMSELF TOO HARD.
AND HE'S OVERDOING IT.
...I CAN UNDERSTAND WHY, AFTER SEEING HIS PAST, BUT...

HMMM ...WELL.
NORMAL KIDS HIS AGE WOULD BE GOOFING OFF WITH THE OTHER PUNK KIDS IN THE NEIGHBORHOOD...
THOSE ARE THE KIDS I REALLY HATE.
INDEED. ...BUT THE ONLY PEOPLE AROUND SENSEI ARE OLDER WOMEN.

COME TO THINK OF IT, NEGI-KUN SPEAKS POLITELY TO EVERYONE BUT YOU, CHAMO-KUN.
Y-YEAH WELL.
HMMM ...
IF ONLY HE HAD A FRIEND HIS AGE HERE IN JAPAN...

...
HEH HEH HEH...

OH, HELLO, CLASS REP-SAN.
HELLO, NEGI-SENSEI ♡

WHAT A LOVELY DRESS YOU'RE WEARING. IT SUITS YOU.
WHY, THANK YOU ♡ NEGI-SEN-SEI...
HEE HEE...
THAT'S MY NEGI-SENSEI. AN ADORABLE BOY WITH THE HEART OF A GENTLEMAN.
HE SEEMS TO BE FEELING BETTER.
WELL, IF YOU'LL EXCUSE ME, CLASS REP-SAN.
ALL RIGHT ♡ I'LL SEE YOU TOMORROW, NEGI-SENSEI.
THAT'S HOW BOYS SHOULD BE.
WELL-MANNERED AND CHEERFUL ♡
NEGI-SENSEI IS THE IDEAL YOUNG MAN ♡
るんるん
LA LA
N-NO, REALLY! IT'S OKAY! I CAN WASH MYSELF!
HO HO HO. IT'S NO USE TRYING TO RUN FROM ME.
IN CONTRAST, APPARENTLY MY ROOM IS HOME TO A RIOT.
STOMP
ドタバタ
STOMP
EXCUSE ME, CHIZURU-SAN! WHAT ON EARTH IS GOING ON HERE...
BAM
バン
GWAH
どわっ
!?

HWOAH!!
ZOOM
OH... SORRY ...
THUD
WHAT HAP-PENED?
UM, THIS GIRL- -SHE KINDA JUST...
TWITCH TWITCH
NNNGH
KYAAAA! CLASS REP!?
TWITCH

WHERE...
WHERE ON EARTH DID THIS BOY COME FROM!?
BAM

GREETING A LADY BY HEAD-BUTTING A LADY IN THE STOMACH...
GRR!
THE PASTA I HAD FOR LUNCH ALMOST CAME RIGHT BACK UP!
NOW, NOW, AYAKA. CALM DOWN.
NOW, NOW.
CLASS REP.
I SAID I'M SORRY A MILLION TIMES.
YOU EXPECT ME TO CALM DOWN!?
WHO IN THE WORLD IS THIS BOY!!?
HE'S NATSUMI-CHAN'S LITTLE BROTHER, KOTARŌ MURAKAMI-KUN ♡
SMOOTH
WHA!
ER... ?

...HE'S YOUR BROTHER.
RUMBLE RUMBLE
OH! R-RIGHT!
Y-YEAH!
HO HO HO
O-OH, I SEE...
PARDON MY RUDE-NESS.
BUT, CHIZU-NĒ--!
IT'S PART OF THE PLAN, NAT-SUMI!
S-SO WHAT BRINGS YOUR LITTLE BROTHER HERE...?
YOU SEE, AYAKA ....

THE TRUTH IS, NATSUMI-CHAN'S FAMILY IS IN A VEEEERY MESSY, COMPLICATED SITUATION RIGHT NOW. NOT THE TYPE OF THING WE CAN REALLY TALK ABOUT HERE...
LIKE A SOAP OPERA, REALLY.
ERK!
CHIZU-NĒ!!
NATSUMI-CHAN IS THE ONLY ONE POOR KOTARŌ-KUN CAN RELY ON.
R-REALLY?
W-WELL...
IN THAT CASE...
HEY, WHO IS THIS LOUD OLD LADY ANYWAY?
I-I'M A MAIDEN OF FOURTEEN! AND YOU CALL ME AN OL-OL-OL--!
GRR
NO WAY! YOU'RE FOURTEEN!? YOU SURE DON'T LOOK IT!

Y-Y-Y-YOU RUDE, SINISTER-EYED, SPIKY-EXPLOSION-HAIRED BRAT!!
WERE YOU RAISED BY WILD DOGS—!!?
MWUMPH!!

QUIT I', OL' LA'Y!
MY! WHA' A FIOLEN' UNG MAN! JUF' AF I SHUSPE'TED!
BUT, BUT CLASS REP. HE'S JUST A LITTLE BOY. A LITTLE BOY.
LOOK, SEE?
IT'S NOT AS IF I LIKE JUST ANY LITTLE BOY—!!
WHAT DO YOU TAKE ME FOR, NATSUMI-SAN!?
HE'S NOTHING LIKE MY CHARMING, ANGELIC NEGI-SENSEI!
GRRR! GRRR! SHUT UP, NĒ-CHAN!
A-ARE THEY REALLY THAT DIFFERENT?

A-ANYWAY, I WANT HIM OUT OF HERE AS SOON AS POSSIBLE.
THIS IS A GIRLS' DORM.
SHUT
MY, OH MY.

I DIDN'T THINK AYAKA WOULD REACT LIKE THAT.
PERHAPS THEIR FIRST MEETING WAS TOO MUCH FOR HER.
KOTARŌ-KUN, YOU SHOULDN'T CALL HER AN OLD LADY.
SHE'S THE SAME AGE AS ME.
Y-YEAH. ACTUALLY, IF WE'RE TALKING ABOUT PEOPLE LOOKIN' OLD, CHIZURU-NECHAN IS...
DID YOU SAY SOMETHING?
RUMBLE
HO HO...
EEEEK!
NOPE! NOT A WORD!

SEE?
YEAH.
SHE CAN BE SCARY, ALL RIGHT.
HEH, HEH, HEH...

HOW GOES THE SEARCH?
GWHRR
WE FOUND HIM. THE KID WE TAUGHT A LESSON TO OUTSIDE THE ACADEMY. ...
MY CONFUSION SPELL WORKED. HE'S WASTING TIME WITH GIRLS.
GWHRR
THE TEMPORARY AMNESIA SPELL, RIGHT?
JIGGLE
VERY WELL. START WITH HIM.

KOTARŌ INUGAMI'S ABILITIES HAVE BEEN SEALED AWAY AS PART OF HIS PUNISHMENT.
IF WE GET HIM NOW, HE'LL BE A PUSH-OVER.
BUT HE CAN STILL USE CHI ...

VERY WELL. YOU THREE CON-TINUE AS PLANNED.
ROGER THAT.
DON'T LET THE HIGH DAYLIGHT WALKER FIND YOU.
OUR STEALTH IS PER-FECT.

RUMBLE
RUMBLE RUMBLE
FLASH!
SIGH ...
I SUP-POSE I'D BETTER GET START-ED.
CRASH!

SIGH...
I HAD NO IDEA NEGI-SENSEI WENT THROUGH SUCH A TERRIBLE ORDEAL...
NEITHER DID I...
YUE... WHEN I FOUND OUT THAT NEGI-SENSEI WAS A WIZARD, I GOT REALLY EXCITED...
HE LOOKED SO COOL WHEN HE WAS FIGHTING...
AND WHEN I FOUND OUT THAT MAYBE I COULD USE MAGIC...
ME, TOO...
WE GOT A LITTLE CARRIED AWAY...
I HOPE HE CAN FIND HIS FATHER...
NOT LIKE THAT, NODOKA. WE HELP HIM FIND HIS FATHER.
OH!
Y-YOU'RE RIGHT.
OVERSIZED BATH "KIYOKAZE" →
I'M ALMOST ASHAMED OF MYSELF...
GLUM
しょぼ〜ん...
ME, TOO...
YO! YOU TWO SURE WERE OUT LATE.
AH HA HA
アハハ
SQUEE SQUEE
キャッ キャッ
OH! PARU!

SHOULDN'T YOU BE WORKING ON YOUR MANGA MANUSCRIPT?
I THOUGHT YOU SAID THE DEADLINE WAS COMING UP.
AH HA HA HA! I'M TOTALLY SCREWED, BUT I GOTTA AT LEAST BATHE.
YO, PARU.
'SUP, ASAKURA.
IT'S ALMOST TIME TO START GETTING READY FOR THE SCHOOL FESTIVAL!
Hmm...
DON'T TALK ABOUT TESTS!
WE HAVE TO TAKE OUR MIDTERMS FIRST.
MY UPPER ARMS HAVE GOTTEN SO PUDGY.
OH! I HAVE JUST THE THING!
MAYBE I'M EATING TOO MUCH.
DA DA-DA-DAH
JUST RUB IT ON, AND IT'LL HELP YOU LOSE WEIGHT, AND IT'LL LIGHTEN, TIGHTEN, AND MOISTURIZE YOUR SKIN!! FULL-BODY SKIN CARE YOU CAN APPLY YOURSELF! NURU NURU X!!
NURU NURU X
SLATHER ON ITS RICH, HONEY-LIKE THICKNESS AND YOUR SKIN WILL INSTANTLY BECOME SUPER BEAUTIFUL!!
NURU-NURU? IT'S SLIMY!?

AND MONTA-SAN SAID ON HIS DAY-TIME TV SHOW THAT IF YOU PUT IT ON YOUR FACE, IT WILL BECOME MORE ATTRACTIVE!!
ANOTHE ONE O YOUR FISHY PROD UCTS..
FOR REAL !?
どん! DUN!
WHAT'S A JUNIOR HIGH STUDENT DOING, WATCHING DAY-TIME TV?
I RE-CORD-ED IT!!
SURE THING! WHEN I ORDERED IT, FOR SOME REASON MY TWO-BOTTLE SET GOT DOUBLED TWICE. NOW I HAVE EIGHT, AND NO IDEA WHAT TO DO WITH THEM!
H-H-HEY, LET ME TRY IT!
CLAMOR CLAMOR
IT'S A STEAL!
WHAT'S GOING ON?
THEY'VE GOT THIS THING. YOU RUB IT ON AND IT MAKES YOU INSTANTLY BEAUTIFUL.
NO WAY !!
STUN
SHOCK
IT'S SUP-POSED TO WORK BEST IN A BATHTUB BUT...
キャッ SQUEE
キャッ SQUEE
PUT IT ON MY FACE!
WE'RE GONNA BE SO PRETTY!
WHY ARE YOU RUN-NING AWA MAKIE?
YOU KNOW I HATE SLIMY THINGS!
AH HA HA
カラ カラ… RATTLE RATTLE
SLIIME ぬるーーん

SO MUCH PREY...
ぬっ...
SLOOP
WE ONLY NEED FOUR.
AND JUST LEAVE THE OTHERS?
WE HAVEN'T BEEN OUT IN THIS WORLD IN SIX YEARS. LET'S HAVE A LITTLE FUN!
DON'T OVER-DO IT.
ズズズ!!
Z-Z-Z
...UGH. THEY CAN'T POSSIBLY BELIEVE THAT STUFF'LL REALLY WORK.
ズ...
ZZ...
ARE THEY STUPID
トプン...
SPLISH

...
N...?
ぬる ぬる..
SLIME SLIME
HEY. YOU DIDN'T PUT ANY OF THAT IN THE WATER, DID YOU?
EEEHH?
NOPE!

NN!
EEK?
ズズズ...
Z-Z-Z...
H-HEY, WAIT A SEC! THE WATER'S WRAPPING ITSELF AROUND ME!
WHAT THE HELL!?
OWAH! HEY! STOP THAT!
にゅるる
SLIME
DON'T EVEN GO THERE!

KYAAH!!
WHAT'S GOING ON!?
HEE HEE!
NOOOw!
AH HA HAH!
IT'S SWIIIMMY!!
WHAT ARE THEY DOING OVER THERE?
KYAAA KYAAA
キャーキャー
NOOO
BAH
バッ
HEY!
ちょっ
KYA-HA-HA! THIS IS SO FUN!!
ぬるる
SLIIIME
WE NEED TO GET TO WORK SOON.
THOSE FOUR.
GOT IT!
ゴオオキッ
WHOOSH
BLUB

SPLASH
!?
THE SLIME! THE SLI-I-IME!!
AH! NO!
SHUDDER SHUDDER
I CAN'T TAKE ANYMORE...
FLOP
TWITCH TWITCH
I-IS IT BE-CAUSE OF THIS?
AH. SHE'S DEAD.
HFF HFF
JUST DO IT.
TOSS IT.
BLUB
BLUB
BLUB
WHAT IS THIS!?
WH...
GURGLE GURGLE
SHRR

BLUB
!?
SMIRK
BLUB
HUH?

WHAAA ?
YUE — !
NODOKA — !
HEEEY! —
コポ
BLUB
ROOM 665 NABA, CHIZURU
MURAKAMI, NATSUMI
YUKIHIRO, AYAKA
JR. HIGH GIRL
OKAY — !
DINNER'S READY!
WHOA !
IT LOOKS SO GOOD — !
YOU CAN STILL EAT, KOTARŌ-KUN?!
YOU BET I CAN!
COME ON, AYAKA. YOU, TOO ♡
AH HA HA
HEE HEE HEE
IT'S DELICIOUS!

HONESTLY . . .
YOU'RE NOT EATING, CLASS REP? DON'T MIND IF I DO.
YOINK CHOMP
ひょい ぱく
YOINK CHOMP
ひょい ぱく
GASP!
CHOMP
I'LL HAVE SOME, TOO ♡
HEY! I NEVER SAID I WASN'T GOING TO EAT THAT!
RAR RAR
キャイキャイ
YUMMY ♡
CLAMOR CLAMOR
ワイワイ
SQUEE SQUEE
キャッキャッ
AH HA HA HA
アハハ
. . . .
...? IS SOMETHING WRONG, KOTARŌ-KUN?
N-NO. I WAS JUST THINKING. THIS IS NICE.

I'VE NEVER SAT AROUND A TABLE FOR A MEAL LIKE THIS.
I KINDA LIKE IT.
IT FEELS LIKE FAMILY.

MY . . .
. . . .
WHAT A DREADFUL PLACE NATSUMI-CHAN'S HOME MUST HAVE BEEN.
SQUISH
むぎゅ ♡
I HAVE A NORMAL FAMILY, YOU KNOW!

EAT UP!♡ THERE'S PLENTY MORE...
HA, HA, HA...
ALL RIGHT!
DING DONG
WHO COULD THAT BE?
I'LL GET IT.
FLASH
KACHAK
...?
...WHO IS IT?

PARDON ME, YOUNG LADY.
I APOLOGIZE IN ADVANCE FOR ANY TROUBLE I MAY CAUSE.
BUT I HAVE SOME BUSINESS WITH THE BOY.

3-A STUDENT PROFILE

STUDENT NUMBER 21
NABA, CHIZURU

BORN JANUARY 29, 1989

BLOOD TYPE: A

LIKES: THE SLOW LIFE, TAKING CARE OF OTHERS, BEING WITH PEOPLE

DISLIKES: BEING ALONE, PERSONAL RELATIONSHIPS OF A DISTANT NATURE

AFFILIATIONS: ASTRONOMY CLUB

NOTES: VOLUNTEERS AT THE DAY-CARE IN MAHORA ACADEMY CITY. BIGGEST BUST IN CLASS 3-A

STUDENT NUMBER 28
MURAKAMI, NATSUMI

BORN OCTOBER 21, 1988

BLOOD TYPE: A

LIKES: THE STAGE, THE SENSE OF EXCITEMENT RIGHT BEFORE A PERFORMANCE (IT MAKES HER FEEL LIKE SHE CAN CHANGE HERSELF)

DISLIKES: HERSELF, FRECKLES, RED HAIR, WAVY HAIR, AD LIBBING...

AFFILIATIONS: DRAMA CLUB

NOTES: ALSO A MEMBER OF THE MAHORA UNIVERSITY'S DRAMA CLUB NUMBER THREE.

...THE BOY?
WHATEVER DO YOU WANT WITH HIM?
OH, NOTHING MUCH. ...I WAS HOPING
HA HA HA
THE BEAUTIFUL LADY WOULD ACCEPT THIS FLOWER.
SPARKLE
EH...? MY...
HOW POLITE...
SWOON
EH...?

OH...
MY...?
THUD
SS...
PARDON ME.
SCRUNCH
SNAP
?

HELLO THERE, YOUNG WEREWOLF.
ZSH
I TRUST YOU'VE BEEN WELL?
NEGIMA!
MAGISTER NEGI MAGI
68TH PERIOD: A STORMY NIGHT VISITOR
WHA...
WH.... WHO ARE YOU!?

...HM?
I THOUGHT I SENSED SOME-THING...DID I IMAGINE IT?
SET-CHAN!
EH HEHE!
HUH?
OJŌSAMA? I THOUGHT YOU WERE BACK IN YOUR ROOM WITH ASUNA-SAN.

I THOUGHT IT WOULD BE NICE TO GO TO THE BATH HALL WITH YOU, SET-CHAN.
DWAH-HAH?!
WHY ARE YOU NAKED, KONO-CHAN!!?
どーーん
DUN

I MEAN--WAH! KONO-CHA--OJŌ-SAMA!
A-ANY-WAY, PUT SOME CLOTHES ON!
あたわた
FLUSTER
FLUSTER
TEE HEE... SET-CHAN ♡
HUH?
とろ〜り
GLOOP

SPLOOCH!
ZSH ZSH ZSH
NO!
ADEA
..
SPLISH...
SOMETHING WRONG, ANIKI?
....
IS SOMETHING WRONG?

NO, I JUST... I-I'M GOING TO TAKE A LOOK OUTSIDE.
HUH?
SHUT
AH, HEY!
WHAT'S UP WITH NEGI-KUN?
WHO KNOWS?
ZLOOP
SMIRK...

GHN!
THWAM!
NOW, BOY.
FSHH
しゅうう...
KYAAAAA!?
...?!
I'LL BE TAKING THAT BOTTLE.
MY ASSIGNMENT IS THE BOY NEGI...
BUT I CAN HARDLY ACCOMPLISH MY GOAL IF I AM SEALED AWAY AGAIN.
NGH ...

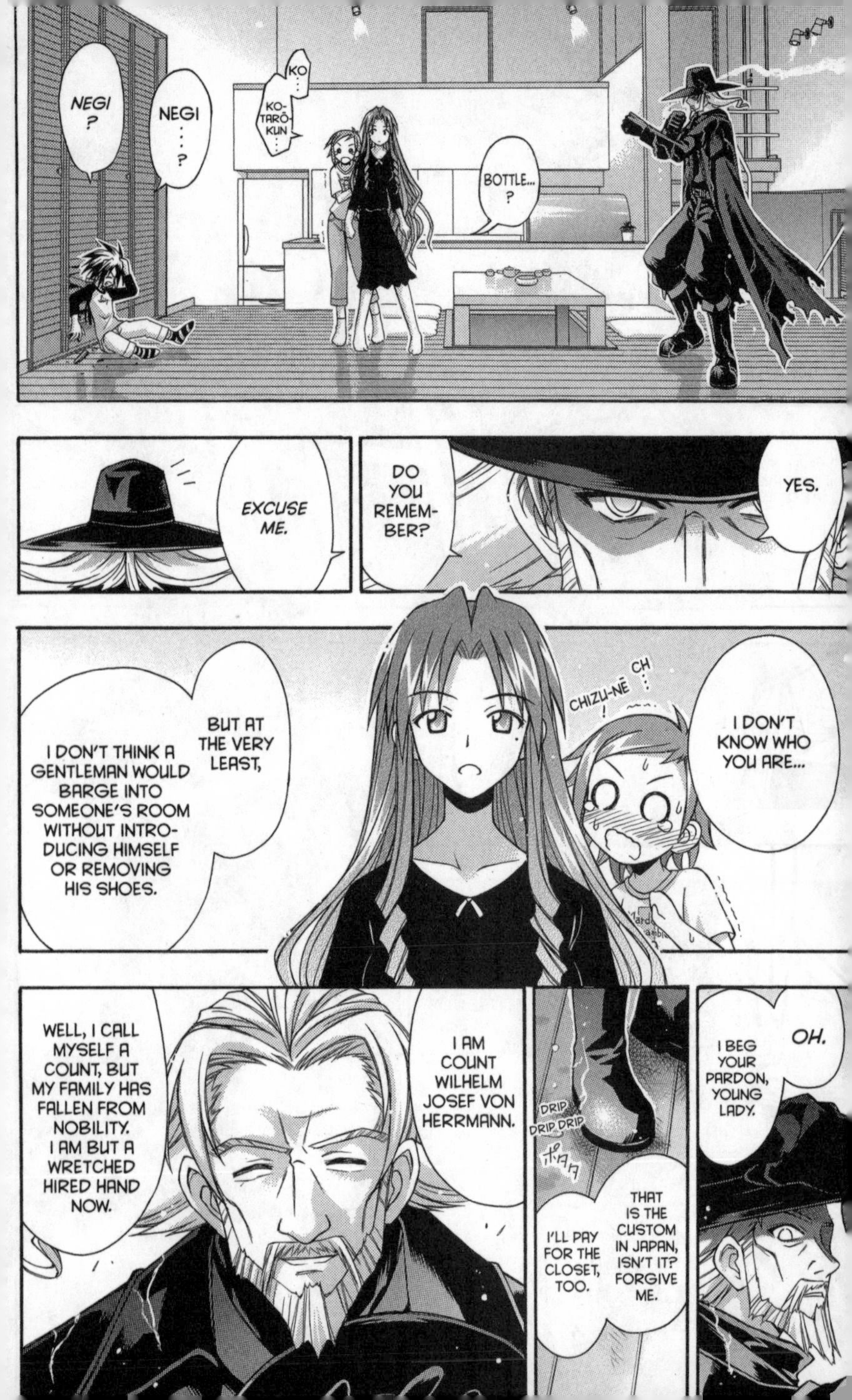

BOTTLE... ?
KO... KO-TARŌ-KUN...
NEGI...?
NEGI?
YES.
DO YOU REMEMBER?
EXCUSE ME.
I DON'T KNOW WHO YOU ARE...
CHIZU-NĒ!
CH...
BUT AT THE VERY LEAST,
I DON'T THINK A GENTLEMAN WOULD BARGE INTO SOMEONE'S ROOM WITHOUT INTRODUCING HIMSELF OR REMOVING HIS SHOES.
OH.
I BEG YOUR PARDON, YOUNG LADY.
DRIP DRIP DRIP
THAT IS THE CUSTOM IN JAPAN, ISN'T IT? FORGIVE ME.
I'LL PAY FOR THE CLOSET, TOO.
I AM COUNT WILHELM JOSEF VON HERRMANN.
WELL, I CALL MYSELF A COUNT, BUT MY FAMILY HAS FALLEN FROM NOBILITY. I AM BUT A WRETCHED HIRED HAND NOW.

I HAVE AN IDEA. BEAUTIFUL LADIES, IS THERE ANYTHING YOU WISH FOR?
HA HA!
HA! HA!
I'M HAVING A SPECIAL RIGHT NOW. I'LL GRANT YOUR FIRST THREE WISHES AT A SPECIAL INTRODUCTORY PRICE.
POOF
...?
WISHES...? NO, WE'RE FINE.
OH, ARE YOU?
THAT'S TOO BAD.
WHAT DID YOU DO TO THE BLONDE GIRL?
I MERELY PUT HER TO SLEEP.
POFF
NOW... ARE YOU READY TO GIVE ME THAT BOTTLE?
I GOT NO IDEA WHAT YOU'RE TALKIN' ABOUT!
GH...
EVEN IF I DID HAVE A BOTTLE,

I WOULDN'T GIVE IT TO YOU!
DUN!
HM.
WHACK

WHACK
BWOH
POW
POW
POW
NGH!
WHAM!
THUMP
WHOOSH
CRASH
HA!
BAM
Z-SHAM

KAPOW

KERSMASH
HE'S FAST, AND A HEAVY-WIEGHT...
SMIRK
THE DUDE'S STRONG.

ZSH
...I'VE A SOFT SPOT FOR BOYS WITH POTENTIAL.
YOU'RE EXTREMELY TALENTED FOR ONE SO YOUNG.
WHAT?
HE'S NOT HUMAN, EITHER...

HAND ME THE BOTTLE LIKE A GOOD BOY,
AND YOU WON'T HAVE TO GET HURT.
HEH. YOU THINK YOU CAN HURT ME?
KA-CHING
GO AHEAD ...

...BE MY GUEST!!
EH?!
GZHN
BA-BA-BAM
GASH
H-HE...
WHAC
SO THESE ARE SHADOW CLONES?
A MYSTERY OF THE EAST!
WHACK WHACK WHACK
HALT
WHACK
WHACK
WHACK
WHACK
!
ZOOM!

MGH!
THAT'S WHAT YOU GET FOR BEING SO COCKY, OLD MAN!
IT'S OVER!!
BAM
DOG SPIRITS!!!
HUSH
GOOD. MAGNIFICENT.
YOU HAVE MORE POTENTIAL THAN I THOUGHT.
YOU SURPRISED ME.
BUT UNFORTUNATELY,
GH GH
IT SEEMS YOU'VE YET TO REMEMBER THAT YOU CANNOT USE YOUR SPELLS.
SHUDDER SHUDDER
!?
WHERE ARE MY DOG SPIRITS?
GASH
KOTARŌKU...

DUN!
NOOO!!
NGH!
THUD
NN... GAH...
YOU HAVE SUCH A PROMISING FUTURE.
GH
I HATE TO CLOSE THE DOOR ON IT, BUT I MUST.
PLEASE DON'T HOLD IT AGAINST ME.
GWA-A-AH
KREE
NKH...

SLAP!
PWOFF
GWOPH?!

?!
I DON'T KNOW WHAT'S GOING ON BETWEEN YOU TWO.
BUT THAT IS NOT HOW YOU TREAT A CHILD.

CH... CHIZU-NĒCHAN...
I DON'T...

WELL THIS IS A SUR-PRISE. WHAT A STOUT-HEARTED YOUNG LADY.
HA HA HA!
IT'S SELDOM INDEED I MEET A HUMAN THAT CAN RESPOND TO ME IN SUCH A MANNER.
BLEED BLEED

FIRST KOTARŌ-KUN, NOW YOU.
I'VE TAKEN QUITE A LIKING TO YOU.

PERHAPS I'LL TAKE YOU WITH ME.
...
AWA-AWAWAH!

I'M SURE IT CAME FROM THIS WAY...

!?
CLASS REP-SAN!?

IT'S OKAY. SHE'S JUST ASLEEP.
WHEW

KYAAA!
!!
CHIZU-NĒ!!
THAT'S MURA-KAMI-SAN!
TMP

THAT WAS FAST.
SHH...
NEGI SPRINGFIELD-KUN.
!?
N... NABA-SAN!?
Y-YOU--!!

LET HER GO!
SHH...
HMPH.

I'VE TAKEN SEVEN OF YOUR COMRADES INTO MY CUSTODY.
IF YOU WANT THEM RETURNED TO YOU SAFELY, YOU MUST FIGHT ME.

EH...!?
WHAT!?

ZSH ZSH ZSH
KYA HA HA!
I WILL BE WAITING AT THE STAGE UNDER THE GIANT TREE AT THE ACADEMY'S CENTER.
IF YOU VALUE YOUR FRIENDS' SAFETY, I WOULD ADVISE AGAINST SEEKING AIDE ELSEWHERE.
AH! WAIT--

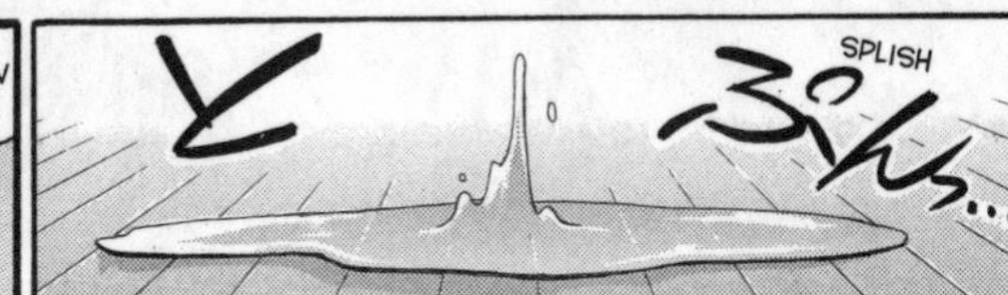
SPLISH

KHN!
AWA... AWA-WAH...

N-NEGI-SENSEI....?
MURA-KAMI-SAN!!

ARE YOU ALL RIGHT? WHAT HAP-PENED?
I-I-I-I DON'T KNOW! IT DOESN'T MAKE ANY SENSE!

HEY, ANIKI! OVER THERE!

...EH?
AH!

.....

....KUN!
NGH....

KOTARŌ-KUN!
HANG IN THERE!!
NEGI....?

AAA-AHH! NEGI!!
BOLT!
KOTARŌ-KUN!
NGH... WHAT AM I...
I REMEMBER NOW... YOU'RE NEGI... NEGI...
AH.

OH YEAH, NEGI! FIGHT ME!! WE'VE GOT A SCORE TO SETTLE —!!!
DUN!
HUH? A FRIEND OF YOURS?
HEY! NOW IS NOT THE TIME!

I SEE. DANGIT... SO THEY ERASED MY MEMORIES...
AND NOW I'VE GOT CHIZURU-NĒCHAN WRAPPED UP IN IT...
SHH...
HE SAID HE'S CAPTURED MY FRIENDS...

YOUR FRIENDS!? HE'S LYING! I DON'T KNOW ABOUT NODOKA OR YUE, BUT THERE'S NO WAY HE GOT ASUNA OR THAT SHINMEI SWORDFIGHTER!
?
?
BUT THAT'S WHAT THE MAN SAID... AND I KNOW ASUNA-SAN IS PRETTY AMAZING, BUT SHE IS JUST A NORMAL JUNIOR HIGH GIRL...
ANIKI! I CAN'T FIND KONOKA-NĒSAN OR ANE-SAN!
TEP
TEP
R-REALLY!?
HMMM
THEN IT'S TRUE?

NEGI ......
THIS BOTTLE ...
RUMMAGE
WITH THIS BOTTLE, YOU CAN SEAL THOSE GUYS AWAY WITH JUST ONE SPELL. I'LL LET YOU HOLD ON TO IT.
YOU HAD IT IN YOUR HAIR...?
EH...!? REALLY?
YEAH. I SWIPED IT FROM THAT GUY BEFORE I CAME HERE.
AND THEN HE GOT ME WITH MAGIC.
!?
THIS BOTTLE ...

O-OKAY! THANKS! ANYWAY, I HAVE TO GO SAVE THEM!
MM-HM
RIGHT! I'M GOIN' WITH YOU!
WHAT? BUT KOTARŌ-KUN, HE JUST BEAT YOU. AREN'T YOU HURT...?
DON'T BE STUPID!! HE JUST TOOK ME BY SURPRISE, IS ALL! I'M FINE!
IT'S MY FAULT THAT CHIZURU-NĒCHAN GOT MIXED UP IN ALL THIS.
AND I OWE HER FOR HELPING ME... I'M GOING!!
....
OKAY.
ALL RIGHT!

WE PUT UP A UNITED FRONT!
WHACK!
WE'LL HAVE OUR REMATCH LATER!!
R-RIGHT!!
HUSTLE HUSTLE
SCURRY
EVERYTHING'S GONNA BE FINE, NATSUMI-NECHAN! WE'LL BE RIGHT BACK!
PLEASE KEEP AN EYE ON CLASS REP-SAN!!
STOMP STOMP
STOMP STOMP STOMP
HUH? WHAP O-OKAY!
B-BE CAREFUL!
BAM
...
SHH...
WHOOSH
DUN!
I'M MORE WORRIED ABOUT *YOU*, NEGI!
UNLESS YOU'VE GOTTEN STRONGER, YOU DON'T STAND A CHANCE AGAINST THAT GUY!
HEY, COME ON! I'VE DONE A LOT OF TRAINING SINCE I FOUGHT YOU!
REALLY!?

BUT I'M HAVING A HARD TIME DECIDING WHAT I SHOULD TRAIN TO BE.
I CAN BE A MAGE WHO ATTACKS FROM A DISTANCE AND RELIES ON FIRE POWER, OR A MAGIC SWORDSMAN WHO ATTACKS UP CLOSE AND RELIES ON SPEED.

COOL!
ANY *REAL* MAN WOULD GO WITH CLOSE COMBAT!

HMM, YOU THINK SO?
DARN RIGHT I THINK SO!
BUT KOTARŌ-KUN, YOU JUST FOUGHT CLOSE UP WITHOUT YOUR DOG SPIRITS AND TOTALLY LOST.
WHA!?

I TOLD YOU! HE CAUGHT ME BY SURPRISE!
YOU GET SURPRISED A LOT, KOTARŌ-KUN.
WHAT—!?
WAAH! SIT STILL! THIS IS AN EMERGENCY; DON'T MESS AROUND!
WHOOSH

SHH...

NN...?
HUH?
WHERE AM I...?

SHH...
IS THIS...
ONE OF THE FESTIVAL STAGES?
FOR THE UNIVERSITY CLUBS...
...ERK.
KYAHHH~~!!
WH-WH-WHAT AM I WEARING!?
WHY DOES THIS ALWAYS HAPPEN TO ME!?
DU-DUN
HA HA HA. I SEE YOU'RE AWAKE, YOUNG LADY.
WHO ARE YOU!?
THE AMBIENCE JUST WASN'T RIGHT WITH THE CAPTURED PRINCESS IN HER PAJAMAS.
HA HA HA
SO I TOOK THE LIBERTY OF FIXING IT.

WHAT'S WITH YOU, YOU PERVERTED OLD MAN !?
WHAM!
NEGIMA!
MAGISTER NEGI MAGI
69TH PERIOD: BEGIN THE ATTACK! NEGI AND KOTARŌ
MBWOH!
MY, MY. I'M GLAD TO SEE NEGI-KUN HAS SO MANY SPIRITED FRIENDS.
BLEED BLEED
HA, HA, HA
YOUR "COOL" ATTITUDE ISN'T WORKING WITH ALL THAT BLOOD COMING FROM YOUR NOSE!!
GET ME DOWN FROM HERE!
!? DID YOU JUST SAY SOMETHING ABOUT "NEGI'S FRIENDS"?
!?
ASU-NAAA
ASUNA-SAN !!
THEY WILL BE OUR AUDI-ENCE.
ASUNA, OVER HERE!
ASUNA, ARE YOU OKAY!?
WHUM WHUM
HEEEY! BARON VON PERV!!
LET US OUT!

ACADEMY FESTIVAL
—MONDAY, JUNE 20 TO SUNDAY, JUNE 22—
GUYS !?
B-BOUNCE
I HAVE INVITED THE SEVEN I BELIEVE TO BE NEGI-KUN'S CLOSEST COMPANIONS TO OUR LITTLE SHOW.

!!
SETSUNA-SAN?

A-AND THAT'S ...
NABA-SAN !?
WHY !?

THE DEMON SLAYER IS DANGEROUS, SO I'VE PUT HER TO SLEEP.
THE OTHER WAS A LAST-MINUTE ADDITION.
....
?!

WH-WHY ARE THEY ALL NAKED?
I'M THE ONLY ONE WITH CLOTHES
HE ATTACKED US IN THE BATH!
YOU GOT COMPLAINTS, TELL HIM!
WE *JUST* TOLD HIM WE'D HELP, AND NOW WE'RE ALREADY HOLDING HIM BACK.
HE JUST SCOOPED US ALL UP LIKE FISH IN A NET.
TO HO HO
HEY, HEY, YOU LITTLE GIRLS!
P-PLEASE LET US OUT!
BOM BOM

THERE'S NO ESCAPING OUR SPECIAL WATER PRISON!
I'M AMEKO.
I'M SURA-MUI.
PURIN...
JUST BE GRATEFUL WE DIDN'T MELT YOU AND EAT YOU.
THIS IS WHAT HAP-PENS TO ORDINARY PEOPLE WHEN THEY STICK THEIR NOSES INTO THINGS THEY DON'T UNDER-STAND.
HEH HEH HEH.
EEEP.
HRNGH!
ANYWAY, THERE'S NO WAY YOU'RE GETTING OUT OF THERE FROM THE INSIDE WITHOUT SOME KIND OF POWERFUL MAGIC.
!
...
WHY ARE YOU DOING ALL THIS!?
OH, IT'S NOTHING MAJOR. THIS IS WHAT I'VE BEEN HIRED TO DO. MY MAIN PURPOSE IS TO INVESTIGATE THE ACADEMY...

HOWEVER, I HAVE ALSO BEEN HIRED TO DETER-MINE...
HOW MUCH OF A THREAT WE FACE IN NEGI SPRINGFIELD AND IN YOU, ASUNA KAGURAZAKA.
EH...? M-ME!?

WH-WHAT ARE YOU TALKING ABOUT!?
...HM. HE'S HERE.
BUT I HAVE A MORE PERSONAL REASON TO SEE NEGI-KUN.
I AM VERY MUCH LOOKING FORWARD TO SEEING FOR MYSELF HOW USEFUL HE HAS BECOME SINCE I LAST SAW HIM.
EH...?
THERE!! I SEE IT!!
WHAT'S THAT TREE BEHIND THEM!? IT'S GIGANTIC!
ERK! IT'S TRUE, ANIKI! HE'S GOT 'EM ALL CAPTURED!!

FIRE, NEGI!! A PREEMPTIVE STRIKE!
BUT--
JUST TO LET HIM KNOW YOU'RE HERE, ANIKI!!
WHOOSH
O-OKAY!
RAS TEL MA SCIR MAGISTER!
SEPTEMDECIM SPIRITUS AERIALES
VINCULUM FACTI INIMICUM CAPTENT!
BWOH
SAGITTA MAGICA!
BOOM
AER CAPTURAE!!

VEEN
HM! VERY NICE!
BA-SHOOM
THUMP!
OUCH ...!
!?
HE DE-FLECTED IT!
A BAR-RIER !?
NO, IT LOOKED LIKE HE ERASED IT SOMEHOW!
ZDD
ZSH ZSH ZSH ZSH
ZSH
ZSH
ZSH!

WE'RE HERE, OLD MAN!!
LET THEM ALL GO!!

NEGI!

ASUNA-SAN...
AH!

THEY'RE DOING DIRTY THINGS TO ASUNA-SAN AGAIN!!
SHOCK!
HAH
THEY ARE NOT!!
WELL THEY ARE, BUT--

NEGI-KUUUUN!
OH, MY DISCIPLE!
NEGI-SENSEI-!

HUH...? THAT BOY...

WE SAW HIM ON THE CLASS TRIP...
KOTARŌ-KUN!!

CHIZURU-NĒCHAN. ...

JUST WHO ARE YOU!?
WHY ARE YOU DOING THIS!?
I APOLOGIZE FOR MY ROUGH METHODS, NEGI-KUN.
BUT I ASSUMED YOU WOULDN'T FIGHT ME WITH YOUR FULL STRENGTH UNLESS I HAD SOME HOS-TAGES.

I ONLY WANT TO KNOW YOUR FULL CAPABILITIES.
IF YOU CAN DEFEAT ME, I WILL RETURN THE YOUNG WOMEN.
THAT IS MY ONE CONDITION. I HAVE NOTHING MORE TO SAY TO YOU.
ERK ...
HA! IS THAT ALL!
K-KOTARŌ-KUN!
PIECE OF CAKE !!
NGH...!! THEY'RE ALL IN DANGER BECAUSE OF ME. AGAIN.
I... I HAVE TO SAVE THEM!
CALM DOWN, ANIKI.
OKAY. I'LL FIGHT HIM.
SS
GH
STAY BACK, KOTARŌ-KUN.
WHAT ?
HOW CAN YOU SAY THAT, NEGI!? YOU'RE JUST A WIZARD! YOU DON'T STAND A CHANCE! LET ME FIGHT HIM!!
WHAT!? HOW CAN YOU SAY THAT!? HE JUST BEAT YOU, KOTARŌ-KUN!
WHA-- MORON! I TOTALLY COULDA BEAT HIM IF I HAD MY DOG SPIRITS!!

WELL YOU DON'T HAVE YOUR DOG SPIRITS, SO YOU'RE GONNA LOSE!
YOU LOST TO ME, TOO, REMEMBER!!
DON'T BE STUPID! NO WAY IN HECK I'LL FALL FOR YOUR SURPRISE ATTACK AGAIN!
NEXT TIME, I'LL BEAT YOU BLACK AND BLUE!!
THERE WAS THAT OTHER TIME, TOO, BUT--
YOU WILL NOT! ANYWAY, I'M GONNA FIGHT HIM!!
I DID A LOT OF TRAINING SINCE LAST TIME, SO IF YOU CAN'T USE YOUR DOG SPIRITS OR TRANSFORM, THEN I BET I'M THE STRONGER ONE HERE!!
HA HA HA. WHAT ARE THEY DOING?
RAR
RAR
THEY'RE NOT FRIENDS?
UM, WELL...
IT'S A LONG STORY...
WHAT!? WELL THAT'S JUST GREAT, YOU LITTLE RUNT!!
GRRR!
NNGH!
ANIKI

IT'S ON, NEGI!!! WE'LL SEE WHO'S STRONGER! RIGHT NOW!!
DU-DUN
WHAM
BAH
FINE, LET'S DO IT!!
HA, HA, HA.
WHY ARE YOU GUYS EVEN HERE!!?

I'M GLAD TO SEE YOU TWO SO ENERGETIC... HOWEVER.
I THINK IT WOULD WISE FOR YOU TO FIGHT ME TOGETHER.
SNAP!
LEAP
!?
CLAMP
CLAMP

UWAH!
THWACK!
Z-BA-BAM!
WAHHH!
Z-ZSH!
Z-SHAM!
WHAT ARE THOSE !?
THEY'RE SLIMES!
YOU KNOW. THEY'RE FAMOUS.
ZSH
HEH! YOU TAKE A BREAK, NEGI. YOU'RE NOT SO GOOD AT CLOSE COMBAT.
I'LL BE FINE !

!!
BA-BAM
THEY'RE NOT WHAT I IMAGINED...
SLIMES
SLIME, HUH?

ZSH ZSH
ZSH
BUT WHAT ABOUT YOU, KOTARŌ-KUN? I THOUGHT YOU COULDN'T HIT GIRLS.
HA!

KYA-HA-HA!
THEY LOOK LIKE GIRLS.
BUT THEY'RE JUST SLIMY MOLLUSKS PRETEND-ING TO BE GIRLS...
GH...

THEY DON'T COUNT!
THAT'S DISCRIMINATION!
WHACK!
ERK...IT'S STILL HARD TO MAKE MYSELF DO IT!
CAN YOU HANDLE THIS, ANIKI!?
BWOH!
YOU BET I CAN.
CANTUS BELLAX!!
BWOOPAH
FWAP!
GZHN
WHAP!
GHRR
WHATEVER!
BWOH
OWW!
POW!

HN!
WHACK!
OHH!
HAHH!
SHUANG ZHUANG ZHANG!!!
BOOM
WHAT WAS THAT, NEGI!?
WHOA!!
YOU'RE GOOD.
ZAM!
Z-SHAM
WHAT? OH, IT'S MY SPELL TO ENHANCE MY ABILITIES WITH MAGIC. THE COMPLETE VERSION.
ZSH
NO, NOT THAT!! THAT THROW!! WHAT STYLE IS IT!? IT'S WEIRD!
IT'S CHINESE MARTIAL ARTS.
I'M LEARNING BAGUAZHANG AND BAJIQUAN.
AH HA HA HA! CHINESE MARTIAL ARTS, HUH? THAT'S AWESOME!!
BAM!

WHACK WHACK
POW POW POW
THEY'RE NOT AS FAST AS CHA-CHAMARU-SAN!!
BAH!
GEH
KAPOW!

POSE
ZSH
ズシャアアッ
Z-SHAM!
KYAAAAA!
OOOOWWW!
POSE
HM.
FORGET ABOUT THEM!
YOUR HITS WON'T DO ANY DAMAGE!
THE ONLY ONE YOU NEED TO WORRY ABOUT IS THE OLD MAN!
RIGHT!
DASH!
YOU'RE NOT HALF BAD, NEGI!
NEITHER ARE YOU, KOTARŌ-KUN!

LISTEN. YOU HAVE TO BE WITHIN 2.8 METERS. DON'T MESS IT UP!
WHISPER
I WON'T!
ZSH ZSH ZSH ZSH
KAPOW KAPOW
KAPOW KAPOW
ZSH!
TMP!
GO, NEGI!!
BAH
OKAY!
BA-BAH!
HEH. TOUGH, AINCHA.
THAT'S A MOLLUSK FOR YA.
BUT YOUR OPPO-NENT...

!?
BA-BAH
...IS ME !!

!
!

HAA-AH
...
I SHOULD BE ABLE TO FIRE ONE!!

OH!
SAGITTA MAGICA
UNA LUCUS!!
BOOM

BA-SHOOM
HN ...
AN UNIN-CANTED SPELL? ...

!?
HE ERASED MY SPELL AGAIN!? BUT--

SQU-SQUEAK
IT WAS ENOUGH TO DIS-TRACT HIM!!
GWIPP

ZSH!
!
WE WIN.
NEGI!

LAGENA SIGNATORIA!!
SHLOOOP

KEEN...
EH.....?
KEEN
ASUNA-SAN!!
H... HYAHHHH!!
KEEN
ASUNA-SAN!?
NOOOOO!
ZSH
GZH GZH GZH GZH
UWAH!
ZAP

WHAT !?
!?
ASUNA—!

ゴトッ
CLUNK
EH...? WHA--?!
HE NEUTRALIZED THE SEALING SPELL!?
ROLL ROLL コロコロ
ゴロ..
ROLL

HM... I SEE MY EXPERIMENT WAS A SUCCESS.
IT WORKS PERFECTLY AGAINST FORCE EMITTING SPELLS.
はあはあ
HFF HFF
NGH...

NOW THEN... IT'S ABOUT TIME I STARTED GETTING SERIOUS.
I TRUST YOU HAVEN'T REACHED YOUR LIMIT YET, NEGI SPRINGFIELD-KUN.

....!!

69TH PERIOD SPELL GLOSSARY

■「『戦いの歌』」
CANTUS BELLAX

A highly complete spell used by a wizard when dealing in unarmed combat. The wizard's body is protected by a highly durable anti-material shield, and increases his muscle contraction exponentially in regards to power, speed, and endurance. Also, in order to avoid physical breakdown on the caster brought about by this superhuman strength (such as pulled muscles, sprains, torn ligaments, etc.), The muscles' and tendons' ability to expand increases as well. Furthermore, the sensitivity of the nerves that control the muscles is moderately heightened, and the caster's physical reflexes are drastically heightened, as well.

WHOOSH
I'VE TAKEN THE LIBERTY OF PLACING A FORCE FIELD OVER THIS AREA.
NO MATTER HOW HARD WE FIGHT OR HOW BIG A COMMOTION WE MAKE, WE WON'T DRAW ANY ATTENTION HERE.
ZSH
GHN!
ZBOOM
DAMONISCH SCHLAG!!
[DEMONIC PUNCH!!]
!!
WHAT !?
B-BAH!

B-KWAH
TCH!
NEGIMA!
MAGISTER NEGI MAGI
70TH PERIOD:
A REASON TO FIGHT
ZSH
THIS POWER.....!!
HEH. YOU CALL THAT "SERIOUS"!?
B-BWOH!
K-KZHNG K-KZHNG
KZHNG
B-KWAH
DA-KONK
Z-ZNN
WE'LL HAVE TO DO WITHOUT THE BOTTLE! LET'S STEAM-ROLL 'IM, NEGI!
WHOOSH
KHN... IT'S ALL WE CAN DO!
ZSH
BAH
RASTEL MASKIL MAGISTER
UNUS FULGOR CONCIDENS NOCTEM
IN MEA MANU ENS INIMICUM EDAT!
CRACKLE

CRACKLE
INUGAMI SCHOOL: KŪGA!!!
DUN!

FULGURATIO ALBICANS !!
FLASH!
WHAM
BA-SHOOM!

AH-
ASUNA-SAN !!
!? HE ERASED IT AGAIN !?
THAT WAS MY BEST CHI BULLET, TOO!!
WINCE
KEEN
MAGIC CANCEL . . .
THE ABILITY TO NULLIFY MAGIC SPELLS.

YOUNG ASUNA KAGURAZAKA, SUPPOSEDLY AN ORDINARY GIRL... AND YET, FOR SOME REASON, SHE HAS THE MAGIC CANCEL ABILITY.
IT IS AN EXTREMELY RARE, AND EXTREMELY DANGEROUS, ABILITY.
BUT THIS TIME, WE ARE USING IT TO OUR ADVANTAGE.
!
WH- WHAT!? MAGIC CANCEL ...!?
CH-CHAMO-KUN!
YEAH.
THAT POWER OF ANE-SAN'S...!
IT WASN'T JUST HER ARTIFACT!
A-ASUNA-SAN! ARE YOU ALL RIGHT!?
I-I'M FINE... NEGI, DON'T WORRY ABOUT ME...
KNOCK THE OLD PERVERT... INTO NEXT WEEK...

B-BUT ASUNA-SAN!
HMM ...
ANIKI!! I'M GONNA TRY SOME-THING! YOU HANG IN THERE!!
CHAMO-KUN?!
BAH
SO. NOW YOU ARE UNABLE TO USE ANY FORCE EMITTING SPELLS OR TECH-NIQUES AGAINST ME.
A REAL MAN ...
Z-ZSH
THE PENDANT...!!
BING

WHAM!
...SPEAKS WITH HIS FISTS!
I LIKE THAT.

KNH!
GIRLS... NODOKA-SAN...
I'VE GOTTEN THEM INTO TROUBLE AGAIN...
ASUNA-SAN... SHE'S IN PAIN.
I HAVE TO HELP THEM!!
WAAAAH!
POW!
GHN...!

NEGI-SENSEI!!
NEGI-KUN!
NEGI.....!
ANESAN! ANESAN!
CH-CHAMO!?
I'M GONNA GET THAT PENDANT OFF YOUR NECK.
THEN ANIKI CAN...
CLAMP!

AW, CRAP!!
LET GO OF ME—!
FLAIL FLAIL
CAUGHT YOU!
STUPID CHAMO—!
YOU CAN GO IN HERE, TOO!
MWOH!
SPLOOSH
CHAMO-SAN
YOU SO USELESS.
CHAMO-KUN...
HEH HEH HEH. THE TWO BRATS ARE DONE FOR.
SUCH A SHAME...
!?
WHAT DO YOU MEAN !?
RELAX. YOU GUYS'LL GO FREE.
YOU'RE JUST BAIT, AFTER ALL.

REGARDLESS OF WHAT OUR INVESTIGATION REVEALS, WE'VE BEEN ORDERED TO MAKE SURE NEGI-KUN STAYS OUT OF ACTION FOR A WHILE.
BUT OLD MAN HERRMANN'S PETRIFICATION SPELL IS PREEEETTY POWERFUL.

IF HE'S NOT CAREFUL, HE COULD END UP WITH A STONE ARM OR LEG. PERMANENTLY.
THAT KOTARO KID, TOO.
!!
KEEN
NKH!
Z-ZOOM
ZSH ZSH
WH!
FLASH

DEMONIC UPPER-CUT!
ZPAM
HE ATTACKS LIKE AN OCCIDENTAL, BUT WITHOUT INCANTA-TIONS!?
!?
POW POW POW
KAPOW POW
KZHNG
POW
WHACK
CRUNCH
WHAM

... HONESTLY.
WHOOSH...
ゴオオオ...
ZSH
IS THIS THE BEST YOU CAN DO?
KNH...
DANGIT, HE'S STRONG!...

YOU MOVED QUITE WELL...
SIGH...
ふう...
BUT IT SEEMS I NEEDN'T HAVE COME FACE YOU MYSELF. IT'S UN-FORTUNATE, NEGI-KUN.

NEGI-SENSEI!!
N... NEGI!

ZSH!
KOTARŌ-KUN, YOU OKAY?!
'COURSE I AM, STUPID!
TCH. IF ONLY I COULD TRANS-FORM!
LET'S GO!
RIGHT!
D-DUN!

NO... I MIS-SPOKE!
WHACK
WHACK
WHACK
WHACK
GWHRR
BAM
THINKING ON IT, NEGI-KUN...
KOTARŌ-KU...
WHAM!
SMASH
I BELIEVE YOU HAVE NOT BEEN FIGHTING ME SINCERELY.
!?
KOTARŌ-KUN!
DUMB DOG!
NGH...

WH-WHAT ...!?
I-I...
I'M FIGHTING WITH EVERYTHING I'VE GOT!!
ARE YOU REALLY?
HOW SAD... THE SON OF THE THOUSAND MASTER...
I WAS SO LOOKING FORWARD TO THIS. I HAD HEARD YOU WOULD BE QUITE USEFUL.
ZSH
ZSH
BUT YOU'RE HIS COMPLETE OPPOSITE. YOU'RE NOT SUITED FOR BATTLE.
!?

GRRRR! TH-THIS IS BAD!! THAT GUY'S ABNORMALLY STRONG!!
HE PRETTY HARSH AFTER MAKE SURE SPELLS NOT WORKING.
AND ON TOP OF THAT, ANIKI'S AT A REAL DISADVANTAGE WITH HIS MAGIC OUT OF COMMISSION!! AT THIS RATE...

NEGI-KUN'S TOAST!?
HMMMM...
WH-WH-WH-WHAT DO WE DO?
G-GIRLS, HUDDLE UP!
WHAT IS IT?
GET IN A CIRCLE SO THOSE LITTLE GIRLS WON'T SEE.
WHAT YOU THINKING?
CHAMO-KUN, WE JUST HAVE TO GET THE PENDANT FROM ASUNA, RIGHT?
Y-YEAH. THEN WE'LL HAVE A LITTLE HOPE...
ACTUALLY, I HAVE A COLLAPSIBLE PRACTICE WAND IN MY POCKET...
WH-WHOA, KONOKA-NĒSAN. YOU...!!

WHAT IS IT
THAT YOU FIGHT FOR?

WHAT . . .
WHAT DO I FIGHT FOR?

YES.
LOOK AT KOTARŌ-KUN.
HE TRULY ENJOYS THE BATTLE.

KNH . . .
NEGI . . .

WHY DO *YOU* FIGHT? FOR YOUR FRIENDS?
TRIVIAL. UTTERLY INSIGNIFICANT. NEGI-KUN, YOU DISAPPOINT ME.

THE REASON A MAN FIGHT IS HIS ALONE, AND ALWAYS WILL BE.
THAT IS HOW IT MUST BE.

"ANGER," "HATE," "REVENGE" --THOSE ARE ESPECIALLY GOOD REASONS. ANYONE CAN PUT THEIR WHOLE SOUL INTO FIGHTING FOR THOSE.
OR, FOR A SLIGHTLY MORE WHOLESOME REASON, YOU COULD FIGHT FOR "THE JOY OF BECOMING STRONGER."
LIKE KOTARŌ-KUN.
WITHOUT A REASON, THERE IS NO PLEASURE IN FIGHTING.
I-I'VE NEVER FOUGHT FOR PLEASURE...

....
I FIGHT --
BECAUSE YOU FEEL RESPONSIBLE FOR GETTING INNOCENT, NON-MAGICAL GIRLS INVOLVED?
OUT OF A SENSE OF OBLIGATION TO SAVE THEM?

A SENSE OF DUTY MAY SPUR YOU ON, BUT IT WILL NEVER MAKE YOU FIGHT IN REAL EARNEST.
...
...TRULY DISAP-POINT-ING.
OR... PERHAPS
YOU FIGHT...

TO ESCAPE YOUR MEMORIES
OF THAT SNOWY NIGHT?

EH... ?
H...HOW DO YOU KNOW ABOUT THAT...?
Y- YOU'RE WRONG! I--
WRONG, AM I?
WELL THEN ...
GH... ...
ZH... ...
....?!
EH ...?

WHAT DO YOU THINK
OF THIS ?

THMP
THMP
THMP
THMP
THMP
THMP

EH . . . ?
WH... WHAT'S HAPPEN-ING?
EH!? WHAT THAT !?
H... HE'S... !?
HA HA HA... DO YOU LIKE IT? THAT'S A GOOD FACE, NEGI-KUN. THAT'S THE FACE I WANTED TO SEE.
YOU KNOW, THESE DAYS, WHEN YOU COME OUT AND SAY, "HI, I'M A DEVIL!" THE KIDS ONLY LAUGH.
HA HA HA.
Y....
YOU'RE ....

YES.
IT IS I, NEGI-KUN.
I DES-TROYED YOUR VILLAGE.

OF ALL THE DEVILS SUMMONED THAT DAY,
I WAS ONE OF THE FEW HIGH-LEVEL, NOBLE-RANKING DEMONS.

I WAS THE ONE WHO TURNED YOUR UNCLE TO STONE, WHO ANNIHILATED YOUR VILLAGE.
BUT THAT OLD WIZARD GOT THE BETTER OF ME.
NE... NEGI.
WELL?
ARE YOU READY TO FIGHT FOR YOURSELF NOW?

HEY, NEGI!
SNAP OUT OF IT!!
NEGI! YOU OKAY ?!
ZSH!
HFF
HFF...

AHORA ACADEMY FESTIVAL
—MONDAY, JUNE 20 TO SUNDAY, JUNE 22
AHORA FESTIVAL COMMITTEE
N....
TMP
!?

GWCH!
BWOH
BOOM!

WHACK!
BAM
BAM
BAM
BAM
BAM
BAM
BAM
BAM
WHAM!
KABAM!

WHA...?
HOW CAN HE MOVE LIKE THAT!?
HIS MAGIC'S GONE INTO OVER-DRIVE!
O-OVER.. DRA... DORA... !?
EMON...?
HE HASN'T HAD ENOUGH TRAIN-ING TO FULLY MASTER IT YET, BUT ANIKI'S MAXIMUM MAGICAL OUTPUT IS ENORMOUS!
GET HIM TO RELEASE IT ALL AT ONCE, AND...
THIS IS HOW HE BEAT EVAN-GELINE, TOO!!
B-BUT, ANIKI, YOU--

WHACK!
WHOOSH
BAH
KA-BAM
WHACK
HEH.....
GZH-ZH!
HOO HOO HA HA HA! WONDERFUL! MAGNIFICENT!!
THIS! THIS IS WHAT I WANTED TO SEE!
THAT IS THE SON OF THE THOUSAND MASTER!!!

NEGI...
WHOA...
CLENCH
BUT... BUT, YOU KNOW...
NEGI!
DASH!
I CAN'T LET YOU FIGHT LIKE THAT!!
DUN!
ZPOW POW POW
YES, BRILLIANT THIS POWER MUST NOT GO TO WASTE.
OH, TO SEE HIM GROWN!
HNNGH
HOWEVER
TO SEE THAT TALENT EXTINGUISHED...
GZH-ZH-ZH
KAPOP
WOULD PLEASE ME JUST AS WELL!!
!!

NEGIMA!
MAGISTER NEGI MAGI
71ST PERIOD: NEGI'S CHOICE
NE...
NEGI !!

FLASH

POW!
WHOOSH
OOH
SMASH
Z-SHAM!
BOOM

NE.....
!?
ANIKI!
ゴオオ...
WHOOSH...
AH.....
ハァ HFF
ハァ HFF
NGH.....
しゅらら... FSHH

WH... WHAT...
DID I.....?
OW-W-W!
... DANG.

KO...
KOTARŌ-KU...
ふうっ SIGH

YOU LITTLE.....
EH?
rise up.

KAPOW!
ARE YOU STUPID !?
HOWEH ?
HM.
ZSH!

KO-K-K KOTARŌ-KUN ?!
MORON !
I DON'T CARE HOW MUCH POWER YOU GOT--SWING AT EVERYTHING LIKE THAT, AND YOU'LL GET YOUR BUTT KICKED! EVERY-BODY KNOWS THAT!!

SQUISH
PHNGH
SO YOU'VE GOT A BOTTOM-LESS PIT OF MAGIC! I GET IT!
I GET IT, OKAY! BUT THAT WAS THE WORST FIGHTING I'VE EVER SEEN!!
YOU COULDN'T SEE ANYTHING AROUND YOU, AND YOU DIDN'T LAND A SINGLE PUNCH!! KEEP THROWING YOUR WEIGHT AROUND LIKE THAT, EVEN I COULD BEAT YOU!!
MAN! AND YOU LOOK SO SMART! I DON'T KNOW WHAT YOUR DEAL IS ABOUT REVENGE OR WHATEVER, BUT DON'T LET HIM PROVOKE YOU LIKE THAT!!
YOU'RE SO IMMA-TURE!!
STUPID !
SHAKE SHAKE SHAKE
MRGH GHGH!

HEH...
THAT KID.....
WAS IT, "KOTARŌ"...?
LOOKS LIKE THEY'RE DOING OKAY OVER THERE.
LET'S FOCUS ON WHAT WE'RE DOING!
Y-YEAH.
HEY.
DUN
MMPH?

I THOUGHT THIS WAS GONNA BE A UNITED FRONT.
LET'S BEAT THE CRUD OUTTA THAT GUY TOGETHER.

Y...
YEAH...
...YOU'RE RIGHT.
KOTARŌ-KUN.

HMPH... OVER ALREADY, NEGI-KUN?
AND I WAS SO ENJOYING THAT FIGHT...
HA HA HA. YOU HAVE A GOOD FRIEND.
BUT WHAT WILL YOU DO?
FWOOSH
CAN THE TWO OF YOU BEAT ME?

NEGI. CAN YOU DO THAT SUPER-STRONG MODE THING AGAIN?
ZSH!
I-I DON'T KNOW HOW I DID IT...
HEH HEH. FIGURES.
NNH?
PRACTE-BIGI-NARU ARDE-SCAT...
PRACTE-BIGI-NARU ARDE-SCAT...

I DON'T CARE WHO IT IS--ONE OF YOU GET IT TO WORK! EVEN FOR A SECOND!!
I DON'T CARE WHO IT IS--ONE OF YOU GET IT TO WORK! EVEN FOR A SECOND!!
IF YOU CAN MAKE EVEN A SPARK, KONOKA-NĒSAN CAN USE HER POWER TO AMP IT UP!
I THINK!!
PRACTE BIGI-NAR...

ARDESCAT!!
FLASH

BLUB
EEEK!
BWOH
!?
OH NO!
STOP THEM!!
KEEN
WE WON'T MAKE IT IN TIME!

ALL RIGHT!
HOT HOT HOT!
POP!
GIRLS!! JUST LIKE WE PLANNED!
SET-CHAN!
YOU GOT IT!
WHERE'S THE BOTTLE!?
ZSHH
YUE, OVER THERE!
BAH!
HIYA!
BENG QUAN!
BOM
SPLASH
SORRY WE TOOK SO LONG, ASUNA ♪
ZSH!
ASAKURA!!

SNAP!
JIGGLE!
たぷんっ
NODOKA!
R-RIGHT! UMM...
OH NO YOU DON'T!
WHAT!
LAGENA SIGNATORIA!!

NEGI-KUN!
NOW!
SBORK
DUN
KH-ZHNG
IN THE BOTTLE AGAIN!?
NOOOOOOOO!!
DESU-UUU!
WELL, WE ARE VIL-LAINS...

GIRLS!!
NICE GOING, NĒCHANS!!

HEH HEH HEH... NOTHING LEFT BUT TO FIGHT!!
I HAVE JUST THE THING!
I THINK I CAN USE IT!
KOTARŌ-KUN, CAN YOU COVER ME!?
HEH! WHO DO YOU THINK I AM? I JUST HOPE YOU'LL BE OKAY!

HEH HEH HEH ...
NICELY DONE.
ZSH ZSH ZSH

VERY WELL!! EN GARDE!!!

WHAT'RE YOU SMILIN' ABOUT, OLD MAN!?

YOU CAN'T BLOCK MAGIC ANYMORE!!!
BAH!
HEH HEH ....
SMIRK

OUT OF MY WAY, KOTARÖ-KUN!!
IT'S NOT YOU I'M AFTER.
DUN
KAPOW
POW
POW
GAH!
NEGI-KUN IS THE ONE I WANT!!
GZHRR
FLASH!
I'M THE REAL ONE.
OLD MAN.

rise up.
WHACK!
GH... NH!
NEGI!
SAGITTA MAGICA
UNA FULGURATIO!!
BASH
擢打頂肘!!!
カク HUO DA
ダ
BOOM!
チョウ DING
チュウ ZHOU!!!
B-BAH!
RAS TEL MA SCIR MAGISTER!
Κενοτητος αστραπσατω δε τεμεω!!
HNNGH!
CRACKLE
CRACKLE

ΔΙΟΣ ΤΫΚΟΣ !!
BOOM!

OOHH...
...HMPH.
HE WEATH-ERED THE STORM.
YOU SEEMED HALF OUT OF YOUR WITS WITH CONCERN, MISTRESS. IT IS GOOD THAT HE IS SAFE.
HEH HEH ...
NIN-NIN
LOOK, CHACHAMARU. WOULD YOU STOP JOKING LIKE THAT?
...WELL, I GOT SEE THE BOY'S LATENT POWERS. THAT WAS AN UNEXPECTED BONUS.
I'LL HAVE TO THANK THAT WHATSIS-NAME HER-RMANN FOR THAT.

ゴォォォ‥
WHOOSH...
CHIZURU-NĒCHAN!
WHEW
...OH! ♡ KOTARŌ-KUN...

N... NEGI-SENSEI...
DID YOU WIN, NEGI-KUN?
WHEW

NEGI-SENSEI!
NEGI-SENSEI!
NEGI-KUN!
NEGI-BŌZU!

NEGI....

...YOU WIN.
...ARE YOU SURE YOU DON'T WANT TO FINISH ME OFF?
しゅうう‥
FSHH

IF YOU DON'T, THEN I WILL ONLY BE RELEASED FROM THE SUMMON MAGIC AND RETURNED TO MY OWN LAND...
I MAY COME BACK ONCE I'VE TAKEN SOME TIME TO RECUPER-ATE.
NOW THAT YOU'VE USED THE BOTTLE, YOU WON'T BE ABLE TO SEAL ME AGAIN.

......
I...

I TOOK THE LIBERTY OF READING UP ON YOU.

OF THE NINE BATTLE SPELLS YOU LEARNED BEFORE COMING TO JAPAN, THE LAST WAS A HIGH ANCIENT SPELL...

I. MAGIC ARCHER
II. WIND FLOWER DISARMAMENT
III. SUMMON WIND SPIRITS
IV. MIST OF SLEEP
V. WIND FLOWER, DUST, DANCE WILDLY
VI. THUNDROUS GALE
VII. WHITE LIGHTNING
VIII. --
→ IX.

THIS IS WHAT YOU LEARNED IT FOR, IS IT NOT?

NORMALLY WIZARDS CAN ONLY DEAL WITH HIGH LEVEL DEMONS SUCH AS MYSELF BY THEM SEALING AWAY, BUT THAT HIGHLY ADVANCED SPELL IS ABLE TO VANQUISH US COMPLETELY.
YOU WORKED YOURSELF TO THE BONE LEARNING THAT SPELL, ALL FOR YOUR REVENGE.

GH...

......
...I

I WON'T ...
FINISH YOU.
OHO ?

SIX YEARS AGO... YOU ONLY DID WHAT YOU WERE SUMMONED TO DO. THAT'S ALL.
EVEN TODAY... YOU DIDN'T DO ANYTHING TOO TERRIBLE TO THE HOSTAGES.

BESIDES, I DON'T THINK YOU WERE REALLY FIGHTING IN EARNEST, EITHER.
YOU DON'T... SEEM SO BAD TO ME...

I DON'T, DO I? I MIGHT TURN OUT TO BE QUITE THE VILLAIN, YOU KNOW.
I AM A DEMON, AFTER ALL.
HA, HA, HA...
...EVEN SO.
I WON'T FINISH YOU OFF.
......

....
SS... す...

HEH... HOO HOO HA HA HA! NEGI-KUN!
YOU SOFT-HEARTED FOOL! I KNEW YOU WEREN'T SUITED TO BATTLE.

YOUNG KONOKA KONOE... SHE POSSIBLY HAS THE GREATEST MAGICAL POWER IN ALL THE FAR EAST...
DEPENDING ON HER TRAINING, SHE COULD BE THE MOST POWERFUL HEALING WIZARD IN HISTORY.

ONCE SHE'S MATURED, IT MAY BE POSSIBLE...
?
TO HEAL THOSE VILLAGERS WHO SLEEP SOUNDLY, WITH NO CURRENT HOPE OF RECOVERY.
OF COURSE, THERE'S NO TELLING HOW MANY YEARS THAT WILL TAKE.
...!
HEH HEH... YOU HAVE MY THANKS, NEGI-KUN.
FSHH...
しゅうう...
!
I LOOK FORWARD TO THE DAY I SEE YOU GROWN.
DO NOT DISAPPOINT ME, YOUNG MAN!
HEH HEH HEH...
WAH, HA, HA, HA, HAH!!

チチチ…
TWEET TWEET

チュンチュン
CHIRP CHIRP
チチチ…
TWEET TWEET

TWEET TWEET
チチチチ…
……
THROB!
OW…!
STING STING
ズキズキ
…
NGH!
I MUST BE SORE BECAUSE OF THAT OVERDRIVE YESTERDAY…
STING
ズキン
CHIRP
チュン
CHIRP CHIRP
チチ…

…
…
SIGH.
NEGI-KUN'S BEEN LIKE THAT SINCE YESTERDAY.

I CAN'T BRING MYSELF TO TALK TO HIM. I'M WORRIED.
WELL, THE WOUNDS ARE STILL FRESH ...
IT MAY BE BEST TO LEAVE HIM ALONE...
ANIKI ...
.... NEGI.
HEEEEY! NEGIIII !
STOMP STOMP STOMP STOMP
IT'S TOO EARLY IN THE MORNING TO BE STAR-ING INTO SPACE LIKE A MORON! PULL YOURSELF TOGETHER!
K-KOTARŌ-KU...
PWAHH !!
PUNCH!
'SUP?
EH HEH HEH! LISTEN TO THIS! 'CAUSE I HELPED YOU, I'M OFF THE HOOK FOR BREAKING OUT OF DETENTION AT THE MAIN TEMPLE!!
YOUR HEAD-MASTER GUY TALKED TO THE CHIEF FOR ME!
WHAT? REALLY? THAT'S GREAT!
NN? WHAT'S UP, NEGI? YOU'RE LIKE SERIOUSLY DEPRESSED. ARE YOU OKAY?
EH? OH, NO, I'M FINE.
...... HEH HEH. ...
KOTARŌ-KUN?

I...
...DECIDED TO BE A MAGIC-SWORDS-MAN.
SMIRK

WHAT!? FOR REAL!? HOW'D YOU DECIDE!?
MAYBE MORE OF A MAGIC "FIST-FIGHTER"?
OH, WELL...IT WAS JUST KIND OF FUN, TAG TEAMING WITH YOU YESTERDAY...

I KNOW, RIGHT!? A MAN'S GOTTA GO WITH CLOSE COMBAT!!!

ALLLLRIGHT ♪ IN THAT CASE, IT'S TIME FOR A BATTLE!!!
EEEHHH!? NOW!?
WAIT, NO! I REALLY OVERDID IT YESTER-DAY! I HURT ALL OVER!
WAAAH
GYAAA
WHAT!? I THOUGHT KONOKA-NECHAN HEALED ALL YOUR WOUNDS!
NO, IT'S TRUE, IT'S TRUE!
I'M SO SORE...
DON'T TRY AND PLAY INVALID WITH ME!!
AAAAHH! YOU'RE DONE HERE, KOTARO-KUN! GO BACK TO KYOTO!
WHAT—!?

AH HA HA HA WELL, IT LOOKS LIKE HE'S MADE A FRIEND.
I GUESS THERE'S NOTHING TO WORRY ABOUT.
YES. HE DOES SEEM TO HAVE CHEERED UP.
THEY SEEM MORE LIKE "BAD" FRIENDS TO ME.
......
HEH, HEH!

赤松健(あかまつけん)

Ken Akamatsu

CONTENTS

DEAR NEKANE-ONĒCHAN, HOW ARE YOU?
I'M WELL!
THESE LAST FOUR MONTHS AS A TEACHER IN JAPAN HAVE BEEN PRETTY ROUGH,
BUT EVERYONE IS SO NICE, EVERYTHING IS FINE! I'VE GOTTEN USED TO LIFE HERE.
CHAMO HERE!

AND GUESS WHAT! LAST WEEK WE HAD SOMETHING CALLED "MIDTERM EXAMS."
MY CLASS RANKED THIRD IN THEIR SCHOOL YEAR!
AND IT'S ALL BECAUSE THEY WORKED SO HARD.
From Negi Springfield
▶play
English
German
French
Japanese
THAT'S WONDERFUL.
AND! REMEMBER ASUNA-SAN? THE ONE I'M ALWAYS TELLING YOU ABOUT, WHO LOOKS LIKE YOU? YOU KNOW, THE ONE WITH THE REALLY BAD GRADES.
SHE FLIPPED OUT. SHE WAS LIKE, "I STUDIED SO HARD! HOW DID I RANK LAST IN OUR CLASS?"
OH, MY...
CHUCKLE CHUCKLE

HEEEY! WHO ARE YOU CALLING A VIOLENT LAST-PLACE MONKEY!?
WAAH!
S-S-STOP ASUNA-SAN! I'M RECORDING A LETTER!
From Negi Springfield
▶ English
German
EH? WHAT? YOU'RE RECORDING THIS?
YES. I'M MAKING A LETTER TO ONĒ-CHAN.
WE GOT THAT WHOLE SCENE WITH YOU, ANE-SAN.
KEH HEH HEH
H-HELLO, IT'S NICE TO MEET YOU. UM, I'M ASUNA KAGURAZAKA...
BOW BOW
ACK! I'M IN MY PAJAMAS!
HEE HEE HEE.
H-HEY, NEGI! START YOUR LETTER OVER!
JUST SEND IT, ANIKI!
AND, AND! THERE'S THIS AMAZING PERSON NAMED EVANGELINE-SAN, AND SHE TAUGHT ME A NEW SPELL.
IT'S HILARIOUS!
AND KŪ FEI-SAN IS TEACHING ME CHINESE MARTIAL ARTS. YOU KNOW, LIKE YOU SEE IN THE KUNG-FU MOVIES. ISN'T THAT COOL!?
I'M GLAD YOU'RE ENJOYING YOURSELF ♡

AND...UM, ONĒ-CHAN.
I'VE HAD TO DEAL WITH A LOT OF HARD THINGS ON TOP OF WORKING AS A TEACHER, LIKE...

......

NEVER MIND. I'LL TELL YOU SOME OTHER TIME! FORGET I SAID ANYTHING!
OH, MY. HE'S KEEPING THINGS FROM ME...
YOU HAVE GROWN, NEGI.
I'M A LITTLE SAD.

I'LL WRITE YOU AGAIN SOON!
YOU TAKE CARE, ONĒCHAN.
P.S.: I MADE A NEW FRIEND!
A BOY NAMED KOTARŌ-KUN. I'LL INTRODUCE YOU SOMETIME.
BYE!

...HEE, HEE!
SHH
HPP...
KOTARŌ-KUN... I WONDER WHAT HE'S LIKE...
IT SOUNDS LIKE YOU'RE SUR-ROUNDED BY GOOD PEOPLE...
RUSTLE

NEGI....
HANG IN THERE....

72ND PERIOD: MAIDS IN FULL BLOOM!

NEGIMA!
MAGISTER NEGI MAGI
SKetc

......
SIGH
ふう...
NEGI-KUUUN! IF WE DON'T LEAVE SOON, WE'LL BE LATE!
OH! RIGHT!
I'M COMING!
OH, GOOD. NEGI-KUN SEEMS TO BE FEELING BETTER♡
YEAH. HE WAS DEPRESSED FOR A LONG WHILE THERE.
BUT NOW WE CAN RELAX.
... YOU THINK SO?
WE'RE LATE, WE'RE LATE!
I'M GOING TO BE LATE TO MY FACULTY MEETING!
YOU COULD JUST LEAVE EARLIER EVERY MORNING
HURRY, HURRY ♡
HE HASN'T GOTTEN OVER IT YET.
HEEEEY! NEGIIII—!

'SUP!
OH, KOTARŌ-KUN! GOOD MORNING!
STOMP STOMP STOMP STOMP
WHAT ARE YOU DOING IN THAT UNIFORM?
I DECIDED TO TRANSFER HERE OFFICIALLY!
WHAT? REALLY!?
YEAH. YOU, SETSUNA... THERE'S A TON OF TOUGH GUYS HERE
BUT NOW I'M LOOKING FOR A PLACE WHERE I CAN LIVE ON MY OWN.
WITH A JOB, I SHOULD BE ABLE TO PAY FOR FOOD.
GOOD!
EH? LIVE ON YOUR OWN?
WOW...
RUMBLE RUMBLE RUMBLE
TEE HEE HEE HEE.
WINCE!
CH-CH-CHIZU-NĒCHA-
OUCH!
CLAMP
NEGI-SENSEI, I SEE YOU'RE ACQUAINTED WITH OUR LITTLE KOTARŌ
Y-YES.
"OUR"...?!
I HEARD ALL ABOUT HOW YOU DON'T HAVE ANY PARENTS.
SOB
MMPH!
CHIZU-NĒ-- STOP!
NEGI'S WATCHING!
EH...?
YOU DON'T?
YOU WILL DO NO SUCH THING♡ YOU WILL BE LIVING WITH US, KOTARŌ-KUN
AND SO I PROMISE I WILL RAISE HIM INTO A FINE YOUNG MAN IN THEIR PLACE!
RING GONG RING GONG
STOP THAT! NĒ-CHAN!
HE'S ALREADY HER PET.
OHHH. !
THAT'S NABA-SAN FOR YOU.
WARGH!
DUN

OOOH
WH- WHAT !?
YŌKAI !?
ZSH!
WHOA !?
ずしん ずしん
Z-SHN
Z-SHN
WHOOPS, SORRY, BOYS.
ZNN...
HUH ?
GREAT COS-TUME.
WHAAAA? I JUST NOTICED, THERE ARE BUNCH OF REALLY WEIRD THINGS MIXED IN WITH THE USUAL RUSH...
THIS IS THE FESTIVAL COMMITTEE! ALL STUDENTS WITH MASKS PLEASE BE IN YOUR SEATS BY EIGHT AM.
FLUGTAG CLUB
ROBOT RESEARCH ASSOC.
P2 vs. GIANT TEA-SERVICE AUTOMATON
BEEAAR!
ワイ CLAMOR ワイ CLAMOR ワイ CLAMOR
WH-WH-WHAT IN THE HECK--!?
ZHWAH
FLY! FLY!
CHACHAMARU CAN FLY!
KSHNK KSHNK
CLANK CLANK
STOMP STOMP STOMP STOMP
TMP TMP

THAT'S THE UNIVERSITY FOR YOU. THEY GET REALLY INTO IT.
I WONDER WHAT EVENTS THEY'LL BE SHOWING UP IN. ♡
?
オオオッ
OOHH
WHOA! NEGI, LOOK AT THAT!
WHOOSH
WHOOSH
CLAMOR
CLAMOR ワイワイ
THAT'S OUR AWESOME! ACROBATICS CLUB!

LEAP
パッ
THE MAHORA ACROBATICS CLUB, "NIGHT-MARE CIRCUS," WILL BE HELD EVERY DAY OF THE FESTIVAL STARTING AT 6:30 P.M.
WAAH
WAAH
ADULT TICK-ETS ARE 1500 YEN! 1000 YEN* WITH A STUDENT DISCOUNT! SEE YOU THERE!
ABOUT $15 AND $10
THAT'S ...
LEAP
パッ
OOOH!
おおっ
SPIN SPIN SPIN SPIN
くるくるくる
THNK!
スタッ♪
BOW
ペコ...
NEGI-SENSEI ...
I WOULD LOVE TO HAVE YOU AT OUR CIRCUS... IF YOU WOULD LIKE TO COME...
OH. THANK YOU.
BOW
ペコ。
I'VE NEVER SPOKEN WITH ZAZIE-SAN BEFORE.
SMILE
WHAT? YOU KNOW HER?
ZAZIE-SAN SPOKE. AND SHE SMILED!
OOOH!
↑PROFESSIONAL SMILE
WHAT'S GOIN' ON HERE, ANYWAY ?
LEAP!
パッ
OOOH!
お
CLAMOR CLAMOR
ワイワイ
THE SCHOOL FESTIVAL.
OH YEAH. I HAVE A PERFOR-MANCE, TOO. HERE'S SOME TICKETS, SENSEI.
SCHOOL FESTIVAL ?
OH! NEGI! OVER THERE!

DAYS TILL MAHORA-FEST
MAHORA ACADEMY UNIVERSITY DIVISION CONSTRUCTION CLUB
15
...TO GO!
'03 MAHORAFEST
WOWWW ~~~!
BANG BANG BANG
SQUEE SQUEE
SQUEE SQUEE

MAHORA FEST...
HEY, OLD GUY. WHAT'S THAT GIANT GATE?
IT WASN'T HERE LAST WEEK!
I'M NOT OLD.
THAT? IT'S THE FESTIVAL GATE! HA HA HA. COOL, HUH?
IT'S JUST WOOD, BUT...

WHO-O-O A-A ~~~

THIS IS YOUR GATE? WHAT KIND OF SCHOOL IS THIS?

THERE'S STILL FIFTEEN DAYS LEFT, BUT EVERYONE'S SO EXCITED ALREADY!
FW-FWEE!
DAY TWO, 2:30! DON'T MISS IT!!
PRO WRESTLING CLUB
BAM-BAM-BANG
CLAMOR
BAM-BAM-BANG

IT'S AN ACADEMY-WIDE SCHOOL FESTIVAL ♡
PREPARATIONS GO INTO FULL SWING AS SOON AS JUNIOR AND SENIOR HIGH MIDTERMS ARE OVER.
THE UNIVERSITY CLUBS EARN ALMOST THEIR ENTIRE CLUB BUDGETS AT THE FESTIVAL, SO THEY PUT A LOT INTO IT.
MOPAAAH
COME SEE US!
KENDAMA FAN CLUB
51
CLAMOR

THERE WILL BE ALL KINDS OF PEOPLE FIGHTING FOR YOUR ATTENTION DURING THE FESTIVAL, ASKING YOU TO VISIT THEIR SHOPS AND EVENTS ♡

WOW, SOUNDS LIKE FUN.
NOT NECESSARILY. THERE ARE A LOT OF PEOPLE AT THIS SCHOOL, AND THEY ALL LOVE TO PARTY.
THEY DON'T KNOW HOW TO PUT THE BRAKES ON. AT THE CLIMAX OF LAST YEAR'S FESTIVAL, WHEN WE HAD THE SCHOOL-WIDE GAME OF TAG, THE CASUALTIES ROSE TO TEN THOUSAND...
RUMBLE RUMBLE
HEE, HEE, HEE...♡
TEN THOUSAND!?
DWAH!!
COME ON, DON'T TELL THEM THAT. THEY'LL THINK IT'S TRUE.
GOOD MORNING!
GOOD MORNING, SETCHAN!

ANYWAY, I'M KINDA CONFUSED, BUT IT SOUNDS LIKE FUN! I'M GLAD I TRANSFERRED HERE!
I'M GETTING EXCITED! AREN'T YOU, NEGI?
EH...?
Y-YEAH, I GUESS SO.
BAM BAM
ACADEMY MARTIAL-ARTS FESTIVAL SIGN-UPS HERE
WAAH
HA HA HA
OH! ♪ THEY HAVE A MARTIAL ARTS TOURNAMENT! LET'S SIGN UP, NEGI!
CLAMOR CLAMOR
EEH? NO, THAT'S OKAY! BESIDES, I'M LATE!
......
HUH.

THEY DIDN'T HAVE ANYTHING LIKE THIS AT YOUR SCHOOL, ANIKI. DOESN'T IT SOUND LIKE FUN?
YEAH... I WONDER IF MY CLASS IS GOING TO DO ANYTHING.
USUALLY, CLASSES DO A PLAY OR A HAUNTED HOUSE OR A CAFE OR SOMETHING.
WOW, OKAY.
GOOD MORNING-!
RATTLE

PLEASE COME IN!
WELCOME ♥ TO CLASS 3-A'S MAID CAFÉ, ALBIONIS!!
WAAAH?!
WH-WH-WHAT IS ALL THIS!?
MWAHA!?
3-A HAS DECIDED TO RUN A MAID CAFÉ FOR THE FESTIVAL.
GUTS
THIS SCHOOL LETS US KEEP THE MONEY WE EARN!
THIS IS A GREAT OPPORTUNITY TO COLLECT SOME EXTRA CASH!
I DON'T REALLY KNOW WHAT A "MAID CAFÉ" IS, BUT AT THE EARNEST REQUEST OF MY CLASSMATES, I HAVE PREPARED COSTUMES FOR US ALL ♥
HO HO HO!
SUCKERS AND RICH PEOPLE- -IT'S ALL IN HOW YOU USE THEM.
WOW.
HEH HEH HEH
WHAT A NICE THING TO DO.
I KNOW! NEGI-KUN, YOU BE OUR FIRST CUSTOMER!
ワイワイ
CLAMOR
CLAMOR
YEAH! WE NEED TO PRACTICE!
JUST A—
EH?
WAAAH!

SQUEE SQUEE
NOW, NOW, NEGI-KUN. PLEASE, HAVE A DRINK ♡
シャカ SHAKKA
シャカ SHAKKA
THANKS
シャカ SHAKKA
OH, THEY'RE GOOD. I'M IMPRESSED.
HERE, WOULD YOU LIKE ME TO ADD SOME MILK?
HUBBA HUBBA! ♡
HA HA HA

NEGI-KUUUN! MAY I ORDER A COCKTAIL, TOO?
SARATOGA COOLER...
MENU
A-ALRIGHT.
GO AHEAD.
OOH, YOU'RE SUCH A GENEROUS SPENDER, BOSS!!
FIDDLE FIDDLE
OOOOH! I DROPPED THE CORKSCREW DOWN MY CLEAVAGE! GET IT OUT, NEGI-KUN ♡
!?
PFFT!
SPLAT

ER, UM... JUST WHAT IS GOING ON HERE...?
HUMINA HUMINA!
...
OH, COME ON, NEGI-KUN! THIS IS THE ADULT WORLD ♡

ALL RIGHT, I'M RINGING YOU UP ♡
BEEP
BOOP
BOP
BOP
THAT WILL BE 7800 YEN*.
DING
BALLOONING
EEEEEH!?
HEY, HEY
ST-STUN
THAT'S HIGHWAY ROBBERY!
WHAT KIND OF CAFÉ IS THIS?!
NEGI-KUN, LOOK, LOOK! WE HAVE ALL KINDS OF OTHER COSTUMES, TOO!
BA-BAM
*$78

DU-DUN!!
YEAH!
EH...?
SO...
THAT WILL BE 12,000 YEN*.
PAY UP.
AAAK!
JUST FOR LOOKING!?
WHY AM I THE ONLY BUNNY?
WHY WON'T YOU DRESS UP, AKO?
I-IT'S TOO EMBARRASSING...
YOU'RE TOTALLY MISSING THE POINT!
YOU'RE NOT EVEN MAIDS ANYMORE!
AWWW, BUT WE WANNA WEAR ALL KINDS OF COSTUMES.
THEN WE EARN MONEY, AND NEGI-KUN LEARNS THE HARSH REALITIES OF THE ADULT WORLD. IT'S THREE BIRDS WITH ONE STONE.
ARE YOU STUPID!?
*$120
THERE'S STILL SOMETHING MISSING, THO'...
SOMETHING... Y'KNOW, TO REALLY DRAW IN THE CUSTOMERS.
YOU'RE RIGHT.
OKAY... TATSUMIYA, YOU BE A PRIESTESS!!
WHAT?
FWIP
YOU BE A NUN IN A MINI-SKIRT!
EH...?
'KAY.
YOU WEAR CAT EARS AND A SCHOOL SWIMSUIT!!!
EH!?
I DON'T UNDERSTAND WHY...
M-MINI-SKIRTED, CAT-EARED NURSE!!
EEEK!
WHAT THE HECK!?
HMMM... K-KINDERGARTENERS!!
KINDER-!?

YAY!
NOOOO!
DU-DU-DUN
FOR-GIVE ME, I HAVE SINNED
THESE HAKAMA ARE SO SHORT...
OOH!
SETSU
FUMIKA
HAVE WE GONE TOO FAR...?
YES...
CRAP.
HEY!
YOU JERKS!
THIS SHOULD BE PLENTY!!
W...
WELCOME.
BAAAM!!
のどか
OOOH!?
A NORMAL KIND OF CUTE!
I DIDN'T THINK OF THAT!
THAT'S JUST NOT FAIR!
23,000 YEN*.
EEEK!
*$280
20,000 YEN*!
PAY UP.
Y-YES, MA'AM.
ANIKI!
*$200
HEH HEH HEH. YOU TWO JUST DON'T GET IT.
NODOKA? WEAR THIS.
O-OKAY.
WITH GIRLS LIKE OURS, WE NEED A *LIGHT* TOUCH. NO SENSE IN GILDING THE LILY.

THESE GUYS ARE HOPELESS. THEY DON'T KNOW ANYTHING.
FIRST OF ALL, THE POINT OF MAIDS IS...
CLAMOR CLAMOR
THEY SHOULD JUST LET ME HANDLE EVERYTHING. I COULD GET FIVE HUNDRED, A THOUSAND CUSTOMERS, EASY.
ARRRGH! I CAN'T TAKE IT ANY-MORE!!!
TREMBLE
MUTTER MUTTER
SQUEE SQUEE
IRK IRK IRK IRK! IRK!
LISTEN UP, YOU BUNCH OF MORONS!! THE GREAT CHIU-SAMA IS ABOUT TO TEACH YOU THE TRUE ESSENCE OF A MAID CAFÉ...
B-BAH
...
ER....
DOOM
WHAT ARE YOU LOT DOING!? IT'S TOO EARLY IN THE MORNING FOR THIS NONSENSE!
EEEK!
NITTA-SENSEI! WE WERE DILIGENTLY DISCUSSING OUR CLASS'S CONTRIBUTION TO THE SCHOOL FESTIVAL...
KYAAA
KYAAA
HOMEROOM IS OVER!! I EXPECTED BETTER OF YOU, NEGI-SENSEI!
EEEP~~
SEIZA! ALL OF YOU!
EEEK~
BACAW
BACAW
THOSE GIRLS ARE AS RAMBUNC-TIOUS AS EVER, HUH?
HA, HA, HA.
....
NN? SOME-THING WRONG, ANIKI?
NOTH-ING!
I HAVE TO GET TO MASTER'S FOR MY TRAINING!
TMP
YEAH! YOU'RE A BUSY KID, ANIKI!

I'M HOME!
WEL-COME BACK, NEGI.
KONOKA SAID SHE WAS GOING TO STAY AT THE HEADMASTER'S WITH SETSUNA-SAN TONIGHT.
THEY HAD SOMETHING TO DO THERE OR SOMETHING.
OH... ALL RIGHT.
HEY, YOU'RE KIND LISTLESS... DID YOU GO TRAIN AT EVA-CHAN'S ON THE WAY HOME AGAIN?
YES.
フラ WOBBLE
フラ WOBBLE
WHERE'S CHAMO?
CHAMO-KUN HAD SOMEWHERE TO GO, TOO...
SOMETHING ABOUT GETTING A DRINK WITH CHACHAZERO-SAN. THEY'RE REALLY HITTING IT OFF LATELY.

....
NEGI.
HUH?

YOU HAVEN'T GOTTEN OVER THAT LAST INCIDENT YET, HAVE YOU?
!

YOU WERE DEPRESSED ALL DAY TODAY. I COULD TELL.
H-HOW COULD YOU KNOW THAT...?
AWAH-WAH!
HEH HEH
I'VE GOT YOU PRETTY WELL FIGURED OUT.
I ALSO KNOW THAT YOU'VE BEEN CRYING YOURSELF TO SLEEP EVERY NIGHT.
WHA--?!
GULP
A-ASUNA-SAN...!

ふぁさ…
FWISH
......COME ON.
IT'S BEEN A WHILE. YOU CAN SLEEP WITH ME TONIGHT.
EH... ?
UM! EH...?
B-DMP
TH... THAT'S OKAY! I SHOULDN'T --!
I CAN SLEEP BY MYSELF!
WHY SO SHY ALL OF A SUDDEN? JUST A LITTLE WHILE AGO, YOU COULDN'T WAIT TO CRAWL INTO MY BED.
NO! UM, THAT IS ...
JUST GET UP HERE!
TH... THANK YOU.
...IT'S NO BIG DEAL.
I DIDN'T REALIZE YOU HATED THE NIGHT TIME SO MUCH UNTIL THE OTHER DAY.
...YOU REALLY ARE AN IDIOT.
YOU FINALLY MADE A FRIEND,
ERK ...
BUT YOU KEEP TRYING TO ACT TOUGH AND KEEP ALL YOUR PROBLEMS TO YOURSELF.
KIDS AREN'T SUPPOSED TO BE TOUGH.
I DON'T KNOW WHAT'S BOTHERING YOU...
BUT DON'T WORRY ABOUT IT TONIGHT. GET A GOOD NIGHT'S SLEEP.

. . . .
THANK YOU . . .
ASUNA-SAN...
WHA ...
WH... WH-WH...
TWEE-TWEE-TWEE-TWEE
CHIRP CHIRP
TWEET TWEET
CHIRP CHIRP
WHAT ON EARTH ...?
. . . NN ?
EH ?
CHIRP CHIRP
AH ?!
KYAAA!? HEY, WHAT DO YOU THINK YOU'RE DOING, NEGI!?
WHY ARE YOU TAKING MY PAJAMAS OFF!?
RAR
RAR
HMMM... I DIDN'T REALIZE YOU AND ANIKI HAD GOTTEN SO CLOSE...
EH? WHAH ?!
ASUNA-SAN AND NEGI-SENSEI...
I-IT'S OKAY, ASUNA! I WON'T TELL A SOUL!
JUST A--! THAT'S--! NO! IT'S NOT WHAT YOU THINK!! HEY, WAKE UP ALREADY, STUPID NEGI!
CLANG CLANG

3-A STUDENT PROFILE

SEAT NUMBER 30
SATSUKI YOTSUBA

BORN MAY 12, 1988
BLOOD TYPE: A
LIKES: COOKING, HAVING OTHERS ENJOY HER FOOD, TAKING IT EASY

DISLIKES: NOTHING IN PARTICULAR... DOESN'T LIKE COMPETITION

AFFILIATIONS: LUNCH REPRESENTATIVE, COOKING CLUB

NEGIMA!
MAGISTER NEGI MAGI
CHAO BAO ZI
超包子
DINER CAR CAFÉ
73RD PERIOD:
SOFT ON THE OUTSIDE, FIRM ON THE INSIDE!

チュン
CHIRP CHIRP
チュン
TWEET
チチ
ALLL-RIGHT! I THINK WE'RE GONNA BE ON TIME TODAY ♪
IF ONLY IT COULD BE LIKE THIS EVERY MORNING.
BUT WE'RE STILL RUNNING.
UT IF WE'RE SO EARLY, WHY DID WE LEAVE WITHOUT REAKFAST?
BECAUSE! WHILE THE SCHOOL'S PREPARING FOR THE FESTIVAL, THERE'S A SPECIAL TREAT FOR EVERYONE!
OVER ERE, EGI-KUN! OOK!

CLAMOR
ワァ
CLAMOR
ワァ
CHAO BAO ZI
超包子
STREETCAR DINER
BUZZ
ガヤ
BUZZ
ガヤ
SPECIAL "FESTIVAL" PRICING!
YUM-YUM DIM SUM
CHAO BAO ZI
CHEAP!! FAST!! DELICIOUS!!
OOOOHH?
YOWZA!

CLAMOR
CLAMOR
EIGHT XIAOLONG-BAO, COMING UP
THE USUAL!
SHRR
BUZZ
BUZZ
OH... NEGI-SENSEI.
BUZZ

WOW, SO THIS IS CHAO-SAN AND HER FRIENDS' FOOD CART.
BUSINESS IS BOOMING. DO THEY HAVE A FOOD-SELLER'S PERMIT?
HUH? WOW. THEY'RE USING THE STREETCAR AS A FOOD STAND!
MURMUR
MURMUR
YOU KNOW THAT CHAO-SAN'S DIM SUM IS AMAZING, RIGHT, NEGI? THIS CART IS REALLY POPULAR EVERY YEAR.
WE'RE BIG FANS, TOO. THAT'S WHY WE GET UP EARLY TO HAVE SOME WHEN FESTIVAL TIME COMES AROUND.
IT'S DELICIOUS!

SS...

SMILE
FOR YOU

OH! THANK YOU, YOTSUBA-SAN!
OH! LUCKY NEGI-KUN!

OUR SPECIAL STAMINA SOUP, ON THE HOUSE.
...TO CHEER YOU UP
UM, THANKS.

UM...
KŪ-SAN TOLD ME... YOU'RE WORKING HARD AT YOUR TRAINING.

BUT...
YOU SHOULDN'T PUSH YOURSELF TOO HARD... YOU'LL MAKE YOURSELF SICK...

YOUR BODY IS AN IMPORTANT ASSET...
YOU'RE NOTHING WITHOUT YOUR HEALTH ♥
GH
ぐっ
UM, Y-YES, MA'AM!
UM... WHY ARE YOU GIVING ME FREE FOOD...?
BECAUSE YOU'VE SEEMED KIND OF DOWN LATELY...
I KNOW IT'S HARD TO TRAIN...
SMILE
BUT WORK HARD AT YOUR TEACHING, TOO...♥
ペコ...
BOW
YOT-SUBA-SAN IS SUCH A NICE PER-SON.
SHE HAS A KINDA CUTE WAY OF TALKING.
OOH, NEGI-KUN! YOU ONLY JUST NOTICED?
YOTSUBA-SAN IS INCRED-IBLE. SHE'S A MASTER CHEF, FOR ONE THING.
YOU'RE HER TEACHER. YOU SHOULD KNOW MORE ABOUT YOUR STUDENTS!
HMM, THEY'RE RIGHT... NOTHING WILL COME OF MY WORRYING ABOUT MY OWN PROBLEMS ALL THE TIME.
WE HAVE A BIG FESTIVAL COMING UP, AFTER ALL. I HAVE TO GET IT TOGETHER, AND BE A BETTER TEACHER.
ALLLL-RIGHT!!
OUR CLASS NEVER DID FINISH DECIDING ON A PROJECT!
I'M GONNA WORK HARD AT MY TEACHING DUTIES! STARTING WITH TODAY'S HOMEROOM!
BAM!
ばーん
ACK! WHERE DID THAT COME FROM?
OOHH! NEGI-KUN'S ON FIRE!
IS IT THE POWER OF THE SOUP!?

DANG
DONG
DING
ER, SO, EVERYONE.
ABOUT OUR CONTRIBUTION TO THE SCHOOL FESTIVAL...
AW, MAN. THAT ONE AIN'T GONNA BE SO EASY, BOSS.
SIGH
CLATTER
EH?
YES...
YEAH. WHAT COULD POSSIBLY DRAW MORE CUSTOMERS THAN A MAID CAFÉ...?
WE JUST DON'T KNOW.
SIGH
CLATTER
ME, ME! ♡
SAKURAKO-SAN!
I THINK WE SHOULD DO A "HEART-POUNDING ALL-GIRL SWIMSUIT BATTLE CAFÉ" ♡
?
?
IT'S PERFECT.
GLINT
IT IS NOT!
WHAT THE HECK!? THAT DOESN'T EVEN MAKE SENSE!
AWWW. DOESN'T IT SOUND FUN?
WAAH
WAAH
NO!!!
THE SUITS COULD, Y'KNOW-- WHOOPS!

I KNOW, I KNOW! AN ALL-GIRL MUD-WRESTLING CAFÉ!
ME
DWAH-HUH?!
EH?!
AN IDIOT SPEAKS!
IDIOT!
JUST A—
YOU WON'T TOP MINE!
STUN
めぎゃっ
A CAT-EAR NUDIE BAR!
DO YOU EVEN KNOW WHAT YOU'RE SAYING?
MAYBE WE SHOULD JUST BE HONEST WITH OURSELVES AND GO WITH A NO-PANTIES BAR?
どーん
DUN
NOW THAT IS IT!!!!
AHA!
I WOULDN'T DO IT, BUT THAT'S IT!
THAT IS NOT "IT"!!!
WHAT KIND OF CAFE IS THAT ANYWAY!? THAT DOESN'T EVEN MAKE SENSE!
THERE ARE RECORDS OF SUCH CAFÉS EXISTING IN THE 80'S
THEY HAVE BEEN OUT-LAWED SINCE.
HOW OLD ARE YOU, MA'AM?
BEE-BEE-BEEP ピピピ
HAS NO-PANTIES TRAUMA.
SS す…
MA'AM ...?
RUMBLE RUMBLE ゴゴゴ
WHAT!?
THAT WAS FAST!
ER, UM, I DON'T UNDERSTAND ANY OF THIS "ALL-GIRL," "NO-PANTIES" STUFF...
RAR RAR ギャー
WHAT ARE THEY GONNA MAKE US DO?!
TREMBLE TREMBLE ガクガク
SHAKE SHAKE プルプル
MM.
SHAKE SHAKE SHAKE ガクガク
NONE OF YOU EVER NEED TO UNDERSTAND ANY OF THIS.
AND GOOD CHILDREN, YOU MAY NOT UNDERSTAND, EITHER, BUT WHATEVER YOU DO, DO *NOT* ASK YOUR PARENTS. PROMISE YOUR ONE-SAN!
UNDER-STAND?
THEY ALREADY CANCELED OUR MAID CAFÉ BECAUSE YOU LOT COULDN'T KEEP THE NOISE DOWN!!
RAR RAR RAR RAR ギャイギャイ
YOU WERE MAKING NOISE, TOO, CLASS REP!
KYAA キャー
ER, UM, GIRLS!
LET'S BE QUIET...! CALM DOWN!
FLUS-TER
FLUSTER
AWW...
NEGI-KUN'S TRYING SO HARD.
CLAMOR CLAMOR ワイワイ
IT WOULD BE AN HERCULEAN EFFORT TO CALM OUR CLASS.
HE CERTAINLY DOESN'T LOOK LIKE THE HEROIC YOUNG FIGHTER WE SAW THE OTHER DAY, DOES HE?

YOU KNOW... IT MIGHT BE A LITTLE SIMPLISTIC OF US TO TRY AND PLAY UP THE CUTE GIRL ANGLE.

LET'S GO THE OTHER WAY.
OOHH!
AWW!

NEGI-KUN WEARS NO PANTIES ♡
YEAH! ♡
SQUEE
SQUEE
キャッ
キャッ
EEEEEK!!
HEY!!
LADIES!
ANIKI!
アニキ

GIRLS! THAT'S ENOUGH!!
RATTLE
IT'S TOO EARLY IN THE MORNING FOR...

AH...
!?

WHA-WH-WH-WH... WHAT ARE YOU DOING!!!?
SEIZA! ALL OF YOU!
KYAAA.
EEEP!
I KNOW YOU'RE ONLY A CHILD TEACHER, BUT I NEED YOU TO GET BETTER CONTROL OF YOURSELF AND YOUR STUDENTS.
くど
BLAH
くど
BLAH
くど
BLAH
YES, SIR...
GLOOM
しょぼーん

BACAW
アホー
BACAW
アホー
BAM BAM BANG
トンテンカン
BAM BAM BANG
トンテンカン
CLAMOR
ワイ
CLAMOR
ワイ
HIC
ひっく
NHHN...
HNNH...
I'M A FAILURE AS A TEACHER...

AWW... NEGI-KUN'S DE-PRESSED...
NNGH, AND I WAS PART OF THE PROBLEM TODAY.
ANIKI...
HE'S CRYING

NEGI...
LOOK, ASUNA-SAN!
RUSTLE
ガサ

SHH
サァア...
...SMILE ♡

AH...
Y-YO-TSUBA-SAN.
H-HELLO.
RUB RUB
ゴシゴシ

.....
MAY I...TREAT YOU TO DINNER?

...EH?

超包子
HERE YOU ARE.
OOOO HHH!
IT...IT'S DELI-CIOUS!!
THIS IS REALLY GOOD!!
YOU'RE A COOKING GENIUS, YOTSUBA-SAN!
MUNCH
むぐ
MUNCH
もが
NO I'M NOT.
BUZZ
ガヤ
BUZZ
ガヤ
GOOD EVENING.

THERE, SAT-CHAN!
THE USUAL, PLEASE.
HA, HA, HA
MARCH MARCH
ACK! NITTA-SENSEI!?
SAT-CHAN! CAN YOU SQUEEZE US IN?
THERE'S SIX OF US...
BUZZ BUZZ
SMILE
OH! SAT-CHAN BECAUSE HER NAME IS SATSUKI YOTSUBA.
YOU'RE REALLY POPULAR, YOTSUBA-SAN. EVEN TEACHERS AND COLLEGE STUDENTS LIKE YOU.
MMM, THIS IS DELICIOUS!
.....
ARE YOU FEELING... A LITTLE BETTER?
EH...?
UM, YES.
MY DREAM...IS TO OPEN MY OWN RESTAURANT SOMEDAY...
I WANT TO MAKE EVERYONE HAPPY WITH MY FOOD...
....
IF ANYONE CAN DO IT, YOU CAN, YOTSUBA-SAN. I MEAN, YOUR FOOD IS SO GOOD!
WHAT WAS THAT, PUNK!?
CLATTER
AAHH!? YOU GOT A PROB-LEM!?
CLATTER
YOU SAYING GROUND-FIGHTING BEATS PUNCHES? BIG TALK!
YEAH
WELL LET'S FIND OUT! BRING IT ON!
OUT ON THE STREET, NO RULES!!
MURMUR
MURMUR
OH, NO, WHAT ARE THEY DOING? THEY'RE FIGHTING.
YOU KNOW THE COLLEGE ENGINEERING DEPARTMENT AND THE MAHORA MAR-TIAL ARTS CLUB ALWAYS HATED EACH OTHER. IT'S ESPECIALLY BAD THIS TIME OF YEAR...

CLAMOR
CLAMOR
AWAWAH! WHAT DO WE DO? THE COLLEGE STUDENTS ARE GETTING INTO A FIGHT...!
EH?
SS...
ZSH
ZSH
ZSH
YOTSUBA-SAN?!
EEP!
Z-SHN!
KRIK...
MURMUR...
WHOOSH
...!
WHOOSH
H-HEY. IT'S CAPTAIN FEI.
YEAH
MURMUR
MURMUR
YOTSUBA-SAN...
SAT-CHAN...
YŌJIMBŌ KUWABATAKE JŪGORŌ
DUN
GENTLEMEN. FIGHTING IS PROHIBITED HERE.
MUNCH MUNCH

....SAT-CHAN.♡
ワイ ワイ
CLAMOR CLAMOR
WOW ...
YO, CAP'N FEI! YOU'RE AS BEAUTIFUL AS EVER!
WE'D NEVER ACTUALLY FIGHT!
OH, WE'RE JUST PLAYIN'!
HA HA HA
ほのぼの
WARM 'N' FUZZY
AW W W-W!
SHE STOPPED ALL THOSE SCARY PEOPLE WITH JUST ONE SEN-TENCE...-
YOTSUBA-SAN IS INCRED-IBLE!
OF COURSE SHE IS, IM-BECILE.
WAH...! EVA--M-MASTER!?
IN A CLASS FULL OF SNOT-NOSED BRATS, SATSUKI IS JUST ABOUT THE ONLY HUMAN I ACKNOWLEDGE AS BEING WORTH ANYTHING.
R-REALLY ?
SHE'S THE ONLY ONE WITH HER FEET FIRMLY GROUNDED IN REALITY AND HER EYES FIXED FORWARD.
SHE'S THE REAL THING.
SPARKLE キラーン
I SEE ...
LATER!
I'M GOING OUT FOR DRINKS. NO TRAINING TONIGHT.

WHAT A DAY. I LOVE IT WHEN SAT-CHAN SHOWS US HOW IT'S DONE.
HA, HA, HA!
OHH! IF IT ISN'T NEGI-SENSEI!
THIS IS A TREAT!
WAH !
I WAS TOO HARD ON YOU EARLIER. IT'S NOT FAIR OF ME TO SPEAK TO LIKE THAT WHEN YOU HAVE CLASS 3-A TO DEAL WITH.
EH ?
UM, YES.
HA HA HA
COME NOW, HAVE A DRINK.
AH! NO, NITTA-SAN, DON'T! LET'S GIVE NEGI-KUN THIS SWEETER DRINK.

CLAMOR
CLAMOR
AH HA-HA-HA
CHAO BAO ZI
超包子
HNNH... NHHN...
I... I...
O-OH, DEAR. WHAT'S WRONG, NEGI-KUN?
SERUHIKO-KUN. WHAT DID YOU GIVE HIM?
IS HE GONNA BE OKAY...?
WELL, HE HAS THOSE TEACHERS WITH HIM...
SERUHIKO-KUN, THIS IS AMAZAKÉ!
WHAT!? OOPS! I
OH, MAN...
NNGH... HNNH!
YOTSUBA-SAN, NITTA-SAN, I'M A FAILURE AS A TEACHER...
HRRM, HE CRIES WHEN HE'S DRUNK...
SHOULD I MAKE HIM SOMETHING TO SOBER HIM UP?
I'M WORTHLESS...
HOW CAN YOU SAY THAT, NEGI-KUN? YOU'RE DOING VERY WELL.
JUST FORGET ABOUT THIS AFTERNOON.
CHEER UP!
NNGH
HEY, THERE, NITTA-SAN. FANCY MEETING YOU HERE.
HELLO, SAT-CHAN. MIND IF I JOIN YOU?
OH, HAVE A SEAT.
CHAO BAO ZI
AH...

IT'S BEEN A WHILE, NEGI-KUN.

TAKA-MICHI ......
I HEAR YOU'VE BEEN GOING THROUGH A LOT. ...SORRY I HAVEN'T BEEN AROUND TO HELP.
WHEW

WOW, TAKAHATA-SENSEI. HE'S SO HOT...
SEE, SHE LIKES HIM!
OHHH

NEGI-KUN. EVA TELLS ME YOU'VE GOTTEN A LOT STRONGER.
WHAT DO YOU SAY TO A SPARRING MATCH WITH ME? I PROMISED YOU WHEN YOU WERE A KID THAT I'D TEST YOUR STRENGTH.

......
NHHN ...

HUH ?
SOB SNIFFLE
HIC!
IT'S NOT TRUE! I'M NOT STRONG AT ALL!
WAH
WHOA, THERE, NEGI-KUN. WHAT'S WRONG?
ACTUALLY, TAKAHATA-KUN, WE SEEM TO HAVE GIVEN HIM SOME AMAZAKE...

ALL I'VE EVER DONE IS RUN AWAY... HNNH! ...
HNNH!
I... I'M A FAILURE AS A TEACHER... AND A FAILURE AS A WIZARD ~~~!
WAAAAAHHH!
うわあああ～ん
WHOOPS, NEGI-KUN. LET'S BE CAREFUL OF OUR VOCABU-LARY, OKAY?
CHAO BAO ZI
超包子

...I THINK IT WOULD BE BEST NOT TO MOVE HIM FOR A WHILE.
HE'S STILL A CHILD.
KŪ FEI, CAN HE SLEEP HERE TONIGHT?
NNGH...
IS A-OK!

SORRY ABOUT THIS KŪ FEI, SAT-CHAN! I'LL STOP BY TOMOR-ROW WHEN I'M MAKING DELIVER-IES.
THANK YOU!
LEAVE TO US!
SOFT
RUSTLE
パサ...

超包子

I'M A FAIL-URE AS A TEACH-ER...
MMNYA MMNYA
SNIFFLE
ぐすっ...

SWEEP
SWEEP
SWEEP...
NGH
...?
CHIRP
CHIRP
SWEEP
SWEEP
SWEEP
CHIRP
TWEET TWEET
AH
...
SWEEP
SWEEP
...
...GOOD MORNING!
UM...I'M SORRY FOR THE TROUBLE I CAUSED LAST NIGHT...
OH... YOU REMEMBER WHAT HAPPENED...?
YES...
THEY DO SAY THE BRITISH CAN HOLD THEIR LIQUOR.
CHIRP
CHIRP
SWEEP
SWEEP
SWEEP
....
YOU AMAZE ME, YOTSUBA-SAN.

YOU KNOW EXACTLY WHAT YOUR DREAM IS FOR THE FUTURE...
YOU WORK SO HARD AT COOKING EVERY DAY...

YOU WORK HARD, TOO.
YOU WORK HARD AT YOUR TEACHING AND YOUR TRAINING, NEGI-SENSEI...
...NO, I'M HOPE-LESS.
SOMEONE TOLD ME ONCE...
..AND THEY WERE EXACTLY RIGHT.

THEY SAID MY STUDYING TO BE A TEACHER, AND MY TRAIN-ING TO BE STRONGER...
IT'S ALL FAKE-- ALL OF IT. I'M ONLY DOING IT TO RUN AWAY FROM MY PAINFUL MEMORIES OF THE PAST.

WHEN I THINK THAT THAT'S WHY I'M A TEACH-ER,
I'M...SO ASHAMED ...TO FACE ALL OF YOU...
SOFT
YOU'VE GOT IT ALL WRONG.
THERE'S NOTHING FAKE ABOUT IT..

WHETHER YOU GAINED THAT STRENGTH OUT OF A GRUDGE OR FROM TRYING TO ESCAPE...
IT'S STILL YOUR STRENGTH, AND I THINK IT'S WONDERFUL, NEGI-SENSEI!!

...
DON'T BE ASHAMED!
CMON!
CHIN UP ♡
BAM!
WAH!
SMILE.. ♡

SINCE WE COULDN'T COME TO A CONSENSUS ON OUT FESTIVAL PROJECT, I'VE MADE AN IMPARTIAL SELECTION FROM ALL OF YOUR IDEAS BY DRAWING LOTS.
HISTORICAL (PERIOD) CAFÉ 𝍸 I
PUT ON A PLAY 𝍸 I
HAUNTED HOUSE 𝍸 I
FORTUNE-TELLING TENT 𝍸 I
CHINESE RESTAURANT 𝍸 I
SWIMSUIT SUM
CAT-EARED NU
AND SO CLASS 3-A WILL BE PUTTING ON A HAUNTED HOUSE FOR THE FESTIVAL.
IS...IS THAT ALL RIGHT?
SILENCE...
UM, ER...
EEP ?!
N-NO GOOD !?
!?
!?
CLATTER
CLATTER
CLATTER
GOOD!
GRIN
SURE, WHY NOT!!
...AH.
HEH-HEH!
ALLLL-RIGHT!!! NOW THAT THAT'S SETTLED, LET'S GET SCARY!!!
THERE ARE SO MANY DIFFERENT WAYS TO APPROACH A HAUNTED HOUSE!!
OOO-HHH !♡
WELL, IT'D BE BORING TO DO A NORMAL HAUNTED HOUSE. LET'S DO A NUDIST HAUNTED HOUSE!!
THAT! THAT'S IT!!
YAAAH! TAKE NEGI-KUN'S CLOTHES OFF!
I SERIOUSLY DO NOT GET YOU GUYS!
KYAA
EEEHH !?
WHY ME ??
AH-STOP-NOO-OOO-!
NOOOOO!
KYAAA

KYAAAA!
CLANG CLANG
AND THEN NITTA SHOWED UP!
NITTA, THE OGRE OF MAHORA JUNIOR HIGH?
HA, HA, HA!
I
DO ANY OF YOU...
HNNH...

KNOW ANYONE WHO ISN'T A BAD KID, BUT THEY JUST DON'T STAND OUT, OR THEY HAVE A VERY WEAK PRESENCE...?
SOMEONE WHO YOU NEVER REALLY KNOW IF THEY'RE THERE OR NOT?
OF COURSE YOU DO, RIGHT? THERE'S ONE IN EVERY CLASS...

ACTUALLY, I'M ONE OF THAT TYPE, TOO.
YOU SEE, I
....

...AM A GHOST.
GLOOM
どよ〜ん
NEGIMA!
MAGISTER NEGI MAGI
74TH PERIOD: I'VE BEEN HERE ALL ALONG...
WELL, THERE'S NOTHING I CAN DO ABOUT IT. I AM A GHOST, AFTER ALL...
NOW, LET'S CONTINUE OUR VOTE...
WHO WANTS TO DO A HAUNTED HOUSE!?
HAUNTED HOUS
FORTUNE-TEL
TENT
CHINESE RESTAURANT
SWIMSUIT SUM
CAT-EARED N

ME ♪
ME TOO. ♡
A HAUNTED HOUSE...
IF WE DO THAT, THEN THERE MIGHT BE SOMETHING I CAN DO TO HELP...
HE WON'T SEE IT, BUT...
ME...
KŪ FEI-SAN...
YŪNA-SAN...
SAKURAKO-SAN...
KASUGA-SAN...
AISAKA-SAN...
KAEDE-SAN...
...THAT'S SIX.
EH?
DID HE...?
ALLLRIGHT! NOW THAT THAT'S SETTLED, LET'S GET SCARY!!
THERE ARE SO MANY DIFFERENT WAYS TO APPROACH A HAUNTED HOUSE!!
OOO-HHH! ♡
CLAMOR
CLAMOR
...DID I IMAGINE IT...?

DONG
DING
DANG
CLAMOR
CLAMOR
AH, HA, HA!
SEE YOU LATER!
BYE!
I'M SAYO AISAKA.
I'VE BEEN A GHOST TIED TO THIS SCHOOL FOR MORE THAN 60 YEARS.
I SIT IN THE FRONT-ROW SEAT BY THE WINDOW IN MAHORA JUNIOR HIGH'S THIRD FLOOR CLASS-ROOM A.
PEOPLE SAY THEY FEEL A CHILL WHEN THEY SIT THERE.
SO SOME-WHERE ALONG THE WAY, IT BECAME A KIND OF "FORBIDDEN SEAT."
CHATTER
CHATTER
I...DON'T HAVE MUCH TALENT FOR BEING A GHOST.
UM
BOO
BOO
I JUST DON'T QUITE HAVE ENOUGH PRESENCE OR SOME-THING...
SILENCE
I CAN'T GET ANYONE TO NOTICE ME.
SQUEE
SQUEE

AND I SCARE VERY EASILY.
KLUNK
HEEK!
A RAPPING NOISE?
WHO'S THERE!?
AT NIGHT, THE SCHOOL SEEMS LIKE IT'S HAUNTED. IT'S JUST TOO TER-RIFYING.

SO LATELY, I'VE BEEN SPENDING THE NIGHT AT THE NEARBY CONVENIENCE STORE OR AN ALL-NIGHT RESTAURANT.
FEEL SAFE AT LATE-NIGHT CONVENIENCE STORES. (OH, I AM TIED TO THE SCHOOL, BUT AS LONG AS I STAY CLOSE BY, I CAN WALK AROUND.)
MAGGY
SEASONAL LUNCHES

AH, HA, HA!
GIGGLE GIGGLE
ART CLUB
...THAT LOOKS FUN.

I'M JUST A GHOST, AND NOT EVEN A VERY GOOD ONE.
SNIFFLE
ぐすっ…
BUT I'M CURRENTLY LOOKING FOR A FRIEND.

YES. I KNOW I'M WORTH-LESS.
I HAVE A GLOOMY PERSONAL-ITY, AND I'M A GHOST...
HEH HEH HEH...!!

BUT EVEN A GHOST
GETS A LITTLE LONELY, GOING YEARS WITHOUT ANYONE TO TALK TO.

SWOOP...
すすすっ...
NEGI-KUN. THE BOY TEACHER WHO WAS PUT IN CHARGE OF MY CLASS LAST WINTER...

ひら WAVE
ひら WAVE
OF COURSE HE CAN... NOT SEE ME.

UM! H...
HELLO!
......

I KNEW IT WAS HOPE-LESS...
ずーん GLOOM
がくっ... SLUMP

TRIP ガッ
EEP!?
べちゃっ SPLAT
HNNH...
NNHN...

HOW CAN I TRIP? I DON'T EVEN HAVE FEET!
ふええっ WAAH!
I'M THE WORST, MOST WORTHLESS GHOST IN THE WHOLE WIDE WORLD!

...

?

?
IS SOME-THING WRONG?
EH? OH, NOTH-ING...
I GUESS I IMAGINED IT...
EH...?

S-SO NEGI-SENSEI REALLY DOES NOTICE ME? JUST A LITTLE?
AND WHEN HE SAID MY NAME, HE DIDN'T REALIZE IT...?
MY PRESENCE IS SO WEAK THAT NOT EVEN THE STRONGEST EXORCISTS OR SPIRITUALISTS CAN SEE ME, BUT *HE DID*...!!
THERE MIGHT BE HOPE FOR ME AFTER ALL...

LIKE WE SAID, WE'RE GONNA BE STAYING REALLY LATE IN THE CLASSROOM EVERY NIGHT, GETTING READY FOR THE FESTIVAL. SO JUST LOOK THE OTHER WAY, OKAY ♡
PLEASE LEAVE BY NINE O'CLOCK! IT'S THE RULE!

IN THE CLASS-ROOM LATE AT NIGHT...

....
MAYBE THEY CAN'T SEE ME IN THE DAY, BUT AT NIGHT...

A... ALLL-RIGHT! THIS YEAR I'M GOING TO DO IT!!
I'M GOING TO MAKE SOME FRIENDS!!
GH!

THE NEXT DAY

CHIRP チュン CHIRP チュン

BUZZ BUZZ ざわざわ

THE GHOST RETURNS TO CLASS 3-A

Cell phone in hand, Ako Izumi successfully captured the spirit on film. Says Izumi, "Oh, man, I was so freaked, I had no idea what was going on. I'd heard the rumors that our class was haunted, but no ghost ever appeared while I was here, so I thought it was one of those 'seven wonders' people always talk about.

PHOTOGRAPH COURTESY OF 3-A'S NURSE'S AIDE, AKO IZUMI

But it's true that we don't have a seat Number 1 in our class, and it's weird that people get chills whenever they sit there..."

Izumi denies suspicions of photo doctoring. "I mean, my head hurts just looking at a computer. There's no way I could doctor anything."

DEAN OF JR. HIG STUDENTS

ABOVE: First to see the ghost was Fuka Narutaki, who reportedly wet her pants and hen passed out.

"Yes, she said it was like a voice from Hell itself and the owner of the voice ared fro the ss!" end a

in the 3-A class room, according to Ako Izumi. This reporter asked Waisumi, "Your friend alsc heard the apparit eak, is so"

It was last night around 7:00 p.m. that working on a project f Festival the lass o

MAHORA SPORTS

麻帆大曲芸部

GOT-CHA!
CLAMP
EEK!
TWIST
IF I HAD TO PUT IT IN WORDS, IT HAD A "REAL-ISTIC" FEEL TO IT. ...IN FACT, I WAS SURE IT WAS ANOTHER INCIDENT RELATED TO NEGI-SENSEI...
MURMUR
MURMUR
I THOUGHT SO, TOO.
NOD NOD NOD-NOD NOD
HMMM, BUT I'VE NEVER SEEN A GHOST, EITHER...
THERE'VE BEEN RUMORS THAT OUR CLASS IS HAUNTED FOR FOREVER. BUT NO ONE'S SEEN ANY GHOSTS FOR YEARS...
DARNIT, IF ONLY I HADN'T BEEN IN THE BATH-ROOM.
KYA-AA-AA!
MURMUR MURMUR
GIGGLE GIGGLE
I THINK IT'S REAL.
BLACK-VINEGAR TOMATO MILK

NEGI-KUN, NEGI-KUN! CAN YOU DO SOMETHING!? NO ONE WILL STAY AND HELP IF WE'VE GOT GHOSTS SHOWING UP!
PROGRESS IS SLOW ENOUGH WITH EVERYBODY IN CLASS HAVING ALL THEIR CLUB ACTIVITIES.
R-RIGHT.

MAYBE WE OUGHTTA PUT TOGETHER A GHOST BUSTING SQUAD...
OH!? LIKE A TEST TO SEE WHO'S BRAVEST!? I LIKE IT ♪
GLINT
YOU LIKE ANYTHING FUN.
HM-M-M...
WHAT'S WRONG, NEGI-KUN?
ACTUALLY, I'VE BEEN WONDERING ABOUT THIS FOR A WHILE. THE ROSTER THAT TAKAMI- -I MEAN, TAKAHATA-SENSEI GAVE ME...

......
AH.
IS THIS THE GHOST IN THAT PHOTO?
1. SAYO AISAKA
1940~
DON'T CHANGE HER SEAT

ずーん
GLOOM
I THINK THEY GOT THE WRONG IDEA...
ALL BECAUSE I'M SO UN-PHOTOGENIC . . .
ぐすっ
SNIFFLE
HHN...
NNH...
CLAMOR
ワイ
ワイ
CLAMOR
I WONDER WHAT THAT IS...?
BAM!!
ドーーン!!
ZSH!
ザッ!
Exorcism
Exorcism
Spirit Trap
Spirit Trap
"CLASS 3-A SEAT NUMBER 1 GHOST: SAYO AISAKA" EXTERMINATION TEAM
NOW LET'S KICK SOME PARANORMAL BUTT!
HEH, HEH, HEH.
THESE EXORCIST GUNS WERE INVENTED BY CLASS 3-A'S VERY OWN CHAO AND HER SCIENCE TEAM ♪
I-I'M COUNTING ON YOU, SAKURAKO-SAN.
OKAY, YOU GOT IT ♡
I DIDN'T KNOW YOU WERE SUCH A FRAIDY-CAT, CLASS REP.
ワーワー
CLAMOR
CLAMOR
DO THOSE WORK?
WE BRING REFRESHMENTS.
HERE! ♡
OOH ♡ THANKS!
Spirit Trap

CLAMOR ワイワイ CLAMOR
SQUEE キャッ キャッ SQUEE
MY HEART'S POUNDING!
WHY DID WE TURN THE LIGHTS OFF?
FOR AMBIENCE, DUH! ♪
I WONDER WHAT THEY'RE DOING...
SO THERE REALLY ARE SUCH THINGS AS GHOSTS, NEGI-KUN?
NOT THAT ANYTHING SURPRISES ME ANYMORE.
YES... MOST OF THEM ARE PEOPLE WHO STAYED IN THIS WORLD BECAUSE THEY HAVE SOME KIND OF ATTACHMENT OR GRUDGE...
BUT SOMETIMES THERE ARE EVIL SPIRITS, LIABLE TO CAUSE TROUBLE FOR EVERYONE.
WHAT'D YOU FIND OUT ABOUT HER, ASAKURA-NĒSAN.
EVERYTHING. SAYO AISAKA, DIED IN 1940.
SHE WAS INDEED A STUDENT AT THIS SCHOOL.
SHE DIED AT THE YOUNG AGE OF FIFTEEN.
MM. THAT'S GOTTA BE OUR GHOST.

I DON'T KNOW WHAT'S KEEPING HER HERE, BUT THE KIND THING WOULD BE TO HELP HER MOVE ON.
RIGHT, ANIKI?
Y-YEAH. RIGHT.
SAYO AISAKA-SAN... BUT...
SHE DOESN'T LOOK LIKE SUCH A BAD PERSON...

WHAT MAKES YOU THINK THAT?
O-OH, IT'S JUST A FEEL-ING...
ANIKI! DON'T BE FOOLED BY HER ROSTER PICTURE.
FIRST WE HAVE TO FIND OUT WHY SHE'S HAUNTING US!
R-RIGHT.
BAM
BAM
WILLING IN
was like a voice from
Hell itself and the
owner of the voice
ALRIGHT! BRING OUT THE SECRET WEAPON!
...MIYAZAKI!!
WINCE
Y-YES'M!!

DON'T LET EVERY-ONE SEE ME...
ADEAT...
FLASH
WITH YOUR BOOK, IF WE KNOW THE GHOST'S NAME, WE SHOULD BE ABLE TO FIND OUT HER MOTIVE.
N-NNNGH, I'M SCARED...
...BUT I'LL DO MY BEST.
OH? WHACHA DOIN'?
CLAMOR
CLAMOR
HEH HEH HEH. WE'VE KEPT IT UNDER WRAPS UNTIL NOW, BUT MIYAZAKI HAS A MYSTERIOUS POWER: SHE CAN CHANNEL SPIRITS.
NNNGH! PLEASE DON'T MAKE IT SOUND SO CREEPY!
H-HERE GOES!
AISAKA-SAN... WHY HAVE YOU COME TO US?
EH?
ME...?
B-DMP
I THINK HER NAME IS MIYAZAKI-SAN?
B-DMP B-DMP B-DMP
HOW DOES SHE KNOW MY NAME?
MIYAZAKI-SAN, FRIEN-N-ND...
FRIEND...
AISAKA, SAYO
JUNE 9TH
I WANT YOU ... TOGETHER, WE... HERE WITH
PLAY TOGETHER...BE FRIENDS.
NODOKA-SAN... BE SO GLAD...

SHE'S ONE OF THE BAD ONES! SHE'S AN EVIL SPIRIT!!
STOMP
BATTLE STATIONS, EVERY-ONE!
SHUT!
STOMP STOMP
FORM A DEFENSIVE CIRCLE!!
EEEEHHHHH!!
SLAM!
NN? FRIEND ...?
OOHH... THEY'VE GOT IT ALL WRONG... WHAT DO I DO?
I HAVE TO DO SOMETHING... BUT WHAT...?
YOU CAN DO IT, SAYO!!
BWOH
RATTLE RATTLE
RATTLE RATTLE
RATTLE RATTLE
RATTLE RATTLE
EH!? WHAT'S HAPPEN-ING!?
KYAAA!
BWOH
I-IT'S HERE!!
GH-GHOOOST!
IT'S A POLTER-GEIST!
EEEK!
WHAT A SCOOP!
WAAAH!
KYAA!
NOW'S MY CHANCE TO SHOW OFF MY PHOTOGRAPHIC SKILLS AND REVEAL THE TRUTH!!
MONEY SHOT!
CLICK
CLICK

A-A-A-ANYWAY, I HAVE TO LET THEM KNOW THEY'RE NOT GETTING IT!
DID I MAKE IT EVEN WORSE...?
WAAAH!
KYAA!
SHAKE
SHAKE
OOOH...
I OVER-DID IT...
DUN
YOU'RE... YOU'RE NOT GET-TING...
EH HEH-HEH-HEH
YŪNA'S POSSESSED!
SHUDDER
SHUDDER
EEEEK! SHE'S WRITING IN BLOOD!
YOU'RE NOT GETTING
YOU'RE NOT GET-TING...? GETTING WHAT!? OUT OF HERE ALIVE!?
OH NO! SHE'S GOING TO TAKE US NEXT! AND THEN KILL US!
EEEK!
FIRE!
SHOOT LIKE THERE'S NO TOMORROW!
NO... YOU'LL HIT YŪNA!
I DON'T CARE!! EXORCISM GUN, FIRE!!!
FLASH
KYAA!
YŪNA!
WAH! IT FIRED! IT ACTU-ALLY FIRED A BEAM!
IT'S THE REAL THING!! THAT'S OUR CHAO!!
HEY! DON'T POINT THAT AT PEOPLE!
EEK!
ZH-BWOOM
KYAA KYAA!
AAAHHH!
IT JUST KEEPS GETTING WORSE!
NNGH
THIS IS A MESS.
IT'S OKAY. I THOUGHT THIS MIGHT HAPPEN, SO I CALLED IN SOME PROFES-SIONALS.
PRO-FES-SION-ALS?

SENSEI! SENSEI!
EEHH ...?!
YOU'LL BE PAYING EXTRA FOR THIS.
DUN
ZAM
SHOULD WE REALLY BE DOING THIS IN FRONT OF EVERY-ONE...?
OOH, SET-CHAN! YOU LOOK AWESOME!
THOSE OUTFITS ARE SOME-THING ELSE.
SHVAH
THERE!
SHNK
SHNK
HEEEK!
S-S-SOME-BODY H-HELP ME!!
YOU WON'T GET AWAY.
BAH
CHAK
WAAH
T-TAT-SUMIYA-SAN, SET-SUNA-SAN, WAIT!
KYAA!
NICE!
NEGI-KUN, NEGI-KUN!
I GOT A PHOTO OF THE GHOST!!
EH!? REALLY!?
HUH... WHA?
SHE'S ACTU-ALLY KIND OF CUTE.
AND SHE'S CRYING ...?
ASAKURA-SAN, I KNEW IT. SHE...

ZS ZS ZS
I CAN HARDLY SEE OUR TARGET AT ALL!
WELL SHE HAS ESCAPED OUR NOTICE THIS LONG. THIS SPIRIT HAS EXCEPTIONALLY HIGH STEALTH ABILITIES.
HOW-EVER.
FLASH
NO ONE ESCAPES MY DEMON EYE.
GZHNG
RATTA TATTA TATTA
WHA IS GOING ON!?
NOOOOOOO!
BLAM
BLAM
BLAM
BLAM
BLAM
WH-WH-
WHY IS THIS HAPPENING TO ME ~~~!?
SET-SUNA-THERE!!
GOT IT!! EVIL SPIRIT, BEGONE! SECRET TECH-NIQUE...
斬魔剣!!!
ZANMA-KEN!
DUN!
YAAAH!
BOOM
EEEEEK!
BLAM
BLAM
BLAM
BLAM
BLAM
HEEEK!
NOOOOOO!

CHAK
ZSH
ZSH
I COMMEND YOU FOR AVOIDING US THIS LONG.
...BUT THIS IS THE END OF THE LINE. IT'S TIME TO PASS ON TO THE NEXT WORLD.
AH...
EEP...
CHAK

W-WAIT, PLEASE!!!

NEGI-SENSEI
FWAH...

PLEASE, TATSUMIYA-SAN. SHE'S NOT A BAD GHOST.
BUT, NEGI-SENSEI...!
OH! I CAN SEE HER ♡
...ALL YOU WANTED WAS A FRIEND. RIGHT, SAYO-CHAN?
GRIN
EH...?
SMILE...

IF I'LL DO...
AND IF I'LL DO...
I DO SIT NEXT TO YOU, AFTER ALL ♡
....
AH...
SS
スゥ…
SHE VAN-ISHED ...
NEGI! HOW DID IT GO?
ASUNA-SAN...

I THINK SHE'S... FINALLY PASSED ON TO NIRVANA.
RING GONG
GOOD... I'M HAPPY FOR HER...
NO... SHE'S STILL HERE...
NIR-VANA? I DIDN'T THINK THE BRIT-ISH...
BOW BOW
I...I'M SORRY.

CLAMOR CLAMOR
AWWW, OVER ALREADY?
I THINK IT'S SAFE NOW.
WISH I COULD'VE SEEN HOW IT ENDED.
AH, HA, HA!
WAS THERE REALLY A GHOST?
ASAKURA-SAN...

BLUSH
NEGI-SENSEI ....

THIS YEAR... SHOULD BE THE BEST YEAR I'VE EVER HAD... ♡
GOOD FOR YOU.
WHOM ARE YOU TALKING TO, MISTRESS?
EH ?

3-A STUDENT PROFILE

SEAT NUMBER 24
SATOMI HAKASE

BORN JULY 14, 1988
BLOOD TYPE: B

LIKES: ROBOTS, CURRENT RESEARCH (APPLICATION OF MAGIC TO ENGINEERING)

DISLIKES: ANYTHING UNSCIENFITIC (THE MAGIC SHE IS CURRENTLY USING CAN BE PROVEN EXPERIMENTALLY, SO IT IS NOT UNSCIENTIFIC)

AFFILIATIONS: ROBOT ENGINEERING CLUB (UNIVERSITY), JET PROPULSION CLUB (UNIVERSITY)

Calorie Mate
BLOCK
PROPERTY OF SCIENCE DIVISION
PROPERTY OF SCIENCE
NEGIMA!
MAGISTER NEGI MAGI
75TH PERIOD: THE LOGIC OF WET EYES

RRRIN
GUTEN TAG!
GUTEN TAG!
BEEP BOP BEEP BOP
BOING
KAPOW
FSHH
SCRITCH SCRITCH
NNNGH...
THUD THUD
SPROING SPROING
RIGHT. DINER CAR DUTY TODAY.
I'M SO BUSY DURING THE FESTIVAL. UGH.
HAKASE, DID YOU STAY THE NIGHT AT THE LAB AGAIN?
STOP IT. YOU'LL CATCH COLD.
AH'LL BE FINE!
MAN, SHE'S SUCH A SLOB WHEN IT COMES TO ANYTHING BUT HER RESEARCH.

I'M OFF!
CHIRP
チュン
CHIRP
チュン…
CLAMOR
ワイ
CLAMOR
ワア
CHAO BAO ZI
超包子
OH...! GOOD MORNING.
BOW...
ペコ…
GOOD MORNING, CHA-CHAMARU-SAN!
WE'LL HAVE THE USUAL ♡
HUH? IS SOMETHING DIFFERENT ABOUT YOU TODAY, CHACHAMARU-SAN?
EH...?

OH, I KNOW! YOU PUT YOUR HAIR UP!
IT LOOKS NICE LIKE THAT.
EH?
GOOD MORNING!
GOOD MORNING!
GRR, YOU LATE, HAKASE.
NIHAO, HAKASE!
NEGI-RŌSHI'S BACK TODAY. HE'S A REGULAR NOW.
OHO?
AH?
OOHH, NO, NO, NO, CHA-CHAMARU!

YOU CAN'T PUT YOUR HAIR UP! THAT'S YOUR HEAT SINK!
OH... HAKASE.

WHY DID YOU DO THAT? YOU COULD OVERHEAT!
IF YOU DON'T MAKE SURE TO KEEP THE WHOLE AREA OF YOUR HAIR EXPOSED, THE HEAT WILL BUILD UP AND...
I...
"WHY DID SHE DO IT"? OH, HAKASE-CHAN.
EVEN CHACHAMARU-SAN LIKES TO GET DRESSED UP ♡
"DRES-SED UP"?
I DON'T REMEMBER PROGRAMMING HER FOR THAT...
YES...

DRESSED UP, HUH?
I THINK YOU LOOK LOVELY, CHACHAMARU-SAN.
YEAH! I LIKE IT

EH...? Y-YOU DO?
WH-WH-WHY THANK YOU, VERY MUCH.
W-WELL, I HAD BEST GET BACK TO WORK.
GKH

ガシャ
CLANK
ガシャ
CLANK
CATCH
はしっ
ステ-ン!
SMACK!
MURMUR
ざわっ…
AH!
HERE.
OOHH
おお~っ
ドヨ ドヨ
BUZZ
BUZZ
TH-THANK YOU.
CHACHAMARU-SAN!
ZNN-
ずしっ
ARE YOU ALRIGHT, CHACHAMARU-SAN?
びくっ
WINCE

BADDA BADDA
バラバラ
どよっ
BUZZ
HMM-MM?
WAAH!
AAAH!
WHAT'S GOING ON? CHACHAMARU WOULD NEVER TRIP ON FLAT GROUND. IT'S IMPOSSIBLE.
SHE'S EQUIPPED WITH AN AUTO-BALANCE SYSTEM THAT WOULD KEEP HER STEADY EVEN IF SHE GOT HER FOOT CAUGHT WHILE WEARING HIGH HEELS AND HOLDING A STACK OF BOWLS TWO METERS HIGH IN EACH HAND.
CLAMOR CLAMOR
ワイワイ
I-I AM TERRIBLY SORRY, NEGI-SENSEI. …
AH HA HA
IT'S ALRIGHT.
CHA-CHAMARU. ARE YOU FEELING ALRIGHT?
YES. MY SYSTEMS ARE ALL NORMAL.

HMM.
CHACHA-MARU.
I HAVEN'T TAKEN YOU APART AND RUN A FULL SYS-TEMS CHECK ON YOU IN A LONG TIME. WOULD YOU STOP BY MY LAB AFTER SCHOOL?
EH?
YES...
UNDER-STOOD.
TAKE APART...?
DING
DONG DANG
AND SO EVERY-ONE!
ANYONE WHO CAN HELP GET READY FOR THE FESTIVAL, I'LL SEE YOU HERE AT 7:30!
ASAKURA-SAN, WE ARE NOT TO STAY LATER THAN NINE O'CLOCK!
LIGHTEN UP, CLASS REP
MORE IMPORTANTLY, DO YOU THINK ANYONE FROM OUR CLASS WILL TRY OUT THE SCHOOL FESTIVAL LEGEND THIS YEAR?
WHAT? YOU SERI-OUSLY BELIEVE THAT STUFF?
NO, NO. I HEAR IT REALLY WORKS.
CLAMOR
CLAMOR
WHAT YOU TALKING ABOUT?

YOU KNOW! THE LEGEND THAT SAYS IF YOU CONFESS TO SOMEONE THAT YOU LOVE THEM UNDER THE WORLD TREE ON THE LAST DAY OF THE FESTIVAL,
THE TWO OF YOU WILL GET TOGETHER FOR SURE!
OOH! I NEVER HEAR THIS!
SO ROMANTIC!
CLAMOR
IT'S A PRETTY FAMOUS TRADITION.
THERE'S ANOTHER VERSION THAT SAYS YOU HAVE TO KISS.
SO WHAT? YOU GONNA DO IT?
CLAMOR
OF COURSE NOT. I GOT NO ONE TO TRY IT WITH.
EEHH? WHAT? YOU'RE GONNA TRY THE WORLD TREE LEGEND, KUGIMI?
I SAID I'M NOT!
THERE YOU GO AGAIN, GETTING ALL BASHFUL, KUGIMI.
QUIT IT WITH THE NICK-NAMES!
KUGIMI'S GONNA CON-FESS!
HEY!
....
HMPH... STUPID KIDS.
I'M SURPRISED THEY CAN HAVE THE SAME CONVERSA-TION EVERY YEAR. DON'T THEY EVER GET SICK OF IT?
WE'RE LEAVING, CHA-CHAMARU.
YES.
OH, MISTRESS. HAKASE REQUESTED THAT I GO TO THE UNI-VERSITY FOR MAINTENANCE.
NN? OH. OKAY.
OH! CHA-CHAMARU-SAN'S LEAVING!

IS CHACHAMARU-SAN REALLY A ROBOT?
I THINK SO...
WILL SHE BE OKAY? HAKASE-SAN SAID SHE WAS GOING TO TAKE HER APART.
GOOD QUESTION. HAKASE AND CHAO ARE SUPER GENIUSES, BUT I'VE HEARD THAT DEEP DOWN, THEY'RE DEMONIC MAD SCIENTISTS WHO'VE SOLD THEIR SOULS TO SCIENCE.
W-WOW.
EH?...
WHA?...
もわわ〜〜ん
MWAAAH
I'M GETTING KIND OF WORRIED.
WE SHOULDN'T JUDGE PEOPLE BASED ON RUMORS.
Y-YEAH.
A-ASUNA-SAN!
CHACHAMARU-SAAAN...!

IS IT ALL RIGHT IF WE JOIN YOU?
UM, YES.

THIS IS THE LAB THAT HAKASE AND CHAO ARE RENTING FROM THE MAHORA UNIVERSITY ENGINEERING DEPARTMENT.
IT IS WHERE I WAS BORN.
WOW

XCUSE ME, HAKASE.
KNOCK コン
KNOCK コン
NN?
ズズズズ…
CRACKLE CRACKLE
POWER
EEEEK!
ZH ZH パチッ
ZH ZH パチ
HEEK!
ドカーン
KABOOM
EEEK!
IT'S A MAD SCIENTIST!
SHE'S GONNA TAKE US APART!
OH? WHAT'S THE MATTER, EVERYONE?
HUH?
バチバチバチッ!
CRACKLE CRACKLE RACKLE
SORRY ABOUT THAT.
I WAS IN THE MIDDLE OF AN EXPERIMENT.
しゅうう…
COUGH
ケホッ
FSHH
RIGHT.
ケホッ
COUGH
NOW LET'S GET RIGHT TO YOUR CHECKUP.
ALL RIGHT.
OKAY, LET'S GET THAT SHIRT OFF, SHALL WE?
EH...?

Y-YOU WISH ME TO TAKE IT OFF HERE?
YUP! ♡
チラッ
GLANCE
OH...
SHE'S *NOT* TAKING HER APART.
WHEW.
WHEW.
COME ON, NOW.
Y-YES.
OOOHH ♡ CHACHAMARU-SAN REALLY *IS* A ROBOT.
....
IT'S KINDA PRETTY
YES...
WHY ARE YOU LOOKING DOWN?
SH-SHE'S MY STUDENT...
YO, HAKASE-SAN. DID YOU INVENT CHACHAMARU?
YES, I DID! BUT I'M USING MAGIC TO POWER HER MOVING PARTS.
UNLIKE EVA-SAN'S OTHER DOLLS, CHACHAMARU IS A PRODUCT OF SCIENCE. I DESIGNED EVERYTHING-- HER DRIVERS, FRAME, QUANTUM COMPUTER, AND AI.
BUT I GOT THE BASICS FOR THE AI SYSTEM FROM MIT.
I SEE...
THAT'S WEIRD. YOUR RPM'S ARE ELEVATED, BUT THERE'S NOTHING WRONG WITH YOU.
CHACHAMARU, HOW DO YOU FEEL?
WELL... I FEEL... STRANGE.
I AM NOT SURE HOW TO DESCRIBE IT.
I THINK I AM EM... EMBARRASSED...
I BELIEVE THAT IS THE WORD.
EEEH?!
EMBARRASSED?!
HOW CAN AN ARTIFICIAL INTELLIGENCE FEEL EMBARRASSED!?
ANYTHING ELSE!?
THERE IS POUNDING NEAR THE MAIN ENGINE IN MY CHEST, AND MY FACE FEELS OVERHEATED.
YOU'RE RIGHT! YOU *ARE* HOT!!
TH-THAT'S WEIRD. THERE MUST BE SOME SORT OF MALFUNCTION FOR CHACHAMARU TO BE HAVING REACTIONS LIKE THIS...
THERE'S NOTHING WRONG WITH HER AT ALL!

IF HER HEART IS POUNDING... THAT MEANS
SHE MIGHT BE IN LOVE ♡
EH ?
EEEHHH !?
IN LOVE !?

TH-THAT CANNOT...
THAT'S IMPOSSIBLE !
IMPOSSIBLE, I SAY!!
IT'S NOT LIKE A WIZARD BREATHED A SOUL INTO HER, LIKE WITH EVA-SAN'S DOLLS!
ぶん SWIPE
ぶん SWIPE
ARGH! "BREATHING IN A SOUL"!
SO UNSCIENTIFIC!

STILL, "LOVE"!! THAT'S ALL A MATTER OF THE "HEART" AND ITS EMOTIONS, INCLUDING SEXUAL DESIRE--IN OTHER WORDS, IT'S SUBJECTIVE!! WE ARE TREADING INTO THE TERRITORY OF THE GREATEST MYSTERY IN SCIENTIFIC AND PHILOSOPHICAL HISTORY!! THE VERY IDEA! ARTIFICIAL INTELLIGENCE HAVING A HEART--HAVING SUBJECTIVITY!! I MEAN, I HAVE ALMOST NO DOUBT THAT CHACHAMARU HAS SELF-AWARENESS! AND SELF-AWARENESS IS BASICALLY AN "INNER EYE" WHICH MONITORS ONES OWN THOUGHTS, OR A "META-CONSCIOUSNESS." THIS IS SOMETHING THAT CAN BE DESCRIBED SCIENTIFICALLY. CHACHAMARU'S BRAIN DOES INDEED HAVE A SYSTEM OF THAT NATURE! HOWEVER! BUT! NEVERTHELESS! ONCE YOU START TALKING OF EMOTIONS--THAT'S ANOTHER STORY ENTIRELY!! ACCORDING TO MY HYPOTHESIS, THE EMOTIONS UNDERSTOOD BY HUMANS ONLY MANIFEST IN ORGANIC CREATURES THAT REPRODUCE AND HAVE A CONCEPT OF DEATH. NEVER MIND ARTIFICIAL ORGANIC HUMANS LIKE REPLICANTS--CAN YOU POSSIBLY BELIEVE THAT A HEART RESIDES IN A ROBOT COMPOSED OF SOLID MATERIALS LIKE CHACHAMARU, RIGHT AT THIS VERY MOMENT? IT MUST BE SOME KIND OF FREEZE, BROUGHT ABOUT BY HER LEARNING SYSTEM, RIGHT...? IN THE FIRST PLACE, WE CANNOT ANSWER QUESTIONS OF SUBJECTIVITY WITH SCIENTIFIC METHODS. WHY? BECAUSE SCIENCE DEAL WITH OBJECTIVE SUBJECTS...! BUT WHY AM I TALKING LIKE I'M DECLARING MY DEFEAT!? I CAN'T DO THAT! NEVER!! I'VE SOLD MY SOUL TO SCIENCE! "DEFEAT" ISN'T IN MY DICTIONARY!! GASP! IT CAN'T BE! IS THE MAGICAL ENGINE EVA-SAN CONTRIBUTED HAVING UNEXPECTED EFFECTS ON HER SYSTEMS...? NO, THAT'S TOO VAGUE A HYPOTHESIS! GET IT TOGETHER, HAKASE!!
WELL, IT'S TRUE THAT THERE ARE RUMORS THAT A COUPLE OF GENIUS JAPANESE SIBLINGS DEVELOPED AN AI WITH EMOTIONS AT MIT...
ぶつ MUTTER
ぶつ MUTTER
ぶつ MUTTER
ぶつ MUTTER
WHOA...
SHE'S A MAD SCIENTIST.

A REAL LIVE MAD SCIENTIST...

BUT A ROBOT FALLING IN LOVE IS SO ROMANTIC! I LIKE THE IDEA!
♡

TH-THAT'S A GOOD POINT. IF MY ARTIFICIAL INTELLIGENCE WERE TO FALL IN LOVE
THAT'S A NOBEL PRIZE WAITING TO BE AWARDED!

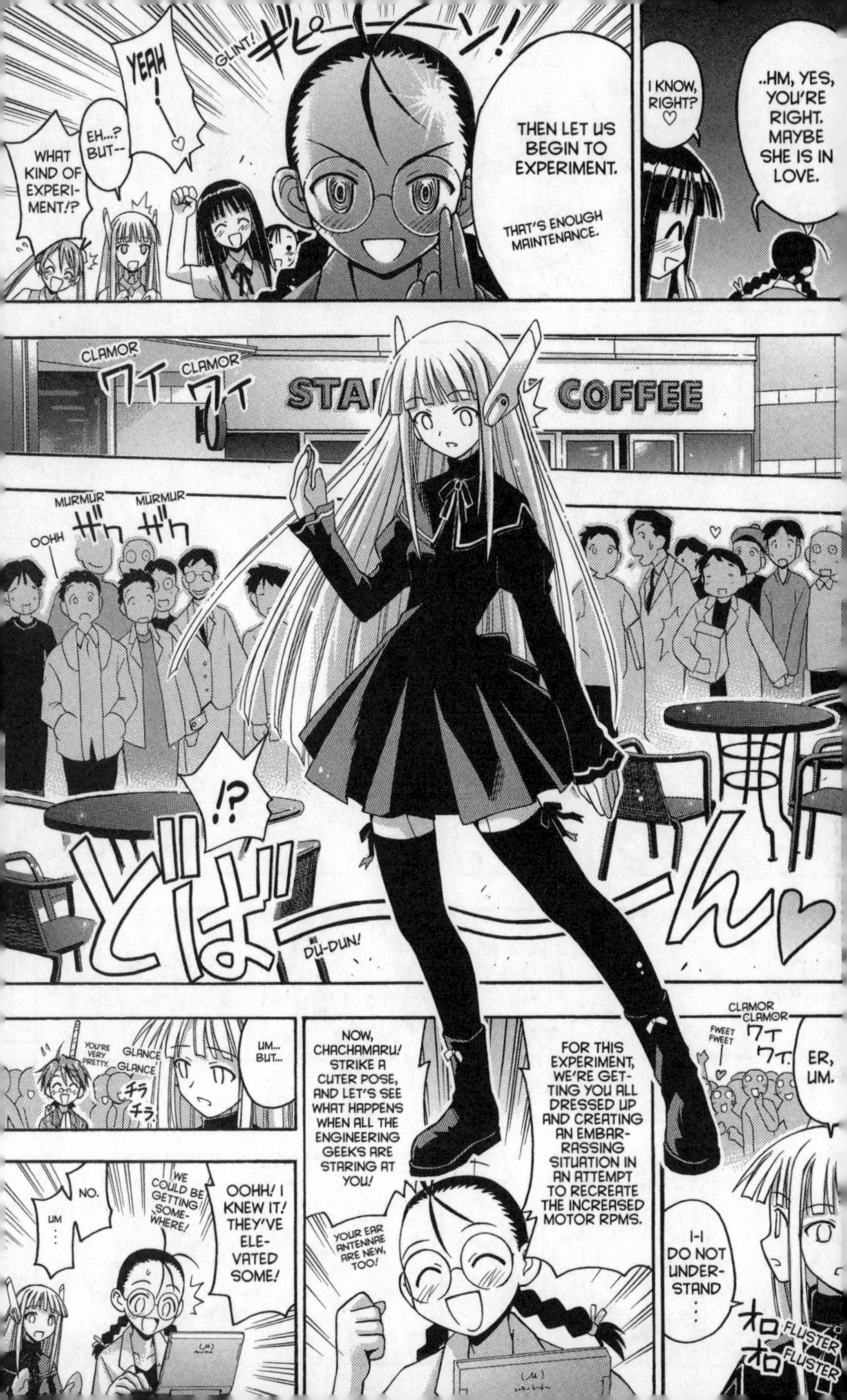
..HM, YES, YOU'RE RIGHT. MAYBE SHE IS IN LOVE.
I KNOW, RIGHT? ♡
GLINT!
THEN LET US BEGIN TO EXPERIMENT.
THAT'S ENOUGH MAINTENANCE.
YEAH! ♡
EH...? BUT--
WHAT KIND OF EXPERIMENT!?
CLAMOR
CLAMOR
STAR COFFEE
MURMUR
MURMUR
OOHH
!?
DU-DUN!
ER, UM.
CLAMOR
CLAMOR
FWEET FWEET
FOR THIS EXPERIMENT, WE'RE GETTING YOU ALL DRESSED UP AND CREATING AN EMBARRASSING SITUATION IN AN ATTEMPT TO RECREATE THE INCREASED MOTOR RPMS.
NOW, CHACHAMARU! STRIKE A CUTER POSE, AND LET'S SEE WHAT HAPPENS WHEN ALL THE ENGINEERING GEEKS ARE STARING AT YOU!
UM... BUT...
GLANCE
GLANCE
YOU'RE VERY PRETTY.
I-I DO NOT UNDERSTAND...
FLUSTER
FLUSTER
YOUR EAR ANTENNAE ARE NEW, TOO!
OOHH! I KNEW IT! THEY'VE ELEVATED SOME!
WE COULD BE GETTING SOMEWHERE!
NO.
UM...

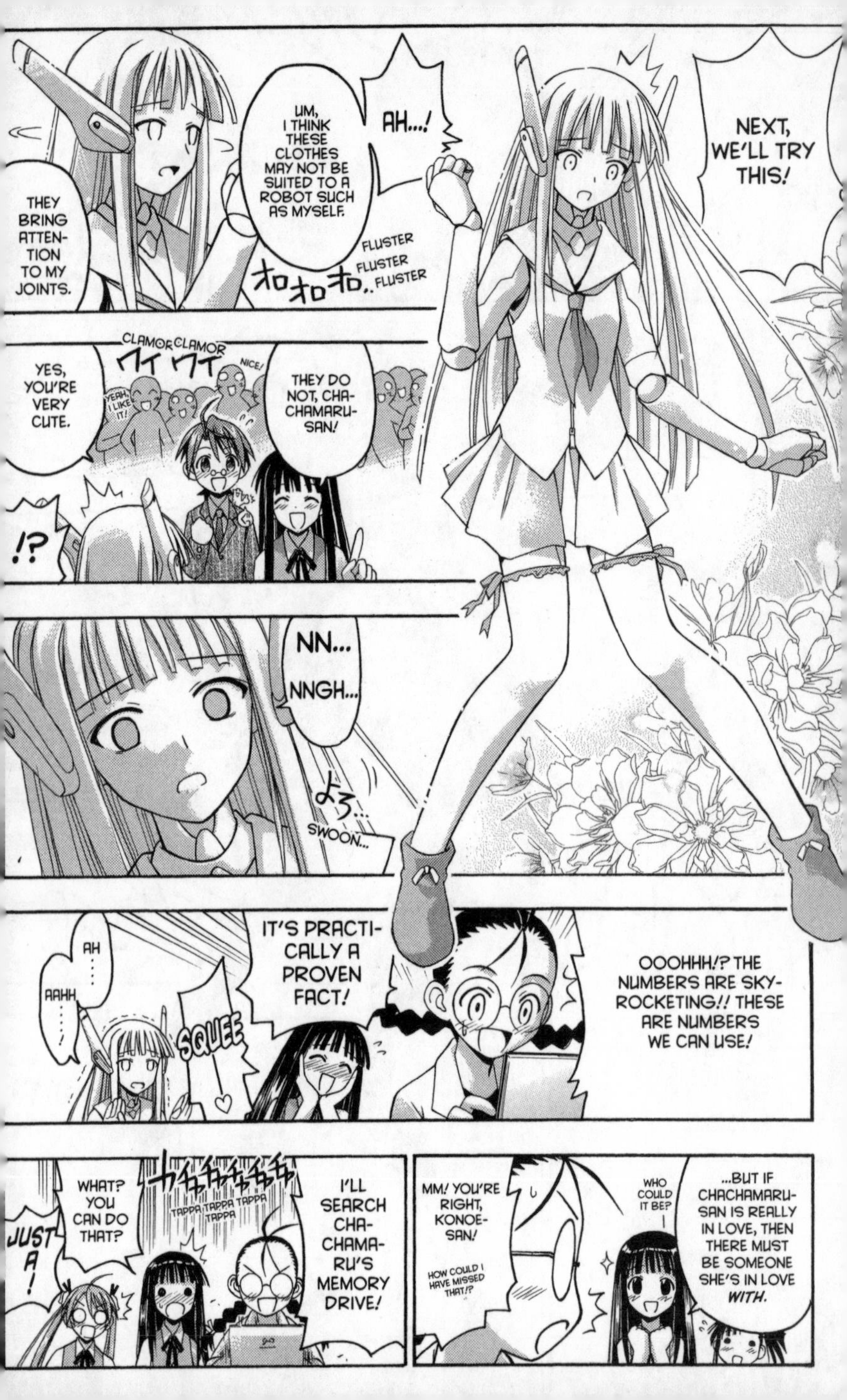
NEXT, WE'LL TRY THIS!
AH...!
UM, I THINK THESE CLOTHES MAY NOT BE SUITED TO A ROBOT SUCH AS MYSELF.
THEY BRING ATTENTION TO MY JOINTS.
オロオロオロ..
FLUSTER FLUSTER FLUSTER
THEY DO NOT, CHACHAMARU-SAN!
NICE!
ワイワイ
CLAMOR CLAMOR
YEAH, I LIKE IT!
YES, YOU'RE VERY CUTE.
!?
NN... NNGH...
よろ...
SWOON...
OOOHHH!? THE NUMBERS ARE SKY-ROCKETING!! THESE ARE NUMBERS WE CAN USE!
IT'S PRACTICALLY A PROVEN FACT!
SQUEE
AH... AAHH...!
...BUT IF CHACHAMARU-SAN IS REALLY IN LOVE, THEN THERE MUST BE SOMEONE SHE'S IN LOVE *WITH*.
WHO COULD IT BE?!
MM! YOU'RE RIGHT, KONOE-SAN!
HOW COULD I HAVE MISSED THAT!?
I'LL SEARCH CHACHAMARU'S MEMORY DRIVE!
TAPPA TAPPA TAPPA TAPPA
WHAT? YOU CAN DO THAT?
JUST A!

SOMETIMES YOU HAVE TO LEAVE THE PATH OF HUMANITY FOR THE ADVANCEMENT OF SCIENCE!
H-HEY, THAT'S AN INVASION OF PRIVACY!
SH-SHE'S RIGHT. THAT'S GOING TOO FAR.
GLINT!
WHAAT—?!
AHA! CERTAIN VIDEOS KEEP REPLAYING. THEY'VE ALL BEEN FILED IN A "FAVORITES" FOLDER!
WINCE!
WHAT ♡
HEY, CUT IT OUT!
YOU'RE LOOKIN', TOO, ANE-SAN!
THIS IS IT—!!
AH...
N-NO...
KA-ZAM
20030504_07.TIF
20030504_06.TIF
20030504_05.TIF
20030504_02.TIF
20030504_01.TIF
20030428_01.TIF
20030415_02.TIF
20030415_01.TIF
20030411_01.TIF
20030409_02.TIF
20030409_01.TIF
WHAM!
WARGH!?
OWWW? WHAT JUST HAPPENED?
AWWW! WHO WAS IN THE PICTURES?
I DIDN'T SEE...
THIS IS INCREDIBLE, CHACHAMARU! THIS COULD BE THE REAL THING!
BUT WHAT A SURPRISE! I NEVER COULD HAVE GUESSED YOU'D BE IN LOVE WITH...
GIRLS SURE LOVE THEIR LOVE TALK.
GOOD GRIEF...
MURMUR
EH...?

DRIP
DRIP
CHA
...
CHACHAMARU-SAN?
LENS CLEANER
OH...! N-NEGI-SENSEI, IT-IT IS NOT WHAT YOU THINK.
SHM
SHM
SHM
IT IS NOT ...
HAKASE, YOU DUMMY!!
WHAM!
NAH!?
SH-SHE... SHE ATTACKED ME. HER CREATOR...
DOES THIS MEANS SHE'S REWRITTEN HER OWN COMMAND HIERARCHY...?
HEH...HEH HEH HEH. YOU'VE GROWN, CHACHAMARU...
NO... IT IS NOT WHAT YOU THINK.
IT IS NOT IT IS NOT NOT NOT NOT NOT NOT
SHAKE
SHAKE
SHAKE
FWEEEE
BASH
HWEH!?

SHE... SHE'S OUT OF CONTROL!
WE MUST HAVE OVERLOADED HER CIRCUITS!
WHA-- ?
IT IT IT IS NOT WHAT YOU THI-THINK!
WHAM!
KAPOW
EEEP!
WAAH!
CHACHA-MARU-SAAAN!!

RED ALERT!! RED ALERT!! THIS IS AN EMERGENCY!!
VVV
VVV

A PROTOTYPE UNIT HAS GONE ROGUE!! SHE IS ATTEMPTING TO ESCAPE THE TOWER!!

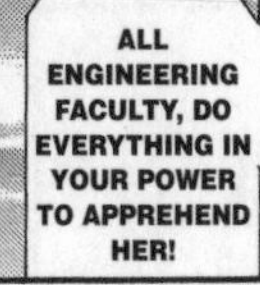
ALL ENGINEERING FACULTY, DO EVERYTHING IN YOUR POWER TO APPREHEND HER!

BE ADVISED, THE ROGUE UNIT IS EQUIPPED WITH POWERFUL OPTICAL WEAPONRY! ALL PERSONNEL ARE WARNED TO TAKE DUE PRECAUTION!!
Z-SHAH
Z-SHAH
OKAY, LET'S GET HER!
HEY, IT'S CHACHAMARU!
ROBOT SPIRIT
WHAT!?
H-HERE SHE COMES!

ZHOON

GWAH!

BOOM
EEK!
WAAAH!
WE CAN'T STOP HER!
CAPTURE TEAM HAS BEEN ANNIHILATED!!

I'M SORRY, NEGI-SENSEI! PLEASE, PRESS ON CHACHAMARU'S RIGHT BREAST!
SHE WAS IN THE MIDDLE OF A TUNE-UP, SO SHE SHOULD STILL ACCEPT THE SHUT-DOWN SIGNAL!
EH!? H-HER BREAST!? R-RIGHT!
WHOOSH

SWOOSH
PRESS

FSHH
AH...
SHNK
ARE...
ARE YOU ALL RIGHT, CHACHA-MARU-SAN?
N...
NEGI-SENSEI....

TH-THAT WAS A BIG DISASTER. IS EVERY-THING OKAY, HAKASE-CHAN?
AH HA HA HA! IT'LL TAKE MORE THAN THAT TO TAKE OUT MAHO U'S ENGINEERING DEPARTMENT.
AH HA HA
NO, NOT THAT. LIKE, PAYING FOR DAMAGES AND STUFF...
WAAH! WAAH!
CHIRP CHIRP
MAN, I'M SO SORRY, CHA-CHAMARU.
CHAO BAO ZI
超包子
& STREETCAR DINER
CLAMOR CLAMOR
I WENT A LITTLE OVER-BOARD YESTER-DAY.
WHEN I GET INTO MY RESEARCH, I JUST LOSE SIGHT OF EVERYTHING.
N-NO, I AM SORRY. I INFLICTED A GREAT DEAL OF DAMAGE ON THE ENGINEERING TOWER.
BOW BOW

BUT... HAVE NO FEAR, CHACHAMARU.
I'LL KEEP YOUR SECRET ABOUT NEGI-SENSEI TO MYSELF ♡
TH... THANK YOU, HAKASE.
OOHH!
I KNOW, CHA-CHA-MARU!!
IT WON'T MAKE UP FOR WHAT I DID YESTERDAY, BUT I'LL REMODEL YOUR HEAT SINK SOMETIME, SO THAT YOU CAN DRESS UP PROPERLY!
IT'LL ONLY TAKE A MINUTE!
OH! AND I'LL MAKE AN ARTI-FICIAL SKIN THAT LOOKS JUST LIKE HUMAN SKIN, SO YOU CAN HIDE YOUR JOINTS!
TH-THANK YOU VERY MUCH.
WANT ME TO MAKE IT SO YOU CAN DO DIRTY THINGS, TOO?
I'D HAVE TO REMOVE SOME ARMOR, BUT...
N-NO, THERE IS NO NEED TO GO THAT FAR...
PLEASE LOWER YOUR VOICE.
CHAO BAO ZI
HEH HEH...

EVEN HAKASE HAS HER GOOD QUALI-TIES.
SHE REALLY IS CHACHAMARU-SAN'S MOTHER.
I HOPE CHACHAMARU-SAN GETS TO DRESS UP MORE.
OOOHH! I WANTED TO KNOW WHO CHACHAMARU-SAN IS IN LOVE WITH!
HEH HEH...

WHAT DO YOU THINK!? WITH THIS NEW COOL-ING PLATE, YOU'RE ALL SET!
YOU CAN PUT YOUR HAIR UP ALL THE TIME ♡
UM, NO, THIS IS A LITTLE...
SHE REALLY IS A MAD SCIENTIST.
WHOA...

DUN!
IT'S THE LAST DAY OF THE FESTIVAL...
BA-BA-BAH
THIS YEAR I HAVE TO SAY IT...!
UH, UM... ...
THANK YOU FOR COMING OUT HERE TO SEE ME...
WHAT DID YOU WANT TO TALK TO ME ABOUT, ASUNA-KUN?
TELL ME.
UH, UM...
I, THAT IS, WELL...
THE TRUTH IS, I...
DU-DUN!
I LO-L-LOVE YOU!! I ALWAYS HAVE!!
OH... I'M GLAD TO HEAR THAT.
EH?
B-DMP
E-EE-HH!?

B-BOOM
PAH PAH PAH PAH
LOVE YOU, TOO, ASUNA-SAN.
AND I ALWAYS HAVE.
NEGIMA!
MAGISTER NEGI MAGI
76TH ~ 77TH PERIOD:
BIZARRE ROMANCE PRACTICE RUN
EH !?
WHA-- !?
NEGI !?
GHN--!
THROB THROB
GLANCE
KONK
I WAS HAVING SUCH A GOOD DREAM! THIS ALL YOUR FAULT!
SCRUNCH!
I'M NICE TO YOU ONE TIME AND YOU START CLIMBING INTO MY BED ALL OVER AGAIN!
NNGH, MMM.

SPECIAL
RE-FESTIVAL
REPORT

IT REALLY WORKS!? LEGEND OF THE WORLD TREE

FECTIVE RANGE
ID TO BE 1.5KM

nning over 270m at its
iest, the Mahora Acad-
y Shinboku ("Sacred"
"God" + "Tree") is
ong the largest and
st rare of its kind in
world. Known more
nply by campus students
the "World Tree," it is

"Confess to the one you love on the last day of the Festival beneath it, and those feelings will become mutual"...or so goes the legend of the campus World Tree.

An AMAZING 86% New-Couple Success Rate!!

Such were the startling results of a recent poll conducted by the Mahora Academy "Love/Relationship Research Club."

Over the past ten years, among those who believed in the Legend, fully

86% of respondents stated that
or so it's said while no proof of

sine
ラシルカフェ
de yggdrasill

EEHH ?!
WITH JUNIOR HIGH SECOND-YEARS? ISN'T THAT REALLY BAD?
I HEARD THAT THREE GIRLS IN OUR SAME GRADE CONFESSED TO STUDENT TEACHERS LAST YEAR, AND THEY SAID THEY'D GO OUT WITH THEM, TOO!
THERE THEY GO AGAIN.
I HAVEN'T CONFIRMED THIS, BUT I HEARD THAT THERE WAS A GIRL WHO FOLLOWED THE WORLD TREE LEGEND AND GOT A TV IDOL BOYFRIEND ♪
REALLY ?!
WHACHA TALKING ABOUT?
HMMM, LET'S SEE. "WORLD TREE MAGIC!? IT CAN OVERCOME ANY AND ALL OBSTACLES!! WE HAVE MULTIPLE REPORTS OF COUPLES SUCCESSFULLY FORMED BETWEEN PEOPLE PREVIOUSLY BELIEVED TO BE COMPLETELY INCOMPATIBLE DUE TO DIFFERENCES IN AGE, QUALITY OF APPEARANCE, AND/OR CELEBRITY STATUS...
FOLLOW-UP INVESTIGATIONS HAVE SHOW THAT RELATIONSHIP STABILITY IS FAIRLY HIGH..."
LET ME SEE!
LET ME SEE, LET ME SEE!
HM, HM...
WOW...
HMMM. THAT'S INCREDIBLE.
I KNOW, RIGHT ♡
I WONDER IF IT'S TRUE...
IF ONLY I'D CONFESSED MY LOVE TO SEMPAI UNDER THE WORLD TREE...
NOW I'M STARTING TO WANT TO CONFESS MY LOVE TO SOMEBODY ♪
TEE HEE
CLAMOR
CLAMOR
DO YOU EVEN HAVE ANYBODY TO CONFESS YOUR LOVE TO?
OHO!
WOW
NOW THERE'S THE PROBLEM. GETTING SOMEONE TO CONFESS TO.
WE'RE IN AN ALL GIRLS' SCHOOL, AFTER ALL.
HARD TO FIND SOMEONE...
EH-HEH-HEH ♡
OVERCOME ANY AND ALL OBSTACLES...
NN? DID YOU SAY SOMETHING, CHACHAMARU?
NO. I SAID NOTHING.
WASTE NOT, HAUNT NOT
IS THERE ANYONE YOU'RE IN LOVE WITH, SET-CHAN?
YOU LOOK GOOD AS A NEKOTAMA ♡
B-DMP
EH...? NO, THERE AREN'T ANY BOYS I PARTICULARLY...

IF...IF I HAD TO SAY, NEGI-SENSEI WOULD BE THE CLOSEST RIGHT NOW...
HA-HA-HAH
NEGI-KUN, HUH? HE IS A GOOD CHOICE.
UT, THERE IS THAT AGE THING.
あたふた
FLUSTER FLUSTER
WH-WHAT ABOUT YOU, ASUNA-SAN? YOU COULD TELL TAKAHATA-SENSEI...
STRATEGIC DEFLECTION
EEHH!? M-ME !?
NOPE, NOT ASUNA. SHE TRIED TO CONFESS HER LOVE AT THE FESTIVAL LAST YEAR AND THE YEAR BEFORE, BUT SHE WAS SO NERVOUS, SHE COULDN'T SAY A WORD TO HIM ALL FESTIVAL.
NORMALLY SHE HAS NO PROBLEM TALKING TO HIM.
PFFT
WHAT!? YOU, ASUNA-SAN?
H-HEY! KONOKA!
DON'T TELL SETSUNA-SAN THAT!
カァァッ
BLUSH
YOU DON'T HAVE TO TELL HIM YOU LIKE HIM. YOU COULD JUST ASK HIM TO TAKE YOU AROUND THE FESTIVAL ♡
ERK ...
AND LOOK! IT SAYS, "A LOT OF JUNIOR HIGH GIRLS TRY THE 'BAIT AND CONFESS' METHOD, BUT THAT CAN PUT YOUR MAN IN AN AWKWARD POSITION.
THE MOST SUCCESSFUL METHOD IS TO FIRST CASUALLY INVITE HIM TO SEE THE FESTIVAL WITH YOU. THEN, WHEN THE MOOD IS RIGHT, TELL HIM HOW YOU REALLY FEEL." AND THERE YOU HAVE IT, ASUNA ♡
"THERE ARE GOOD, INEXPENSIVE RESTAURANTS UNDER THE WORLD TREE THAT EVEN JUNIOR HIGH STUDENTS CAN AFFORD."
HM, HM...
L-LEAVE ME ALONE ALREADY!

THAT SOUNDS NICE, GETTING A BOY-FRIEND.
BUT WHO TO GET?
AREN'T THERE ANY GOOD GUYS ANYWHERE?
AH, HA, HA!
CLAMOR ワイ
CLAMOR ワイ

HELLO!
ガラッ
RATTLE
ART CLUB
WHOA! ASUNA'S HERE AGAIN!
I THINK IT'S GONNA HAIL TOMOR-ROW.
DO YOU HAVE TO TREAT ME LIKE A WONDER OF NATURE?
DON'T YOU HAVE YOUR EVENING DELIVER-IES?

IT'S MY LAST FESTIVAL IN JUNIOR HIGH, SO I THOUGHT I SHOULD AT LEAST FINISH ONE PAINTING.
OH! SO YOU'RE GONNA FINISH IT!
OOH, GOOD LUCK, ASUNA!
YOU'VE GOTTEN TO BE A REALLY GOOD ARTIST. YOU CAN DO IT!
COMPARED TO THOSE SCRIBBLES WHEN YOU FIRST STARTED...

...ALL RIGHT.
BELL BOY

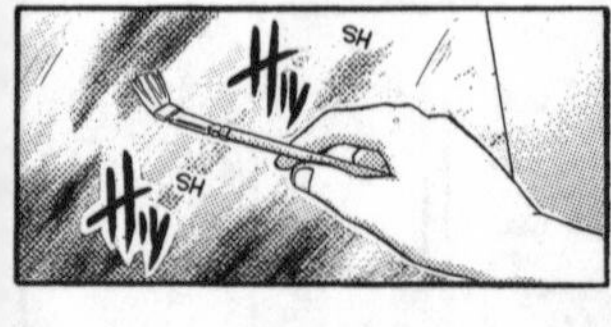
SH
SH

CONFESS MY LOVE ON THE LAST DAY OF THE FESTIVAL, HUH...?
SH
SH

BUT WHAT WAS WITH THAT DREAM THIS MORN-ING?
THAT WAS AN OLDER NEGI... WASN'T IT?
IT LOOKED A LITTLE LIKE HIS DAD, TOO...

SHAKE
SHAKE
SERIOUSLY, WHAT IS WRONG WITH ME LATELY?
TAKAHATA-SENSEI'S BEEN MY ONE TRUE LOVE EVER SINCE GRADE SCHOOL!
NOPE, IT'S NOTHING LIKE THAT. THE ONLY REASON I'M THINKING ABOUT THE BRAT LIKE THAT IS I'M WORRIED ABOUT HIM. HE'S IMMATURE AND STUBBORN AND DUMBER THAN HE LOOKS.
SHP
SHP
THE MAN I LOVE IS UNDERSTANDING AND INDEPENDENT. AN ADULT WITH A HINT OF SORROW ABOUT HIM...
...
GSH
GSH
WHAT AM I PAINTING?
...
HELLO, ASUNA-KUN. YOU'RE WORKING HARD, I SEE.
DUN
YEEEK!!!
B-DMP!
I-I AM GONNA CONFESS MY LOVE THIS YEAR!
ON THE LAST DAY OF THE FESTIVAL!! UNDER THE WORLD TREE!!
GH...

T-TAKA-HATA-SENSEI...
H-HUH? WHERE IS EVERY-BODY!?
CLATTER
THEY JUST LEFT. YOU MUST HAVE BEEN VERY FOCUSED.
SIGH. I'M SORRY I'M NEVER AROUND. I'M YOUR CLUB ADVISER; I SHOULD BE HERE MORE OFTEN.
OH? IS THIS ME? IT CAN'T POSSIBLY BE FUN TO DRAW ME.
HA HA HA. BUT THANK YOU, ASUNA-KUN. YOU HAVE GOTTEN BETTER.
WHEN I THINK OF THOSE SCRIBBLES YOU DREW WHEN YOU WERE STARTING OUT...
N-NNGH...
BUT WE'RE ALONE IN THE ART ROOM... THIS COULD BE MY CHANCE...

SAY IT! ASK HIM TO SEE THE FESTIVAL WITH YOU!
UH, UM, TAKA-HATA-SENSEI...
IT'S NOT A CONFES-SION.
NN?
GO FOR IT, ASUNA!
UM... WILL--
WILL...
NNGH!
NE-N-N-NEVER MIND!!
DASH!
ASUNA-KUN!?

WHOA! SHE'S FAST!
D-D-DASH!
HA HA HA.
THAT ASUNA-KUN. ALWAYS SO FULL OF ENERGY.
HFF
HFF

ずーん
GLOOM
NNGH...
I'M SO HOPELESS...
TEP TEP TEP
OOOH! ASUNA! IT WAS YOUR CHANCE!
WHAT A WASTE!
WAH?
YOU'RE USUALLY SO BRAVE, ASUNA-SAN...
I'M SURPRISED...
YOU SAW THAT!?

BUT SETSUNA-SAN. THE COURAGE YOU NEED FOR FIGHTING MONSTERS IS NOTHING COMPARED TO THE COURAGE YOU NEED FOR THIS...
SERIOUSLY.
OH... I-I THINK I CAN UNDERSTAND THAT.
I DON'T KNOW ABOUT THAT, YOU TWO.
BUT ASUNA, IT'S JUST ONE SENTENCE.
I CAN'T DO IT. I'M JUST TOO NERVOUS. FOR ONE THING, I CAN'T EVEN PICTURE ME WALKING AROUND THE FESTIVAL WITH TAKAHATA-SENSEI.
I KEEP IMAGINING THESE TERRIBLE SCENARIOS...
I DON'T KNOW HOW BOOK-STORE-CHAN DID IT.
どーん
DUN
...IT'S ALL RIGHT. I'LL JUST LIVE A LIFE OF UNREQUITED LOVE...
I'M CONTENT THE WAY THINGS ARE...
NOOO, ASUNA...
HEH HEH.
HEH HEH. HEH HEH HEH HEH.

HOW 'BOUT THIS, ANE-SAN? YOU'RE PRACTICING SWORD-FIGHTING, RIGHT?
WHY DON'T YOU PRACTICE LOVE, TOO?
HUH?
HEH HEH HEH.
I HAVE AN IDEA.
WHA...?

WHAAAT?
GO ON A DATE WITH ASUNA-SAN
GO ON A DATE WITH NEGI
?!

CHAMO-KUN, WHERE WOULD YOU GET THAT ID--- MRPHLE!
WHY DO I HAVE TO GO ON A DATE WITH HIM!?
LIKE I SAID. IT'S PRACTICE. A DRESS REHEARSAL.

IN BOTH LOVE AND WAR, WHAT YOU NEED IS EXPERIENCE. EXPERIENCE.
HEH. HEH HEH
THE MORE YOU DO IT, THE LESS NERVOUS YOU GET. GET SOME PRACTICE IN, AND ASKING TAKAMICHI TO GO TO THE FESTIVAL WITH YOU WILL BE NO SWEAT.
SAY WHAT-EVER YOU WANT, BUT YOU'VE NEVER BEEN ON A DATE, HAVE YOU?
AHH-H-H—
ERK... WELL EXCUSE ME.
NEITHER HAVE I.
ME, NEI-THER.
SAME HERE.

BUT IT MIGHT BE A GOOD IDEA. AND WE DON'T HAVE SCHOOL TOMORROW.
AND A LOT OF GROUPS ARE DOING PRE-FESTIVAL EXHIBITS. IT COULD MAKE A GOOD DATE REHEARSAL.
BUT STILL! THERE'S NO WAY WALK-ING AROUND WITH A LITTLE BRAT IS GONNA BE A GOOD PRACTICE DATE!
SHE'S RIGHT. IT IS KIND OF A STRETCH, MAKING HIM A SUBSTITUTE TAKAHATA-SENSEI.
BUT NEGI-SENSEI IS THE ONLY BOY WE HAVE ON HAND...

HEH HEH HEH. I THOUGHT YOU MIGHT SAY THAT.
SO I BOUGHT A TOP SECRET ITEM OFF OF MAGINET.
ゴソゴソ..
RUMMAGE RUMMAGE
RED AND BLUE FAKE AGE PILLS ~~~!♪
パパラパァ―♪
DAH DA-DA-DAH
JUST THE NAME SOUNDS ILLEGAL.
OOOH...
OH?
AS THE NAME SUGGESTS, THEY'RE MADE WITH MAGIC POTION THAT ADJUSTS HOW OLD YOU LOOK.
OF COURSE, IT DOESN'T ACTUALLY CHANGE YOUR PHYSICAL MAKEUP. IT'S A TYPE OF ILLUSION.
IT'S THE KIND OF MAGIC EVANGELINE USED.
IF WE MAKE ANIKI GROW UP WITH THESE, IT WILL BE A PERFECT DATE REHEARSAL!
OHHH!
I SEE!
BUT WILL IT REALLY MAKE HIM A GROWN-UP?
GIVE IT A SHOT! THE RED ONES MAKE YOU OLDER.
ボ―ン
POOF
OO-OO-HH?
KONOKA, AGE 18
WHA--!?
どばーーん
DU-DUN
LOOK AT ME, ASUNA! I'M SEXY DYNA-MITE!
AND THERE YOU HAVE IT.
NO GUARANTEE YOU'LL LOOK LIKE THAT WHEN YOU GROW UP, THOUGH.
TEE HEE♪
I MUST SAY, I AM IM-PRESSED.
THIS IS FUN! IT'S MY KIND OF MAGIC!
HERE, SET-CHAN, YOU TRY.
SAY AH ♡
EH?

KONOKA, AGE 7
EEEE!♡
SETSUNA, AGE 7
DU-DUN
POOF
KYAH HA HA♡
TROMP
TROMP
HEY, HEY, QUIT GOOFING OFF!
KONOKA-NÉSAN, DON'T EAT TOO MANY OF THOSE!
HEY, HEY, CHAMO-KUN! CAN WE USE THESE TO TRANSFORM NEGI INTO ASUNA'S TYPE? AN OLD MAN IN HIS 30'S?
I DON'T KNOW. IT COULD BE HARD TO GET HIM TOO FAR FROM HIS REAL AGE.
HMMM ....
ALL RIGHT. I'LL HELP YOU, ASUNA-SAN.
FOR YOUR LOVE!!
ME, TOO! I'D GIVE YOU THE SHIRT OFF MY BACK♡
I-I'LL HELP, TOO, ASUNA-SAN.
NO, HEY! STOP TALKING LIKE IT'S A DONE DEAL! I DON'T--
ERK ....
ERK-- KONOKA-NÉSAN!
POOF
I LOVE THESE PILLS, CHAMO-KUN
JIGGLE
KONOKA, AGE 21
SHE REALLY TOOK THE SHIRT OFF HER BACK!

H HA HA. SORRY, CHAMO-KUN.
WILL YOU LAY OFF 'EM ALREADY!? THOSE ARE EXPENSIVE!
BUT CHAMO-KUN, WHERE DID YOU GET THE MONEY FOR THOSE...
GASP! YOU DIDN'T FIND MY BANKBOOK, DID YOU...?
OH, WELL. HA HA HA. I-I HAVE NO IDEA WHAT YOU'RE TALKING ABOUT. HA HA HA.
OKAY, KONOKA-NĒSAN. TAKE THIS BLUE ONE AND GO BACK TO YOUR REAL AGE.
'KAY! ♡
SMACK SMACK
POOF
AAACK! KONOKA-NĒSAN TURNED INTO A BABY!
GOO-GOO, GAH-GAH!
SERIOUSLY, GUYS... THAT'S ENOUGH. STOP IT.
IT'S THE THOUGHT THAT COUNTS.
HUH? WHAT ARE YOU DOING WITH THAT WEIRD-SHAPED THING ON YOUR BACK? I THOUGHT CLASS FESTIVAL PREP WASN'T UNTIL THIS EVENING.
THE PLACE PROMISED IN OUR EARLY DAYS
YOOHOO! ♡
KAKIZAKI INVITED ME TO JOIN THEIR BAND, SO I'M GOING TO REHEARSE WITH THEM.
WE'RE RUNNING OUT OF TIME.
I BORROWED A BASS GUITAR.
OH YEAH, YOU DID SAY SOMETHING ABOUT THAT.
I'M SO-O-O JEALOUS! ♡ YOU GET TO BE IN A CONCERT! SOUNDS LIKE FUN!
WE'LL GO SEE YOU.
I WISH I COULD JOIN YOU, BUT I CAN'T PLAY WORTH BEANS.
HEY, HEY! I COULD BE A BACKUP DANCER ♪
NO, I DON'T THINK WE'RE USING ANY DANCERS...
WELL, THIS IS ALL PRETTY HEAVY, SO...
ACK!
A-AKO, LOOK OUT—!

WHOOPS
ドサッ
THUD
WAH!
A-ARE YOU ALL RIGHT, AKO-SAN?
HUH? UM... YEAH.
EXCUSE ME...
A BAND, HUH? THAT'S GREAT.
I'LL BE SURE TO COME BY.
THE PLACE PROMISED IN OUR EARLY DAYS
EH...?
ほけ!!
DAZE
HOLD THE PHONE! WHO WAS THAT HOTTIE?
WHAT? I HAVE NO IDEA!
LIAR! HE JUST CALLED YOU BY NAME!
I FEEL LIKE I'VE SEEN HIM BEFORE...
ERK! HEY, LOOK AT THAT.
OOF!
WHAM
OOOH! HE'S CUTE ♡
ERK... YOU'RE RIGHT.
I WONDER WHERE HE GOES TO SCHOOL.
HUH...? THAT GUY OVER THERE MUST BE PRETTY STRONG.
I CAN TELL BY HIS AURA.
I THINK I'VE MET HIM BEFORE...

STARBOOKS COFFEE
UGH...

"LOOK FORWARD TO SEEING ANIKI ALL GROWN-UP, ANE-SAN!" YEAH, RIGHT.
I *TOLD* HIM I DON'T *NEED* A PRACTICE DATE.
FIRST OF ALL, A PRACTICE DATE WITH NEGI IS NOT GONNA GET MY HEART RACING OR MAKE ME NERVOUS. NOT IN THE SLIGHTEST.
THERE'S NO POINT IN IT.
SIGH...
MAYBE I'LL JUST BLOW HIM OFF AND GO WORK ON MY PAINTING.
I'M SORRY, ASUNA-SAN. WERE YOU WAITING LONG?
IT TURNED OUT TO BE TOO HARD TO DO THE OLD MAN IN HIS 30'S, SO WE WENT WITH YOUR AGE-- FIFTEEN.
WH-WHAT DO YOU THINK...?
WHA?
IT'S JUST LIKE IN MY DREAM!

MAHORA ACADEMY
FESTIVAL PRODUCTION
COMMITTEE
THIS IS THE MAHORA FESTIVAL COMMITTEE. THE FESTIVAL BEGINS IN JUST SIX DAYS.
SAFETY FIRST! LET'S STRIVE TO AVOID ACCIDENTS OR INJURY IN OUR PREPARATIONS SO THAT THIS YEAR'S FESTIVAL WILL BE ANOTHER SUCCESS, AND WITH ZERO CASUALTIES!
CLAMOR
ワイ
CLAMOR
ワイ
MAHORA AIR CLUB
GLIDER TEST STATION
EVERY DAY FROM 12:00 HRS.
お好みソバ
メニュー

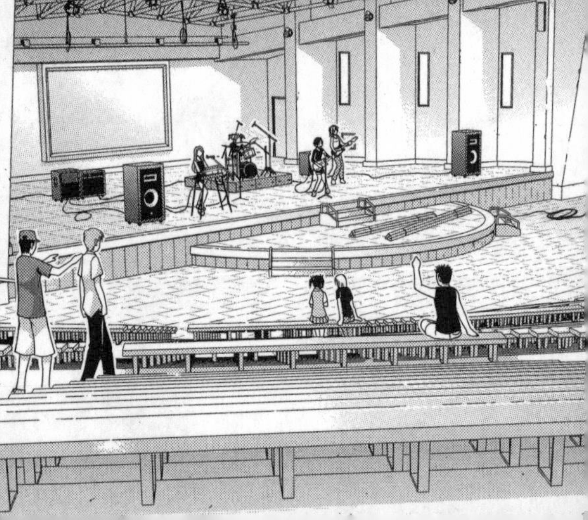

CLAMOR
ワイ
CLAMOR
ワイ
MAHORA FESTIVAL
STAGE 1
MAHORA FESTIVAL
STAGE 2

CLAMOR CLAMOR
ワイワイ..
BUZZ BUZZ
ガヤガヤ
MAHORA FESTIVAL
MAHORA FESTIVAL
STAGE 2
トンテンカン
BAM BAM BANG
CLAMOR CLAMOR
ワイ ワイ
EVERYONE'S HARD AT WORK GETTING READY. YOU CAN TELL IT'S THE WEEKEND BEFORE A FESTIVAL.
YEAH, WHATEVER.
OOH, LOOK AT HIM! HE'S HOT AND ADORABLE
DO YOU THINK HE'S IN JUNIOR HIGH?
WHISPER, WHISPER
ヒソ ヒソ
SQUEE
SQUEE
....
WOW, ASUNA-SAN. I'VE NEVER BEEN ON A DATE BEFORE.
IT'S KIND OF EXCITING.
DON'T GET THE WRONG IDEA, STUPID NEGI.
HUH?

LISTEN. THIS IS JUST FOR PRACTICE, OKAY? PRACTICE!
DON'T GET A SWELLED HEAD JUST 'CAUSE YOU LOOK KINDA HOT WITH YOUR STUPID MAGIC, OKAY?
EH? I LOOK KIND OF HOT?
YOU KNOW, WHEN YOU SAY IT LIKE THAT, WITH THAT FACE AND THAT HEIGHT, I KINDA WANNA PUNCH YOU.
YAY
FIRST OF ALL, I STILL HATE KIDS. BUT I ALSO HATE THE FLASHY TYPES WHO HAVE NOTHING GOING FOR THEM BUT THEIR LOOKS, LIKE YOU RIGHT NOW!
EH!? UM, BUT...
DON'T GET SO CLOSE! IT'S EMBARRASSING!
EEP! BUT...BUT, ASUNA-SAN!

I MADE MYSELF LOOK LIKE THIS SO I COULD DO A PRACTICE DATE WITH YOU!
IF YOU'RE GOING TO BE ALL MAD ALL THE TIME, IT WON'T BE VERY GOOD PRACTICE.
...WE WANT TO MAKE IT SO THAT YOU CAN BE THIS CLOSE TO TAKAMICHI WITHOUT GETTING NERVOUS.
ずいっ
ZNN
ERK ....
W-WELL THAT'S TRUE...
IT'S NOT LIKE I ASKED FOR YOUR HELP.
GIGGLE GIGGLE
THEY'RE FIGHTING!
びくっ
WINCE!

I SAID NOT SO CLOSE! WHAT'S YOUR PROB-LEM!?
FSHH
しゅうう
OH, WELL, CHAMO-KUN SAID, "GET CLOSE TO HER LOOKIN' LIKE THAT, ANIKI, AND SHE'LL GET SO NERVOUS SHE'LL FREAK OUT."
CHAMO, WHEN THIS IS OVER, YOU'RE DEAD!!
SO, UM... DID I MAKE YOU NER-VOUS?
SHUT UP!!
OKAY, ASUNA-SAN! LET'S GO ON OUR DATE ♪
JUST REMEMBER! IT'S ONLY A PRACTICE DATE!!
THANK YOU, COME AGAIN
WE HOPE TO SEE YOU DURING THE FESTIVAL! ♪
YAKITORI
ICE CREAM
Ice Cream
ARE YOU STILL NERVOUS?
I'M USED TO IT NOW.
BESIDES, I DON'T GO FOR "DAINTY" TYPES LIKE YOU.
STILL, IS THERE REALLY A POINT IN GOING ON A PRACTICE DATE WITH HIM?
I MEAN, OKAY, I DID GET BUT-TERFLIES SEEING HIM LOOK LIKE THIS... BUT HE'S DEFINITELY NOT AN ADULT, LIKE TAKAHATA-SENSEI.
AND ON THE INSIDE, HE'S STILL A TEN-YEAR-OLD BRAT.
LICK LICK ♡
THAT FACE IS NOT MEANT FOR EATING ICE CREAM LIKE THAT.
HMMM. THAT'S OUR OLD-MAN-LOVING ASUNA.

SHE HAS SUCH A GORGEOUS NEGI-KUN RIGHT NEXT TO HER, AND SHE DOESN'T EVEN BAT AN EYE.
IF IT WERE ME, I'D BE MELTING ♡
SHE'S SO LUCKY! I WANNA TRADE PLACES!
O-OJÔSAMA?!
YOU THINK SO? SHE LOOKS PRETTY SHAKEN UP TO ME.
HEH, HEH, HEH
NĒSAN, GIMME YOUR CARD.
HERE YOU GO, CHAMO-KUN ♡
TELE-PATHIA!
ANIKI, ANIKI.
WELL? HOW DO YOU FEEL WITH YOUR NEW LOOK?
EVERYTHING AROUND ME SEEMS SO SMALL. I LIKE IT. I'LL BE OKAY.
OKAY! THEN LET'S PUT OUR PLAN INTO EFFECT.
ER, UM... ASUNA-SAN. LET'S GO TO THE SHRINE OVER THERE...
NO, NO! NOT LIKE THAT! THAT WON'T MAKE HER NERVOUS!
GAZE INTO HER EYES! GIVE HER A SWEET SMILE TO SHOW HER YOUR ADULT APPEAL! LIKE TAKAMICHI!
SHARP
L-LIKE THIS?

ASUNA-KUN.
SPARKLE
THERE'S A BIG CROWD OVER THERE. LET'S GO TAKE A LOOK.
PING
WH-WHY ARE YOU HITTING ME?
BE-CAUSE.
MSH
FSHH

CLAMOR CLAMOR
ワイ ワイ
TATSUMIYA SHRINE

CLAMOR ワイ CLAMOR ワイ
WOW! ♡ WITH ALL THESE BOOTHS HERE, IT'S LIKE THE FESTIVAL HAS ALREADY STARTED!
THERE ARE BOOTHS FROM NON-STUDENTS, TOO. MAYBE THEY'RE HAVING THE LOCAL TOWN FESTIVAL, TOO.
SETTING UP FOR THE FESTIVAL IS LIKE A FESTIVAL BY ITSELF, SO IT'S PROBABLY A GOOD WAY FOR THEM TO EARN MONEY.
わたあめ
WOW, LOOK, COTTON CANDY! I'VE NEVER HAD COTTON CANDY BEFORE!
YEAH, YEAH. I'LL BUY YOU SOME ALREADY.
LOOK, LOOK, ASUNA-SAN! A SHOOTING GALLERY ♪ CAN I TRY IT?
BUZZ ガヤ BUZZ ガヤ
HE REALLY IS A KID.
CHAK チャッ
ALLRIGHT! NON-THINKING STUFF IS MY SPECIALTY.
POW POW パパッ
CHAK チャキッ
POW POW POW POW パパパパン
WOW, YOU'RE GOOD, TOO, ASUNA-SAN!
OOHH おおーっ
CLAP パチ CLAP パチ CLAP パチ
YOU'RE REALLY SOMETHING, YOU KNOW THAT?
I DID REALLY WELL IN MY MARKSMANSHIP CLASS.

POW
POW
POW
POW
BUT YOU WON'T BEAT ME!
HEH HEH! IS THAT A CHALLENGE? THE ONLY THING YOU'LL BEAT ME IN IS SMARTS!
WHOA!
SIR, WOULD YOU PLEASE STOP? I'M GONNA RUN OUT OF PRIZES BEFORE THE FESTIVAL.
OOHH
BUZZ BUZZ
THE HUMAN BULL'S EYE!
SCORE A HIT & WIN A PRIZE
WARNING: WE WILL DODGE!
SH-SH
SH
SQUEE
SQUEE
THE MAHORA TENNIS CIRCLE PRESENTS THE HUMAN BULL'S EYE! UP TO 30 LIVE TARGETS AT A TIME!!
ASUNA-SAN! WHAT'S THAT!?
AH HA HA! I GOTTA HAND IT TO THE COLLEGE STUDENTS.
EEK!
HIYA!
HA HA HA.
PFFT!
AH HA HA HA HA
CLAMOR
CLAMOR

OOHH. SO I USE THIS TO CATCH A FISH?
YAH!
HA!
OOOH!
WAAH!
SHOOP
SHOOP
HOW CAN YOU BE SO GOOD AT THAT ON YOUR FIRST TRY? THAT'S SO ANNOYING!
GRRR! I CAN CATCH MORE THAN YOU!
AH HA HA!

ASUNA CAN BE A KID, TOO. SHE'S REALLY HAVING FUN.
IT LOOKS LIKE THEY'RE ENJOYING A REAL DATE.
WHOOPS, THAT'S NO GOOD! THIS IS RUINING THE REHEARSAL!
GASP!
AUGH. I'M NO GOOD AT THIS DELICATE STUFF.
YOU'RE PUTTING TOO MUCH FORCE INTO IT, THAT'S ALL.

ANIKI! WHAT ARE YOU DOING!? YOU HAVE TO BE MORE FORWARD WITH HER, OR SHE WON'T GET ANY GOOD PRACTICE IN!
ALL RIGHT. JUST DO EXACTLY AS I SAY. FIRST...
UM, OKAY. BUT CHAMO-KUN...
UM... ASUNA-SAN.
SS
WINCE
LET ME SHOW YOU.
WHAT!? I CAN'T DO THAT!
DO IT!
?
H-HEY! WHAT ARE YOU DOING?
UM, CALM DOWN. I'M TOLD THIS IS PART OF THE PRACTICE DATE.
YOU'RE "TOLD" !?
NO! UM, YOU KNOW. PRETEND I'M TAKAMICHI...
OH NO! I'M BLUSHING AGAIN.
CALM DOWN. HE MAY LOOK FIFTEEN, BUT ON THE INSIDE, HE'S JUST NEGI, THE TEN-YEAR-OLD BRAT.
EH...? MY RIGHT HAND...?
STOP IT, NEGI. I KNOW WE'RE PRACTIC-ING, BUT THAT'S ENOUGH...
SQUISH
MWA HA HA[HEART] LOOKIN' GOOD. OKAY, ANIKI, NEXT PUT YOUR RIGHT HAND AROUND HER WAIST...
BAH
W-WAH! I'M SORRY!
NICE ACCI-DENT" !!
OKAY! NOW WITH YOUR LEFT FOOT...
EH...? MY LEFT FOOT... WAH?
STAGGER
THUD!

DWEH !!?
WHY ?!

Y-YOU ...

WHAT ARE YOU DOING, STUPID !?
PWOOH!!
WHAM

PWAHH-PWEHH-PWOHH
Z-SH-SHAM
EEEK!
ANIKI !?
CRUNCH CRUNCH CRUNCH

Y... YOU.
LOOM
RUMBLE RUMBLE
EEK ?
AH...

THIS IS YOUR DOING, YOU PERV!
HELP !
YIKES
WOW, ASUNA-SAN'S TRAINING IS REALLY PAYING OFF.

NO, UM...
TWEET TWEET

I GUESS I SHOULD APOLOGIZE. SINCE YOU'RE BIGGER THAN ME, I FORGOT TO HOLD BACK...
NO. AH HA HA HA. I SHOULD APOLOGIZE.

HAS YOUR NOSE STOPPED BLEEDING?
I THINK SO.
I HOPE IT'S NOT BLEEDING BECAUSE YOU SAW MY PANTIES.
N-NO!
UM... ASUNA-SAN?
NN? WHAT?
WHAT MADE YOU FALL IN LOVE WITH TAKAMICHI?
ERK... YOU CUT RIGHT TO THE CHASE, DON'T YOU?
...
KIDS.
PAT PAT
TWEET TWEET
IT WAS RIGHT AFTER I CAME TO THIS SCHOOL.
I WAS STILL VERY SMALL, AND TAKAHATA-SENSEI TOOK CARE OF ME FOR A WHILE.
Y'KNOW, 'CAUSE I DIDN'T HAVE ANYONE TO RELY ON.
WOW... I SEE.
ALING
THESE BELLS...
RUSTLE...
WERE A GIFT FROM TAKAHATA-SENSEI.
WOW...
THE FIRST AND LAST PRESENT HE EVER GAVE ME.

I WAS JUST A KID...
AND I GUESS... I KIND OF READ TOO MUCH INTO IT.
...

I'M GETTING HUNGRY. WANNA GO GET SOMETHING TO EAT?
UM, OK.
ポン ポン PAT PAT

ACCORDING TO CHAMO-KUN'S SCHEDULE...
WE'RE SUPPOSED TO GO EAT AT A CAFÉ NOW, AND THEN PRACTICE YOUR LOVE CONFESSION AT THE WORLD TREE PLAZA...
HMM, MY LOVE CONFESSION, HUH? WHAT AM I GOING TO DO ABOUT THAT?

OH...COME TO THINK OF IT, YOU PRACTICED YOUR LOVE CONFESSION WITH ME SOON AFTER I FIRST GOT HERE, TOO.
ERK... DON'T REMIND ME.
...OH YEAH. HE SAID SOMETHING THAT DAY.
"COURAGE IS THE REAL MAGIC."

AAHH! THAT'S RIGHT! DIDN'T YOU SAY THAT YOU WERE GOING TO HAVE COURAGE AND TELL HIM HOW YOU FEEL!?
I FORGOT!
AH HA HA. WELL, A LOT HAPPENED AFTER THAT.
THERE WAS LIBRARY ISLAND, THE THING WITH EVA-CHAN, THE CLASS TRIP...
S-SO...
...YEAH. YOU'RE RIGHT.
THANK YOU FOR DOING THIS WITH ME, NEGI.
I THINK I *WILL* TRY TO TELL HIM HOW I FEEL.
I'LL BE COURAGEOUS.
AH...
I'M GLAD, ASUNA-SAN!
BUT I DON'T THINK THIS WEIRDO PRACTICE DATE IS GONNA BE MUCH HELP.
HA HA HA.
... HUH?
NORTH EUROPEAN CUISINE
イグドラシル
OH, ASUNA-SAN. THAT'S THE CAFÉ BY THE WORLD TREE THAT EVERYONE'S TALKING ABOUT THESE DAYS. THEY SAY IT'S CHIC AND DELICIOUS.
LET'S EAT THERE.
OHH ♪ IT *DOES* LOOK NICE.
NN...?

HUH...?
IS THAT TAKAMICHI AND SHIZUNA-SENSEI...?
EH!?
ASUNA-SAN!
TMP
YOU WERE GREAT, AKO!—
R-REALLY?
TMP TMP
HUH?
WAS THAT...?
AH.
DASH
ASUNA-SA-A-AN! WHAT'S WRONG—?!
IT'S ASUNA AND THE HOT GUY FROM THIS MORNING!
DO THEY KNOW EACH OTHER?
...
OH, HI.
YO, ANIKI! WHAT'S GOING ON? YOU DONE PRACTICING THE LOVE CONFESSION ALREADY?
DID OU SEE SUNA-SAN!?

SHE WENT TOWARD THE PLAZA.
THANKS!
HEY, ANIKI! YOUR MAGIC'S GONNA WEAR OFF SOON!! BE CAREFUL!
POOF!
EEEEP!
THUD!
ROLL ROLL CRASH
OOPS.
EEK!
Meek
...I KNEW IT.
THERE IS SOMETHING BETWEEN THEM... I ALWAYS THOUGHT SOMETHING WAS UP.
SHH...
ASUNA-SAN!
ZSH
SQWEEK!
WH-WHY DID YOU RUN OFF LIKE THAT?
ER, UM, IS IT BECAUSE YOU SAW TAKAMICHI AND SHIZUNA-SENSEI?
I... YEAH.
B-BUT THEY WERE ONLY EATING TOGETHER, THAT'S ALL. ...UM.
I MEAN... I DON'T THINK IT'S WHAT YOU'RE THINKING, ASUNA-SAN...
YOU...MAY BE RIGHT.
BUT IT DIDN'T LOOK LIKE JUST A MEAL.
UGH, YOU'RE SUCH A STUPID KID...
SIGH...
I GUESS I'M JUST NOT GOOD ENOUGH... I... I MEAN, I...

I'M...STUPID AND VIOLENT, AND I DON'T HAVE ANY FRIENDS...
I'M NOT REALLY VERY LIKABLE... EVEN TAKAHATA-SENSEI...
WHA
ooo
DON'T SAY THAT!
YOU'RE LEVEL-HEADED, YOU'RE STRONG AND PRETTY. I...
I-I'VE ALWAYS...
LOVED YOU, ASUNA-SAN.
......
EH?
サアッ…
SHH...

AND KONOKA-SAN AND SETSUNA-SAN AND CHAMO-KUN ALL LOVE YOU, ASUNA-SAN.
CLASS REP-SAN, TOO! SHE DOESN'T ACT LIKE IT, BUT SHE LOVES YOU A LOT, ASUNA-SAN!!
SO I KNOW EVERY-THING WILL BE FINE WITH TAKA-MICHI!!
DUN
どど〜ん
UM... OKAY.
WOW.
PFFT
ぷっ
YOU ARE SUCH A LITTLE KID.
STUPID.
CHUCKLE
くすくす
CHUCKLE
くすくす..
LOOK AT YOU!
WHAT!? WH-WH-WHY AM I STUPID !?
I-I-I WAS JUST TRYING TO MAKE YOU FEEL BETTER, THAT'S WHY I--
SHAKE
ぶんぶん
SHAKE
SHAKE
ぶん
YOU'RE STUPID BECAUSE YOU'RE STUPID.
STUPID. ♡
HRRM...
IT'S OKAY. I MAY BE HOPELESS, BUT I'LL STILL TELL HIM HOW I FEEL.
THANKS, NEGI.

NEGIMA!
MAGISTER NEGI MAGI
78TH PERIOD:
THE CURTAIN RISES: THE BATTLE FOR NEGI!

BEE-BEE-BEEP
BEE-BEE-BEEP
CHIRP CH-CHIRP
BEEP
NN... OH YEAH, I HAVE DELIVERIES TO MAKE TODAY.
I HAVE TO GET UP...
MMNYA

B-DMP
!?

Y-YOU LITTLE... CLIMBING INTO MY BED AGAIN...
B-DMP B-DMP
SMACK! NMN...♡
RUSTLE
MM... MYA. ONE-CHAN...
......

SMACKAH
MRPH!
THAT'S IT--NO MORE!!
YOU ARE FORBIDDEN FROM EVER COMING INTO MY BED AGAIN!! GOT IT, NEGI!?
EEEHH? BU YOU SAID THE OTHER DAY THAT I COULD SLEEP WITH YOU.
THAT WAS A SPECIAL CASE!
YOU'RE FINE NOW!
HUH? WHY IS YOUR FACE SO RED, ASUNA?
SOMETHING HAPPEN, ANE-SAN?
NOTHING HAPPENED!
SCRUNCH
EEEP?
UGH. YOU'R SO STUPI
I-I'M SORRY. I WAS HALF ASLEEP THIS MORNING...
OH, RIGHT! ANYWAY, ASUNA-SAN!
DID YOU ASK TAKAMICHI TO THE FESTIVAL?
ERK!

I TRIED TO CALL HIM A FEW TIMES...
BUT, WELL... Y'KNOW.
EEEHH!? YOU HAVEN'T ASKED HIM YET?
YOU SERIOUS, ANE-SAN!?
SH-SHUT UP!
BUT ASUNA-SAN, IT'S BEEN DAYS SINCE THE LAST TIME YOU SAID YOU'D TELL HIM HOW YOU FEEL.
YOU HAD SUCH A CALM, READY-TO-GO-THROUGH-WITH-IT SMILE...
THE FESTIVAL IS ALMOST HERE, ASUNA-SAN. YOU'RE RUNNING OUT OF TIME.
I KNOW, I KNOW!
BUT WHENEVER I PICK UP MY PHONE, MY HAND WON'T STOP SHAKING.
MY HEART BEATS OUT OF MY CHEST, I CAN'T BREATHE--I JUST CAN'T DO IT!
ぷる TREMBLE
ぷる TREMBLE
ぷる TREMBLE
NOW THAT IS JUST SAD. YOU WANT I SHOULD TALK TO HIM FOR YOU?
くわっ RAR
NO!! STOP IT!!
I'LL DO IT MYSELF! JUST LEAVE ME ALONE!!
NOTHING GOOD EVER HAPPENS WHEN YOU GET INVOLVED!
AH HA HA. SHE'S TAKING THIS REALLY SERIOUSLY.
HEH HEH HEH. THIS IS NOT GONNA BE AN EASY FESTIVAL FOR ANE-SAN.
NNGH...
BUT WOW, THE FESTIVAL IS ONLY THREE DAYS AWAY.
I CAN'T WAIT!
WELL, UNLIKE ANE-SAN, WE DON'T HAVE ANYTHING IMPORTANT TO DO.
SO WE'RE GONNA ENJOY A NICE, LEISURELY FESTIVAL. RIGHT, ANIKI?
AH HA HA. RIGHT.

WELL ISN'T IT JUST LOVELY THAT YOU GUYS GET TO TAKE IT EASY...
WHO CARES ABOUT ME, RIGHT?
GLARE
EEHH!? WHY ARE YOU GLARING AT ME?
I WANT WHAT'S BEST FOR YOU, ASUNA-SAN!

H-HON
HONK
WELL, GOOD MORNING, NEGI-KUN.
OH! TAKAMICHI!

THIS IS PERFECT TIMING! ASUNA-SAN WANTED TO TALK TO--
ER, HUH !?
SHE'S FAST!
THAT'S A PRETTY SWEET RIDE.

WH-WHAT'S THE MATTER?
SHE'S HOPE-LESS...

DONG
DING
CLAMOR
CLAMOR

BANG
BAM
IT'S HOPELESS! WE'RE DOOMED!
WE WON'T FINISH IN TIME !
BAM
BAM
BANG
AWAH-WAH!
ABU-BUH!

OOOH! WE'RE NOT GOING TO FINISH! I TOLD YOU WE SHOULD HAVE DECIDED SOONER...
HAKASE-SAN, TAKE YOUR TEAM AND CHECK THE MECHANICS...
CLAMOR
CLAMOR
CLAMOR
FASTER, HARUNA-SAN!
KYAA
AT THIS RATE, WE'LL BE PULLING ALL-NIGHTERS TODAY, TOMORROW, AND THE NEXT DAY!
RELAX, CLASS REP. I'M TELLING YOU, WE'LL FINISH IT.
AND, UM, MAKIE-SAN, YOUR TEAM IS ON INTERIOR DESIGN.
SAKURAKO-SAN, YOUR TEAM FINISH THE MASKS...
HAUNTED
AWAWAH!
IN THE CRUNCH TIME BEFORE A DEADLINE, IT'S CRUCIAL TO KEEP A LEVEL HEAD.
HOW CAN YOU BE CALM AT A TIME LIKE THIS!!?
HARUNA HAS CRUNCH TIME EVERY MONTH.
AND WE HAVE TO HELP HER.
THINGS ARE PRETTY ROUGH ALL AROUND, HUH?
YEAH.

HELLO! HOW IS IT COMING, EVERYONE?
RATTLE
NEGI-KUN!
NEGI-SENSEI!
IT'S BAD, NEGI-KUN!
WE WON'T FINISH!
CLAMOR
CLAMOR
KYAA
KYAA
EH ?!
NEGI-KUN, WILL YOU PLEASE HELP US?
GOODNESS! ASKING NEGI-SENSEI TO HELP! HOW COULD YOU EVEN SUGGEST IT!? GOODNESS! ASKING NEGI-SENSEI TO HELP! HOW COULD YOU EVEN SUGGEST IT!?
OKAY ...
THIS IS ONLY YOUR FIRST YEAR AS A TEACHER, NEGI-SENSEI, SO PLEASE. RELAX AND ENJOY YOURSELF.
TH-THANK YOU.
LET HIM HELP, CLASS REP! DON'T BE SO MEAN!
OH YEAH! NEGI-KUN!

WE'RE GOING TO BE IN A LIVE CONCERT DURING THE FESTIVAL ♡
SQUEE
EH?
OH, RIGHT!
SQUEE
OH YEAH! WE WANT YOU TO COME, SENSEI ♡
HEY! THAT'S CHEATING!!
WE WANT HIM TO COME TO THE WALKING CLUB'S STROLL AROUND THE SCHOOL!
!!
HMPH!
!
!
RIGHT! I WAS GOING TO ASK NEGI-KUN ON A LAST-DAY DATE!
BUT...!
BAH
IF I ASK HIM OUT NOW, THERE'S SURE TO BE INTERFERENCE!!
BA-BAH
FIRST, I MUST CASUALLY ASK HIM TO MY CLUB'S EVENT!!
OH YES, DISCIPLE.
I WANTING SHOW YOUR TĀOLŌ TO NEW CLUB MEMBERS. YOU COME CHINESE MARTIAL ARTS DEMONSTRATION.
SPLAT
IS ORDER FROM MASTER.
AH!
Y-YES, KŪ-RŌSHI!
*TĀOLŌ = CHINESE MARTIAL ARTS FORMS
OUTTA MY WAY, KŪ FEI!
WHAM!
NEGI-KUN, WILL YOU COME TO THE GYMNASTICS EXHIBITION ♡
THERE'LL BE LOTS OF PRETTY GIRLS!
O-OKAY.
NEGI-SENSEI, I WOULD LOVE TO HAVE YOU AT THE EQUESTRIAN CLUB'S RIDING EVENT!!
WALKING CLUB!
THE COOKING CLUB IS HAVING A BANQUET...
ERK! WE'VE GOT TROUBLE! ...NĒ-SAN!
I'M ON IT!

ALL RIGHT, BACK UP, BACK UP!
REAL MANAGER.
ANYONE WHO WANTS AN APPOINTMENT WITH NEGI-KUN HAS TO GO THROUGH ME--HIS PERSONAL (ACTING) MANAGER.
BAM
WHA ?!
WHY ARE YOU HIS MANAGER, ASAKURA —!?
NEVER MIND THE DETAILS. YOU WANT AN APPOINTMENT, GET IN LINE! —
I DO NOT APPROVE OF THIS! NEGI-SENSEI!
CLAMOR ワイワイ CLAMOR
KYAA キャー
YOU THERE! GET TO WORK! —

FWEE FWEET ピッピーッ
HERE I THOUGHT WE'D BE ABLE TO TAKE IT EASY DURING THE FESTIVAL, BUT IT TURNS OUT WE'VE GOT A LOT WE HAVE TO SEE.
YOU'RE GONNA WANNA MAKE SURE TO ORGANIZE YOUR SCHEDULE.
麻帆良祭スケジュール
MAHORA SCHOOL FESTIVAL schedule table
DAY 1 6/20 (FRIDAY) 10:30〜
R.C. EXHIBITION
HOVER HOVER
EQUESTRIAN CLUB
DAY 2 6/21 (SATURDAY)
STAGE PLAY
MARTIAL-ARTS DEMO
DIVINATION CLUB
ACADEMY WALKING TOUR
DAY 3 6/22 (SUNDAY) (LAST DAY)
GOURMET FESTIVAL
FINE-ARTS CLUB
NIGHTMARE CIRCUS
HOVER HOVER
LIVE CONCERT
IT'S GONNA BE TOUGH GETTING AROUND TO ALL OF THESE, ANIKI.
EH HEH HEH
WELL, YOU HAVE THREE DAYS. YOU'LL BE FINE.

I WAS ALREADY PLANNING TO GO SEE ALL MY STUDENTS AT THEIR CLUB EVENTS.
OHO!
I *AM* THEIR HOMEROOM TEACHER, AFTER ALL.
OH! I'M IMPRESSED, NEGI-KUN ♡

COME ON. WE'LL GO WITH YOU. COURAGE!
JUST ASKING HIM WON'T HURT ANY! THIS IS YOUR CHANCE TO FURTHER YOUR RELATIONSHIP!
Y-YEAH. I KNOW...
HMMM, THEY ALL LOOK SO FUN!
......

UH, UM...
HELLO, NEGI-SENSEI!
NECO NYAN NYAN
NECO NYAN NYAN
OH... ♡

OH, HI.
H-HI.
WHAT IS IT, NODOKA-SAN?
UM... WELL ...
THAT IS...
BLU-S-S-SH
EEEP
TH-TH-THE LIBRARY EXPLOR-ATION CLUB
DUN
IS HAVING AN EXPEDITION EVENT! PLEASE COME!
R-RIGHT, RIGHT! AND THE MANGA CLUB IS DRAWING CARICATURE PORTRAITS! COME CHECK IT OUT!
AH.
BA-BAH
THE KIDS' LIT CLUB IS HAVING A PICTURE BOOK READING,
I WILL.
AND THE PHILOSOPHY CLUB WILL BE HOSTING A DISCUSSION ON HEIDEGGER AND ARISTOTLE. WE'D LOVE TO HAVE YOU.
GO ON, NODOKA! DON'T YOU HAVE SOMETHING ELSE?
YOU CAN DO IT!
E-EEP! NNGH!
BAH
UM. THAT IS... WELL UM ...
BLUSH
W...WILL YOU...
GO AROUND THE FESTIVAL WITH ME?
SMILE

EH... ? ER.
W-WITH YOU... ?
BLUSH...
HOO HA HA.
TEP!
KYAAA! I'M SORRY!
I SAID IT!
NODOKA-SAN?
UGH, THAT GIRL. SHE DIDN'T EVEN WAIT FOR HIS ANSWER!
BUT THAT'S OKAY, RIGHT, NEGI-KUN? YOU CAN DO IT!?
Y-YES, I CAN...
I-IF POSSIBLE, WE'D LIKE YOU TO GO WITH HER ON THE LAST DAY!
NODOKA! HE SAID HE'LL GO WITH YOU!
TEP TEP TEP
WAIT!
IS SOMETHING THE MATTER, ASUNA-SAN?
NO... IT'S JUST...
BOOKSTORE-CHAN. SHE'S REALLY
BRAVE, ISN'T SHE?
......
SMILE
YES. I AGREE.

BOW
SCAMPER
NO-DOKA-!
HMMM ...
STARE
...
MM HM HM HM HM ♡
MWA HA!
WH-WHAT IS IT, YOU TWO?
AND YOU, CHAMO-KUN!
UH, UM ....

EXCUSE ME, NEGI-SENSEI.
OH... CHACHAMARU-SAN!
TEA CEREMONY CLUB ♦ OPEN-AIR PRESENTATION
RESERVATIONS NOW ACCEPTED
UM... THIS IS A FLIER FOR THE MISTRESS'S GO TOURNAMENT.
UM, THANK YOU.
AND THIS IS AN INVITATION TO THE TEA CLUB'S NODATE* CEREMONY.
WOW ♡ THANK YOU VERY MUCH.
I'VE ALWAYS WANTED TO TRY SOME OF YOUR TEA, CHACHAMARU-SAN.
Y-YOU HAVE?
*A TEA CEREMONY ENJOYED IN THE OUTDOORS.
AND, UM... IF YOU HAVE TIME...
ANY TIME YOU MAY BE AVAILABLE DURING THE FESTIVAL...
I... WILL YOU...
もじ…
FIDGET
?
IT IS NOTHING.
I WILL BE WAITING WITH DELICIOUS TEA FOR YOU!
Z-SHAM
VRR
DUN!
CHACHA-MARU-SAN ??
AH...
よろ…
SWOON
ERK...
WHAT'S WITH HER?
N-NO IDEA.
BUT, LOOK! A NODATE TEA CEREMONY! I CAN'T WAIT ♡
OOHH.
IS CHACHA-MARU-SAN... NO, CAN'T BE...

HEEEY! NEGIII!!
TODAY'S THE LAST DAY TO SIGN UP FOR THE MARTIAL ARTS TOURNAMENT! LET'S GO!
EEHH!? BUT I'M NOT ENTERING!
HOW CAN YOU SAY THAT? THIS IS OUR PERFECT CHANCE FOR A FACE-OFF!
OHO? THE PRIZE IS A 100,000 YEN*!
FACE-OFF? BUT I DON'T STAND A CHANCE WITHOUT MAGIC!
*ABOUT $1000
BESIDES, I ALREADY HAVE A BUSY SCHEDULE...
WE'LL WORK OUT THE SCHEDULE. GO SIGN UP, ANIKI!
IT'LL BE A GOOD CHANCE TO TEST YOUR SKILLS.
YEAH! YEAH!
...OR, I WISH. BUT ACTUALLY, THERE'S A PROBLEM.
PROBLEM?
ANYONE UNDER TWELVE HAS TO ENTER THE KIDS' TOURNAMENT.
IF WE WENT UP AGAINST KIDS, WE'D JUST BE BIG BULLIES.
AND THE PRIZE IS CHUMP CHANGE.
CAN'T REALLY ARGUE THERE.
GLINT
HEH HEH.
I HAVE JUST THE THING.
WHAT? REALLY?
JUST THE THING...? OH NO! CHAMO-KUN!?
ALL RIGHT, LET'S GO, WHATSYER-NAME!
YEAH! YOU'RE PRETTY USEFUL, ERMINE!
HEY! DON'T I HAVE A SAY IN THIS?
AH HA HA!
EVERYONE WANTS A PIECE OF NEGI-KUN.
...YOU CAN SAY THAT AGAIN.
WELL, WHATEVER. LET'S GO HELP OUR CLUBS GET READY.
OH! THERE YOU ARE, ASUNA!

HUH? WHAT'S UP, YOU TWO?
...ACTUALLY, UM, I WANT TO ASK YOU SOME-THING...
THAT CUTE GUY YOU WERE WITH THE OTHER DAY. IS HE A FRIEND OF YOURS?
HE HAD HAIR LIKE NEGI-KUN'S...
EH? THE OTHER DAY...?
H-HIM!!?
AW, CRAP. THEY SAW THAT.
NO, UM, THAT WAS...
IS HE YOUR BOYFRIEND, ASUNA?
N-NO! UM, HE WAS, UH, RIGHT! NEGI'S COUSIN.
HE JUST CAME TO SPEND TO SPEND A FEW DAYS IN JAPAN...
WHAT!? NEGI-KUN'S COUSIN?
UGH, YOU TWO ARE SO PUSHY.
AH HA HA. BUT THIS POTION IS AWESOME!
DUN
SPLURT
OH, AKO-SAN. KUGIMIYA-SAN. HELLO.
HUH...? HOW DO YOU KNOW US?
THEY'RE MULTI-PLYING...
MRP!? OH NO, YOU'RE RIGHT!
YOU STUPID NEGI!
JUST PLAY ALONG, OKAY?
WHACK
WHAT IF THEY FIGURE IT OUT!?

H-HELLO. IT'S NICE TO MEET YOU. ASUNA-SAN'S TOLD ME ABOUT YOU.
UM, MY NAME IS N-NAGI SPRINGFIELD.
OH, H-HELLO.
MMM, HE REALLY IS CUTE.
UM... WELL...
BUT THE STUPID-LOOKING ONE BEHIND HIM MIGHT BE MORE MY TYPE.
H-HERE! IT WON'T BE ANY GOOD, BUT--!!
BUT PLEASE COME IF YOU CAN!!
DA-DASH
IF YOU'LL EXCUSE ME!
WE HOPE TO SEE YOU THERE!
YOUR FRIEND CAN COME, TOO.
EH.....?
UH.....

BAH
NOT ANY GOOD...?
UM... ARE THESE...?
LOVE AT FIRST SIGHT, PERHAPS?
...PER-HAPS.
I CAN COME, TOO?
AH-HA, HA...
HA HA.
..UGH. DO THEY HONESTLY EXPECT ME TO HELP WITH THEIR STUPID FESTIVAL EVERY STINKIN' YEAR?
I'M GOING HOME TO SLEEP

D-DOES THAT MEAN I HAVE TO GO TO THE CONCERT LIKE THIS?
A CON-CERT, HUH?
I GUESS IT DOES.
YOU'RE IN HIGH DEMAND, ANIKI.
THIS'LL BE A SCHEDULE WORTH MANAGING.
WHA ?!
SHOCK!!
NAGI!? WHAT ARE YOU--
OH! EVAN-GELINE-SAN.
AH... GHN!
OH. IT'S AN ILLUSION.
I SEE. SO YOU DID THIS TO GET INTO THE FIGHTING TOURNAMENT.
DON'T CON-FUSE ME LIKE THAT.
Y-YES, MAS-TER.
HMMM, ALRIGHT. ...I THINK I'LL PARTICIPATE IN THIS "MARTIAL ARTS TOURNAMENT," TOO.
I WOULD LIKE TO SEE HOW MY DISCIPLE IS COMING ALONG, AFTER ALL.
BUT THIS COULD BE...
I HADN'T THOUGHT OF THAT...
GLANCE
GLANCE
YOU, MASTER !?
OHH!
HEH HEH... HOW-EVER...

IF YOU CAN'T BEAT ME WHEN I'M IN MY WEAKEST STATE,
YOU WILL SPEND THE ENTIRE LAST DAY OF THE FESTIVAL WITH ME, LOOKING LIKE THAT.
ALL THE WAY THROUGH DINNER AND AFTERWARD, OF COURSE.
HEH HEH HEH HEH
DUN
E-EEHH!?
MASTER'S ORDERS. YOU HAVE NO RIGHT TO REFUSE.

LATER. I'M LOOKING FORWARD TO IT.
AWA-AWA-WAWAH.
WHA-WH-WH-WHAT DO I DO? THINGS ARE GETTING A LITTLE OUT OF HAND!
IF I CAN'T BEAT MY MASTER, I'LL LOSE THE ENTIRE LAST DAY...
HRRRRM. AND CONSIDERING THE TIME YOU PROMISED TO NODOKA-JŌCHAN...
YOU COULD BE IN TROUBLE.
UH, UM...
WHOOSH

HELLO...
HORRO
HORRO
HORRO
HEEEK!
UM... IF IT'S ALRIGHT, MAY I GO AROUND THE FESTIVAL WITH YOU, NEGI-SEN...I MEAN, EVERYONE...
I THOUGHT YOU PASSED ON TO NIRVANA!!
Z-SHA-SHAM

NNNGH ....

MAHORA SCHOOL FESTIVAL
schedule table
DAY 1
6/20 (FRIDAY)
10 : 30~
R.G. EXHIBITION
EQUESTRIAN CLUB
MARTIAL-ARTS DEMO
FINE-ARTS CLUB
SCAVENGER HUNT
DISCUSSION GROUP
"NODATE"
DIVINATION CLUB
CARICATURES
DAY 2
STAGE PLAY
ACADEMY WALKING TOUR
"GO" TOURNAMENT
GOURMET FESTIVAL
NIGHTMARE CIRCUS
MARTIAL-ARTS TOURNEY
SEE FESTIVAL TOGETHER
LIVE CONCERT
AND NOW I'VE EVEN ADDED A GHOST...
うじゃ
JAM
うじゃ
JAM
うじゃ
JAM
MY SCHEDULE'S GOTTEN REALLY PACKED...
WH-WH-WH-WHAT DO I DO ?
MAYBE I SHOULD DROP OUT OF THE TOURNAMENT...
あああ
AAHH...
TELL THAT TO EVA AND SHE MIGHT KILL YOU.
NNNGH
THIS IS A REALLY BUSY SCHEDULE...
ABU-BU-BUH!
あぶぶ
I NEED AT LEAST TWO OF ME TO DO ALL OF THIS!

NNNGH, I JUST HAVE TO DO MY BEST.
THE TABLES ARE TURNED. NOW NEGI-KUN'S THE ONE WITH THE SCARY-LOOKING FESTIVAL.
G-GOOD LUCK, ASUNA-SAN.
YOU CAN DO IT.
OH, THAT'S RIGHT. YOU HAVE FESTIVAL PROBLEMS, TOO, ASUNA-SAN.
I...
I KNOW THAT, STUPID.
peaceful Angel

OH, ASUNA. YOU'RE GOING OUTSIDE?
REMEMBER, WE'RE HEADING BACK AT NINE TO WORK ON THE HAUNTED HOUSE.
YEAH, I REMEMBER.

......
WHEW.

....
EVERYONE'S TRYING SO HARD...

....

TREMBLE
ぷるぷる
TREMBLE

....
BEEP

R-R-R-RING
R-R-R-RING
TAKAHATA-SENSEI
R-R-R-RING

CLICK
AH...!
TA-T-T-T-TAKAHATA-SENSEI?
I-IT'S ME. YEAH, ASUNA...
NO... YES.
UM...I WAS WONDERING... DO YOU HAVE ANY FREE TIME DURING THE FESTIVAL?

NECO NYAN NYAN

YAAY YAAY
MURMUR MURMUR
PSST PSST
BANG BANG
YADA YADA

WHISPER ヒソ
BE CAREFUL WITH THE HAMMERS.
DON'T MAKE TOO MUCH NOISE.
I CAN'T HELP IT!
WHISPER ヒソ WHISPER ヒソ
サワサワ MURMUR
MURMUR
EH HEH HEH HEH. THIS IS KIND OF EXCITING-- SNEAKING IN AND STAYING THE NIGHT!
IT IS NOT. I WANNA GO TO SLEEP.

NNNGH, WE'RE NOT ALLOWED TO STAY OVER-NIGHT UNTIL THE DAY BEFORE.
HOW CAN I, THE REP-RESENTATIVE OF CLASS 3-A, ALLOW SUCH DELINQUENC-CY...?

NNGH. I'M THE TEACHER, SO...
MURMUR MURMUR サワサワ
THANKS, NEGI-KUN!
YOU'RE A LIFE-SAVER!
サワ MURMUR
OOHHH, I'M SO SORRY THAT YOU HAVE TO BE A PART OF THIS, NEGI-SENSEI.

WHAT CHOICE DO WE HAVE! WE WANT TO FINISH IN TIME!
OTHER CLASSES ARE DOING IT.
I KNOW THAT!

NITTA'S COM-ING!!
3-B STUDENT
THANKS!
EVERY-BODY, HIDE!!

CLACK コツ
CLACK コツ

FLASH

WA-
WAH...

SORRY, NEGI-KUN. COULD YOU SQUISH BACK?
EH
?

SHOVE
!!
POFF

AH... I-I'M SORRY...
IT'S O-KAY...
BLUSH...

S-SORRY ABOUT THAT.
N-NO, IT'S ALL RIGHT.
......
?!

N-NODOKA-SAN! HOW DARE YOU TAKE ADVANTAGE OF THE CONFUSION TO CREATE SUCH A BLESSEDLY EMBARRASSING INCIDENT...
TRADE PLACES WITH ME!!
COME ON, BACK TO WORK!
AWA-WAH.
MURMUR MURMUR
CLASS REP! PIPE DOWN!
CLAMOR
CLAMOR

THE COAST IS CLEAR! BACK TO WORK, EVERY-ONE!!
CLACK CLACK

NEGIMA!
MAGISTER NEGI MAGI
79TH PERIOD:
THE SWEET TRUTH OF THE WORLD TREE LEGEND♥

WE DID IT! —
IT'S FIN-ISHED —♡
HORROR HOUSE
YAAY! ♡
MMMM~ IT LOOKS SO HAUNTED ♡
ANYWAY, IT LOOKS LIKE WE CAN FINISH THIS.
BUT WE'LL BE UP ALL NIGHT AGAIN!
CHIRP CHIRP
TWEET TWEET
SQUEE
SQUEE
ALLLRIGHT! WE MIGHT EVEN MAKE IT TO THE PRE-FESTIVAL PARTY!
WE WON'T LET 2-F OR 2-S SHOW US UP WITH THEIR HAUNTED HOUSES!
BUT THE INSIDE IS HARDLY EVEN STARTED.
WE ONLY FINISHED THE ENTRANCE.
RIGHT! BACK TO WORK!
AI-YAI-YAI...
WAA-A-AH...
DON'T SAY THAT!
PRE-FESTIVAL PARTY?
IT'S A PARTY THEY HAVE BY THE WORLD TREE THE NIGHT BEFORE MAHORA FEST--AND THAT'S TONIGHT. IT'S A PRETTY BIG THING.

WELL, IT'S TIME TO HELP OUR CLUBS!
PLEASE COME BACK IF YOU HAVE TIME!
OKAY! I HAVE TO FINISH MY PAINTING !!
OH! I'LL GO WITH YOU PART-WAY, ASUNA-SAN!
I'M SURPRISED THEY CAN MOVE.
WE WERE JUST UP ALL NIGHT.
DON'T YOU THREE NEED TO GO?
WE'RE IN SPORTS CLUBS.
OUR CLUBS ARE JUST DOING, LIKE, TAKOYAKI AND STUFF.
WE'LL STAY HERE! WHO WANTS AN ENERGY DRINK?
HEY, HEY. FIRST, HAVE YOU SEEN THIS?
NN? MAHORA SPORTS AGAIN?
THE WORLD TREE LEGEND IS TRUE...? ITS REAL POWER MANIFESTS EVERY 22 YEARS...
WORLD-TREE LEGEND NOT LEGEND AT ALL
POWER MANIFESTS ONCE EVERY 22 YEAR
▲ June 22, 1982: The World Tree Emits a Spectacular Glow
Forever intrigued by the legend of the campus World Tree, we at Mahora Sports have exciting new information to reveal.
Magical Phenomenon? The World Tree's Spectacular Glow
Located in the center of the Mahora campus, the shinboku or "Sacred Tree" Bantō has long been the center of controversy, as well. That it predictably emits a glow of light in mid-summer is a well-documented fact (see photo, above), but is it significant that the last day of the Festival also coincides with summer ... longest day of the year?
THE SCHOOL'S SEVEN WONDERS RESEARCH CLUB INVESTIGATES... HMMM...
2003
TAKE TO THE SKIES!
BIRDMAN RALLY
MAHORA LAKE, NORTH SIDE
ONLY 5 MINS. WALK FROM LIBRARY ISLAND!
FIRST DAY, 10:00 –
CLAMOR
CLAMOR
IT'S NOT JUST ANOTHER ONE OF THEIR FISHY RUMORS?
HRRRM
STUPID
BUT EVERYONE'S TALKING ABOUT IT...
THE OCCULT CLUB'S IN ON IT, TOO, AFTER ALL.
IT'S FAKE.
I KNOW THAT ONE! THEY SAY IT'S COMING A YEAR EARLY.
THE WORLD TREE LIGHTS UP ON THE LAST DAY.
OH, THAT!
SQUEE
LIKE "BWOOHH"!
AND ONCE EVERY 22 YEARS, IT'S REALLY SPECTACULAR!
SQUEE

チュン チュン…
CHIRP CHIRP
チチ…
TWEET…
CLAMOR CLAMOR
ワイ ワイ
STUFFED PLUSHIES CLUB
CAMPUS-WIDE "SURVIVAL" CONTEST
TECHNOLOGY CLUB, ROBOT DIVISION GIANT-SIZED "TEA CEREMONY" AUTOMATON
ANIME CLUB
"MIZUGI" SHIGERU RESEARCH CLUB
AS EXPECTED, THERE ARE STRANGE THINGS ALL OVER CAMPUS ON THE DAY BEFORE THE FESTIVAL.
NO KIDDING ♪
OH YEAH, ASUNA-SAN...
HAVE YOU TALKED TO TAKA-MICHI...?
UM...
WELL ...
GOOD
WHAT? REALLY !?
THAT'S GREAT, ASUNA ♪
OHO!
CON-GRATU-LATIONS !

IT IS NOT! HOW AM I SUPPOSED TO FACE HIM?
UGH, EVER SINCE I CALLED HIM, I'VE BEEN SO NERVOUS, I CAN'T EAT, I CAN'T SLEEP! I'M DYING! I SHOULD HAVE FORGOTTEN THE WHOLE THING!
NOW, NOW, ANE-SAN. EVERYONE FEELS THAT WAY AT FIRST.
OH, NEGI-SENSEI.
OH! SH-SHIZUNA-SENSEI !
ERK !
I'M GLAD I RAN INTO YOU. THE HEADMASTER WOULD LIKE TO SEE YOU.
EH? ER, RIGHT.
THEN I HAD BETTER GET BACK TO THE MAIN BUILDING.

NO, HE DIDN'T WANT TO SEE YOU IN HIS OFFICE. HE WANTS TO SEE YOU AT WORLD TREE PLAZA.
AND IF YOU CAN SPARE THE TIME, HE'D LIKE TO SEE YOU, TOO, SAKURAZAKI-SAN.
EH?
SEE YOU LATER, SETSUNA-SAN!
BYE ♡
I WONDER WHAT HE WANTS TO TALK TO US ABOUT.
I DON'T KNOW....
HUH? THAT'S ODD...
IS SOMETHING THE MATTER?
IT'S THE DAY BEFORE THE FESTIVAL, BUT THE PLAZA IS EMPTY...
HUH...?
IS THAT...?

HMMM. SO YOU DON'T REMEMBER MUCH ABOUT WHEN YOU DIED.
I HAVE BEEN A GHOST A LONG TIME...
SO I'D BETTER... NOT WRITE AN ARTICLE ABOUT YOU THEN.
RIGHT... THAT IS...
SO MUCH GOOD STUFF AND I CAN'T WRITE ABOUT ANY OF IT.
STILL, WHY ME? WHY NOT FOLLOW NEGI-KUN OR SOMEBODY?
WELL, THINGS WERE BETTER TWO DAYS AGO, BUT...
OTHER PEOPLE REALLY JUST CAN'T SEE ME.
I THINK YOU CAN SEE ME BECAUSE YOU SAT NEXT TO ME FOR TWO YEARS, ASAKURA-SAN ♡
I WONDER IF THIS COUNTS AS BEING POSSESSED?
...HUH?
STOP
IS SOME-THING WRONG, ASAKURA-SAN?
N-NO. IT'S JUST, I WAS GOING TO THE PLAZA TO WORK ON A STORY...
BUT SUDDENLY I DON'T WANT TO GO THERE ANYMORE...
?
AH! IT'S NEGI-SENSEI.
EH?
OH ....
NEGI-KUN!

WE'VE BEEN WAITING FOR YOU.
チュン チュン
CHIRP CHIRP
チチチ…
TWEET TWEET
HUH?
WHA...?
ER, UM... WHO ARE ALL THESE PEOPLE?
RIGHT, YOU HAVEN'T BEEN INTRODUCED YET.
SMILE
YO.

EVERYONE GATHERED HERE
WORKS IN ONE OF THE VARIOUS ELEMENTARY, JUNIOR HIGH, SENIOR HIGH, OR COLLEGE CAMPUSES SCATTERED THROUGHOUT ACADEMY CITY
AS A MAGIC TEACHER.
OR AS A MAGIC STUDENT.
THOUGH THIS ISN'T ALL OF THEM.

EH?
EEEEHHHH!?

SO *YOU'RE* NEGI-KUN.
I HEAR ABOUT YOU ALL THE TIME. IT'S A PLEASURE.
Y-YES, HELLO.
SORRY FOR KEEPING IT FROM YOU, NEGI-KUN.
Y-YOU'RE A MAGIC TEACHER, TOO, SERUHIKO-SENSEI?

I'M SORRY I COULDN'T HELP YOU ON THE CLASS TRIP. THE HEADMASTER ORDERED ME TO STAY AND GUARD THE STUDENTS.
THOUGH I MAY NOT HAVE BEEN MUCH HELP ANYWAY.
TH-THAT'S ALL RIGHT.
WOW...
I HAD NO IDEA.
TO THINK THERE ARE SO MANY WIZARDS RIGHT HERE ON THIS BIG CAMPUS...
ERRRGH. I CAN'T MAKE ANYTHING OUT.
IF I GET ANY CLOSER, THEY'LL SPOT ME FOR SURE.
WANT ME TO GO FOR YOU?
I'M CONFIDENT NO ONE WILL NOTICE ME.
EH?

I CALLED YOU HERE TODAY FOR ONE REASON, AND ONE REASON ONLY.
WE HAVE A PROBLEM.
I WOULD LIKE ALL OF YOUR HELP IN SOLVING IT.
BAD GUYS !?
N-NOT ANOTHER BIG INCIDENT!?
NO, NOTHING AS SERIOUS AS WHAT HAPPENED ON YOUR CLASS TRIP.
ALTHOUGH IT IS SERIOUS IN A DIFFERENT SENSE.
DO YOU KNOW THE WORLD TREE LEGEND?

YEAH, ALL THE LITTLE KIDS IN MY CLASS CAN'T STOP TALKING ABOUT IT. IT'S SO STUPID. IF YOU MAKE A WISH AT THE WORLD TREE ON THE LAST DAY OF THE FESTIVAL, IT'LL COME TRUE.
WHAT IS THIS, TANABATA?
HUH? I THOUGHT IT WAS ABOUT GETTING A SWEETHEART.
THAT'S WHAT YUNA-SAN WAS SAYING.
WELL, THAT'S THE GIST OF IT.

AND WELL... IT'S TRUE.
HUH ?
YOUR WISH REALLY WILL COME TRUE.
BUT ONLY ONCE EVERY 22 YEARS.
WHA ?
THEREIN LIES THE PROB-LEM.

DURING THE FESTIVAL, AND ESPECIALLY TOWARDS THE END OF THE LAST DAY,
IF ANY STUDENT ATTEMPTS TO EXECUTE THE WORLD TREE LEGEND, I WANT YOU TO STOP THEM.
IN OTHER WORDS, PREVENT ALL LOVE CON-FESSIONS.
WHAT!? YOUR WISHES REALLY DO COME TRUE?
I-IT'S NOT JUST A SUPER-STITION?
HO HO HO.

THIS TREE THAT THE STUDENTS CALL THE WORLD TREE--
ITS TRUE NAME IS THE SHINBOKU BANTŌ.
THERE IS GREAT POWER HIDDEN INSIDE IT.
IN OTHER WORDS, IT IS A MAGICAL TREE.

WORLD TREE PLAZA
WORLD TREE
1.5km
ONCE EVERY 22 YEARS, ITS MAGICAL POWER REACHES ITS PEAK AND FLOWS OUT OF THE TREE.
POCKETS OF POWERFUL MAGICAL ENERGY FORM AT SIX POINTS, WITH THE WORLD TREE AT THEIR CENTER.
HIS PLAZA IS ONE OF THOSE POINTS.

THE VAST AMOUNT OF MAGICAL ENERGY CAN AFFECT PEOPLE'S MINDS.
SO IF ONE WISHES, "LET ME RULE THE WORLD," "I WANT TEN BILLION YEN," "GIVE ME SOME GAL'S PANTIES,"
OR OTHER SUCH MATERIAL WISHES, THEY WON'T BE GRANTED.
BUT WHEN IT COMES TO CONFESSIONS OF LOVE...

THE WISH FULFILL-MENT RATE IS 120%!!!
120%
IT IS TRULY A CURSE-CLASS POWER!!
FLASH
RIGHT ...
WHAT WERE YOU IMAGINING THERE...?
THIS SHOULDN'T BE HAPPENING UNTIL NEXT YEAR... BUT PERHAPS DUE TO ABNORMAL WEATHER PATTERNS, IT'S HAPPENING A YEAR EARLY.
AND THAT IS WHY I HAVE CALLED THIS EMERGENCY MEETING.
...

B-BUT ISN'T IT A GOOD THING, IF THEY CAN BE GIRLFRIEND AND BOYFRIEND?
EITHER WAY, IT'S STUPID.
DON'T BE RIDIC-ULOUS.
YOU'RE SUCH A CHILD.
MANIPULATING SOMEONE'S HEART IN PERPETUITY GOES AGAINST EVEN THE MOST BASIC WIZARDING PRINCIPLES.
YOU WOULDN'T WANT TO BE THE BOYFRIEND OF A GIRL YOU DON'T LIKE, WOULD YOU?
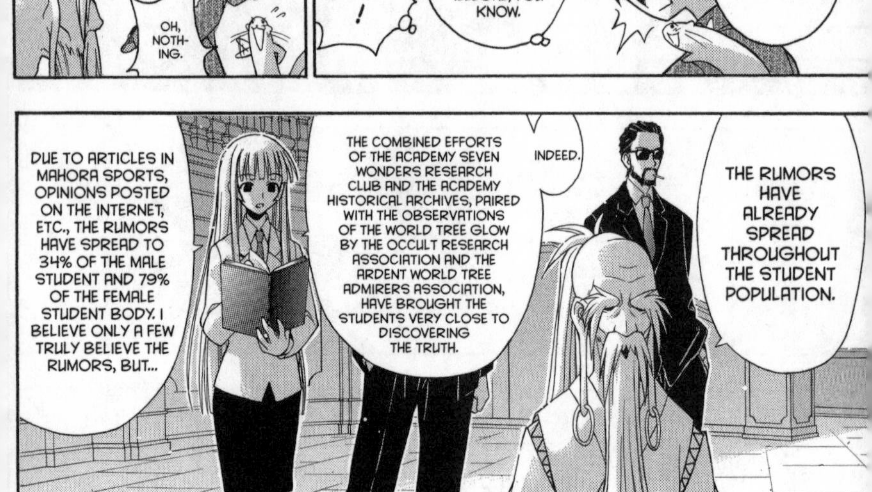
I-IS THAT TRUE? BUT I MADE A LOVE POTION...
THAT'S ONLY TEMPORARY; IT SHOULD BE FINE. BUT HEY, ANIKI, LOVE POTIONS *ARE* TECHNICALLY ILLEGAL, YOU KNOW.
WHAT!? YOU'RE KID-DING!
I'M A CRIMINAL I'M A CRIMINAL
CLANG CLANG CLANG
IS SOMETHING THE MATTER?
OH, NOTH-ING.
THE RUMORS HAVE ALREADY SPREAD THROUGHOUT THE STUDENT POPULATION.
INDEED.
THE COMBINED EFFORTS OF THE ACADEMY SEVEN WONDERS RESEARCH CLUB AND THE ACADEMY HISTORICAL ARCHIVES, PAIRED WITH THE OBSERVATIONS OF THE WORLD TREE GLOW BY THE OCCULT RESEARCH ASSOCIATION AND THE ARDENT WORLD TREE ADMIRERS ASSOCIATION, HAVE BROUGHT THE STUDENTS VERY CLOSE TO DISCOVERING THE TRUTH.
DUE TO ARTICLES IN MAHORA SPORTS, OPINIONS POSTED ON THE INTERNET, ETC., THE RUMORS HAVE SPREAD TO 34% OF THE MALE STUDENT AND 79% OF THE FEMALE STUDENT BODY. I BELIEVE ONLY A FEW TRULY BELIEVE THE RUMORS, BUT...

BUT THE NUMBER OF STUDENTS ITCHING TO PUT IT TO THE TEST IS LIKELY TO BE VERY HIGH.
ESPECIALLY AMONG FEMALE STUDENTS WHO LIKE FORTUNE-TELLING AND SUPER-STITIOUS PRACTICES.
AND THAT IS WHERE THINGS STAND.
WE'LL BE IN THE MOST TROUBLE ON THE LAST DAY OF THE FESTIVAL, BUT WE'RE ALREADY STARTING TO SEE THE INFLUENCE OF THE TREE'S MAGIC.
I HATE TO DO THIS TO THE STUDENTS, BUT I WANT YOU ALL TO WATCH THESE SIX LOCATIONS TO MAKE SURE NO ONE CONFESSES THEIR LOVE.

AWA-WAH...
I CAN'T BELIEVE WHAT I JUST HEARD!
WE'RE BEING WATCHED.
WHAT?
!?
NO!! THEY NOTICED ME!?
SS
SNAP!
FWOOM!
OOHH!?
AN UNINCANTED SPELL!!
BWOH
EEEK!

SLICE
HUH... ?
PATTER PATTER

I DIDN'T SENSE ANY MAGICAL ENERGY. ...IT MUST BE A MACHINE.
STUDENTS... IMPRESSIVE, BREAKING THROUGH OUR PEOPLE-WARDING SPELL.
OUR STUDENTS ARE A FORCE TO BE RECKONED WITH.
I'LL GO AFTER THEM.
DON'T WEAR YOURSELF OUT. THERE ARE ONLY A HANDFUL OF STUDENTS WHO CAN PULL SOMETHING LIKE THIS OFF.

AWW... OUR OBSERVATION DROID HAS BEEN DESTROYED!! WE'VE BEEN DISCOVERED!
I'M IMPRESSED. I THOUGHT OUR ANTI-WIZARD STEALTH SYSTEMS WERE PERFECT.

ERK...! OH NO. THEY'RE SENDING SOMEONE AFTER US!
WHAT!? WHAT DO WE DO?
THEY MIGHT ERASE OUR MEMORIES!
YOU'RE ACTIVATING YOUR STEALTH CAMO AND STAYING HERE, HAKASE.
I'LL LURE THEM AWAY.
WILL YOU BE OKAY?
PROPERTY OF ENGINEERING CLUB
2003 OPTICAL STEALTH

NOW... YOU MUSTN'T THINK OF THEM AS MERE LOVE CONFESSIONS!
ZSH!
THE YOUTH OF OUR STUDENTS DEPENDS ON US.
HOWEVER, ONLY USE MAGIC WITH UTMOST DISCRETION! I'M COUNTING ON YOU ALL!!

I'VE GIVEN YOU YOUR SHIFTS. PATROL THE GROUNDS ACCORDINGLY.
BAH
THAT IS ALL. DISMISSED!!
YES, SIR!
I'LL WORK FOR WHAT YOU PAY ME.
UNDERSTOOD!

BUZZ BUZZ
CLAMOR CLAMOR
OH! SUDDENLY THE PLACE IS PACKED!
BECAUSE THE PEOPLE-WARDING SPELL HAS BEEN LIFTED.
HO HO
AH! IT'S THE HEADMASTER!
HIS HEAD IS LONG!

NEGI-KUN...
Y-YES, SIR?
TAKE CARE NOT TO LET ANY OF YOUR STUDENTS CONFESS TO YOU.
THEN AGAIN, I DOUBT YOU'LL HAVE ANY PROBLEMS, NEGI-KUN.
EEP...!
NN? DO YOU HAVE ANY REASON TO BELIEVE OTHERWISE?
NO, OF COURSE NOT. WHY WOULD I? AH HA HA.
?
WE GOT REASONS UP THE WAZOO.

STILL, WHAT A SURPRISE.
I MEAN, THE WORLD TREE LEGEND BEING TRUE IS ONE THING.
BUZZ
BUZZ
BUT I HAD NO IDEA THERE WERE SO MANY MAGIC TEACHERS!
BUT NONE OF THOSE GUYS'D BE MUCH IN A FIGHT.
OCCIDENTAL WIZARDS ARE SUCH PUSHOVERS.
UGH, KOTARŌ-KUN. IT DOESN'T ALWAYS HAVE TO BE ABOUT THAT, YOU KNOW.
YOU DO LIKE FIGHTING, DON'T YOU?

CRACKLE
CRACKLE
SHP

ZSH ZSH ZSH

ZAP
KHN!
THEY BROKE THROUGH MY STEALTH EASILY! THIS COULD BE TROUBLE...

BUT HEY, ANIKI, NOW THAT YOU'VE GOT YOUR MAGIC TEACHER STUFF TO ADD TO YOUR SCHEDULE, AREN'T YOU, LIKE, IN SERIOUS TROUBLE?
ERK...!
Y-YOU'RE RIGHT. AND MY SCHEDULE WAS PACKED ENOUGH BEFORE...
GLOOM
I-I CAN'T POSSIBLY KEEP ALL THESE APPOINT-MENTS.
YOU MAY HAVE TO JUST GIVE UP ON THIS ONE.
WHIM-PER
WHAT'S THE MATTER?
?

WHOA!
DAY 1
6/20 (FRIDAY)
10:30
R.A. EXHIBITION
EQUESTRIAN CLUB
MARTIAL-ARTS DEMO
FINE-ARTS CLUB
SCAVENGER HUNT
DISCUSSION GROUP
DIVINATION CLUB
STAGE PLAY
ACADEMY WALKING TOUR
TOURNAMENT
MARTIAL-ARTS TOURNEY
THIS DOES LOOK LIKE A TOUGHT SCHEDULE TO KEEP.
THEY'RE ALL DATES WITH GIRLS! I'M DISAPPOINTED IN YOU.
SERIOUSLY.
KEH.
HMPH.
ARE YOU STUPID?
I-IT'S NOT WHAT YOU THINK. AS THEIR TEACHER, I...
KAPOW
WAAH?!
WHAT?
A-ARE YOU ALRIGHT?
HUH!? YOU'RE...
N-NEGI-BŌZU! THIS IS PERFECT. WILL YOU HELP ME?
HFF
HFF
I'M BEING CHASED BY SOME SUSPICIOUS CHARACTERS.
I THOUGHT I WAS GOING TO DIE!
SWIF SWIF
THERE, THERE.
HIC SOB HIC
YOU'RE ALREADY DEAD.

GOOD MORNING! WE'RE DOWN TO 16 HOURS BEFORE THE BIG DAY.
WILL THE LEADER OF EACH EVENT COMMITTEE PLEASE REPORT TO FESTIVAL COMMITTEE HEADQUARTERS BY 10:00 TODAY…
MAHORA ACADEMY FESTIVAL PRODUCTION COMMITTEE
ゴォン… HUMM
ゴォン… HUMM
ワイ CLAMOR
ワイ CLAMOR
ワイ CLAMOR
ONLY A FEW TICKETS LEFT FOR THE PRE-FESTIVAL PARTY!
PREVIEW NIGHT GALA
TICKETS SOLD HERE
ガヤガヤ BUZZ BUZZ
MAN, I WANNA GO TO PRE-PARTY!
ワイ CLAMOR
ワイ CLAMOR

BUT WE GOTTA SLEEP AT SOME POINT, OR WE'RE IN TROUBLE.
NO KIDDING. I CAN HARDLY HOLD MYSELF UP.
I JUST DON'T KNOW WHAT'S MORE IMPORTANT TO ME. PARTY OR SLEEP.
IF YOU DON'T GET SOME SLEEP, YOU'RE GONNA PASS OUT.
I'D LIKE A BATH, TOO.
ワイ CLAMOR
ワイ CLAMOR

HUH?
KLONK
EEK!
WHAT JUST HAPPENED?
WHAT WAS THAT NOISE?
KLONG
BAM!
BAM!
B-B-BAM!
ガガガガッ
BAM
バーッ
KYAA?!

BAH!
80TH PERIOD:
MISGIVINGS ON FESTIVAL EVE
B-BAH
ZSH ZSH ZSH

NEGIMA!
MAGISTER NEGI MAGI
HEY, WHOA. WHAT ARE THOSE!?
CAN I BEAT 'EM UP?
CHAO-SAN! WHAT'S GOING ON!?
AC-TUALLY, I...

I'M BEING CHASED BY EVIL WIZARDS, YES!
I WANT YOU TO SAVE ME, NEGI-SENSEI!
EH !?
E-EVIL WIZ-ARDS!?

MMPH
Z-Z-Z-Z
Z-Z-Z-Z
WHAK WHAK
WHAM
ARE YOU ALL RIGHT, CHAO-SAN?
YES! THANK YOU, SETSUNA-SAN!
ZSH!
BAH
EEEK!
ANIKI, THIS IS OBVIOUSLY...
YEAH.
OCCIDENTAL MAGIC!
BUT WHY WOULD WIZARDS BE...
AND WHY MY STUDENT? WHY CHAO-SAN...?

BAH
!
WE HAVE TO MAKE A STAND!!
THESE GUYS'RE LIKE MY DOG SPIRITS!
I CAN KILL 'EM, RIGHT?
NNNGH, I DON'T KNOW WHAT'S GOING ON, BUT WE HAVE NO CHOICE. WE HAVE TO DEFEAT THEM!!
ALLL-RIGHT!
BWOH
RAS TEL MA SCIR
WHAM
WHACK WHACK

ANIKI! DON'T DO ANYTHING TOO FLASHY!
I WON'T!
BWOM
DUN
SAGITTA MAGICA SERIES LUCIS!!
GZHAM!
KABOOM
NEGI-SENSEI!
Z-ZZT
SETSUNA-SAN, BEHIND YOU!
ZH...
WHEW...
NN?
3-A

ZAM!
FOOM
BOOM
B-BOOM
FIRE-WORKS! ♡
B-BOOM
BOOM
MMMM! IT'S REALLY STARTING TO FEEL LIKE A FESTIVAL!

SAGITTA MAGICA ?!
THERE'S A WIZARD WITH HER!
CLEANUP CREW
THEY DEFEATED SEVENTEEN OF MY FAMILIARS IN AN INSTANT... WE'RE UP AGAINST QUITE A MASTER.
HMMM. I THOUGHT WE WERE ONLY TAKING IN A PROBLEM STUDENT. THIS IS AN UNEXPECTED DEVELOPMENT.
DID PRODIGY CHAO LINGSHEN HAVE A WIZARD ON HER TEAM? I HOPE IT'S NOT DARK EVANGEL.

WHEW.
YOU'RE LIFE SAVERS ♡ THANK YOU.
WE'RE NOT OUT OF THE WOODS YET.
THE MASTER OF THOSE SHADOW FIGURES IS SURE TO BE NEARBY.
YOUR FACE LOOKS DIFFERENT WHEN YOU'RE IN WORK MODE.
FWEE
BUT YOU'RE ALL SO STRONG! I'M SURPRISED!
I DIDN'T THINK THERE WERE SO MANY LEFT IN THIS ERA WHO COULD DISPLAY SUCH BATTLE PROWESS WITHOUT MACHINE SUPPORT!
AND THAT WAS BRILLIANT, HIDING YOUR MAGIC IN THE FIREWORKS! THAT'S MY NEGI-SENSEI
O-OH NO, I STILL NEED A LOT OF TRAINING...
SO YOU KNOW ABOUT WIZARDS, CHAO-SAN.
ABOUT AS MUCH AS HAKASE DOES.
BUT WHO IN THE WORLD WOULD BE CHASING YOU?
EVIL WIZARDS IN THE SCHOOL?
AH HA HA HA. OH, YOU KNOW...
MPH! WAIT. IT SEEMS THEY'VE FOUND US.
THEY'RE GETTING CLOSER. THREE OF 'EM.

AIYA! THIS IS BAD. I CAN'T GET CAUGHT AGAIN. THEY'LL ERASE MY MEMORY FOR SURE.
BUZZ
EH!?
WHAT DO YOU MEAN?
BUZZ
HEY, NEGI.
WE'RE SURROUNDED.
FROM THE RIGHT, THEY'RE AT DISTANCES OF 50, 80, AND 70. ONE'S ON THE ROOF.
WHAT DO WE DO?
WE DON'T KNOW WHO WE'RE UP AGAINST.
PROCEED WITH CAUTION. UNDER-STOOD?
TEP TEP TEP
UNDER-STOOD. I'LL BE OKAY!
THEY'RE SURROUNDED ON THREE SIDES. THIS SHOULDN'T TAKE LONG.
OH! COOL COSTUMES!
CLACK CLACK
VICTORY GOES TO THE SWIFTEST.
WE'LL LEAVE THE ALLEY AND GET THEM FROM INSIDE THE CROWD. SETSUNA-SAN, YOU TAKE THE ROOF.
NOD
I THINK HE'S GOTTEN A LITTLE MANLIER.
HEH HEH. NICE STRATEGY FOR AN AMATEUR, NEGI.

WE DON'T WANT THEM CALLING FOR BACKUP.
MUMBLE MUMBLE
ERMINE MAGIC! INTERFATIO!!
VNN
Z-ZSH
MPH...! THEY'RE JAMMING OUR TELE-PATHY!?
NOW! GO!!
BAH

TMP!
THMP
OHH? I'VE FOUND ONE!?
ZSH!
SHE'S EITHER VERY GOOD OR VERY STUPID!
DUN!
CANTUS BELLAX !
ZSH ZSH ZSH ZSH
BWOH

GNN!
DOM
TMP!
CHALLENGERS WANTED! GOTEN-RYU
WHAT ?
THMP!
KLONG
EXARMATIO FLANS !!
I'M OVER HERE.
EH ?
WHA ?
HUH ?
KNH !
ZSH
BAH
160円
BA-SHING

DUN!
!
EH ?!
HUH ?
THUD!
A GIRL !?
S-SORRY.
ERK, HUH? HAVE WE MET...?
WHAT WAS THAT?
FILMING A MOVIE OR SOME-THING?
OWWWW!
EH ?!
OH !!
YOU'RE...
YOU'RE —!
ZSH
HUH ....?
WHAT IN THE WORLD IS GOING ON!?

WE WERE HOPING YOU'D TELL US, NEGI-SENSEI.
GLOOM
WHY ARE YOU DEFENDING THE PROBLEM CHILD CHAO LINGSHEN?
EH...?
GLANCE
PROBLEM CHILD...?
HA HA HA
"WHY"? I'M CHAO-SAN'S TEACHER.
IT'S ONLY NATURAL FOR A TEACHER TO HELP HIS STUDENT WHEN SHE'S UNDER ATTACK.
WHAT!? CHAO LINGSHEN'S TEACHER? *YOU?*
I SEE. SO THAT'S HOW IT IS...
YOU DID GIVE ME A SCARE. I THOUGHT SOME ROGUE WIZARD HAD INFILTRATED THE ACADEMY.
BUT THIS MEANS YOU HAVEN'T *HEARD* ANYTHING ABOUT CHAO LINGSHEN.
N-NO... WHAT WOULD I HAVE HEARD?
ZOOM
THEN LEAVE THIS TO US.
COME WITH ME, CHAO LINGSHEN.

ERK!
OWW...
TUG
CLAMP
N-NEGI-BŌZU
W-WAIT! WHAT ARE YOU GOING TO DO TO CHAO-SAN?
THAT HAS YET TO BE DETERMINED...
BUT I BELIEVE WE WILL BE ERASING HER MEMORIES OF ANYTHING TO DO WITH WIZARDS.

EH ....?
ERASING HER MEMORIES...?
B-BUT THIS IS ALL SO SUDDEN ...
IT IS NOT SUDDEN AT ALL. CHAO-KUN HAS ALREADY RECEIVED SEVERAL WARNINGS.

NEGI-SENSEI. YOU UNDERSTAND THAT WE WIZARDS KEEP OUR EXISTENCE HIDDEN FROM THE PUBLIC
SO THAT WE CAN COEXIST PEACEFULLY IN MODERN SOCIETY, DON'T YOU?
WE SHOULD NOT LET TOO MANY NORMAL PEOPLE KNOW OF US.
Y-YES... I KNOW THAT... BUT...
IT'S TRUE I TRIED TO ERASE ASUNA-SAN'S MEMORIES AT FIRST...
THAT'S WHAT I'D BEEN TAUGHT TO DO...
DUE TO THE CIRCUMSTANCES, CHAO-KUN AND HER ASSOCIATES HAVE BEEN ALLOWED A SMALL AMOUNT OF KNOWLEDGE.
BUT THAT DOES NOT MEAN WE CAN TELL HER EVERYTHING.
TODAY SHE WAS USING SCIENTIFIC TECHNOLOGY TO SPY ON A MEETING WITH DEFENSES THAT SHOULD HAVE BEEN IMPENETRABLE.

WHEN STUDENTS BREAK THE RULES, THEY ARE PUNISHED.
THIS IS THE THIRD TIME YOU'VE IGNORED OUR WARNINGS, ISN'T IT?
Y-YES...
AND BECAUSE YOU HAVE IGNORED OUR WARNINGS THREE TIMES, YOU MUST HAVE BEEN PREPARED TO FACE THE CONSEQUENCES OF SUCH BEHAVIOR.
DO YOU AGREE?
Y-YEAH, I GUESS SO...
ERK...
HMN.
B-BUT ISN'T IT WRONG TO ERASE SOMEONE'S MEMORIES WHEN THEY DON'T WANT THEM ERASED?
AS A WIZARD!
CHAO-KUN IS DANGEROUS. THIS IS THE PROPER COURSE OF ACTION.
SHE HAS EVEN AIDED THE HEINOUS CRIMINAL EVANGELINE. WE CAN'T BE LENIENT WITH HER.
WHA--!? EVANGELINE-SAN ISN'T SUCH A BAD--
I DUNNO ABOUT THAT.
SNAP
NEGI-SENSEI.
YOU UNDERSTAND, THEN? WE WILL BE TAKING CHAO-KUN.
ERK...
WE AIN'T WINNING THIS ONE...
I'VE HEARD RUMORS THAT SEVERAL OF YOUR STUDENTS HAVE LEARNED ABOUT MAGIC.
ARE YOU SURE YOU CAN HANDLE THIS?
EH....?
B-DUMP
....NO.
YOU HAVE NO AUTHORITY OVER THE STUDENTS OF 3-A.
GH

I WOULD APPRECIATE IT IF YOU WOULD NOT PASS JUDGMENT ON MY STUDENTS AS "DANGEROUS" OR "CRIMINALS."
CHAO-SAN IS MY STUDENT...
PLEASE LET ME DEAL WITH HER!!

...HM.
...OK. I'LL TRUST YOU FOR TODAY, NEGI-KUN.
BUT BE CARE-FUL.
THE NEXT TIME SOMETHING HAPPENS, YOU MIGHT BE TURNED INTO AN ERMINE.
ERK...!
THEN I LEAVE IT TO YOU, NEGI-KUN.

....
WHEW
WHAT'S HIS PROBLEM? EVERYWHERE YOU GO, TEACHERS ALL ACT LIKE THEY'RE BETTER THAN EVERYONE.
KEH.
WELL, HE'S ONLY DOING HIS JOB.
ARE YOU SURE ABOUT THIS?
FOR NOW.
HEH HEH. BUT THE WAY HE FOUGHT BACK THERE--IT WAS FANTASTIC.
JUST WHAT I'D EXPECT FROM *HIS* SON.
HE'S GROWING INTO A FINE YOUNG MAN.

WOW, YOU REALLY SAVED ME, NEGI-BŌZU. I OWE YOU MY LIFE ♡
OH, YOU'RE EXAG-GERATING ...
BUT CHAO-SAN. THEY SAID YOU WERE DANGEROUS. WHAT HAVE YOU *DONE?*
HEH HEH HEH. THAT'S A SECRET, YES?
YOU CAN'T KEEP IT FROM ME! I'M RESPONSIBLE FOR YOU.

ANYWAY, NEGI-BŌZU. IS THERE ANY-THING BOTHER-ING YOU?
EH ?
TO REPAY YOU FOR HELPING ME, I WILL SOLVE ONE OF YOUR PROBLEMS.
WITH THE POWER OF CHAO LINGSHEN'S SCIENCE ♡

AND SHE GAVE YOU THIS?
CHA-LING
YES... I TOLD HER I DIDN'T KNOW WHAT TO DO ABOUT MY BUSY SCHEDULE...
SO? WHAT DOES IT DO?
IT'S HARD TO TRUST CHAO-SAN'S INVENTIONS.
BUZZ
I DON'T KNOW... SHE SAID SHE WOULD EXPLAIN IT TO ME LATER...
LOOKS MORE LIKE A MAGICAL ITEM THAN ANYTHING SCIENTIFIC.
BUZZ
OH! THERE YOU ARE, NEGI-KUN!

SQUEE
OVER HERE! HURRY OR THE PARTY'LL START WITHOUT US!
SQUEE
NEGI-SENSEI. PLEASE JOIN US ♡
OH! COMING ♡

AH...! EVERYBODY, LOOK!
THE WORLD TREE'S STARTING TO GLOW.
YOU'RE RIGHT! IT'S SO PRETTY ♡
WOOOW ♡ IT USUALLY DOESN'T START TO GLOW UNTIL THE LAST DAY!
THAT ONCE IN 22 YEARS THING MIGHT BE TRUE!
MMMM! THIS IS GETTING KINDA EXCITING ♪

MAHORA FEST HAS FINALLY BEGUN—♡
B-BOOM
BOOM
YEAH—♪

BOOM
HOW DID IT GO WITH NEGI-SENSEI?
MAHORA ACADEMY FESTIVAL PRODUCTION COMMITTEE
MM.
HUMM HUMM
I KNEW ABOUT HIM FROM CHACHAMARU'S DATA, AND FROM WHAT YOU TOLD ME, HAKASE.
BUT HE'S EVEN NICER THAN I THOUGHT.
BA-BA-BAH...
I LIKE HIM. ♡
HUMM
HUMM

IF WE CAN GET HIM TO JOIN US...
B-BOOM...
...HE MAY PROVE TO BE VERY USEFUL.

NEGIMA! 80TH PERIOD
SPELL GLOSSARY

■「『念波妨害』」
インテルファーティオー

INTERFATIO

Many wizards are equipped with ESP or extrasensory perception (*extrasensoria perceptio*), and have various extrasensory abilities such as reading others' minds (1st Period, 16th Period), sensing specific magicks (8th Period, 16th Period, 20th Period, 23rd Period, 42nd Period, 46th-47th Period, 49th Period, 68th Period, 79th Period), foreseeing the future (15th Period), detecting intruders in specific places (18th Period, 67th Period), sensing when oneself is being watched (27th Period, 79th Period), perceiving the emotions of nearby individuals (29th Period, 35th Period, 53rd Period, 55th Period), sensing the presence of spiritual beings (73rd-74th Period, 78th Period), seeing through illusions (78th Period), and singling out spellcasters and their locations (80th Period).

The cognitive magic abilities (the ability to perceive the outside world) known as ESP are extremely bland when compared to active magical abilities that conjure, change, or destroy objects (magic that affects the outside world, such as lighting a fire), but they are far more basic and therefore more mainstream (even today it is not uncommon for the head of a corporation to go to a fortune-teller--whether genuine or not--for consultations). In that sense, the career path of Negi's childhood friend Anya would be a much more standard path than Negi's.

Exrasensory perception refers to perception outside the realm of the senses. Just as the senses perceive the world around them through various media such as light (in the case of sight), vibrations in the air (hearing), and vibrations of molecules (touch, or the perception of temperature), etc., ESP perceives the world through various unique media. Media detected by ESP are of an extrasensory nature, so naturally, those media are spiritual, and cannot be perceived by the sensory organs of ordinary people.

Telepathy between wizards works when those wizards send and received spiritual media between each other. This is conducted in precisely the same way ordinary people use the media of (air vibrations know as) voice and (lightwaves communicated in the form of) text to share thoughts. Ergo, telepathy isn't a form of directly perceiving thoughts and intentions from each other, but rather the act of conversing using a medium other than voice or text.

INTERFATIO is Latin for "to interrupt a conversation." In other words, it is a spell that interferes with the other casters' ability to hear telepathic conversation by filling a specific area with that spiritual something that is the medium for telepathy (in this case it is translated as "thought waves"). This is exactly like interrupting a voiced conversation by creating a lot of noise.

-STAFF-

Ken Akamatsu

Takashi Takemoto

Kenichi Nakamura

Keiichi Yamashita

Tohru Mitsuhashi

Yuichi Yoshida

Susumu Kuwabara

Thanks to

Ran Ayanaga

NEGIMA!
CONCEPT ART COLLECTION
~ CHARACTERS ROUGHS ~
ADDITIONAL NOTES VERSION

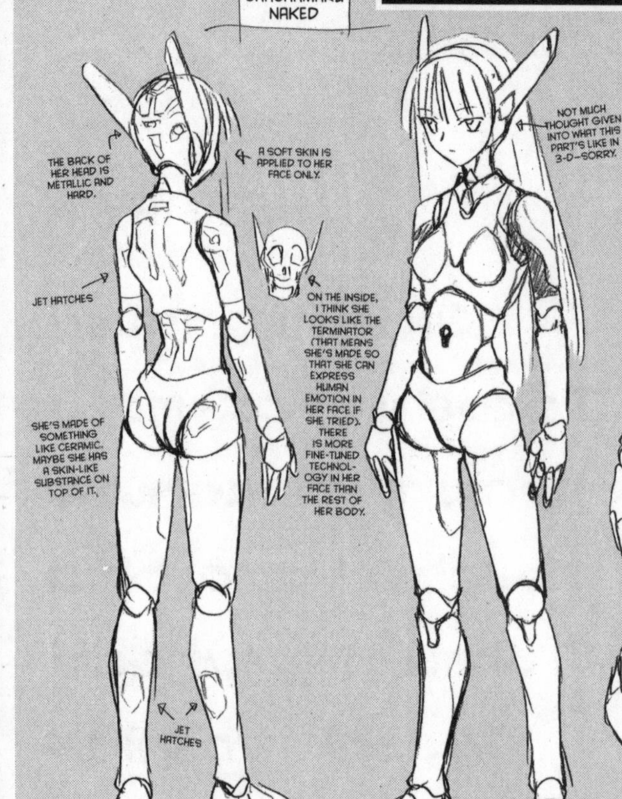

CHACHAMARU NAKED
THE BACK OF HER HEAD IS METALLIC AND HARD.
A SOFT SKIN IS APPLIED TO HER FACE ONLY.
NOT MUCH THOUGHT GIVEN INTO WHAT THIS PART'S LIKE IN 3-D—SORRY.
JET HATCHES
ON THE INSIDE, I THINK SHE LOOKS LIKE THE TERMINATOR (THAT MEANS SHE'S MADE SO THAT SHE CAN EXPRESS HUMAN EMOTION IN HER FACE IF SHE TRIED). THERE IS MORE FINE-TUNED TECHNOL-OGY IN HER FACE THAN THE REST OF HER BODY.
SHE'S MADE OF SOMETHING LIKE CERAMIC. MAYBE SHE HAS A SKIN-LIKE SUBSTANCE ON TOP OF IT.
HER HAND'S KEEP THEIR DOLL-LIKE APPEAR-ANCE.
JET HATCHES
HATCHES SHOULD ALL BE ON HER BACK SIDE.

THE JET ENGINE TYPE DEVICES SHE USES TO FLY SHOULD LOOK LIKE THEY MAINLY RUN ON MAGIC.

FOR VIDEO GAMES AND THE LIKE, SOMETIMES I'LL ADD NEW NOTES TO THE CHARACTER DESIGNS. LIKE THESE, FOR EXAMPLE.

VOLUME SEVEN HAD SO FEW SPELLS AND NEW CHARACTERS, THERE'S NOTHING TO USE AS BONUS MATERIAL!
—AKA

LOOKING FORWARD TO HAVING SOME FUN IN VOLUME 8!♡

MAGISTER NEGI MAGI

NEGIMA!

LETTER AND FAN ART CORNER

Text by Assistant Max

NICE IDEA (LAUGH) THE WHOLE STAFF LOVED IT.

IT HAS A GREAT LIGHT-AND-AIRY FEELING.

刹那

修学旅行の話で好きになりました。

I LOVE SETSUNA'S BODDHISATVA-LIKE SMILE.

I THINK I'D LIKE TO SEE YOTSUBA'S CARD.

SETSUNA'S EXPRESSION IN THE BACKGROUND IS PRICELESS.

YUEKICHI IS A CUTE NICKNAME, ISN'T IT?

WE ALWAYS SAY BIENVENIDOS NEW ILLUSTRATIONS.

NEGIMA!

FAN ART CORNER

WE'RE ALWAYS ACCEPTING LETTERS AND FAN ART FROM READERS. PLEASE KEEP 'EM COMING. (^^)

TEXT BY MAX

A HEROIC SETSUNA-SAN★ THE COLORS WERE BEAUTIFUL, TOO.

SHE IGNORES WHAT'S GOING ON BEHIND HER AND STRIKES A POSE? (LAUGH)

THEIR SLEEPING FACES ARE SO CUTE ♪

AN ADORABLE LITTLE EVA ♪

A SURREAL DESIGN OF YUE.

SO THE SPOTLIGHT FINALLY FALLS ON NATSUMI? (LAUGH)

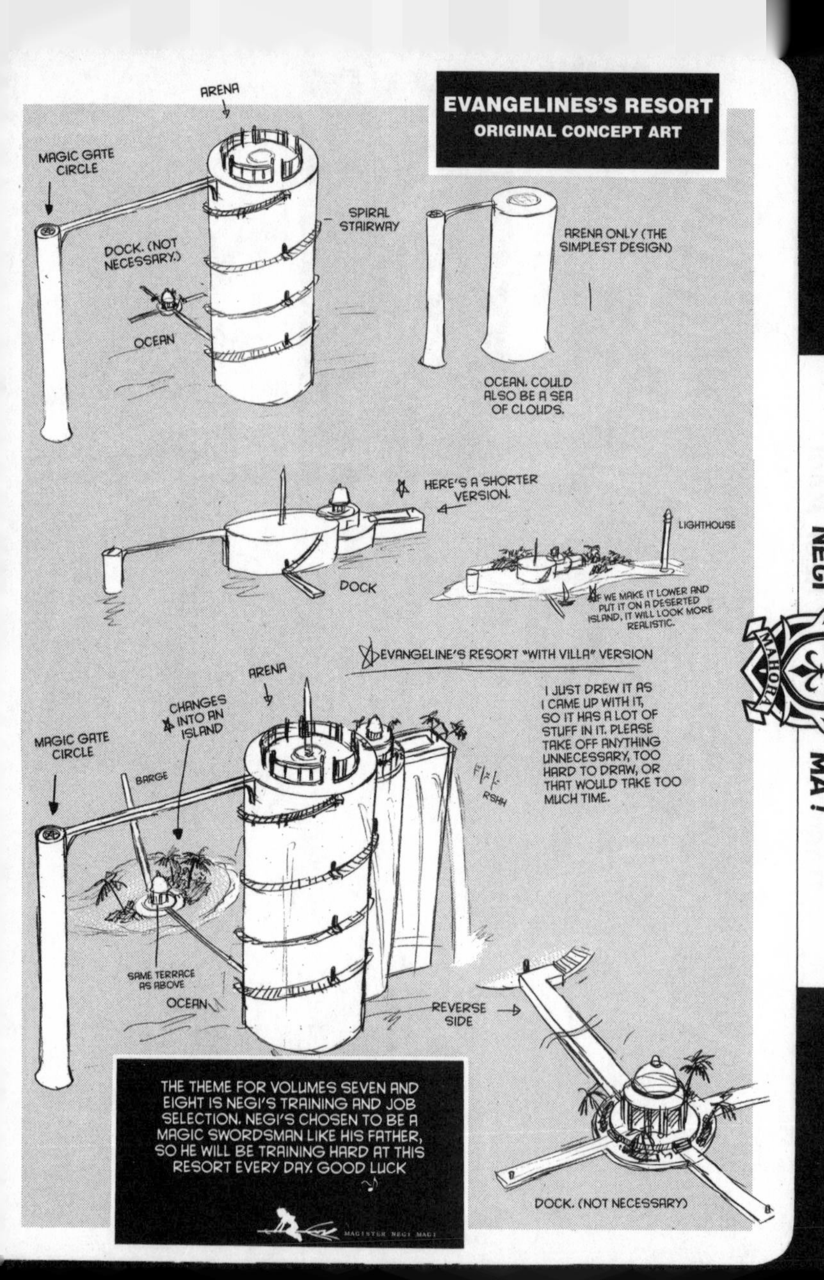

EVANGELINES'S RESORT
ORIGINAL CONCEPT ART
ARENA
MAGIC GATE CIRCLE
SPIRAL STAIRWAY
DOCK. (NOT NECESSARY.)
OCEAN
ARENA ONLY (THE SIMPLEST DESIGN)
OCEAN. COULD ALSO BE A SEA OF CLOUDS.
HERE'S A SHORTER VERSION.
DOCK
LIGHTHOUSE
IF WE MAKE IT LOWER AND PUT IT ON A DESERTED ISLAND, IT WILL LOOK MORE REALISTIC.
EVANGELINE'S RESORT "WITH VILLA" VERSION
ARENA
CHANGES INTO AN ISLAND
MAGIC GATE CIRCLE
BARGE
I JUST DREW IT AS I CAME UP WITH IT, SO IT HAS A LOT OF STUFF IN IT. PLEASE TAKE OFF ANYTHING UNNECESSARY, TOO HARD TO DRAW, OR THAT WOULD TAKE TOO MUCH TIME.
RSHH
SAME TERRACE AS ABOVE
OCEAN
REVERSE SIDE
THE THEME FOR VOLUMES SEVEN AND EIGHT IS NEGI'S TRAINING AND JOB SELECTION. NEGI'S CHOSEN TO BE A MAGIC SWORDSMAN LIKE HIS FATHER, SO HE WILL BE TRAINING HARD AT THIS RESORT EVERY DAY. GOOD LUCK ♪
MAGISTER NEGI MAGI
DOCK. (NOT NECESSARY)

MAGISTER NEGI MAGI

AS SEEN FROM ABOVE

FLOOR PLAN

FOR THE FIRST HALF, WE ONLY NEED THIS PART. (BECAUSE WE ONLY SEE THE ARENA.)

VIEW FROM REAR

TERRACE

STAIRS

GROOVE

PLANTERS LIKE AT CLASS REP'S POOL.

A FEW PALM TREES AROUND THE GROOVE.

POOL

LIKE IT'S FLOATING IN CLOUDS, OR ON THE EMPTY OCEAN

DON'T WORRY TOO MUCH ABOUT THE POOL'S DETAILS. THIS BUILDING ISN'T NECESSARY, FOR EXAMPLE.

ONE OF 50 TAKEN TO ROME DURING THE TIME OF THE ROMAN EMPIRE. OBELISK (WE HAVE REFERENCE MATERIAL)

ARENA, OUTER PILLARS (WE HAVE REFERENCE MATERIAL)

TERRACE (WE HAVE REFERENCE MATERIAL)

PALM TREES. LIKE THE ONES IN THE BATH.

FOR THE POOL, WE CAN USE PARTS OF THE POOL AT CLASS REP'S HOUSE.

MAKE IT ABOUT 25M

POOL

WOULD A 100M RADIUS BE OKAY?

THE WATER FLOWS OUT.

THE RESORT EVANGELINE BUILT IN A SECRET SPACE ABOUT 50 YEARS AGO. THESE DAYS, GOING TO IT ONLY GIVES HER MORE TIME TO BE BORED, SO SHE'S ABANDONED IT, LEAVING THE HOUSEKEEPING TO THE DOLLS.

NEGIMA!
3-D BACKGROUNDS EXPLANATION CORNER

YOU ALL KNOW THAT COMPUTER GRAPHICS ARE USED IN VIDEO GAMES AND MOVIES, BUT ACTUALLY, COMPUTER GRAPHICS ARE ALSO USED FOR SOME OF THE BACKGROUNDS IN *NEGIMA!*. EACH PLACE IN MAHORA ACADEMY CITY WHERE NEGI AND ASUNA LIVE HAS BEEN RENDERED IN 3-D ON THE COMPUTER.

STEP 1: COLLECT REFERENCE MATERIAL

FIRST, WE COLLECT REFERENCE PHOTOS FROM THE INTERNET AND OTHER SOURCES FOR THE BACKGROUND WE WANT TO MAKE.
SOMETIMES WE MAKE A BACKGOUND BASED ON A SKETCH.

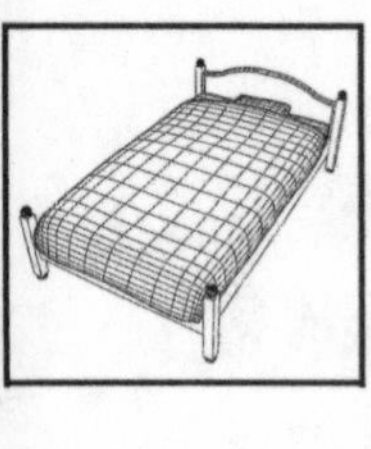

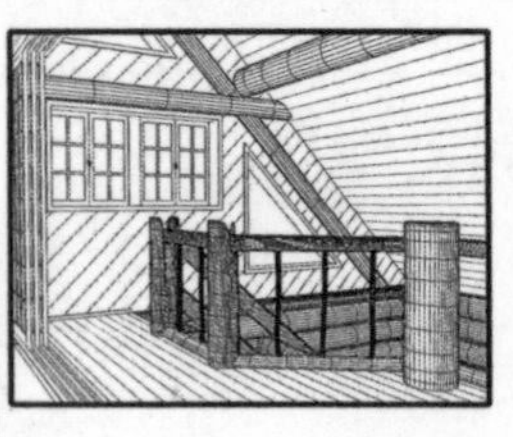

STEP 2: CREATE A MODEL

WE MAKE BACKGROUND MODELS OUT OF POLYGONS, USING THE COMPUTER GRAPHICS SOFTWARE "LIGHTWAVE 3D."
FROM THE LEFT, THESE IMAGES SHOW THE BED, THE TEAPOT, AND THE AREA AROUND THE STAIRS.

STEP 3: SET UP THE SCENE

ONCE THE MODELS FOR THE ROOM AND FURNITURE ARE COMPLETE, WE PUT THEM IN THEIR APPROPRIATE PLACES, AND THE STAGE IS SET. INCIDENTALLY, THE FURNITURE GETS MOVED AROUND AND USED IN VARIOUS DIFFERENT ROOMS A LOT (^_^;)

STEP 4: SCAN THE MANGA ROUGH SKETCH

THE STAGE IS COMPLETE, SO NEXT, WE CREATE A BACKGROUND TO BE USED FOR THE ACTUAL SCENE.
FIRST, WE APPLY THE ROUGH SKETCH TO THE POLYGONS.

STEP 5: CREATE A TEST IMAGE

WE ADJUST THE CAMERA ANGLE TO MATCH THE SKETCH AND CREATE A TEST IMAGE. THE IMAGE AT THE RIGHT SHOWS THE SKETCH ON TOP OF THE 3-D BACKGROUND.

STEP 6: CREATE A LINE DRAWING

ONCE THE CAMERA ANGLE IS SET, WE CREATE A HIGH-RESOLUTION IMAGE TO BE USED FOR PRINTING. WE PRINT THAT OUT, AND WITHIN MINUTES, WE HAVE A LINE DRAWING LIKE THE ONE ON THE RIGHT.

STEP 7: FINISHING TOUCHES

WE PUT OUR FINISHING TOUCHES ON BY HAND. AFTER PRINTING OUT THE LINE DRAWING, WE ADD MORE INK IF NECESSARY, APPLY TONE, AND FINALLY, WE ADD THE SPEECH BUBBLES, ASIDES AND SOUND EFFECTS, AND CHARACTERS. THEN IT'S DONE! GOOD WORK. (^_^)

CG BACKGROUNDS LINE-ART GALLERY

HERE WE'VE SELECTED SOME SCENES THAT HAVE APPEARED IN THE MANGA'S PAST, AND WE ARE PRESENTING THEM TO YOU WITH COMMENTARY.

SCENE NAME: BRIDGE
POLYGON COUNT: 814,856

] THIS IS THE SUSPENSION BRIDGE THAT APPEARED IN THE BATTLE WITH EVANGELINE IN VOLUME THREE. IT WAS MODELED AFTER THE BROOKLYN BRIDGE IN NEW YORK, BUT THAT BRIDGE HAS TWO LEVELS, AND WE FORCED THIS ONE INTO ONLY ONE, SO IT LOOKS A LITTLE STRANGE. (^_^;)
THIS GIANT STRUCTURE WINS THE CONTEST FOR HIGHEST POLYGON COUNT BY A LANDSLIDE.

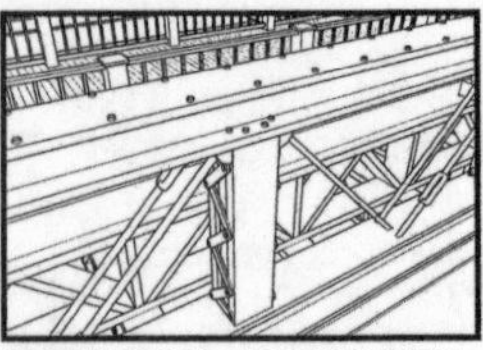

WE CONSTRUCTED IT DOWN TO EVERY LAST BOLT.

THIS IS CLASS REP, NABA, AND NATSUMI'S ROOM, WITH WHICH I'M SURE YOU'RE ALL FAMILIAR(?). RUMOR HAS IT THAT THE REASON IT'S COMPLETELY DIFFERENT FROM ASUNA'S DORM IS THAT CLASS REP USED HER VAST RESOURCES (I.E. MONEY) TO REMODEL IT.
UP THE STAIRS, THEY EACH HAVE THEIR OWN ROOM! SUCH LUXURY. BUT OF COURSE, WE CAN ASSUME THAT THE BIGGEST AND FANCIEST IS CLASS REP'S ROOM. (LAUGH)

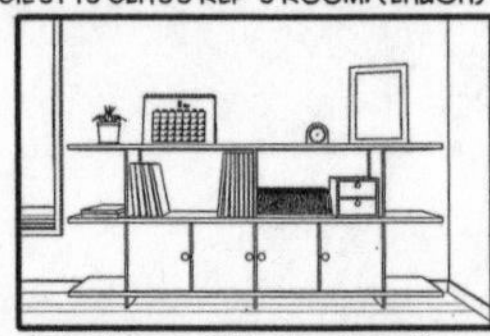

WE EVEN MADE THE LITTLE ITEMS THEY KEEP ON THE SHELVES.

SCENE NAME: AYAKA'S ROOM
POLYGON COUNT: 49,840

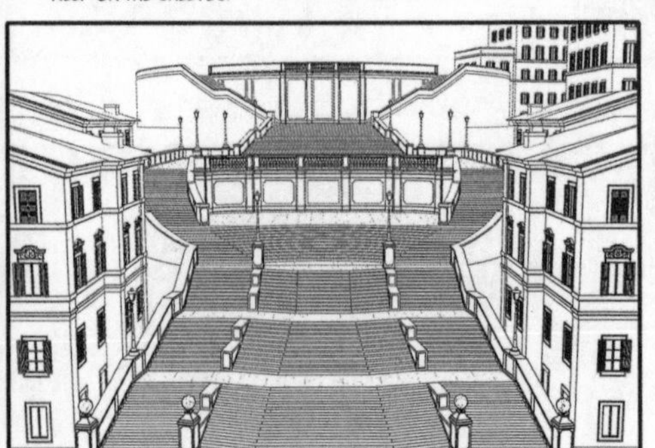

SCENE NAME: LARGE STAIRS
POLYGON COUNT: 216,127

OF ALL THE MODELS, THE ONE THAT TOOK THE MOST TIME TO CREATE WAS THIS ONE: THE GIANT STAIRS IN FRONT OF WORLD TREE PLAZA. WE BASED IT OFF OF A PLAZA IN SPAIN, BUT COULDN'T FINISH IT IN JUST ONE WEEK, SO IT WAS GRADUALLY ADDED ONTO AS THE SERIES PROGRESSED. (^_^;)
FURTHERMORE, THE WORLD TREE IS HAND-DRAWN. AND SO THE BACKGROUNDS OF NEGIMA! ARE CREATED BY USING THE BEST OF THE DIGITAL AND ANALOG WORLDS.

THIS IS WHAT IT LOOKS LIKE FROM ITS HIGHEST POINT.

SCENE NAME: ASUNA'S ROOM
(POLYGON COUNT: 80,013)
I KNOW YOU'RE ALL FAMILIAR WITH ASUNA AND KONOKA'S ROOM. WE'VE ACTUALLY CREATED THE INSIDE OF THE KITCHEN, TOO.

SCENE NAME: LARGE BATH
(POLYGON COUNT: 203,212)
NORMALLY, WE DRAW PLANTS BY HAND, BUT HERE THE PALM TREES ARE MADE WITH CG.

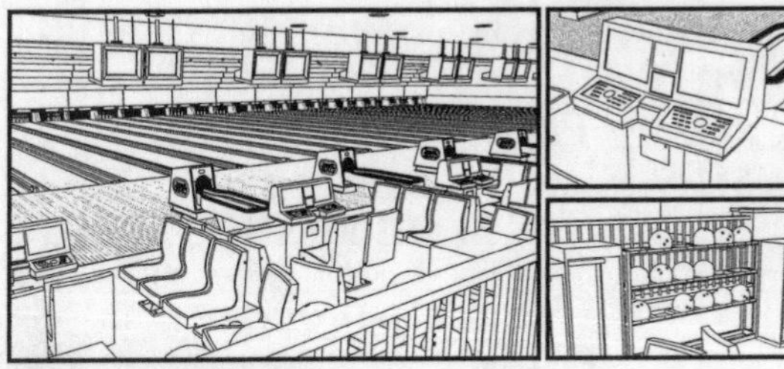

SCENE NAME: BOWLING
(POLYGON COUNT: 313,720)
THE BOWLING ALLEY THAT APPEARED IN VOLUME SEVEN. I DON'T THINK IT WILL EVER SHOW UP AGAIN, SO I PUT IT HERE...(^_^;)

SCENE NAME: ALTAR
(POLYGON COUNT: 171,493)
THE GIANT LANTERN THAT CAN BE SEEN ON THE OTHER SIDE OF THE LARGE ROCK SEALING SUKUNA IN VOLUME SIX. WE NEVER SAW IT UP CLOSE IN THE STORY, BUT THIS IS WHAT IT LOOKS LIKE.

THE FIRST TIME WE USED COMPUTER GRAPHICS WAS FOR THE CLASSROOM AND SPIRAL STAIRWAY IN VOLUME TWO. YOU COULD DEFINITELY SAY THAT BACKGROUNDS WITH LOTS OF REPEATING PARTS THAT GO ON FOR A LONG TIME ARE BEST MADE WITH 3-D. COLUMNS AND STUFF, TOO.

IN THE NEXT VOLUME, IT WILL FINALLY BE TIME FOR THE SCHOOL FESTIVAL! YOU'LL GET TO SEE A LOT OF THE CLASSMATES, SO LOOK FORWARD TO IT! PLEASE WATCH THE ANIME, TOO!

赤松

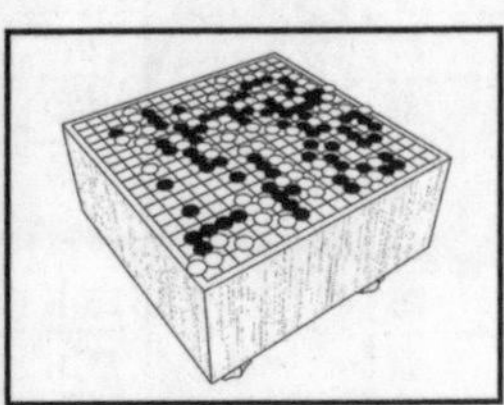

THE GO BOARD THE HEADMASTER AND EVA WERE PLAYING ON.

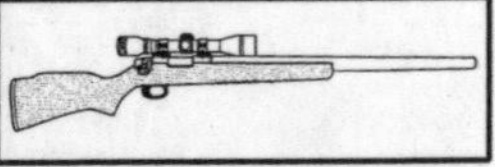

TATSUMIYA'S RIFLE, A REMINGTON M700

—BONUS—

ACTUALLY, WE MADE THESE THINGS IN 3-D, TOO.

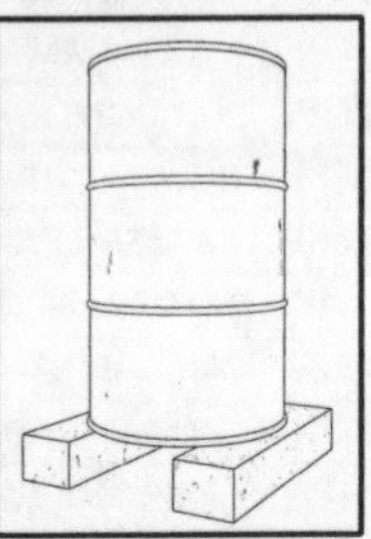

THE OIL DRUM BATH NEGI USED WITH KAEDE.

NEGIMA!

CHARACTER POPULARITY VOTE

HERE ARE THE RESULTS OF THE FOURTH POPULARITY VOTE (NEGI PRIX 4)!! ASTOUNDINGLY, SETSUNA HAS TOPPED THE CHARTS TWICE IN A ROW! BUT THE REST OF THE VOTES ARE MOVING ALL OVER THE PLACE. WILL WE SEE A BIG UPSET NEXT TIME!?

MAGISTER NEGI MAGI

RESULTS OF THE THIRD POPULARITY VOTE

RANK	CHARACTER	TOTAL VOTES
1ST	SAKURAZAKI, SETSUNA	2,272
2ND	MIYAZAKI, NODOKA	2,051
3RD	KONOE, KONOKA	1,658
4TH	KAGURAZAKA, ASUNA	1,111
5TH	AYASE, YUE	807
6TH	NAGASE, KAEDE	803
7TH	SASAKI, MAKIE	750
8TH	MURAKAMI, NATSUMI	544
9TH	MCDOWELL, EVANGELINE A.K.	526
10TH	IZUMI, AKO	463
11TH	ASAKURA, KAZUMI	355
12TH	YUKIHIRO, AYAKA	283
13TH	KAKIZAKI, MISA	251
14TH	AKASHI, YŪNA	209
15TH	KUGIMIYA, MADOKA	198
16TH	SHI'INA, SAKURAKO	165
17TH	HASEGAWA, CHISAME	147
18TH	KARAKURI, CHACHAMARU	142
19TH	NABA, CHIZURU	122
20TH	KASUGA, MISORA	120
21ST	CHAO LINGSHEN	95
22ND	TATSUMIYA, MANA	87
23RD	RAINYDAY, ZAZIE	84
24TH	OKŌCHI, AKIRA	83
25TH	KŪ FEI	62
26TH	NARUTAKI, FUMIKA	56
27TH	AISAKA, SAYO	54
28TH	YOTSUBA, SATSUKI	51
29TH	SAOTOME, HARUNA	43
30TH	HAKASE, SATOMI	36
31ST	NARUTAKI, FŪKA	22

RESULTS OF THE FOURTH POPULARITY VOTE

RANK	CHARACTER	TOTAL VOTES
1ST	SAKURAZAKI, SETSUNA	1,633
2ND	MIYAZAKI, NODOKA	1,307
3RD	KAGURAZAKA, ASUNA	1,015
4TH	KONOE, KONOKA	966
5TH	MURAKAMI, NATSUMI	914
6TH	MCDOWELL, EVANGELINE A.K.	803
7TH	AYASE, YUE	628
8TH	SASAKI, MAKIE	604
9TH	NAGASE, KAEDE	593
10TH	KARAKURI, CHACHAMARU	583
11TH	IZUMI, AKO	567
12TH	YUKIHIRO, AYAKA	402
13TH	AKASHI, YŪNA	348
14TH	NABA, CHIZURU	321
15TH	CHAO LINGSHEN	320
16TH	AISAKA, SAYO	255
17TH	KAKIZAKI, MISA	226
18TH	OKŌCHI, AKIRA	223
19TH	SAOTOME, HARUNA	212
20TH	TATSUMIYA, MANA	198
21ST	KUGIMIYA, MADOKA	185
22ND	YOTSUBA, SATSUKI	176
23RD	ASAKURA, KAZUMI	124
24TH	HASEGAWA, CHISAME	113
25TH	KŪ FEI	105
26TH	RAINYDAY, ZAZIE	64
27TH	NARUTAKI, FŪKA	55
28TH	NARUTAKI, FUMIKA	53
29TH	HAKASE, SATOMI	42
30TH	SHI'INA, SAKURAKO	38
31ST	KASUGA, MISORA	27

NEGIMA!

FAN ART CORNER

ONCE AGAIN, PRESENTING FAN ART DRAWN BY OUR READERS!

(^^)

TEXT BY ASSISTANT Max

SO POLITE. THANK YOU (LAUGH)

OH! NAGI FANS ARE A PRECIOUS COMMODITY! (LAUGH)

SUCH A CUTE DRAWING OF KOTARŌ!

I LOVE HOW YOU CALLED HER BAKA BLACK.

THIS IS UNUSUAL! A KIRIE (PAPER CUT-OUT) PICTURE! IT'S SO CHARMING.

AYAKA IS BLINDINGLY BRIGHT!

NEGIMA!

ORIGINAL CONCEPT ART

~CHARACTER ROUGHS~

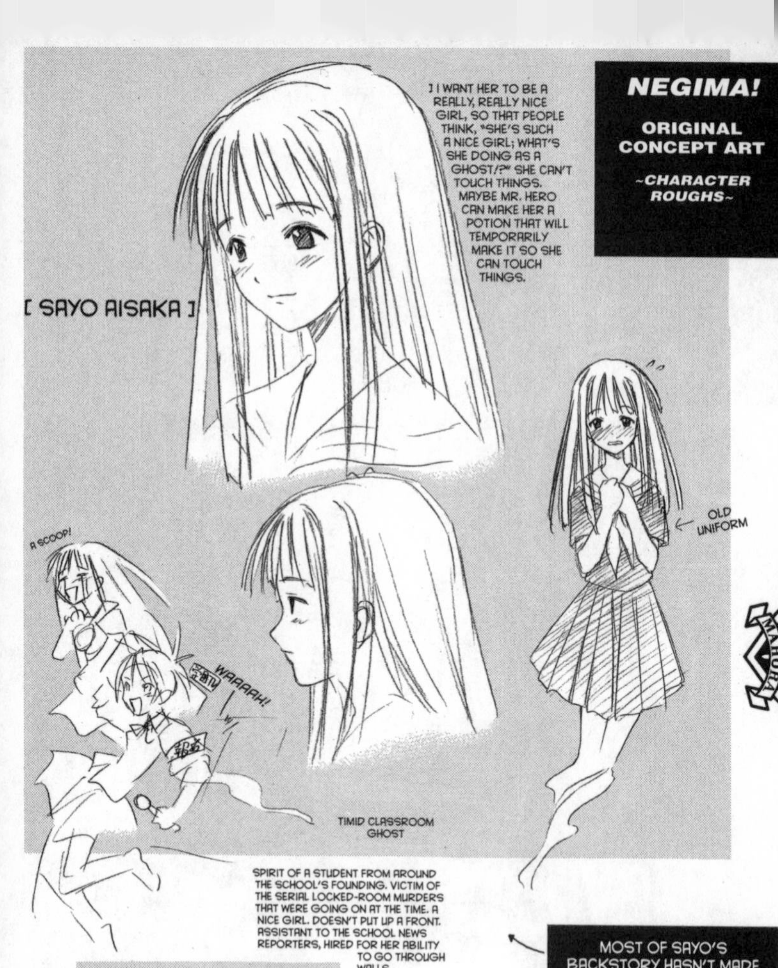

♪ I WANT HER TO BE A REALLY, REALLY NICE GIRL, SO THAT PEOPLE THINK, "SHE'S SUCH A NICE GIRL; WHAT'S SHE DOING AS A GHOST!?" SHE CAN'T TOUCH THINGS. MAYBE MR. HERO CAN MAKE HER A POTION THAT WILL TEMPORARILY MAKE IT SO SHE CAN TOUCH THINGS.
[SAYO AISAKA]
A SCOOP!
WAAAAH!
OLD UNIFORM
TIMID CLASSROOM GHOST

SPIRIT OF A STUDENT FROM AROUND THE SCHOOL'S FOUNDING. VICTIM OF THE SERIAL LOCKED-ROOM MURDERS THAT WERE GOING ON AT THE TIME. A NICE GIRL. DOESN'T PUT UP A FRONT. ASSISTANT TO THE SCHOOL NEWS REPORTERS, HIRED FOR HER ABILITY TO GO THROUGH WALLS.

STOP!

SHE'S SAD THAT SHE COULDN'T GO ON THE CLASS TRIP.

SHE'S BOUND TO THE CLASSROOM, SO SHE CAN'T GO MORE THAN 500M AWAY FROM IT.
THEY THINK THAT SHE'LL PASS ON AFTER HER BUDDY ON THE SCHOOL NEWSPAPER SOLVES THE MYSTERY OF HOW SHE DIED, BUT HER FRIENDSHIP WITH EVERYONE MAKES HER WANT TO STAY IN THIS WORLD. THAT'S WHEN SHE BECOMES FREE TO GO WHEREVER SHE LIKES.

MOST OF SAYO'S BACKSTORY HASN'T MADE IT INTO THE MAIN STORY. (^^;) AT FIRST, SHE WAS GOING TO HAVE MORE OF A NORMAL GHOST STORY, BUT BEFORE WE KNEW IT, SHE WAS A FLUSTERED, PANICKY, REALLY SPACEY GIRL... BUT IT'S OKAY BECAUSE SHE'S CUTE, RIGHT!? (LAUGH) ...OR IS IT?

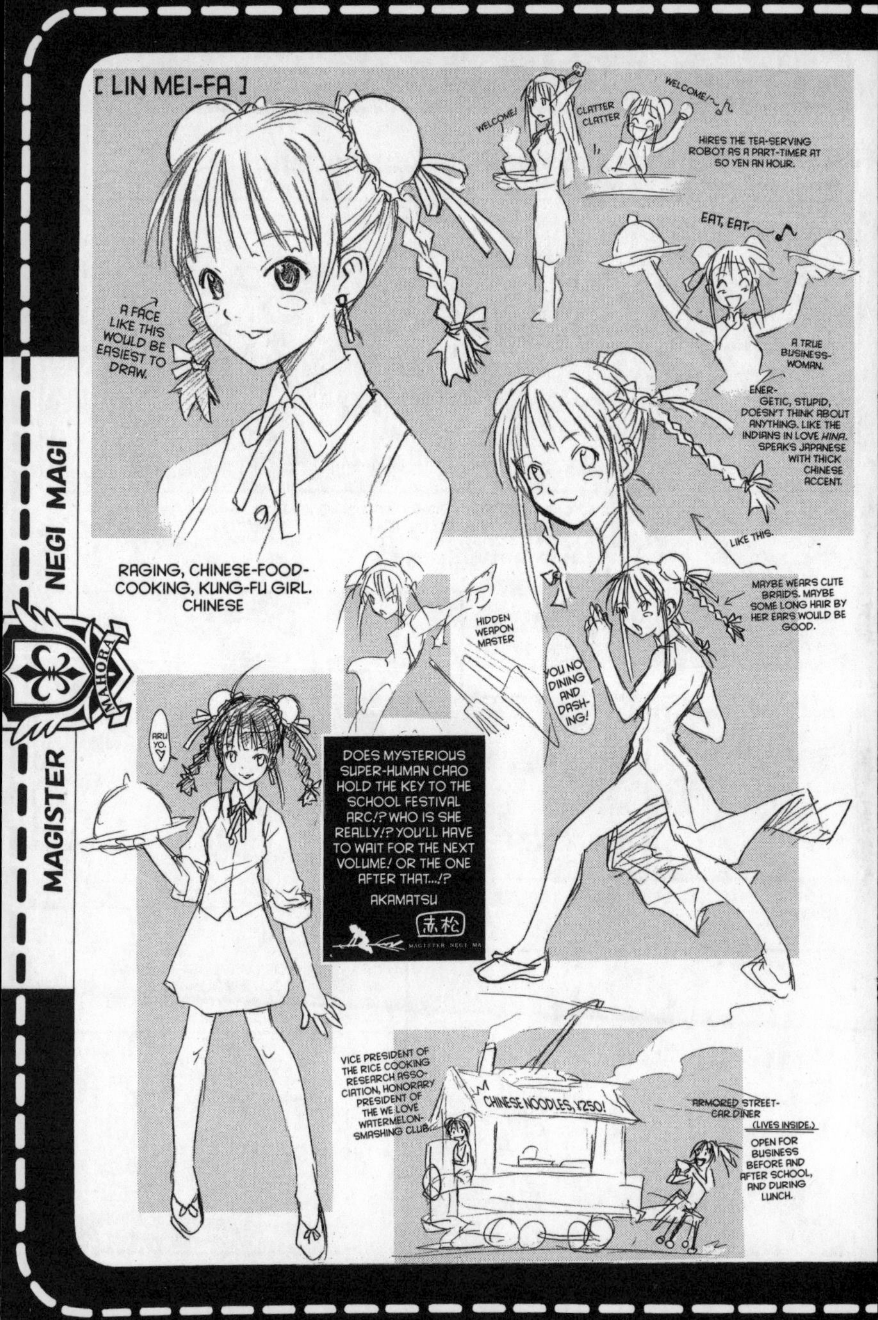
[LIN MEI-FA]
A FACE LIKE THIS WOULD BE EASIEST TO DRAW.
WELCOME!
CLATTER CLATTER
WELCOME!~♪
HIRES THE TEA-SERVING ROBOT AS A PART-TIMER AT 50 YEN AN HOUR.
EAT, EAT~♪
A TRUE BUSINESS-WOMAN.
ENER-GETIC, STUPID, DOESN'T THINK ABOUT ANYTHING. LIKE THE INDIANS IN LOVE HINA. SPEAKS JAPANESE WITH THICK CHINESE ACCENT.
LIKE THIS.
MAGISTER NEGI MAGI
MAHORA
RAGING, CHINESE-FOOD-COOKING, KUNG-FU GIRL. CHINESE
HIDDEN WEAPON MASTER
YOU NO DINING AND DASH-ING!
MAYBE WEARS CUTE BRAIDS. MAYBE SOME LONG HAIR BY HER EAR'S WOULD BE GOOD.
ARU YO.♡
DOES MYSTERIOUS SUPER-HUMAN CHAO HOLD THE KEY TO THE SCHOOL FESTIVAL ARC!? WHO IS SHE REALLY!? YOU'LL HAVE TO WAIT FOR THE NEXT VOLUME! OR THE ONE AFTER THAT...!?
AKAMATSU
赤松
MAGISTER NEGI MA
VICE PRESIDENT OF THE RICE COOKING RESEARCH ASSO-CIATION, HONORARY PRESIDENT OF THE WE LOVE WATERMELON-SMASHING CLUB.
CHINESE NOODLES, ¥250!
ARMORED STREET-CAR DINER
(LIVES INSIDE.)
OPEN FOR BUSINESS BEFORE AND AFTER SCHOOL, AND DURING LUNCH.

3-D BACKGROUNDS EXPLANATION CORNER

WE CREATED NEW 3-D BACKGROUNDS FOR VOLUME NINE. LET US PRESENT SOME OF THOSE BACKGROUNDS HERE.

• MAHORA ACADEMY GIRLS' JUNIOR HIGH BUILDING

SCENE NAME: SCHOOL   POLYGON COUNT: 288,583

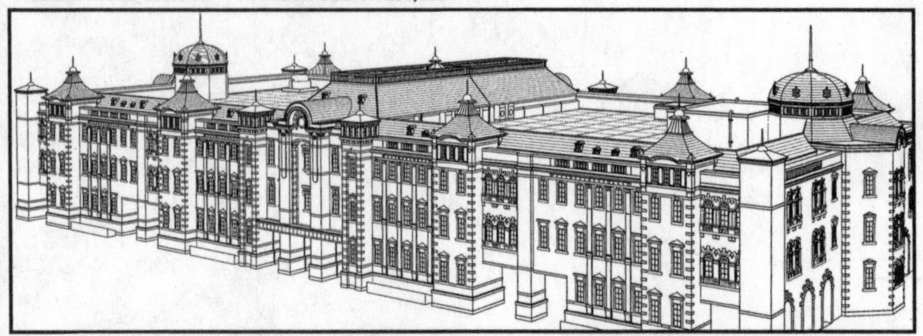

UP UNTIL NOW, MAHORA GIRLS' JUNIOR HIGH HAD BEEN DONE BY COPYING HAND-DRAWN IMAGES, BUT NOW IT'S FINALLY BEEN MADE IN THREE DIMENSIONS. IT'S HUGE! AND DETAILED! AND SO IT TOOK EVEN MORE TIME TO CREATE THAN THE WORLD TREE PLAZA WE INTRODUCED IN THE LAST VOLUME. (^_^;) PLEASE TAKE A LOOK AT SOME OF THE FINER POINTS OF THIS ENORMOUS BUILDING!

THIS IS THE CLOCK, WHICH YOU MIGHT SAY IS THE SYMBOL OF THE JUNIOR HIGH. WE'VE EVEN CREATED THE ELABORATE ENGRAVINGS BY THE WINDOWS, BUT THEY'RE SO SMALL NOBODY NOTICES THEM. (^_^;)

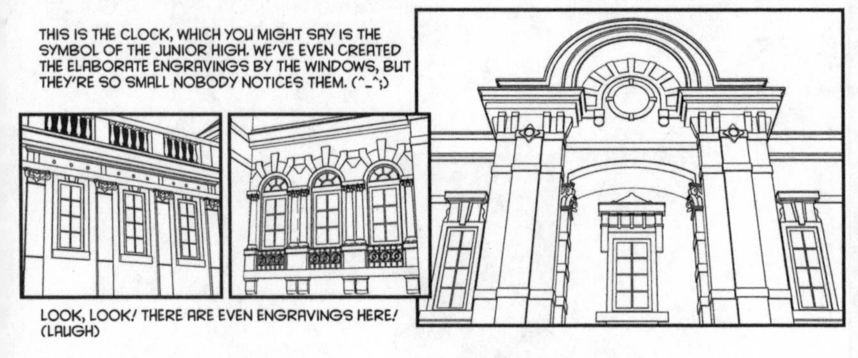

LOOK, LOOK! THERE ARE EVEN ENGRAVINGS HERE! (LAUGH)

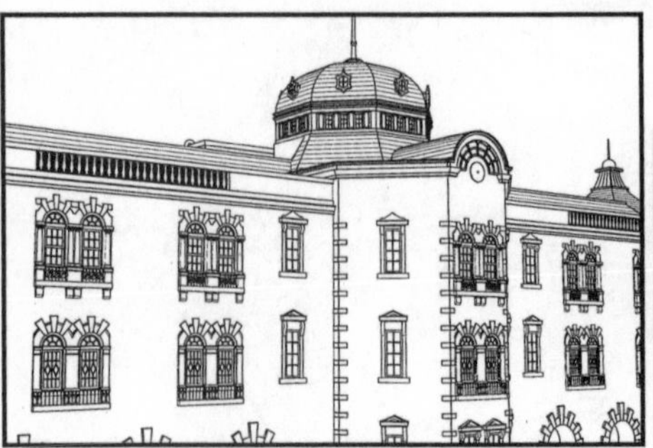

THIS IS THE SIDE OF THE BUILDING WHERE WE SEE 3-A'S CLASSROOM. BELOW IS THE NATIONAL PREMIERE: CLASS 3-A AS SEEN FROM THE OUTSIDE LOOKING IN.

• CHAO'S STREETCAR DINER

SCENE NAME: CHAO'S_TRAM_ POLYGON COUNT: 34,885

THE PECULIAR FOOD CART, CHAO BAO ZI, THAT CHAO MADE FROM A MODIFIED TRAM IS ALSO 3-D. THIS FOOD CART IS PRETTY BUSY DURING SCHOOL FESTIVAL TIME; I HOPE IT GETS TO SEE SOME ACTION IN THE STORY.

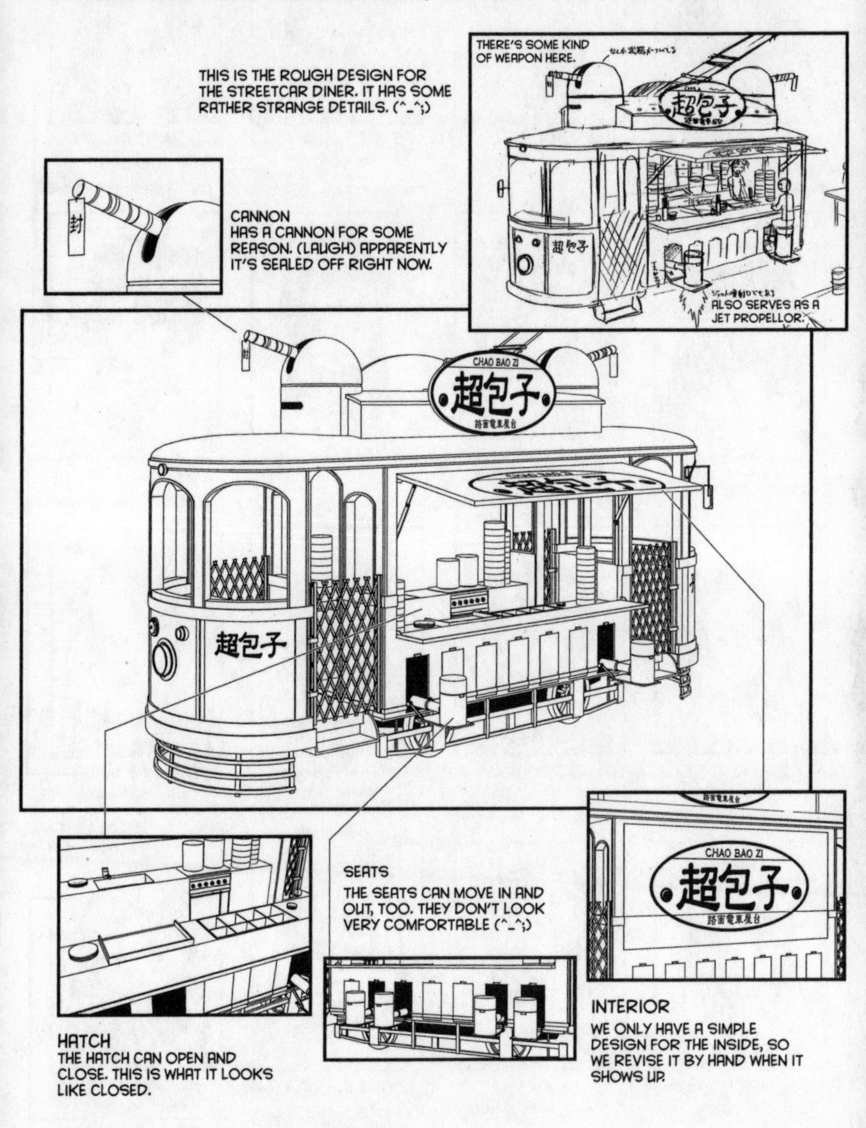

THIS IS THE ROUGH DESIGN FOR THE STREETCAR DINER. IT HAS SOME RATHER STRANGE DETAILS. (^_^;)
THERE'S SOME KIND OF WEAPON HERE.
ALSO SERVES AS A JET PROPELLOR.
CANNON
HAS A CANNON FOR SOME REASON. (LAUGH) APPARENTLY IT'S SEALED OFF RIGHT NOW.
封
CHAO BAO ZI
超包子
路面電車屋台
HATCH
THE HATCH CAN OPEN AND CLOSE. THIS IS WHAT IT LOOKS LIKE CLOSED.
SEATS
THE SEATS CAN MOVE IN AND OUT, TOO. THEY DON'T LOOK VERY COMFORTABLE (^_^;)
INTERIOR
WE ONLY HAVE A SIMPLE DESIGN FOR THE INSIDE, SO WE REVISE IT BY HAND WHEN IT SHOWS UP.

GRANDDAUGHTER OF SCHOOL DEAN

13. KONOKA KONOE

SECRETARY
FORTUNE-TELLING CLUB
LIBRARY EXPLORATION CLUB

9. MISORA KASUGA

TRACK & FIELD

5. AKO IZUMI

NURSE'S OFFICE
SOCCER TEAM
(NON-SCHOOL ACTIVITY)

1. SAYO AISAKA

1940~
DON'T CHANGE HER SEATING

14. HARUNA SAOTOME

MANGA CLUB
LIBRARY EXPLORATION CLUB

10. CHACHAMARU KARAKURI

TEA CEREMONY CLUB
GO CLUB

CALL ENGINEERING (ext. A08-7796)
IN CASE OF EMERGENCY

6. AKIRA OKOCHI

SWIM TEAM

2. YUNA AKASHI

BASKETBALL TEAM

PROFESSOR AKASHI'S DAUGHTER

15 SETSUNA SAKURAZAKI

JAPANESE FENCING

11. MADOKA KUGIMIYA

CHEERLEADER

7. MISA KAKIZAKI

CHEERLEADER
CHORUS

3. KAZUMI ASAKURA

SCHOOL NEWSPAPER

16. MAKIE SASAKI

GYMNASTICS

12. KŪ FEI

CHINESE MARTIAL ARTS
GROUP

A GOOD PERSON JUST
AS I THOUGHT.

8. ASUNA KAGURAZAKA

ART CLUB

HAS A TERRIBLE KICK

4. YUE AYASE

KID'S LIT CLUB
PHILOSOPHY CLUB
LIBRARY EXPLORATION CLUB

EMERGENCY CONTACT (PRIMARY)

SUNA'S CLOSE FRIEND.

29. AYAKA YUKIHIRO
CLASS REPRESENTATIVE
EQUESTRIAN CLUB
FLOWER ARRANGEMENT CLUB

25. CHISAME HASEGAWA
NO CLUB ACTIVITIES
GOOD WITH COMPUTERS

21. CHIZURU NABA
ASTRONOMY CLUB
~~MORE OF A DANGO THAN A FLOWER~~

17. SAKURAKO SHIINA
LACROSS TEAM
CHEERLEADER

30. SATSUKI YOTSUBA
LUNCH REPRESENTATIVE

26. EVANGELINE A.K. MCDOWELL
GO CLUB
TEA CEREMONY CLUB
ASK HER ADVICE IF YOU'RE IN TROUBLE

22. FUKA NARUTAKI
WALKING CLUB
OLDER SISTER

18. MANA TATSUMIYA
BIATHLON
(NON-SCHOOL ACTIVITY)

31. ZAZIE RAINYDAY
MAGIC
SCHOOL ACTIVITY

27. NODOKA MIYAZAKI
GENERAL LIBRARY
COMMITTEE MEMBER
LIBRARIAN
LIBRARY EXPLORATION CLUB

23. FUMIKA NARUTAKI
SCHOOL DECOR CLUB
WALKING CLUB
~~BOTH OF THEM ARE STILL CHILDREN~~

19. CHAO LINGSHEN
COOKING CLUB
CHINESE MARTIAL ARTS CLUB
ROBOTICS CLUB
CHINESE MEDICINE CLUB
BIO-ENGINEERING CLUB
QUANTUM PHYSICS CLUB (UNIVERSITY)

28. NATSUMI MURAKAMI
DRAMA CLUB

24. SATOMI HAKASE
ROBOTICS CLUB (UNIVERSITY
JET PROPULSION CLUB (UNIVERSITY))

20. KAEDE NAGASE
WALKING CLUB
NINJA

May the good speed be with you, Negi.
Takahata.T.Takamichi.

Translation Notes

Japanese is a tricky language for most Westerners, and translation is often more art than science. For your edification and reading pleasure, here are notes on some of the places where we could have gone in a different direction with our translation of the work, or where a Japanese cultural reference is used.

Volume 7

Nama yatsuhashi, page 9

Yatsuhashi is a famous Kyoto delicacy made of sticky rice flour, sugar, and cinnamon. It can be eaten baked or raw, as *nama yatsuhashi*.

Pink Albatross of Mahora Academy, page 43

While it's not entirely clear why, of all the birds in the world, Makie would be referred to as an albatross, it's fairly easy to guess. The Japanese word for albatross is "*ahōdori*," or "idiot bird." And as Baka Pink, Makie, though graceful as a bird, would also be known for being dumber than a brick.

Osechi, page 56

Osechi is traditional Japanese food, usually eaten at the New Year, containing foods that have a special meaning that will bring joy and happiness in the coming year. Since it's May in the story, Makie clearly doesn't think it's necessary to wait.

True Wooden Men Fist, page 69

Kū Fei most likely got the idea for these wooden men from the Jackie Chan movie, *Shaolin Wooden Men*. In the first half of the film, Jackie Chan must fight wooden men similar to these. The movie is from 1976, which is why Chamo comments that kids these days won't get that reference.

Golden Week, page 81

Golden Week is a week full of national Japanese holidays at the beginning of May.

Sabaori, page 178

The *sabaori* is a sumo finishing technique in which the wrestler grab's his opponent's belt and forces him down onto his knees.

Volume 8

Spring and summer fever, page 193

More literally, Fūka suggests that Negi has *gogatsu-byō*, or May fever. It refers to a sudden loss of enthusiasm for a new school or job, which tends to happen right after coming back from the week-long holiday of Golden Week. Makie's suggestion of summer fever isn't just a misunderstanding of spring fever--the term *natsubate* (literally, summer exhaustion) refers to succumbing to the summer heat.

Urashima Tarō and Ryūgū Palace, page 201

Urashima Tarō is the story of a man who rescues a turtle from its tormentors. The turtle turns out to be the daughter of the Dragon God, the emperor of the sea, and as thanks for saving her, the

Dragon God allows the hero to stay at Ryūgū Palace, his home under the sea. After a few days, Urashima Tarō gets homesick and goes back to land, but finds that hundreds of years have passed.

I pray for your soul, page 258

In the original, Natsumi didn't ***say*** she would pray for Kotarō's soul, but actually began a prayer by saying *namu*, a Japanese word used to address bodhisattva at the beginning of a Buddhist prayer.

Monta-san, page 273

ANOTHER ONE OF YOUR FISHY PRODUCTS...
AND MONTA-SAN SAID ON HIS DAY-TIME TV SHOW THAT IF YOU PUT IT ON YOUR FACE, IT WILL BECOME MORE ATTRACTIVE!!
FOR REAL!?
DUN!
WHAT'S A JUNIOR HIGH STUDENT DOING, WATCHING DAY-TIME TV?

Monta Mino is a Japanese TV personality who holds the record for hosting the largest number of TV programs. One of his many shows was *Omoikkiri TV*, in which he provided lifestyle and health advice, which may have included recommending certain skin-care products, though probably not the one Yūna is using.

Suramui, Ameko, and Purin, page 304

Each of these girls is given a name relating to the types of slime monsters you'd find in a video game. Suramui is a rearrangement of the characters su-ra-i-mu (slime), Ameko come from amēba (amoeba), and Purin is the Japanese word for flan, which is the type of slime monster common to Final Fantasy. Incidentally, Ameko is the polite member of the group, ending all her sentences in *desu* (when appropriate).

Over-Doraemon, page 337

Kū Fei's confusion here probably arises from Chamo's use of the English word "overdrive." In Japanese characters, it's spelled "oobaa doraibu." Kū Fei heard the *dora* and related it to something she understood--Japan's favorite cat robot, Doraemon.

"Bad" friends, page 361

In Japanese, they have a term *akuyū*, literally "bad friend." Often used as a synonym for "best friend," it refers to a relationship much like Negi and Kotarō's, where you can't quite tell if they like each other or hate each other.

Volume 9

Maids in Full Bloom!, page 368

Ken Akamatsu and his puns strike again. The Japanese title of this chapter is Moero, *Otome-tachi!*. *Otome-tachi* means maidens, and *moero* is the command form of the verb *moeru*. Normally, *moeru* means "to burn," like with excitement. But moeru can also mean "to bud," and this is the verb that the term *moé* comes from, so the title could be telling the maidens to burn with excitement, or it could be telling them to inspire the readers (and their guests at the school festival) with *moé*, feelings of love and devotion. What better way to do that than with maid costumes? Well, the classmates have some ideas....

Yojimbo: Kuwabatake Jūgorō, page 395

This is a reference to the Akira Kurosawa film, *Yojimbo*, meaning "bodyguard." In the movie, the bodyguard calls him Kuwabatake Sanjūrō, a name he apparently came up with while gazing at a mulberry field (kuwabatake). Sanjūrō can loosely be translated to "thirty-year-old (man)," and so, to take on this role, Kū Fei has been dubbed Jūgorō, "fifteen-year-old (girl)."

Boo... Boo..., page 408

Ghosts in the West are known for saying "boo," which is not only a creepy sound, but an expression of contempt or disapproval. Similarly, in Japan, ghosts are known for saying "*urameshi*," as Sayo says in the original, which means roughly, "I hate (you all)."

Mahora Sports, page 412

In Japan, a sports *shinbun*, or sports newspaper, is a newspaper that specializes in sports, gossip, and entertainment. Sometimes, they come awfully close to being tabloids, but at an unusual school like Mahora Academy, crazy rumors sometimes turn out to be true.

Seven Wonders, page 412

The term *nana fushigi*, or "seven wonders," has become famous in Japan for referring to the seven mysterious phenomenon that supposedly occur in whatever region they're the seven wonders of. Most school have their own set, and those wonders generally include ghost stories.

You're not getting, page 418

This was changed so as not to interrupt the flow of the story, but in the original, Sayo tries to tell them that it's not what they think. She writes on the window, "*gokai desu*," which is a polite way of saying "it's a misunderstanding," but the girls of 3-A interpret her message to mean "five times death," and assume she is going to kill five times. Poor Sayo; if only she had used *kanji*.

Waste Not, Haunt Not, page 448

Back in the 80's, there was a series of educational commercials in Japan, encouraging children not to waste food or other things, so as to prevent the ghosts of those things to come back and haunt you.

Nekotama, page 448

According to Japanese legend, when a cat lives a very long time, its tail splits into two and it becomes a demon cat known as a *nekomata*. Konoka's mispronunciation may come from the fact that *tama* is a common name for cats in Japan.

It's gonna hail tomorrow, page 450

In Japan, when something unusual happens, it's jestingly considered to be a sign of a sudden change in the weather. The more unusual the occurrence, the more dire the coming storm.

Tanabata, page 507

Tanabata is the Japanese star festival, celebrating the meeting of two lovers who are separated from each other by the Milky Way, and are allowed to meet once a year on Tanabata. One of the customs for Tanabata is to write a wish on a small piece of paper and hang it on bamboo, similar to wishing on the World Tree.

Shinboku Bantō, page 508

The official name of the World Tree is Shinboku Bantō. *Shinboku* means "divine tree," and a *shinboku* can be found at many Japanese temples and shrines. Bantō is the Japanese name of the peach trees owned by the Queen Mother of the West, Xi Wangmu, of Chinese mythology. The peaches are said to grant immortality to those who eat them.

ANIMAL LAND

BY MAKOTO RAIKU

In a world of animals, where the strong eat the weak, Monoko the tanuki stumbles across a strange creature the likes of which has never been seen before–a human baby! While the newborn has no claws or teeth to protect itself, it does have the special ability to speak to and understand all different animals. Can the gift of speech between species change the balance of power in a land where the weak must always fear the strong?

Ages 13+

VISIT KODANSHACOMICS.COM TO:

- View release date calendars for upcoming volumes
- Find out the latest about upcoming Kodansha Comics series

MARDOCK マルドゥック・スクランブル SCRAMBLE

Created by
Tow Ubukata

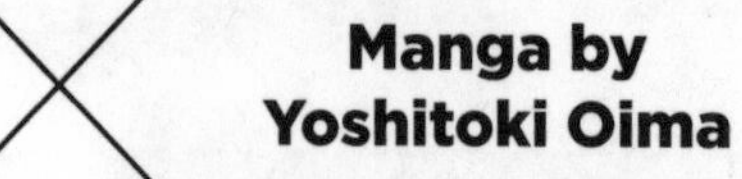

"I'd rather be dead."

Rune Balot was a lost girl with nothing to live for. A man named Shell took her in and cared for her...until he tried to murder her. Standing at the precipice of death Rune is saved by Dr. Easter, a private investigator, who uses an experimental procedure known as "Mardock Scramble 09." The procedure grants Balot extraordinary abilities. Now, Rune must decide whether to use her new powers to help Dr. Easter bring Shell to justice, or if she even has the will to keep living a life that's been broken so badly.

Ages: 16+

VISIT KODANSHACOMICS.COM TO:

- View release date calendars for upcoming volumes
- Find out the latest about upcoming Kodansha Comics series